HELP
YOURSELF
NOW

HELP
YOURSELF
NOW

HELP YOURSELF NOW

A Practical Guide to Finding the Information and Assistance You Need

JAN YAGER, PhD

ALLWORTH PRESS
NEW YORK

Allworth Press books may be purchased in bulk at special discounts for sales promotion, corporate gifts, fund-raising, or educational purposes. Special editions can also be created to specifications. For details, contact the Special Sales Department, Allworth Press, 307 West 36th Street, 11th Floor, New York, NY 10018 or info@skyhorsepublishing.com.

25 24 23 22 21   5 4 3 2 1

Published by Allworth Press, an imprint of Skyhorse Publishing, Inc. 307 West 36th Street, 11th Floor, New York, NY 10018. Allworth Press® is a registered trademark of Skyhorse Publishing, Inc.®, a Delaware corporation.

www.allworth.com

Cover design by Mary Belibasakis

Library of Congress Cataloging-in-Publication Data

Names: Yager, Jan, 1948- author.
Title: Help yourself now: a practical guide to finding the information and assistance you need / Jan Yager.
Description: New York: Allworth Press, [2019]
Identifiers: LCCN 2018056781 (print) | LCCN 2019002098 (ebook) | ISBN 9781621536314 (ebook) | ISBN 9781621536307 (pbk.: alk. paper)
Subjects: LCSH: Social service—Directories. | Human services—Directories. | Consumer protection—Directories. | Legal aid societies—Directories. | Family life education—Directories.
Classification: LCC HV41 (ebook) | LCC HV41 .Y38 2019 (print) | DDC 361.0025/73—dc23
LC record available at https://lccn.loc.gov/2018056781

Print ISBN: 978-1-62153-630-7
eBook ISBN: 978-1-62153-631-4

Printed in the United States of America

This book is dedicated to my wonderful family
and devoted friends as well as to everyone who needs or offers help.

Disclaimer

This publication contains the opinions and ideas of its author and is designed to provide useful advice and general information regarding the subject matter covered. It is sold with the understanding that the author and publisher are not engaged in rendering financial, relationship, legal, psychological, business, medical, or other professional services in this publication. Laws vary from state to state and country to country, and if the reader requires expert assistance or financial, medical, or legal advice, a competent professional should be consulted. Companies, agencies, associations, street or website addresses, or apps may change or even become defunct overnight. The accuracy of any entries in this book, unfortunately, cannot be guaranteed.

The publisher and the author disclaim any liability to any person, organization, or agency for any loss or damage caused by omissions or errors in *Help Yourself Now*, whether such omissions or errors result from accident, negligence, or any other cause. All names, street or website or email addresses, descriptions, phone numbers, titles, and prices are subject to change.

Contents

Introduction:
A Guide to Getting Help

We all need help with something. It can be anything from finding a lawyer who specializes in whatever issue you're facing or a doctor who treats whatever illness you think you have, to funding a new business, to dealing with a bully, to overcoming an addiction, to finding a romantic partner or even a new friend.

Where do you usually go for help? Your family, friends, the internet, Google? The problem with Google and the internet is that there's too much information and too many choices. Plus, many of those choices are made for you by advertisers who may fill your first page of results with entries that have been paid for but might not be right for you.

Help Yourself Now cuts through the information clutter by giving you a manageable place to start. I should know. I've been researching where to get help for more than four decades, beginning with my eight-page article and directory, "Help! How to Cope with It All," in the October 1977 issue of *Redbook* magazine followed by *The Help Book*, published in 1979.

Help Yourself Now covers getting help in thirty areas, from Addiction to Volunteerism, with dozens of issues and concerns in between. For example, Chapter 11, Crime: Victims, Witnesses, and Prevention covers multiple issues such as domestic violence, sexual assault and rape, sexual harassment, stalking, homicide, property crime victimization including cybercrime, as well as being a crime witness and crime prevention.

Whether you're a veteran having problems with depression or PTSD or a parent who is wondering how you're going to pay for your teen's college education, there is help available, if you know how and where to look and also how to ask for it.

The most important piece of advice I have is: do not give up if the first person you ask, whether an employee at a private company or a government worker at a local, state, or federal agency, says "no," or their answers are incomplete or questionable. Keep on asking. Ask at the same agency or company, or if you exhaust all the possibilities at those organizations, keep looking and start over seeking help at new ones.

So much happened to the United States and around the world in the three years that I spent researching, and writing, *Help Yourself Now*. Beginning in December 2019 in China, followed by Europe, and then in the United States from March 2020. The COVID-19 pandemic led to more than 1.5 million deaths globally as of December 2020 with more than 300,000 deaths in the US. But vaccines became available beginning on December 8, 2020 in the UK and soon afterwards in the US.

In the United States, most were in shock and disbelief that in just seven months since announcing on October 4, 2019, that America had its lowest unemployment in fifty years could there could be thirty million seeking unemployment benefits. Those who were either still employed, running businesses that were able to continue to operate despite the shutdowns, as well as those who had emergency funds or savings to see them through these tough periods, did better than those living paycheck to paycheck.

Americans found themselves standing in a line in person, six feet away from the person in front of them, or driving through in their cars, at local food banks to get enough to eat after their sudden job loss. Some moved in with friends or relatives to save on rent or if they thought other less-populated areas might be safer. Stimulus checks helped many but so many still needed assistance feeding themselves and their families. The government business loans helped those businesses who met the requirements which included employing below a certain number of workers and keeping those workers on the payroll rather than laying them off.

One of the many lessons of the COVID-19 pandemic has been the importance of knowing what local and even statewide or national resources are available if you and your loved ones need food, or other essential services. If you are in a bountiful situation now, consider donating money or your time to organizations that are feeding the hungry, such as Feeding America, to your community food bank, such as Connecticut Food Bank, or to a local food program for seniors, such as Meals on Wheels. Whether in New York City; Peoria, Illinois; Rome, Italy; or Kolkata, India, no child or adult should have to be undernourished or go hungry.

The pandemic also emphasized the need for help in so many other areas, matters addressed in *Help Yourself Now*. Just some of those many key issues covered in the thirty chapters that follow are business (see Chapter

6, Business, Entrepreneurship, and Employment), economic hardship or financial assistance (see Chapter 17, Financial Assistance), dealing with death (see Chapter 14, Dying, Death, and Dealing with Grief), mental and physical health (see Chapter 19, Health and Wellness and Chapter 9, Counseling, Depression, and Mental Health), suicide prevention (see Chapter 27, Suicide: Prevention and Related Issues), transportation concerns (see Chapter 28, Transportation, Travel, and Recreation), how to volunteer (see Chapter 30, Volunteerism), adopting or fostering animals (see Chapter 4, Animal Rights and Care), homeschooling or distance learning (see Chapter 15, Education and Chapter 7, Children and Teens), dealing with loneliness and social isolation (see Chapter 28, Relationships), and dealing with emergencies (see Chapter 16, Emergencies, Disasters, and Preparedness), to name just a few.

RELUCTANCE TO SEEK HELP

Some people see the need for help as a sign of weakness. The opposite of that is true. Being able to seek help shows strength, whether you're looking for help in overcoming an opioid addiction, dealing with suicidal thoughts, finding a job, getting a place to stay if you are suddenly homeless, seeking money to start or grow your business, directing a friend whose spouse recently died to a grief group, or perhaps figuring out the best way to get out of debt. Remember the National Parent Helpline's catchphrase: "Asking for help is a sign of strength."

Asking for help also reflects a self-awareness that someone else has the knowledge, expertise, services, or information that you or someone you care about could use.

Being reluctant to ask is the first and biggest mistake too many make when it comes to needing help. The second major error is giving up too soon if assistance isn't immediately offered to you. Keep trying! Yes, there is help available—and lots of it. You just need to be persistent in looking for it and applying some of the strategies and guidelines you know or will learn about in *Help Yourself Now* to judge each source of help that you're considering till you find the help provider or information that clicks with you.

HOW TO USE THIS BOOK

The way you read this book is up to you. You could start from page one and read through to the end like any other book, or after you finish this introduction, you could read only the chapters that pertain to your areas of interest and concern. Each chapter is self-contained, although there is cross-referencing throughout the book so you could skip around from chapter to chapter if you choose to read it that way.

Information sometimes changes; therefore, I apologize in advance for anything that is outdated or incorrect. Updates will be made whenever feasible or practical. However, the publisher and the author disclaim any liability to any person, organization, or agency for any loss or damage caused by omissions or errors in *Help Yourself Now*, whether such omissions or errors resulted by accident, negligence, or any other cause. All names, addresses, descriptions, titles, prices, websites, or social media handles are subject to change.

Here are some other considerations as you read and make use of *Help Yourself Now*:

- Categories may overlap, so be sure to check related chapters or cross-references.
- Some groups are problem-oriented, such as Alcoholics Anonymous, but others cover many concerns and offer a variety of programs, such as the YMCA (Young Men's Christian Association) or the American Heart Association.
- For most listings, you will find the name of the agency, organization, company, or association and its website. Whenever possible, you will find a street address. Since telephone numbers may change often and so much communication today is done through email, telephone numbers are included very selectively, usually just for key crises or lifelines, such as the National Suicide Prevention Lifeline (1-800-273-8255) or the crisis hotline for runaway children and teens (1-800-RUNAWAY). If you do not find a phone number for a listing, go to its website, which will often have a phone number to call (as well as an email address).
- Today there are hundreds of thousands of apps—some free, some for a fee—available on your smartphone for some or most of the listings in *Help Yourself Now*. Whether a listing in this book has a related app or not, most websites today can at least be accessed on your smartphone as well as on your laptop or desktop computer. The goal is to provide a listing that is a starting point for your search for information or a referral to direct help.

- At the end of each chapter, any works that were cited are listed. There are also selected additional reading and/or video references for that chapter.
- *Help Yourself Now* may also be useful if you want to do volunteer work. Nearly every organization, association, or self-help group listed in this book relies heavily on the efforts of volunteers. For targeted volunteer suggestions, consult Chapter 30, Volunteerism.
- The author and publisher do not endorse any of the organizations, associations, agencies, companies, individuals, or publications included in this book; it is only a directory. You must use your own judgment when seeking out and evaluating any place, service, or individual for help.
- No one was charged any fee nor contributed any donation whatsoever for being listed.
- You may want to start locally to see if or what help is available to you. Your community or city may have implemented a help line, like the one that is available in New York City, 311. (911 is still for actual life-threatening emergencies like reporting a crime in progress, a fire, or a medical emergency.) For referrals to local help, try www.211.org. This is a nationwide service, originally started by the United Way of Atlanta, which can refer you to local help throughout the United States and in many parts of Canada. They are available 24/7. You can also try calling 2-1-1 locally and see if your community has a helpline service in place.

Please note that most of the resources in *Help Yourself Now* offer additional ways to contact the organization, agency, or company, besides their website, including via Twitter, related Facebook groups, Instagram accounts, LinkedIn profiles, YouTube videos, or Pinterest images. You may also find an app version. Rather than listing each and every one of these additional options for every listing, when you go to the website or other main listing in *Help Yourself Now* for a particular organization, agency, or company, from that initial listing, explore any of the social media or app options related to the basic entry.

GUIDELINES FOR JUDGING A HELP SOURCE

Once you decide to check out a listing, go to their website and consider the following:

- Who is this individual, agency, or company? You can usually find that out by going to the "About" or "History" section of the website,

which usually gives you the background of the nonprofit organization, company, or government agency.

- Although how long a listing has been doing business is not the only factor to consider, it does at least indicate if this resource has a track record of providing help.

- What is the domain name? Is it associated with an educational institution (.edu), the government (.gov), a nonprofit organization (.org), the military (.mil), or is it commercial (.com)?

- How timely is the information on the website? Is it updated recently or on a regular basis—or is it years or even decades old?

- Is there an email address, contact form, phone number, or a physical mailing address for further information or follow-up?

- If you do call the resource, do you get a person on the other end of the phone, an automated response asking you to leave a message, or are you asked to have a "live chat" with someone via the internet?

- Is this the national or international organization, or a local chapter without any other related resources?

- Are there any testimonials or examples of media exposure related to this listing?

- Are you looking for direct help or just information? That will be a factor in your evaluation of a specific help source. Here are the basic categories of help:

    a. Direct help: you need someone to talk to or deal with your issue now.

    b. Information: this type of resource serves as a clearinghouse of knowledge in a certain area but no direct help is available, although you may be referred to direct help.

    c. Professional membership association: this is for those working in a given field and there are usually dues to join, although some associations also provide information to the general public and/or make referrals to members who provide direct services.

    d. Advocacy groups: these organizations do not provide direct help or even information, but they do advocate on behalf of their cause in an effort to influence leaders or the government to pass or change laws.

WHY I WROTE *HELP YOURSELF NOW*

I wrote *Help Yourself Now* because there are too many dying from preventable causes such as alcoholism, drunk driving, texting-while-driving-related car accidents, drug overdoses, or crime. These life-and-death issues should motivate us to seek intervention and help, before it's too late. In 2017, an estimated 47,000 Americans committed suicide, there were 70, 237 drug overdose deaths, and 17, 284 homicides, not to mention the countless people who could use some support dealing with anxiety, financial problems, homelessness, being bullied, infertility, grief, or compulsive overeating, or relatively lighter concerns such as finding like-minded people to join you as you pursue your dream of learning how to cook, share about parenting challenges, or even how to become a successful entrepreneur.

This book is for everyone who needs help, whether it's for something as monumental as dealing with suicidal ideation or as commonplace yet pressing as finding a job. All of us need help sometimes. I wrote *Help Yourself Now* for all of us.

A NOTE TO READERS

This book is a way to *find* help, not provide help. What I mean is that what you read here is not a substitute for getting professional medical, legal, or psychological advice. It's a starting point. There are tens of thousands of organizations, companies, agencies, and informational clearinghouses, but this book offers a collection of selected sources. At the back of the book, you will find a form titled "Suggestion for an Additional Entry/Resource." If you have a resource you want me to consider for a revised edition of *Help Yourself Now*, please make a copy of the form, complete it, and mail it to Dr. Jan Yager, 1127 High Ridge Road, #110, Stamford, CT 06905, USA. Alternatively, especially if this is a library book, send the information that is requested by filling out the contact form at my website, www.drjanyager .com or fill out the confidential survey at https://www.surveymonkey .com/r/D7S6F6H.

Although individual responses cannot be guaranteed, I thank you in advance for sending referrals for any services or information sources as well as any books that you think should be considered for inclusion.

Reading and Video Materials

Abraham H. Maslow. *A Theory of Human Motivation.* Eastford, CT:
    Martino Fine Books, 2013. First published 1943 in *Psychological Review.*

Council of Economic Advisors, The White House. October 4, 2019. "U.S.
    Unemployment Rate Falls to 50-Year Low." https://www.whitehouse.gov
    /articles/u-s-unemployment-rate-falls-50-year-low/

*Chase's Calendar of Events: The Ultimate Guide to Special Days, Weeks
    and Months.* 62nd ed. Lanham, MD: Bernan Press, 2019. (Updated and
    published annually.)

Doris B. Wiley. "J. L. Barkas Has All the Answers." *The Evening Bulletin*
    (Philadelphia, PA), December 9, 1979.

Encyclopedia of Associations. 58th ed. Farmington Hills, MI: Gale, 2019.

Erving Goffman. *Stigma: Notes on the Management of Spoiled Identity.*
    New York: Simon & Schuster, 1986.

Heidi Grant. *Reinforcements: How to Get People to Help You.* Brighton,
    MA: Harvard Business Review Press, 2018.

J. L. Barkas (aka Jan Yager). *The Help Book.* New York: Scribner's, 1979.

—. "Help! How to Cope with It All." *Redbook*, October 1977, 81-88.

Jan Yager, "Getting Help," selected listings, posted at https://www
    .drjanyager.com/resources/.

Joy Stilley. "Book Offers Guide to Sources of Help." Associated Press,
    December 1979.

Leonard D. DuBoff and Amanda Bryan. *The Law (in Plain English)® for
    Nonprofit Organizations.* New York: Allworth Press, 2019.

Liz Campeze. "Top 20 Movies with a Therapy Focus from Talkspace."
    Talkspace. Last modified July 14, 2015. https://www.talkspace.com
    /blog/top-20-movies-with-a-therapy-focus-from-talkspace/.

Maura A. Matarese. *Finding Hope in the Crisis: A Therapist's Perspective
    on Love, Loss, and Courage.* Carlsbad, CA: Balboa Press, 2018.

Nadine Brozan. "A Guide to Sources of Help." *New York Times*, December 9,
    1979. https://www.nytimes.com/1979/12/09/archives/a-guide-to-sources
    -of-help.html.

Nick Benas and Michele Hart, LCSW. *Mental Health Emergencies: A First-
    Responder's Guide to Recognizing and Handling Mental Health Crisis.*
    NY: Hatherleigh Press, 2017. See especially Chapter 21, "Mental Health
    Self-Care" (for first responders).

PBS NewsHour. "The Stigma That Stops Veterans from Getting Help for
   PTSD." *PBS* video, 9:06. March 29, 2017. https://www.pbs.org/video/the
   -stigma-that-stops-veterans-from-getting-help-for-ptsd-1498008595/.
"PTSD: A Growing Epidemic." *NIH Medline Plus* 4, no. 1 (2009): 10–14.
   https://medlineplus.gov/magazine/issues/winter09/articles/winter
   09pg10-14.html.

CHAPTER 1

Addiction: Alcohol, Drugs, Nicotine, and Gambling

ADDICTION

It is fitting that the first chapter in *Help Yourself Now* is Addiction because it exemplifies how many chapters, or issues, and most concerns are interrelated. Addiction includes alcoholism as well as the abuse of prescription and illegal drugs, plus gambling, but it also involves homelessness (the subject of Chapter 20, Housing and Homelessness) since some with addiction problems may find themselves out on the street because of their habit. Addiction may sometimes also lead to getting arrested and incarcerated (the subject of Chapter 12, Criminal Justice, and Chapter 23, Offenders, Inmates, and the Formerly Incarcerated) as feeding any habit usually requires money, the desperation for which may result in driving some to steal.

There is also too often a connection between addiction and death (see Chapter 14, Dying, Death, and Dealing with Grief), as signified by the 72,000 deaths in just the United States from drug overdoses estimated for 2017. (See the *New York Times* article by Katz and Katz, "'The Numbers Are So Staggering.' Overdose Deaths Set a Record Last Year.") Furthermore, as the Addiction Center points out, there is a complicated relationship between addiction and both suicide and suicidal thoughts (see Chapter 27, Suicide: Prevention and Related Issues) because addiction increases the risk of both those situations.

There are some positive developments in the effort to help drug addicts to get out of the cycle of drug addiction, crime, incarceration, and relapse. Drug courts are developing an option to divert offenders with a drug addiction problem to rehabilitation in lieu of jail or prison time in programs that are known as Restorative Justice. I was able to observe an innovative Drug Court Restorative Justice program in Brooklyn, New York, that is offering drug addicts and even violent offenders an alternative to incarceration if they agree to be in a multifaceted program that includes dealing with their addictions, making restitution to their victims, doing community service, and writing apology letters, among other requirements. Each offender is handled separately, so what is required of them will vary. This is a chance to turn their lives around that is not to be taken lightly, since the alternative is jail time.

I interviewed Pastor Mike Casey, founder of the Bridge, a yearlong recovery program for thirty-four men and women who are healing from addiction. The Bridge is located in Pacific Grove, California, two hours south of San Francisco in the Monterey area. Twenty years ago, Pastor Mike found himself out of a job and homeless because of a twenty-year heroin addiction. He had been a firefighter and paramedic as well as a family man with children. He was able to turn his own life around, and today, along with his wife Michele, he runs the Bridge Restoration Ministry, which he founded fourteen years ago. What do they charge for their unique treatment program, which requires a stay of one year? Nothing. The Bridge is a nonprofit addiction recovery program with an annual operation budget of $500,000 that is supported by private donations, as well as by some income from the thrift shop and culinary arts program that the program runs to offer vocational training to its residents.

In addition to helping residents overcome their addictions, Pastor Mike wants to change the stereotypes about addicts. As he says, "Our residents are moms, dads, uncles, aunts, business owners, photographers, chefs. Over the years, we've had influential people. They're from every walk of life. Addiction knows no bounds."

Here is an association for those who are working with these people dealing with all kinds of addictions:
NAADAC, the Association for Addiction Professionals
44 Canal Center Plaza, Suite 301
Alexandria, VA 22314
https://www.naadac.org/
naadac@naadac.org
Founded in 1972, this professional membership organization represents more than 100,000 addiction counselors, social workers, and others in the health care field who deal with addiction. NAADAC supports the annual National Recovery Month held each September.

ALCOHOL

The opiate drug crisis has become a huge focus in the fight against addiction in the US, but alcoholism is still an addiction that leads to physical problems and even death. Unchecked, it negatively affects jobs and relationships. I am not referring to an occasional glass of wine, but drinking to excess and a dependency on drinking.

But how should alcoholism be treated? Is the abstention advocated by Alcoholics Anonymous (AA) the only answer? Here are excerpts from interviews with former alcoholics who followed different roads to recovery.

The Total Abstinence Approach

"I drank heavily for ten years and was an alcoholic for five. I joined AA and I've been sober for eight years. I'm still an AA member. I don't think controlled drinking works. If you have just one drink, the retroactive effects of alcoholism catch up with you and you're right back where you started. I've buried three friends—recovered alcoholics—who tried to go back to an 'occasional' drink. The latest one was a fifty-year-old friend who had been sober for four years. He took a drink, went on a two-day binge, fell through his glass shower doors, and died."

The Controlled Drinking Approach

"I went into an inpatient alcoholism treatment center when I was eighteen; I had been drinking heavily for two years. My father was an alcoholic. His fourth wife shot and killed him one night when they were both drunk. I'm twenty-five now. I was in AA for two years and I didn't touch a drink until about a year ago. Now I let myself have a social glass of wine, once in a while. I don't want it to be a big deal whether or not I drink. But I am really careful after I take that first drink."

Total abstinence or controlled drinking: just one of the many controversies in helping the out-of-control alcoholic eliminate his or her dependency on alcohol. Stephanie Taylor, a former addiction counselor in a women's prison in Texas, shares what she has learned from her work experience, as well as from being the daughter of parents with addiction challenges—her mother was an alcoholic who died a few years ago in her late fifties from liver failure. Taylor, the author of *Animals That Heal*, says:

I've learned that you can't make a person stop unless they want to, no matter how you try or how many felonies they get or how many negative consequences [there are] to their addiction. If they want to use, they're going to find a way to use. We have to learn to just understand that the person doesn't always have control over it. We talk about addiction as a disease, but it can be a compulsion. I struggle with the notion that it is fully a disease where a person can't control it, where someone has to be abstinent forever. Some people can control and moderate it in a harm reduction method. Each person has to decide for themselves what they can handle and what is best for them. Forcing everyone into a specific modality of recovery isn't going to work.

Exactly how widespread a problem is alcoholism? According to the fact sheet published by the National Institute on Alcohol Abuse and Alcoholism (NIAAA), in 2015 there were 15.1 million adults with Alcohol Use Disorder (AUD) and another 623,000 teenagers (ages 12–17). Christopher Ingraham, in writing in the *Washington Post* about a study published in 2017 in *JAMA Psychiatry*, states that one in eight American adults is an alcoholic. NIAAA further estimates that 88,000 men and women die from alcohol-rated causes annually—62,000 men and 26,000 women. This makes alcohol-related deaths the third leading preventable cause of death, behind smoking tobacco and poor diet and physical inactivity. In 2016, according to the CDC, 10,497 deaths, or 28 percent of the total driving fatalities, were caused by alcohol-impaired driving.

Alcohol is often a factor in violent crimes and suicides. There is also a correlation with increased job absenteeism and such health problems as cirrhosis of the liver, heart disease, lowered resistance to infection, and mental disorders. Other related issues are binge drinking, when a lot of alcohol is consumed in a short period of time, which can be fatal, and fetal alcohol syndrome, when a pregnant woman's alcohol consumption is linked to severe physical and cognitive problems in her newborn.

Alcoholism is still a major problem in America today, but the US is not alone. Belarus is considered a country with excessive drinking. (See Hess et. al., "The Heaviest-Drinking Countries in the World," *USA Today*, May, 17, 2014.) Binge drinking, according to the UK newspaper *The Guardian*, is "glorified in Australia," and New Zealand has a "big binge-drinking culture among the youth." To those afflicted by alcoholism, or family or friends who watch their loved ones unsuccessfully try to cope with it, it is not as important if it is labeled a disease, an allergy, or a symptom, as long as it can be overcome. What is key is that a solution to alcoholism is found so that the problem drinker can, once again, control his or her life and not be controlled by the heavy drinking.

Government agencies that offer free information on drinking and alcoholism (and drug addiction) and referrals to local treatment centers for direct help:

Substance Abuse and Mental Health Services Administration (SAMHSA)
5600 Fishers Lane
Rockville, MD 20857
https://www.samhsa.gov/find-help
National Helpline 1-800-662-HELP (4357)
Provides a treatment locator by state. Just put in your state and related listings will be provided. You can also find listings for self-help groups for addiction as well as lists of additional federal government health, behavioral, and human service agencies and information clearinghouses.

SAMHSA also operates a 24-hour crisis helpline, offering free and confidential help for those dealing with addiction issues, available in English and Spanish, 24/7. However, its website suggests that in a true crisis or emergency, contact 911 instead.

National Institute on Alcohol Abuse and Alcoholism (NIAAA)
National Institutes of Health (NIH)
9000 Rockville Pike
Bethesda, MD 20892
https://www.niaaa.nih.gov
This federal agency is a research and information clearinghouse on alcohol use and abuse, including related issues such as binge drinking, Alcohol Use Disorder (AUD), underage drinking, and alcohol-impaired driving fatalities.

National Institute on Drug Abuse (NIDA)
Office of Science Policy and Communications, Public Information and Liaison Branch
6001 Executive Boulevard, Room 5213, MSC 9561
Bethesda, MD 20892
www.drugabuse.gov
There is a lot of information at this site covering all the various types of drugs that can be abused. Information sheets: https://www.drugabuse.gov/drugs-abuse

One of many noteworthy programs for research into overcoming alcoholism (and drug addiction):
Helping Others Live Sober
Cleveland, OH

helpingotherslivesober.org

From their website: "The mission of the 'Helping Others' Research Project at Case Western Reserve University School of Medicine, Department of Psychiatry, Division of Child Psychiatry, is to improve the quality of life for youth, families, and communities by providing a continuum of scientific information, education, and personal experiences on the role of service in addiction recovery."

Self-help groups offering weekly in-person peer support groups or phone help on an ongoing basis:
Alcoholics Anonymous (AA)
A.A. World Services, Inc.
475 Riverside Drive at West 120th Street, 11th Floor
New York, NY 10115
https://www.aa.org
Started in 1935 in Akron, Ohio, AA is a free self-help support group with weekly in-person meetings for those who have a drinking problem and are willing to tackle it through abstinence and the AA Twelve Steps. Meetings are free, although a small donation is suggested. The AA system works by pairing someone starting on their abstinence journey with a sponsor who has been there and successfully overcome their drinking problem. There are meetings throughout the US and internationally.

Women for Sobriety (WFS)
PO Box 618
Quakertown, PA 18951
https://womenforsobriety.org
contact@womenforsobriety.org
Started in 1976 by Jean Kirkpatrick, PhD, WFS is an abstinence-based self-help program for women seeking to break free from alcohol or drug addictions.

HAMS: The HAMS Harm Reduction Network, Inc.
PO Box 498
New York, NY 10012
http://hams.cc/
From their website: "HAMS is a peer-led and free-of-charge support and informational group for anyone who wants to change their drinking habits for the better. The acronym HAMS stands for Harm reduction, Abstinence, and Moderation Support."

For the families and friends of those with a drinking problem:
Al-Anon
1600 Corporate Landing Parkway
Virginia Beach, VA 23454-5617

https://al-anon.org
wso@al-anon.org
Weekly meetings for family members or friends of those with a drinking problem. The goal is to help those affected by a loved one's drinking to find a way to cope with it and keep the focus on themselves and not on trying to change their loved one, who needs to be the one to deal with their drinking problem.

National Association for Children of Alcoholics (NACoA)
11426 Rockville Pike, Suite 301
Rockville, MD 20852
www.nacoa.org
nacoa@nacoa.org
A national nonprofit membership organization founded in 1983 to help the children of alcoholics.

For those concerned with reducing and eventually eliminating alcohol-related driving accidents or death:
MADD (Mothers Against Drunk Driving)
https://www.madd.org/
See expanded listings in Chapter 28, Transportation, Travel and Recreation and Chapter 30, Volunteerism.

Student Safety Month
http://www.tellcarole.com/student-safety-month.html
See complete listing in Chapter 7, Children and Teens, under "Teens."

DRUGS AND DRUG ABUSE

Associations, agencies, or companies that deal with prescribed or appropriate over-the-counter use of drugs for physical or mental problems are explored in Chapter 9, Counseling, Depression, and Mental Health and in Chapter 19, Health and Wellness. In this section of Chapter 1, we will explore drug abuse. I taught Drugs and Society in 2002 at the University of Connecticut, Stamford campus and Sociology of Deviance in 2020 at Kean University. In Howard Abadinsky's comprehensive textbook, *Drugs: An Introduction* (in the 2001 edition), six out of fourteen chapters dealt with drug abuse. Unfortunately, one cannot usually discuss drugs and drug use without also exploring drug abuse. Those who find themselves with a drug abuse problem will often share how the line between use and abuse can be quite thin and blurry.

To say we have a drug abuse problem in America has become a dramatic understatement. The statistics are mind-boggling: As mentioned in the beginning of this chapter, in 2017, there were 72,000 drug overdose deaths in the United States. Nearly 30,000 were related to fentanyl and fentanyl analogs (synthetic opioids), according to the National Institute on Drug Abuse.

Let's compare that number to two other statistics that represent preventable tragedies:

- Car accidents leading to death: 40,000
- CDC estimates of fatal car accidents related to alcohol impairment: 28% in 2016, or 10,497 people. In addition, 16% of car crashes were related to legal and illegal drugs.
- Murders: 17,000

Obviously, addiction, including drug abuse, has reached epidemic proportions in the United States as well as globally, with International Overdose Awareness Day noting that the United Nations Office on Drugs and Crime (UNODC) estimates that in 2017 there were a minimum of 190,900 premature deaths caused by drugs. Opioids are blamed for the majority of those deaths.

The situation has become so desperate that for the first time in thirteen years, there is a nationwide advisory that anyone with friends or family members with an opioid problem—and possibly even anyone who might encounter someone who has overdosed—should learn how to administer the opioid antidote naloxone and should carry it at all times.

The emphasis on opioid-related deaths is definitely needed, but we need to also remember that many other legal and illegal drugs, if done to excess and to the point of dependency and abuse, can cause serious addiction problems and even death. If the drugs are very expensive, the abuse may also cause financial problems. As mentioned, needing to "feed the beast" is often the reason that drug addicts turn to crime, and unless they get a second chance with an alternative-to-prison program, they may find themselves incarcerated with a felony conviction.

Here are the main drugs that can be abused with grave consequences:

- Opioids
- Cocaine

- Heroin
- Amphetamines
- Tranquilizers/sedative (benzodiazepines)
- Hallucinogens, including LSD (lysergic acid diethylamide)
- PCP (phencyclidine)
- Ecstasy
- Mushrooms
- Marijuana (Even though marijuana is legal in several states in the United States and in some countries, marijuana abuse is possible.)
- Nicotine

The National Institute on Drug Abuse lists even more drugs that can be abused, including:

- Club drugs (GHB, ketamin, MDMA (ecstasy) and methamphetamine
- Fentanyl (synthetic opioid)
- Inhalants
- Over-the-counter medicines
- Prescription medicines
- Steroids (anabolic)
- Synthetic cannabinoids (K2/Spice)
- Synthetic cathinones (bath salts)
- E-cigs

In *Drugs: An Introduction*, Abadinsky outlines three steps on the road to becoming a cocaine abuser (based on the article by David Smith, "Cocaine-Alcohol Abuse" in the *Journal of Psychoactive Drugs*): (1) experimental use; (2) compulsive use; and (3) dysfunctional use.

Whether you want to break your two-pack-a-day nicotine addiction or you have become addicted to opioids, there is help available. If you are not in a crisis situation, information clearinghouses can be a place to explore your options as you seek out direct help, whether on an outpatient or inpatient rehab basis. There is help available to provide you with the physical and emotional support you need to break free of a drug addiction that has become unmanageable as well as expensive.

If you need immediate help, dial 911.

This national government helpline offers confidential crisis counseling, but it is suggested that you call 911 for genuine immediate help:
Substance Abuse and Mental Health Services Administration (SAMHSA)
5600 Fishers Lane
Rockville, MD 20857
https://www.samhsa.gov/find-help
National Helpline 1-800-662-HELP (4357)
Provides a treatment locator by state. Just put in your state and related listings will be provided. You can also find listings for self-help groups for addiction, lists of additional federal government health, behavioral, and human service agencies, and information clearinghouses.

Remember, if you or your loved one is having a life-threatening drug-related crisis, call 911 immediately.

Other programs within SAMHSA or additional organizations that may be helpful:
SAMHSA
Behavioral Health Treatment Services Locator
https://findtreatment.samhsa.gov/
Link to find treatment programs throughout the US for drug or alcohol addiction or mental health issues.

Opioid Treatment Program Directory
https://dpt2.samhsa.gov/treatment/directory.aspx
Link to treatment programs by state for those addicted to opioids, including prescription pain relievers and heroin.

Drug-Free Workplace
1-800-WORKPLACE (967-5752)
https://www.samhsa.gov/workplace/resources/drug-free-helpline
Link to help employers establish all the various components of a drug-free workplace.

Johnny's Ambassadors
johnnysambassadors.org
In 2020, Laura Stack founded this nonprofit organization after her 19-year-old son Johnny died from suicide on November 20, 2019. As Laura wrote to me: "Our mission is to educate parents and teens about the dangers of dabbing high-THC marijuana wax and extracts."

Victoria's Voice Foundation
5601 Windhover Drive
Orlando, FL 32819
VictoriaSiegelFoundation.org
This foundation was started by Jackie Siegel, star of "The Queen of Versailles," and her husband David, after their 18-year-old daughter, Victoria "Rikki" Siegel, died from a drug overdose. Victoria's Voice Foundation is an advocacy and educational foundation. It also provides speakers to organizations to help families stop their kids from experimenting with drugs and how to avoid accidental overdoses, among other life-threatening issues. In 2019, Momosa Publishing published *Victoria's Voice*, which includes Rikki's diary as well as a useful illustrated "Guide to Abused Substances," covering alcohol, nicotine, fentanyl, opioids, cocaine, heroine, and marijuana, among others, and a Resources section.

Referrals to a drug treatment specialist:
American Academy of Addiction Psychiatry (AAAP)
400 Massasoit Avenue, Suite 307, 2nd floor
East Providence, RI 02914
https://www.aaap.org
A professional membership organization for psychiatrists, faculty, residents, medical students, and related healthcare professionals who are specializing, or interested in, addiction treatment. To search for specialists: https://www.aaap .org/patients/find-a-specialist/.

American Society of Addiction Medicine (ASAM)
11400 Rockville Pike, Suite 200
Rockville, MD 20852
https://www.asam.org/
Founded in 1954, a professional membership association for those treating people with an addiction problem. To search for addiction specialists: https://asam .ps.membersuite.com/directory/SearchDirectory_Criteria.aspx.

Self-help organization for those with a drug addiction problem:
Narcotics Anonymous (NA)
PO Box 9999
Van Nuys, CA 91409
https://www.na.org/
From their website: "Narcotics Anonymous is a global, community-based organization with a multi-lingual and multicultural membership. NA was founded in 1953, and our membership growth was minimal during our initial twenty years as an organization. Since the publication of our Basic Text in 1983, the number of members and meetings has increased dramatically. Today, NA members hold

nearly 67,000 meetings weekly in 139 countries. We offer recovery from the effects of addiction through working a twelve-step program, including regular attendance at group meetings."

Inpatient programs:
The Bridge Restoration Ministry
P.O. Box 113
Pacific Grove, CA 93950
https://www.tbrm.org/
This is a privately-funded program, free to anyone with an addiction problem. Residents are overcoming their addiction to heroin and other opioids, alcohol, or methamphetamines. The Bridge is a residential program with a one-year stay, although many residents stay as long as nineteen months. They have a culinary program and a thrift store where residents may eventually work. Founded and run by Pastor Mike, a former firefighter/paramedic who was addicted to heroin and opioids for seventeen years. When he achieved his own recovery, he was determined to give back to others, which he has done through this nonprofit addiction recovery program as well as his book about his life, entitled *Comfortably Numb.*

Phoenix House
164 W. 74th Street
New York, NY 10023
https://www.phoenixhouse.org/
Since 1968, it's been an independent nonprofit organization profit treatment for addiction problems in ten states and through 120 programs.

The Recovery Village
633 Umatilla Boulevard
Umatilla, FL 32784
https://www.therecoveryvillage.com
Founded in 2013, The Recovery Village has locations in Florida, Colorado, Washington, and Ohio. They treat drug abuse and addiction, alcohol abuse and addiction, and co-occurring disorders, including but not limited to depression, anxiety, eating disorders (bulimia, anorexia, etc.), and post-traumatic stress disorder (PTSD).

Warriors Heart®
756 Purple Sage Road
Bandera, TX 78003
https://www.warriorsheart.com
From the website: "Warriors Heart is a privately funded treatment center located in San Antonio, where we only treat active military, veterans, firefighters, police,

EMTs, and active members from across the United States that belong to organizations that protect and serve the citizens of the United States." Located outside of San Antonio, the 40-bed treatment center offers help for those who have alcohol, opioid, and drug addiction challenges. Warriors Heart® started in 2013 when Former Special Forces Tom Spooner joined with Josh Lannon and his wife Lisa Lannon. The Lannons moved their family from Arizona to Texas to open Warriors Heart®.

Information clearinghouses, referrals, research, and advocacy:
Addiction Center (Recovery Worldwide LLC)
https://www.addictioncenter.com/
To find a treatment facility for alcohol or drug-related addiction issues: https://www.addictioncenter.com/about/contact/

Addiction Group
https://www.addictiongroup.org/
Information resource for those dealing with alcohol and drug addiction, and related mental health issues. At their website, you will find articles as well as referrals to other organizations offering help.

Helping Others Live Sober
See complete listing above under "Alcohol."

National Council on Alcoholism and Drug Dependence, Inc. (NCADD)
217 Broadway, Suite 712
New York, NY 10007
Advocacy organization started in 1944.

Smart Approaches to Marijuana (SAM)
Alexandria, VA
https://learnaboutsam.org
From their website: "Our mission is to educate citizens on the science of marijuana and to promote health-first, smart policies and attitudes that decrease marijuana use and its consequences."

Shatterproof
135 West 41st Street, 6th Floor
New York, NY 10036
https://www.shatterproof.org
A national nonprofit founded by CEO Gary Mendell after his son Brian's death from drug addiction. It is "committed to ending the devastation that addiction causes families."

To Write Love on Her Arms (TWLOHA)
PO Box 2203
Melbourne, FL 32902
https://twloha.com
From the website: "To Write Love on Her Arms is a nonprofit movement dedicated to presenting hope and finding help for people struggling with depression, addiction, self-injury, and suicide. TWLOHA exists to encourage, inform, inspire, and invest directly into treatment and recovery." Started in 2007 as the outgrowth of founder Jamie Tworkowski's posts about helping a friend with addiction and other issues.

DRUGS AND THE CRIMINAL JUSTICE SYSTEM

Another issue related to drugs and drug abuse is what happens to those who are arrested, convicted, and incarcerated for possession of an illegal drug and/or possession with intent to sell. According to the Federal Bureau of Prisons, based on data from July 2018, 46.1 percent of the inmates in federal prisons, or 78,511 men and women, were incarcerated because of drug offenses. In the last few years, we have seen the legalization of marijuana for recreational use in several states in the United States, including Colorado, Washington, California, New Jersey, Alaska, the District of Columbia, Idaho, Illinois, Maine, Massachusetts, Nevada, Oregon, Vermont, and Michigan. Even more states have legalized the medical use of marijuana. In California, there is a movement to expunge the records of an estimated 54,000 who were incarcerated for marijuana-related convictions including possession. In New York City in September 2018, it was announced that arrests will not be made for using marijuana. Instead, users will be issued a summons for $100.

Organizations with information about these and related issues:
ACLU (American Civil Liberties Union)
125 Broad Street, 18th Floor
New York NY 10004
See complete listing in Chapter 23, Offenders, Inmates, and Formerly Incarcerated.

The Drug Policy Alliance (DPA)
131 West 33rd Street, 15th Floor
New York, NY 10001
http://www.drugpolicy.org/
An advocacy nonprofit organization concerned with drug policy reform. There are state offices in California, Colorado, New Jersey, New Mexico, and Washington, DC.
    From their website: "Vision. The Drug Policy Alliance envisions a just society in which the use and regulation of drugs are grounded in science, compassion, health and human rights, in which people are no longer punished for what they put into their own bodies but only for crimes committed against others, and in which the fears, prejudices and punitive prohibitions of today are no more."

Families Against Mandatory Minimums (FAMM)
1100 H Street NW, Suite 1000
Washington, DC 20005
https://famm.org
The history of FAMM, from its website: "In 1990, Julie Stewart was public affairs director at the Cato Institute when she first learned of mandatory minimum sentencing laws. Her brother had been arrested for growing marijuana in Washington State, pled guilty, and–though this was his first offense–was sentenced to five years in federal prison without parole. The judge criticized the punishment as too harsh, but the mandatory minimum law left him no choice. Motivated by her own family's experience, Julie created FAMM in 1991."

NORML and the NORML Foundation
1100 H Street NW, Suite 830
Washington, DC 20005
norml.org
From their website: "NORML's mission is to move public opinion sufficiently to legalize the responsible use of marijuana by adults, and to serve as an advocate for consumers to assure they have access to high quality marijuana that is safe, convenient and affordable."

United Nations Office on Drugs and Crime (UNODC)
https://www.unodc.org/
UNODC, through its field offices, operates in 150 countries. Some initiatives are the International Anti-Corruption Day every December 9, and International Day against Drug Abuse and Illicit Trafficking every June 26.

NICOTINE AND SMOKING

Few will deny that smoking is an addiction and that there are health consequences of continued smoking. Still, it bears repeating that smoking is the number-one cause of illness and death that is preventable. Yes, preventable. According to the American Cancer Society, based on the US Surgeon General's 1990 and 2010 reports, ten years after someone quits smoking they have reduced their chances of dying from lung cancer to half of what it would be for someone who is still smoking. Fortunately, in the United States there has been a decrease in the number of people who smoke cigarettes: according to the CDC (Centers for Disease Control and Prevention), smoking declined from 20.9 percent in 2005 (or 21 of every 100 adults) to 15.5 percent in 2016 (fewer than 16 out of every 100 adults). So, there are improvements. But if you multiply that percentage by the adult population, that means that more than 37 million Americans were still smoking in the United States in 2016: 17.5 percent of men and 13.5 percent of women. Here are some statistics from the CDC "Fast Facts" sheet related to smoking:

- Cigarette smoking causes more than 480,000 deaths annually in the United States.
- Secondhand smoke is included in that number, causing an estimated 41,000 deaths.
- The life expectancy of a smoker is 10 fewer years than a nonsmoker.
- Smoking is linked to diseases besides cancer, including diabetes, COPD (chronic obstructive pulmonary disease), stroke, heart disease, and lung diseases.

What about the newer trend to e-cigs, also known as e-cigarettes or vaping? An article in *Medical News Today*, "Are e-cigarettes a safe alternative to smoking?" by Yvette Brazier, estimated that e-cigarette use had risen 900% among high school students between 2011 and 2015, becoming the most popular type of tobacco product. Note, however, that in the article, "5 Vaping Facts You Need to Know," published at the Johns Hopkins Medicine website, fact number 1 is: "Vaping Is Less Harmful Than Smoking, but It's Still Not Safe."

Center for Disease Control and Prevention, Office on Smoking and Health (OSH)
National Center for Chronic Disease Prevention and Health Promotion
1600 Clifton Road
Atlanta, GA 30329-4027
https://www.cdc.gov/tobacco/about/osh/index.htm
tobaccoinfo@cdc.gov
From their website: "Tobacco use is the leading cause of preventable disease, disability, and death in the United States. Every day, about 2,300 young people under age 18 try their first cigarette. Each year, nearly half a million Americans die prematurely of smoking or exposure to secondhand smoke. Another 16 million live with a serious illness caused by smoking. The Centers for Disease Control and Prevention (CDC) is at the forefront of the nation's efforts to reduce deaths and prevent chronic diseases that result from tobacco use. The agency and its partners promote tobacco control interventions, including actions to prevent youth from starting to use tobacco, smoke-free environments, programs to help tobacco users quit, and steps to eliminate tobacco-related health disparities in different population groups."

There is a lot of free information at this site, including statistics and health effects: https://www.cdc.gov/tobacco/data_statistics/index.htm. CDC information on quitting: https://www.cdc.gov/tobacco/data_statistics/fact_sheets/cessation/quitting/index.htm.

Help for quitting is also available. I personally quit my three-pack-a-day habit more than thirty years ago by going cold turkey, and so did my mother. My sister quit decades ago by attending a program that is still helping smokers to quit, although it is now an online twenty-eight-day course: Smokenders (see listing below).

Smokenders
3590-B Highway 31 South, Suite 263
Pelham, Al 35124
http://www.smokenders.org/
support@SmokendersOnline.com
Some cities still have the in-person course that has been helping smokers to quit for the last forty years. If there is no course in your vicinity, there is an online option. It is a fee-based program.

American Cancer Society
https://www.cancer.org
See complete listing in Chapter 19, Health and Wellness.
At the main website there is a wealth of information on how to stop smoking, including prescription drugs that might help to quit (with alerts about potential side effects of each drug).

American Lung Association
http://www.lung.org
See complete listing in Chapter 19, Health and Wellness.
Offers a Freedom from Smoking program: http://www.lung.org/stop-smoking/join-freedom-from-smoking/. The "Stop Smoking" area of their website has a lot of information about smoking, how to quit for yourself, and what you can do to help someone else quit. For more information on their Employee Wellness Program, write to workplacewellness@Lung.org

QuitGuide Mobile App
Available on the App Store (Apple) and Google Play in Android.
Helps to track cravings and monitor smoking habits. Shares helpful motivational messages.

D.A.R.E.
Reducing or ending tobacco use among kids and teens is one of the many goals of D.A.R.E. (Drug Abuse Resistance Education).
See complete listing in Chapter 7, Children and Teens.

Partnership for Drug-Free Kids
https://drugfree.org
At their site you will find information about vaping, which has become a new epidemic. Many teens get addicted to vaping, also known as e-cigs or e-cigarettes, because of their misunderstanding that it would be less harmful and less addicting than smoking cigarettes. The answer about whether vaping is safe is stated emphatically at their website: "The short answer is no, vaping is not considered safe for teens and young adults, especially since their brains are still in a period of active development."
    See complete listing in Chapter 7, Children and Teens.

SmokeFree
https://smokefree.gov/
Website created and maintained by the US government to help you or a loved one to quit. There is lots of useful information as well as tips for quitting, tailored to various groups of smokers such as teens, veterans, women, and those sixty and over.

GAMBLING

Gambling is another kind of addiction that can take its toll. In 2013, GamingHill.com published an article, "100 Best Gambling and Poker Movies," which is now posted at the Internet Movie Database, IMDB. Since that time, even more movies about gambling have been released including the 2017 film

Molly's Game, starring Jessica Chastain, a true story of a woman who ran a high-stakes poker game, and the 2014 remake of the 1974 movie *The Gambler*, starring Mark Wahlberg. The life of the gambler is often the subject of novels, TV shows, and movies, and sometimes it is even glamorized or romanticized. But the reality is far from romantic. Compulsive gamblers—not those who occasionally play bingo at church or the singles or couples who go to a casino once every year or two to play a set amount at the slot machines, but those unable to stop—often feel as driven and as hopeless as alcoholics, compulsive overeaters, or drug addicts. Fortunately, there is help for the compulsive gambler. However, some gamblers, who feel that their debt has gotten so out of control that they no longer can think clearly about their options, may resort to embezzlement, thievery, or lying to gain the needed gambling funds or to pay off the debts they have incurred. The gambler's family also suffers. Some inmates attribute their imprisonment in part to their compulsion to gamble. Bankruptcy, depression, alienation, and the ultimate act of desperation, suicide, are just some results of compulsive gambling.

How many addicted gamblers are there in the United States? Gamblers Anonymous (GA) estimates at least six million; about fifty million citizens regularly gamble to the tune of $100 billion a year. Unfortunately, with legal online gambling, the potential for gambling addiction is greater than ever.

Withdrawal symptoms from a gambling addiction resemble those of other addictions: diarrhea, severe headaches, restlessness, and shakiness. Whatever the number of compulsive gamblers, and however severe their problems, gamblers need as much help and support as other addicts in coping with their affliction.

In theory, gambling should not be a problem with children or teens since in most states the legal age to gamble is twenty-one; in some states, at casinos that do not serve liquor, it might be eighteen. Despite these age limits to gambling, it is a fast-growing addiction among teens.

The two main self-help support groups for gamblers and their families, friends, and children are Gamblers Anonymous (GA) and Gam-Anon. Both groups follow the principles of Alcoholics Anonymous and Al-Anon, All these groups have local chapters throughout the United States and provide the direct service of self-help peer counseling at weekly meetings. You should be able to find a local chapter by going to the website for the international headquarters.

National Council on Problem Gambling
730 11th Street NW, Suite 601
Washington, DC 20001
https://www.ncpgambling.org/
ncpg@ncpgambling.org
24 Hour Confidential National Helpline 1-800-522-4700
From their website: "Purpose: To serve as the national advocate for programs and services to assist problem gamblers and their families." Go to https://www .ncpgambling.org/about-us/regional-affiliates/ to find the regional affiliated groups.

Gamblers Anonymous (GA)
National Headquarters
PO Box 17173
Los Angeles, Calif. 90017
http://www.gamblersanonymous.org/ga/
isomain@gamblersanonymous.org
GA started in Los Angeles one Friday the thirteenth in 1957. Since then the GA movement has grown to have hundreds of chapters throughout the US and globally. All services are free; no outside contributions are solicited. Like Alcoholics Anonymous, telephone communication after meetings is encouraged. Also like AA, sessions begin with gamblers announcing their first name followed by the declaration, "I am a compulsive gambler." There are even chapters of GA in US prisons, such as the California Institute for Men in Chino, California, and a publication is directed to that population entitled "Toward Recovery in Prison." As GA states at its website: "The only requirement for membership is a desire to stop gambling."

Gam-Anon
PO Box 307
Massapequa Park, NY 11762
https://gam-anon.org
A self-help group modeled after Alcoholics Anonymous (AA) and Al-Anon groups for the spouses, romantic partners, friends, parents, and children of the gambler. It has confidential weekly meetings, telephone contact between meetings, and an annual convention. It tries to keep the focus on the group attendee, not on the gambler or the gambler's compulsion.

Reading and Video Materials

28 Days. Starring Sandra Bullock. Directed by Betty Thomas. 2000. 1 hour 43 minutes. Written by Susannah Grant.

Addiction Center, "Addiction and Suicide," https://www.addictioncenter.com/addiction/addiction-and-suicide/

Alene Tchekmedyian. "Prosecutors move to clear 54,000 convictions in California." April 1, 2019, *Los Angeles Times*.

Alexander E. M. Hess, Thomas C. Frolich and Vince Calio. "The Heaviest-drinking Countries in the World." *USA Today*, online site, posted May 17, 2014.

Allen Carr. *Allen Carr's Easy Way To Stop Smoking*. Clarity Marketing USA, 2011.

Center for Disease Control and Prevention (CDC). "Fact Sheets—Binge Drinking." Updated May 10, 2018. https://www.cdc.gov/alcohol/fact-sheets/binge-drinking.htm.

Christopher Ingraham, "One in eight American adults is an alcoholic, study says," *Washington Post*, August 11, 2017. https://www.washingtonpost.com/news/wonk/wp/2017/08/11/study-one-in-eight-american-adults-are-alcoholics.

Days of Wine and Roses. Starring Jack Lemmon and Lee Remick. 1962. Directed by Blake Edwards. 1 hour 57 minutes. Written by J.P. Miller.

Dennis Thompson. "Kids Who Vape Face Toxin Dangers, Study Finds." Posted at WebMD.com, March 5, 2018.

Emma Ockerman. "US Urges Public to Carry Opioid Overdose Drug in Rare Move." Bloomberg.com, April 5, 2018. https://www.bloomberg.com/news/articles/2018-04-05/u-s-urges-public-to-carry-opioid-overdose-antidote-in-rare-move

"Fast Facts" Disease and Death (Cigarette Smoking). Page last updated: February 6, 2019, Content source: Office on Smoking and Health, National Center for Chronic Disease Prevention and Health Promotion.

Federal Bureau of Prisons. "Offenses." August 25, 2018. Posted online at https://www.bop.gov/about/statistics/statistics_inmate_offenses.jsp

GamingHill.com, "100 best gambling and poker movies." IMDB, April 13, 2013. https://www.imdb.com/list/ls051320004/

Howard Abadinsky. *Drug Use and Abuse: A Comprehensive Introduction*. 9th edition. Boston: Cengage, 2017.

International Overdose Awareness Day, "Facts & Stats," https://www.overdoseday.com/resources/facts-stats/

John Collopy. *The Reward of Knowing*. Charleston, SC: Advantage Media
    Group, 2018.

John Katz and Margot Sanger-Katz. "'The Numbers Are So Staggering.'
    Overdose Deaths Set a Record Last Year." *New York Times*, November
    29, 2018, posted at nytimes.com.

Justin George, "Inmates face problem habit," *Baltimore Sun*, October 8,
    2014. http://www.baltimoresun.com/news/maryland/baltimore-city
    /bs-md-gamblers-in-prison-20140917-story.html#

The Lost Weekend. Starring Ray Milland and Jane Wyman. 1945. 1 hour
    41 minutes. From the novel by Charles R. Jackson. Directed by Billy
    Wilder. Screenplay by Charles Brackett.

Michelle Alexander. *The New Jim Crow*. NY: The New Press, 2012.

Michael Joseph Blaha, M.D., M.P.H., "5 Vaping Facts You Need to Know,"
    posted at hopkinsmedicine.org

Mike Casey. *Comfortably Numb*. Digi-Tall Media, 2016.

Nathan Bomey. "US vehicle deaths topped 40,000 in 2017, National Safety
    Council estimates." Published February 15, 2018 in *USA Today*.
    https://www.usatoday.com/story/money/cars/2018/02/15/national-safety
    -council-traffic-deaths/340012002/

National Institute of Alcohol Abuse and Alcoholism, National Institutes of
    Health. "Alcohol Facts and Statistics." Updated June 2017. https:
    //www.niaaa.nih.gov/alcohol-health/overview-alcohol-consumption
    /alcohol-facts-and-statistics

National Institute on Drug Abuse, NIH (National Institutes of Health).
    "Overdose Death Rates." Revised August 2018. https://www.drugabuse
    .gov/related-topics/trends-statistics/overdose-death-rates

Sarah Marsh, Eleni Stefanou, and the *Guardian* Readers. "Which countries
    have the worst drinking cultures?" *The Guardian*, April 15,
    2016. https://www.theguardian.com/society/2016/apr/15/which-countries
    -worst-alcohol-binge-drinking-cultures

Stephanie L. Taylor. *Animals That Heal*. Independently published. 2018.

"Teen Addiction to Online Gambling" by CRC Health. https://www
    .crchealth.com/troubled-teenagers/teen-gambling/

Yvette Brazier. "Are e-cigarettes a safe alternative to smoking?" Reviewed
    by Alana Biggers, MD, MPH. Published in Medical News Today and
    posted at their online site on June 25, 2018.

CHAPTER 2

Adoption and Foster Care

It used to be that most of the couples who adopted children or became foster parents were unable to have children of their own. Although infertility is still a major reason for adoption or foster care, those who are physically able to have children and who already have children are adopting children of all ages or participating in foster care.

ADOPTION

Famous men and women who were adopted include: Dave Thomas, founder of Wendy's; Apple co-founder Steve Jobs; pastor Jesse Jackson; singer Faith Hill; and many more. The list of adoptive parents has countless famous names as well, including *Today Show* co-host Hoda Kotb; actresses Angelina Jolie, Sandra Bullock, Meg Ryan, Nicole Kidman, and Diane Keaton; actors Tom Cruise and Brad Pitt; and singer Sheryl Crow, to name just a few.

It used to be that only legally married couples of the same religion and race, who were certified as sterile and were below a certain age limit, could adopt a child. They tended to prefer a healthy infant of their own race; the younger, the better. Older or handicapped children were too often overlooked and either remained in institutions or were brought up in one or multiple foster homes.

But adoption practices have changed. Straight and gay single men and women are now adopting children. Parent or parents and adopted child need not be of the same race or religion. Older and handicapped children are finding permanent homes. Many couples with biological children are adopting a second or third child.

There are four types of adoption: independent adoptions of minors (arranged directly with the natural parents); adoption of minors through a licensed agency or agent; adoption of minors by stepparents; and adoption of an adult by another adult at least ten years older than the adopted "child." Requirements vary from state to state as to which court has jurisdiction over adoption proceedings, how long a probation period is necessary before the adoption is final, the age at which the child's consent is also required, and whether an adopted child still has the right to inherit through his or her biological parents who die without leaving a will.

Legally, there are private or state adoptions. Private adoptions are more expensive than adoptions through government agencies. The cost may range from $25,000 to $50,000. It may also take less time, and there is a greater likelihood that it will be possible to adopt an infant.

Adoption through a state agency is free but may take longer, from a year to five years, and the children may be older. Private agency adoptions are more expensive, but one cannot say which service will arrange a "better" adoption. In both cases, however, there is a severe shortage of infants for adoption. One consequence of that shortage has been the notorious "black market" baby farms. One of the most famous cases is that of a doctor who sold 200 babies on the black market between 1950 and 1965. According to a 2015 *Daily News* article by Ashley Lewis, he would tell the mothers that their babies had died in childbirth and then sell the babies for $800 to $1,000. Lewis's article describes the joyful reunion of a birth mother with one of those black market babies, fifty-one years later.

When I wrote the original *Help Book*, the most controversial issue in adoption was the sealing of a birth record. "Sealing" refers to the prac-tice—after a legal adoption—of replacing the original birth certificate with a new revised document. The original one is "sealed" and separately filed. It is then up to the "discretion" of the adoption agency whether to reveal the identity of any of the parties involved in the adoption. Until very recently, practically all agencies refused to release any records. Even at maturity, and even if an adoptee knew that he or she had natural sib-lings, the information was not obtainable. The traditional reasoning for this secrecy was that it was for the child's own good, since it was believed that many adopted children were illegitimate. Now, however, the ethics and even the constitutionality of sealed records have been questioned. The trend is toward what is known as an "open" adoption, whereby the adoptive parents know the identity of the birth parents and, in some cases, may even agree to allow them to communicate with the adopted child throughout the child's formative years.

Related to the issue of "sealed" versus "open" adoptions is the issue of when or even whether the adoptive parents should tell the child that he or she is in fact adopted. The current consensus is that at some point the child should be told. More than ever before, agencies, societies, and the adoption triangle—adoptees, birth parents, and adoptive parents—are asking, "Is all this secrecy necessary?" and answering "No."

For direct assistance in adoption, consult your local telephone directory in the state, city, or county government listings under any of the following categories: Child Welfare, Health, Social Services, Welfare, Bureau of Adoption, Human Resources, or Child Services. To find out what state department offers adoption services, contact your state information office in your state capital. State agencies may also be able to provide referrals to private licensed adoption services in your area.

You can search for adoption information for your state at: https://www. childwelfare.gov/topics/adoption/adopt-assistance/.

Organizations or associations related to adoption:
Adoptive Families
https://www.adoptivefamilies.com/
A website and network with information on adoption for prospective adoptive families and those who have adopted.

Child Welfare League of America, Inc. (CWLA)
727 15th Street NW, 12th Floor
Washington, DC 20005
http://www.cwla.org
cwla@cwla.org
Founded in 1920, the Child Welfare League of America, Inc., is a private membership organization that is devoted to developing standards in areas that have been specified as child welfare services including adoption, foster parenting, day care, services to children in their own homes, and unmarried parents. From their website: "Our primary objective is to make children, especially our most vulnerable children, a priority in the United States. To do that, we must engage all Americans in promoting the well-being of children and young people and protecting them from harm." CWLA offers extensive related publications as well as training and workshops, including online webinars. There is also an annual conference, usually held in Washington, DC.

North American Council on Adoptable Children (NACAC)
970 Raymond Avenue, Suite 106
Saint Paul, MN 55114
https://www.nacac.org
info@nacac.org
Founded in 1974, this is a membership organization of adoptive-parent groups and individuals concerned about children in need of adoptive homes. A key mission is advocating for adoption from foster care, especially for children who are harder to place because of their age or mental, emotional, or physical disabilities. NACAC is an information clearinghouse for those interested in adopting a child (American or foreign) or in foster care. Public education programs include extensive information on everything from the federal adoption tax credit to how to adopt to post-adoption advocacy, conferences, and special publications.

A unique nonprofit offering a way for families to fund their adoption goals through a crowdfunding platform:
AdoptTogether
251 W. Central Avenue, #278
Springboro, OH 45066
https://adopttogether.org/
From their website: "AdoptTogether is a nonprofit, crowdfunding platform that bridges the gap between families who want to adopt and the children who need loving homes." At their website, you can read the March 2017 story about how Andrea Wittig's family, the first ones to adopt a baby through AdoptTogether's crowdfunding platform, raised over $35,000 to adopt their child from Uganda. For information on how it works, go to: https://adopttogether.org/how-it-works/

Selected adoption agencies. In addition to my own research, I relied on the information provided by AdoptTogether (described above) and their list, "Top Domestic Agencies," created in consultation with their adoption expert Chloe Briggs:
American Adoptions
7500 W. 110th Street, Suite 500
Overland Park, KS 66210
http://www.americanadoptions.com
From their website: "American Adoptions is currently one of the largest domestic adoption agencies of its kind in the United States, completing more than 300 domestic adoptions per year. We are a fully licensed, nonprofit domestic adoption agency that works with both pregnant women and adoptive families across the nation."

Barker Adoption Foundation
http://www.barkeradoptionfoundation.org
Barker is a nonprofit adoption agency licensed in Washington, DC, Maryland, and Virginia. From their website: "Ruth and Richard Barker founded the agency in 1945 in response to a request from the US Navy to address the needs of pregnant WAVES (Women Accepted for Volunteer Emergency Service). Since then, Barker has evolved from a traditional domestic infant-placing adoption agency into a highly regarded, comprehensive adoption center." There is a long list of services that Barker offers, but a couple of key ones are that it does domestic infant adoptions, older-child foster care adoptions, and international adoptions from South Korea, China, Columbia, and India.

Gladney Center for Adoption
6300 John Ryan Drive
Fort Worth, TX 76132-4122
https://adoptionsbygladney.com/
With regional offices in Texas, Oklahoma, and Florida, this service has a 125-year history of placing children for adoption.

Nightlight Christian Adoptions
1528 Brookhollow Drive, #100
Santa Ana, CA 92705
https://www.nightlight.org
Offices in California, Colorado, Oklahoma, Missouri, Georgia, South Carolina, and Kentucky. Helps with domestic and international adoptions.

Snowflakes Embryo Adoption Program
A division of Nightlight Christian Adoptions (see listing above)
https://www.nightlight.org/snowflakes-embryo-adoption-donation/embryo-adoption/
From the website: "What is Embryo Adoption? When couples use in vitro fertilization to achieve pregnancy, they will often have embryos remaining after they complete their family. One option available to them is to donate those embryos to another couple. Embryo adoption allows the family with remaining embryos to select a recipient family for their embryo gift. That family could be you. The adopting family is able to use the donated embryos to achieve a pregnancy and give birth to their adopted child."

WACAP (World Association for Children & Parents)
315 S. Second Street
Renton, WA 98057
(additional offices in New York and Wisconsin)

https://www.wacap.org
Started in 1976. They place children from the US and a large number of international countries including Korea, Bulgaria, Haiti, and Vietnam. For a full list of countries, see their website.

Spence-Chapin
410 East 92nd Street, 3rd Floor
New York, NY 10128
https://www.spence-chapin.org
Since 1908, Spence-Chapin, a licensed nonprofit organization, has been helping with domestic, international, and special-needs adoptions as well as with foster care.

FOSTER CARE

According to the Child Welfare Information Gateway, part of the Children's Bureau of the US Department of Health and Human Services, as of September 30, 2016, there were an estimated 437,465 children in foster care. The median age of children in foster care at that time was 7.8 years.

In many ways, foster care is a much more difficult journey than ordinary parenting or adoption, since the child may still be returned to his or her natural parents, and the foster care placement may therefore turn out to be temporary. The child also may be transferred to another placement home or facility. Foster care may be short-term or for all of the child's dependent years.

Abuses are sometimes publicized in the media, such arrest in Florida of a foster father who pleading "no contest" to raping a thirteen-year-old foster-turned-adoptive daughter since the age of five. (See "Foster Kids Lived with Molesters. No One Told Their Parents.," Josh Salman, et. al., *USA Today Network*.) When such abuses are exposed, there is a heightened public awareness that potential foster parents need to be investigated carefully.

Through organizations such as the National Foster Parent Association, higher standards for foster care are being established and enacted. That foster parenting is a unique and demanding skill is finally being recognized: The Foster Parent Dissemination Center of the Child Welfare League of America, in cooperation with the US Children's Bureau of the Office of Child Development, is helping social workers educate foster parents. They emphasize that even though a child's placement is usually temporary, foster parenting is a challenging and important role.

Some of the questions that must be answered by potential foster parents:

- How does caring for a foster child differ from having a relative or friend visit in one's home?
- How will the foster child affect the relationships already established in the foster care family, where there are often other foster care or biological children?
- How does the foster care parent explain why the child's biological parent or parents are unable to care for him or her?
- How can the foster care family best utilize the services and skills of the cooperating social service agency?

I interviewed a twenty-two-year-old, Leroy, who along with his younger brother was placed in foster care at the ages of eight and six because their only parent, their father, was unable to care for them. His foster parents adopted them when they reached middle school age. Leroy shared with me the importance of an organization called Treehouse in helping him to do well in school and develop the self-esteem that has enabled him to enroll in college. In addition to the help of his foster parents, Treehouse provided Leroy with mentors, educators that they refer to as "education specialists," who helped him throughout his school years, including starting him on his music education by giving him a saxophone. As Leroy explains, "My education specialist was really good about pushing me to get to my goals. Without them, I don't think I would have the strong foundation in who I am."

In addition to emotional and educational support, Treehouse provided material needs so Leroy and his brother would not be at a disadvantage compared to their classmates. Says Leroy, "They had almost anything I needed. Books, and shoes, and clothes, and toys and board games. Really, anything a child should need, they had in their warehouse." He also participated in their summer programs as well as going on lots of field trips. "I had a lot of opportunities," Leroy concludes, opportunities that enabled him to graduate from community college with an A in music. He is now pursuing a BA in math education and a second major in music education, with the goal of teaching in middle school.

Foster care information and assistance (see also "Adoption"):
AdoptUs Kids
https://adoptuskids.org
info@adoptuskids.org
From their website: "A national project working to ensure that children and teens in foster care get safe, loving, permanent families . . . We also maintain the nation's only federally funded photolisting service that connects waiting children with families."

National Foster Parent Association (NFPA)
1102 Prairie Ridge Trail
Pflugerville, TX 78660
https://nfpaonline.org/
Info@NFPAonline.org
This is an information clearinghouse and membership organization about foster care and the rights of foster care parents and foster care children. There are twenty-six state affiliates to NFPA: https://nfpaonline.org/stateaffiliates.

National Adoption Center
1500 Walnut Street, Suite 701
Philadelphia, PA 19102
www.adopt.org
nac@adopt.org
From their website: "When we opened our doors in 1972, we didn't know whether anyone would want to adopt a child who was 11 years old or brothers and sisters who were siblings and wanted to stay together. Would anyone consider a child who was blind or who had Down syndrome? We are thrilled at our success: more than 23,000 families created. It turned out that once the public knew about the children, they came forward to adopt them."

My Stuff Bags Foundation
5347 Sterling Center Drive
Westlake Village, CA 91361
www.mystuffbags.org
From the website: "The My Stuff Bags Foundation's ultimate goal is to provide a My Stuff Bag filled with new belongings to each of the nearly 300,000 children each year who must enter crisis shelters and foster care with nothing of their own."

Federal volunteer program available locally:
Foster Grandparents (Corporation for National and Community Service (CNCS))
1201 New York Avenue NW
Washington, DC 20525
http://www.seniorcorps.gov/about/programs/fg.asp
Established in 1993, the Foster Grandparents program is part of a government-funded effort to provide service to children "with exceptional or special needs." Those fifty-five and over who have limited income and meet the income eligibility requirement may apply to be a Foster Grandparent. If accepted into the program, they will be volunteers but will receive a nominal stipend, assistance with payment of their meals related to their services, and reimbursement for transportation to the foster child or children that they are assigned to. For more information, go to https://www.nationalservice.gov/programs/senior-corps/senior-corps-programs/fostergrandparents

Local programs serving children and teens in foster care:
The New York Foundling
590 Avenue of the Americas
New York, NY 10011
https://www.nyfoundling.org
On October 11, 1869, the first abandoned infant was brought to their East 12th Street brownstone by Sister Mary Irene Fitzgibbon and two other Sisters of Charity. In 1973, they opened their first foster care department in Puerto Rico.

From the website: "No child should fall through the cracks. No family in crisis should be ignored. While our mission has expanded since our founding in 1869, we remain committed to those who might otherwise be abandoned by society. Today, The Foundling is not only one of the largest providers of foster care and adoption services, we provide services across the entire spectrum of needs: child welfare, juvenile justice, education, services for single mothers, support for young people aging out of foster care, programs for the developmentally disabled and much more."

Treehouse
2100 24th Avenue S, Suite 200
Seattle, WA 98144-4643
https://www.treehouseforkids.org
info@treehouseforkids.org

Two of the many adoption agencies that assist with foster care adoptions:
Barker Adoption Foundation
http://www.barkeradoptionfoundation.org
See complete listing above.

The New York Foundling
https://www.nyfoundling.org
See complete listing above.

Reading Materials

AdoptTogether with Chloe Briggs. "Top 10 Domestic Agencies." https:
  //adopttogether.org/top-10-domestic-agencies/
American Adoptions. "The Differences Between Private and Foster
  Adoption." 2018. https://www.americanadoptions.com/adopt/private
  _or_state_adoption
Ashley Lewis, "'Hicks baby' reunited with her mother and brother." *New
  York Daily News*, August 5, 2015. http://www.nydailynews.com/news
  /national/black-market-baby-reunited-family-51-years-article-1.2315946
Child Welfare. "Foster Care Statistics 2016" and "Numbers and Trends
  April 2018." https://www.childwelfare.gov/pubPDFs/foster.pdf.
Chris Beam. *To the End of June: The Intimate Life of American Foster Care.*
  NY: Mariner Books, Houghton Mifflin, 2014.
Havocscope. "Human trafficking victim prices." 2018. https://www.havoc
  scope.com/black-market-prices/human-trafficking-prices/
Josh Salman, Daphne Chen and Pat Beall. "Foster Kids Lived with
  Molesters. No One Told Their Parents." *USA Today* Network, Updated
  October 16, 2020.
Kaitlin Roig-DeBellis with Robin Gaby Fisher. *Choosing Hope.* NY:
  Putnam's, 2016.
Meredith Hall. *Without a Map: A Memoir.* Boston, MA: Beacon Press, 2007.
Randall Hicks. *Adopting in America: How to Adopt Within One Year.* San
  Diego, CA: WordSlinger Press, 2018.
Sherrie Eldridge. *Twenty Things Adopted Kids Wish Their Adoptive Parents
  Knew.* New York: Random House, 1999.
Wendy Salisbury Howe. *Like Rain on a Dry Place: A Birth Mother's Story.* 2016.

CHAPTER 3

Aging

We all need to know someone like eighty-six-year-old Bill Hennessey to challenge our preconceived ideas about the elderly. "I've just slowed down," said Bill during one of his numerous daily walks. "That's all. Slowed down, but I'm much keener and more knowing in most areas of life than I was at twenty-six." Bill's voice was strong, his ideas were clear, and his words were spoken with deliberation. "Now I analyze much more than I did and I'm not so quick-tempered—in politics, in working relations, in striving for a certain point and not getting it."

When I lived on Irving Place in Manhattan, for four years I shouted out, "Hello, Bill," as I walked down my street or, if I had more time, I stopped to chat with him. We would talk about the play he was writing or theater in general. Playwriting was Bill's fourth career. The first, after he graduated from Swarthmore College in 1921, was as a reporter for a Philadelphia newspaper. After that, he began his second career as an actor. After serving as a Red Cross field supervisor during World War II, he next became a cabinetmaker like his father. When he was thirty-eight, he wrote his first play and went on to write two more. Bill took a course in Native American folklore for background for his play, which takes place in the Old West. Bill told me that he worked on his play for about four hours each day; he was also taking an art course. In addition, he began learning Latin the year before, studying two hours a day. "I've never been bored," Bill explained. "The whole thing is to keep busy and not just sit around. You've got to do things. I don't think of my age. I don't think of what's behind me. I think of what's ahead of me."

I also think of ninety-two-year-old Irwin Zucker, a book publicist who is legendary in the publishing community. Based in Beverly Hills, California, Irwin grew up in Brooklyn, but he moved west and never looked back. Irwin is still working as a book publicist, obtaining radio interviews and other media opportunities for his clients, just as he has done for the last sixty-plus years.

When most people think of aging in America today, do they think of the Bill Hennesseys or the Irwin Zuckers? Or is the general view of the 49.2 million Americans who, as of 2016, were 65 years of age or older (15.2 percent of the population) that they are dependent, depressed, and despondent old people living in nursing homes under constant supervision—or, at the other extreme, living the life of Riley with $1 million in retirement funds as they sail around the world on a cruise with other wealthy retirees?

Neither extreme is really the norm, especially for those in their 60s through late 70s and even into their 80s or 90s, as long as someone's health is reasonably good. Although the rate at which people age has not changed, better health care and living conditions have increased the average life span. In 2017, according to the CDC (Centers for Disease Control and Prevention), life expectancy in the US for men is 76.1 and for women is 81.1 years, compared to only 47 years for men and 49 years for women in the year 1900 and, in the year 1950, only 67 for men and 72 for women. To give a bit of an international perspective, in 2015, according to Infoplease.com, the country with the highest life expectancy is Monaco (89.52) followed by Japan (84.74) and Singapore (84.68). On their list, the United States ranks 43rd (79.68).

We even have to define what you are talking about when you refer to someone as a senior, or elderly. AARP, the Washington, DC-based membership and advocacy organization for seniors with an estimated 38 million members, lowered their membership age requirement to 50; others, like Medicare government health insurance, require that you be 65; some movie theaters offer senior discount tickets to those age 60 and over. Certain jobs, like air traffic controllers and airline pilots, may have a mandatory retirement age. US pilots must retire by 65, up from age 60 through the 2007 Fair Treatment for Experienced Pilots Act. For air traffic controllers, the mandatory retirement age is 56, although there may be exceptions up to 61. By contrast, entrepreneurs or those who are self-employed can continue working as long as their health allows. In theory, a Supreme Court justice serves for life, although some do retire, like Justice Anthony Kennedy, who retired July 31, 2018 at the age of 82 after serving thirty years. In 2020, Associate Supreme Court Justice Ruth Bader Ginsburg was still working at age eighty-seven, but she died on September 18, 2020.

Taking a global view, mandatory retirement is a common practice in South Korea, for example. In 2017, the average mandatory retirement age for salaried workers rose to 61.1, up from 58.8 in 2013 and 60.3 in 2016. Even France has taken a more progressive look at the concept of mandatory retirement, which is illegal in the United States except in certain professions, as noted above. A 2008 law in France made it possible to retire at 70 if someone chose to continue to work. Mandatory retirement at 67 or even earlier seems to have previously been the rule.

It is clear that how someone defines a senior, and when or if someone wants to, or should, retire, and at what age, covers a wide spectrum in the United States.

How many unhappy elders have purely physical ailments? How much discontent is due to the prejudice against the elderly and the overemphasis on youth?

In interviews with the elderly in different places and professions, and with the added firsthand experience of finding myself in the 65+ category, I discovered that there are four groups of seniors who fare better than others 65 and over:

1. Those who were always self-employed or self-reliant, so they are used to making the most of unstructured time
2. Those who are still working, so they have somewhere to go regularly and something to do that keeps them occupied and feeling relevant
3. Those who are retired, financially stable, and healthy enough to enjoy their retirement because they travel and/or have hobbies that preoccupy them, as well as friends and/or family to connect to
4. Those whose dependence on their families is welcomed and encouraged and not resented

By contrast, those who can no longer work for physical or mental reasons but lack the financial resources to live comfortably, those who do not have any hobbies or volunteer jobs to make their 24/7 free time interesting, or those without children or nearby family or friends, often feel lonely, isolated, and useless. These are the elderly people who seem to get caught in a vicious circle of mental and physical problems, including depression and doctor's visits or even hospitalizations, that seems to be broken only by death.

A movement against "ageism," led by such national groups as the Gray Panthers started by Maggie Kuhn in 1970, is trying to eliminate the prejudices and misconceptions that prematurely render too many of our older population "useless." Fortunately, as more and more seniors elect to keep working, whether for personal, professional, or financial reasons, younger generations are being forced to rethink, or at least confront, their outdated views about the elderly for the sake of a harmonious workforce.

For those who either do not have enough money or prefer to use their retirement income or savings for the "extras," there is a wide range of direct services offered to the elderly at the local, city, and state levels. A "model" program might offer free or reduced transportation for the elderly, especially if the transportation is "wheelchair compliant," such as the off-peak reduced rate for seniors that the MTA in New York City offers; food programs, such as free or low-cost meals, available through nonprofit, community, or religious centers; free or low-cost transportation pick-up and return services for those who can no longer drive or are in wheelchairs; reduced or free tickets to movies or cultural events; recreational facilities; employment counseling; free hotline or online information; medical services, such as Medicare, for those 65 and over who meet the eligibility requirements; discounts on rent or mortgage payments; a telephone reassurance program for those who live alone; crime prevention education; advocacy courses; friendly visitors; legal information, and more. Check with your local, city, or state government listings.

The private sector is helping seniors out as well. The Senior List publishes an annual list of senior discounts: https://www.theseniorlist.com /biggest-list-of-senior-discounts/ . Here are just some of the discounts listed: 10 percent discount for 60+ at Burger King; 10 percent for 60+ at selected Ben & Jerry's; 10 percent senior discount for 55+ at Chili's Restaurant; and many more.

Numerous federal programs are also available to assist the elderly (in health care, food, housing, Social Security benefits for those who qualify) and are administered through state agencies. Consult your regional office of the federal US Department of Health, Education, and Welfare (https://www.hhs.gov/) , US Department of Agriculture (https://www.usda .gov/), US Social Security Administration (https://www.ssa.gov/) and US Department of Labor (https://www.dol.gov/) for information on those programs. Also see separate listings in this book in Chapter 9, Counseling, Depression, and Mental Health; Chapter 14, Dying, Death, and Grief; Chapter 6, Business, Entrepreneurship, and Employment; Chapter 18, Food,

Hunger, Nutrition, and Eating Disorders; Chapter 19, Health and Wellness; Chapter 27, Suicide: Prevention and Related Issues; Chapter 29, Veterans and Chapter 30, Volunteerism.

Information on aging and services for the elderly:
American National Red Cross
17th and D Streets, NW
Washington, DC 20006
https://www.redcross.org
Seeks to enable every older person to maintain independence in community life and, when needed, to insure dignified protection and assistance. Through a nation-wide network of chapters, the American Red Cross determines which services are most needed, and senior volunteers are often a mainstay in carrying them out.

The expanded mission of the American National Red Cross is explained at their website: "The Red Cross organization has expanded its services, always with the aim of preventing and relieving suffering. Today, in addition to domes-tic disaster relief, the American Red Cross offers compassionate services in five other areas: community services that help the needy, support and comfort for military members and their families, the collection, processing and distribution of lifesaving blood and blood products, educational programs that promote health and safety, and international relief and development programs."

FINRA Securities Helpline for Seniors
Call 844-57-HELPS (844-574-3577) Monday – Friday 9 a.m. – 5 p.m. Eastern Time
FINRA, authorized by Congress, is a not-for-profit organization overseeing U.S. brokers and dealers. It also offers a helpline especially for senior investors.

Gray Panthers
244 Madison Avenue, #396
New York, NY 10016
www.graypanthersnyc.org
This is a membership organization founded in 1970 by Maggie Kuhn who, at the age of sixty-five, had just retired after working for twenty-five years. The group is international in scope, advocating for the rights of seniors. There are active Gray Panther networks in several states including California, New York, Florida, Michigan, Minnesota, Pennsylvania, Texas, Wisconsin, and Washington, DC.

Association of Mature American Citizens (AMAC)
5 Orville Drive, Suite 400
Bohemia, NY 11716
https://amac.us/
A membership and advocacy organization that started in 2007.

AARP, the American Association of Retired Persons
601 E Street NW
Washington, DC 20049
https://www.aarp.org/
A membership and advocacy organization for those fifty and older offering discounts on insurance, travel, car rental, and other services and products. Founded in 1947 by a retired high school principal, Dr. Ethel Percy Andrus. There are more than 38 million members of AARP, which covers the entire United States, Puerto Rico, the District of Columbia, and the US Virgin Islands.

A Place for Mom, Inc.
701 5th Avenue, Suite 3200
Seattle, WA 98104
https://locate.aplaceformom.com
This is a free referral service about available local assisted living communities throughout the US and Canada. (FYI: The participating senior communities pay to be part of this service.)

National Council on Aging, Inc. (NCOA)
2511 18th Street South, Suite 500
Arlington, VA 22202
https://www.ncoa.org
NCOA started in 1950, and you will find much at this website including information about fall prevention (a leading concern for the elderly), as well as advocacy for health and work-related issues associated with aging. The organization sponsors webinars and conferences such as the 2018 National Senior Center Conference.

Senior Business Directory
c/o Florence Belsky Charitable Foundation
PO Box 786
340 W 42nd Street
New York, NY 10108
https://seniorbusinessdirectory.org
The Senior Business Directory is a project of the Florence Belsky Charitable Foundation, a foundation set up by the late Florence Belsky, a philanthropist who worked her way through Hunter College and law school. It is free for seniors with a product or service to be listed in the business directory. Fill out the form at the website and the administrator will advise you if your listing has been approved.

The Transition Network
505 Eighth Avenue, Suite 1212
New York, NY 10018
www.thetransitionnetwork.org
info@thetransitionnetwork.org
Founded in 2000, this membership organization offers support to women who are going through the transition from working and/or raising children to retirement/the next phase in their lives. There are local chapters in Atlanta, Billings, Boston, Central Ohio, Chicago, Long Island, North/Central New Jersey, New York City, Philadelphia, San Francisco Bay Area, Santa Fe, South Florida, Washington, DC.

Free services for seniors living independently:
Senior Companions
https://www.nationalservice.gov/programs/senior-corps/senior-corps-programs/senior-companions
A public-private partnership created in 1993 with support from Congress, the President, and community groups from around the country, Senior Companions has volunteer seniors age fifty-five and over who qualify for the program who offer services, companionship, and friendship to elders who are living independently and who need help with daily tasks such as paying their bills or going grocery shopping.

Specifically for Baby Boomers, those born between 1946 and 1964:
Snabbo
www.snabbo.com
Started in 2009 by CEO Barbara Crowley, this is a membership/social media site where Boomers and those interested in Boomers can share.

US government sources of help for seniors:
Administration on Aging (AoA)
330 Independence Avenue SW, #4760
Washington, DC 20237
https://eldercare.acl.gov
Per the Older Americans Act of 1965, the goal of AoA is to help seniors to live independently, including offering transportation, caregiver help, health promotion, and adult day care programs. It provides grants to states to aid in offering food to the elderly.

National Center on Elder Abuse (NCEA)
c/o University of Southern California Keck School of Medicine
Department of Family Medicine and Geriatrics
1000 South Fremont Avenue, Unit 22, Building A-6
Alhambra, CA 91803
https://ncea.acl.gov/
Conducts research and offers help and information to prevent abuse of the elderly. At the site, you are cautioned not to report suspected cases of elder abuse to this research center but to call 911 instead.

Elder Justice
https://www.elderjustice.gov
Resources to help prevent elder abuse. Additional information about what to do if elder abuse is suspected at https://www.justice.gov/elderjustice/find-support-elder-abuse

Medicare
https://www.medicare.gov/
Offers information as well as a way to register for Medicare. See more complete listing in Chapter 19, Health and Wellness.

US Social Security Administration (SSA)
https://www.ssa.gov
After creating an account, you can apply for your Social Security benefits online. In a nutshell, the longer you hold out filing for your SSI benefits, the more money you will receive monthly. You can qualify for a reduced benefit at age 62. Based on your age, you will qualify without a reduced rate beginning at 66 or thereabouts, depending on your birth year (go to https://www.ssa.gov/planners/retire/ageincrease.html to find your exact full retirement age). However, if you are able to hold off till 70 to file, you will get the largest amount in your monthly check. There is no value to waiting till after 70 since the monthly amount will not increase. Remember, however, that you may be taxed by the federal government on your monthly Social Security benefits. Depending on your individual situation, you may want to voluntarily ask the government to withhold federal income tax on your benefits. They will withhold any of these four percentages, based on your written request: 7 percent, 10 percent, 12 percent, or 22 percent.

See also listings in Chapter 9, Counseling, Depression, and Mental Health; Chapter 17, Financial Assistance; Chapter 18, Food, Hunger, Nutrition, and Eating Disorders; Chapter 19, Health and Wellness; Chapter 20, Housing and Homelessness; Chapter 29, Veterans; and Chapter 30, Volunteerism.

Reading and Audiovisual Materials

About Schmidt (2002). Starring Jack Nicholson. Directed by Alexander Payne.

Administration for Community Living, Administration on Aging, US Department of Health and Human Services. "2017 Profile of Older Americans." 2018. https://www.acl.gov/sites/default/files/Aging%20 and%20Disability%20in%20America/2017OlderAmericansProfile.pdf

Atul Gawande. *Being Mortal: Medicine and What Matters in the End*. NY: Metropolitan Books, 2014.

The Bucket List. (2007) Starring Jack Nicholson and Morgan Freeman. Directed by Rob Reiner.

FBI. "Scams and Safety" and "Fraud Against Seniors." https://www.fbi.gov /scams-and-safety/common-fraud-schemes/seniors

Fraser Smith, MD, and Ellie Aghdassi, PhD. *Keep Your Brain Young*. Ontario, Canada: Robert Rose, 2014.

Fred Yager and Jan Yager. *Idiot's Guide: Social Security*. New York: Penguin Random House, Alpha Books, 2015.

Infoplease.com, "Life Expectancy for Countries: What Life Expectancy Really Means."

Jonny Bowden, PhD. *The Most Effective Ways to Live Longer*. Beverly, MA: Fair Winds Press, 2010.

Mitch Albom. *Tuesdays With Morrie: An Old Man, a Young Man, and Life's Greatest Lesson*. NY: Doubleday, 1997.

S Shim. "S. Korea's average retirement age rose to 61.1 in 2017: ministry." Yonhap News Agency, January 28, 2018. http://english.yonhapnews.co .kr/news/2018/01/28/0200000000AEN20180128001400315.html

Todd Campbell. "What's the Maximum Social Security at Age 62, 65, or 70?" Published in www.Fool.com and Posted at https://www.fool.com /retirement/2018/01/27/whats-the-maximum-social-security-at-age-62 -65-or.aspx

Understand France. "Retiring in France." https://www.understandfrance .org/Paris/Life4.html

CHAPTER 4

Animal Rights and Care

ANIMAL RIGHTS

Most activities generated by citizens' concern for animal protection focus on a few distinct areas:

- Finding non-animal ways to experiment for scientific, health, and nutritional reasons (anti-vivisection)
- Preventing excessively cruel and painful means of capturing and confining animals (humane and anti-zoo activities)
- Prohibiting the trapping, killing, or imprisonment of animals in danger of extermination (endangered species, conservation)
- Bettering the care of household pets and curbing their numerical explosion as well as safeguards against their potential threats to the human population (animal shelters, pet adoption centers, spaying, and other birth control methods)
- Finding means of nourishment and dress outside the animal kingdom (vegetarianism, veganism, synthetic furs and shoes, non-animal testing of cosmetics)

This last issue will be explored in Chapter 18, Food, Hunger, Nutrition, and Eating Disorders. All the other concerns will be the subject of this chapter on Animal Rights and Care.

The treatment and rights of animals have concerned humankind throughout history and have been debated by such philosophers as Aristotle, Voltaire, and Schweitzer. In sixth-century BC Greece, Pythagoras, upon seeing his neighbor beating a dog, supposedly cried out that he should stop, exclaiming, "It is the soul of my late friend; I can tell from his voice!"

Ancient India ascribed religious and sacred qualities to the cow, a custom that still prevails and is at the basis of that country's widespread vegetarianism among the Hindu population. With the nineteenth-century increase in vivisection—the use of live dogs, cats, rats, mice, and other creatures for dissection and other scientific purposes—the rights of animals began to involve even more issues than whether a person had the right to hunt, beat, or even eat an animal.

How many animals are used in vivisection? According to the figures compiled by the US Department of Agriculture and reprinted at the website for the American Anti-Vivisection Society (AAVS), there were 767,622 used in 2015, down from 834,453 the year before. You can find out details on what kind of animals were used at aavs.org/animals-science/animals-used/.

ANIMAL CARE

Many notables have joined in the cause of preventing the killing of wildlife and certain species in danger of extermination, such as dolphins, coyotes, doves, seals, and whales. Another concern is the very real household pet explosion. It was estimated that in 2017 there were 89.7 million dogs in the US, up from 68 million in the year 2000. Cats were estimated at 70 million in 2015 nationwide

Because of neglect and abandonment, animal shelters in the United States are forced to euthanize hundreds of thousands of dogs and cats each year. The ASPCA reports that 1.5 million pets (670,000 dogs and 860,000 cats) are euthanized each year, but at least the number has gone down since 2011, when 2.6 million pets were euthanized. The ASPCA attributes the improvement in these statistics to an increase in pet adoptions as well as an improvement in the number of stray animals successfully returned to their owners. The problem with strays is not just the ethical issue of killing those that are captured, but the potential health hazards from dog bites and dog waste. Unfortunately, abandoning an unwanted dog or other pet is still one of the most common ways of getting rid of a pet. Surgical birth control is one way of decreasing the household pet population, but many owners fail to "fix" their pets because of ethical commitments, indifference, or an inability to pay the fees of private veterinarians. As an alternative, lower-cost facilities, such as the Spay Neuter Project of Los Angeles, offer free spaying or neutering so that cost is no longer a factor in helping to keep down the pet population. Controlling the pet population without resorting to extermination is usually the responsibility of the pet owners. These goals can be accomplished through public education and animal birth control.

Part of educating the public about animal care is letting potential pet owners know about some of the less obvious costs involved in pet ownership. There is of course the cost of food and an initial visit to a veterinarian, but one of the costs that may not be considered initially is the financial burden when you have to travel—even, with some dogs that require being walked every few hours, on a day trip. One option might be "doggie day care." Doggie day care may mean the animal has more interaction with people or other dogs than a traditional kennel, but you have to check out each situation since the opposite might be true: there may be more interaction at the kennel than there is at the doggie day care. Do not be fooled or taken in by the name of the facility alone. Check it out yourself, and get referrals from other satisfied pet owners that have used it before. Some doggie day care facilities have webcams installed so that you can watch your pet on your phone or computer screen to see what your pet is up to throughout the day.

Pets need care and supervision. Some people may be tempted to leave their pets alone for long periods of time because of work or other commitments, or to save the money and the inconvenience of getting their pet to the care facility. Others may be unaware that most domestic animals need some attention from their master or a surrogate caregiver on a regular basis for their physical and emotional well-being.

Alternatives to doggie or pet day care or using a kennel include having a dog or cat sitter or a dog walker come to your apartment or home to take care of your pet. This might be less disruptive for the pet and the owner. You will have to compare how much it will cost you versus convenience, since there are so many factors to consider. Make sure the pet sitter or walker is reliable and consistent. Since you will not be there to check up on them, unless you install a baby monitor or camera, make sure you have confidence in your pet care arrangement. If you are going to use some kind of surveillance equipment in your home, make sure you follow the laws in your state about such usage. Is advance consent required from the party being watched? There are also, of course, occasional innovative solutions to these challenges, such as the car salesman in Norwalk, Connecticut, who brings his oversized but well-behaved dog to the office each day.

Being kind to domestic pets seems like an obvious approach for those who own dogs, cats, rabbits, or other typical pets. Sadly, there are those who are cruel to animals. You have probably seen the commercials on television asking you to donate to organizations that protect animals. A leader in this area is the American Society for the Prevention of Cruelty to Animals, known as the ASPCA (https://www.aspca.org/). In addition to their work preventing cruelty to animals, and rescuing abandoned ones, they help when disasters occur, like the wildfires in Northern California in July and August 2018, to rescue animals that are left behind.

In researching my book, *Career Opportunities in the Film Industry* (Checkmark Books, 2003, 2009), coauthored with Fred Yager, I conducted interviews related to the unique job of Animal Safety Representative. There is a long history in the film industry of protecting animals used in movie production. Dating as far back as 1925, a formal program for monitoring the use of animals in filmmaking was set up with American Humane (AH), which had actually been protecting animals (and children) from abuse or mistreatment as early as 1877.

As we point out in *Career Opportunities in the Film Industry*, a more concerted effort to protect animals happened after the 1939 accident during the filming of the movie *Jesse James*. A horse and its rider plunged over a seventy-foot cliff. The rider survived the fall but the animal, which had broken its back, died. The next year, the Hollywood office of AH was authorized to start monitoring movie productions that used animal actors.

By adhering to the AH's "Guidelines for the Safe Use of Animals in Filmed Media" and by having an AH Certified Animal Safety Representative on the set, a film is able to earn and display this end-credit disclaimer: "No Animals Were Harmed," a trademarked and coveted distinction for a film. According to the American Humane website, over 1,000 productions a year are monitored.

Laws about animal welfare, registration, and maintenance may vary from state to state. Check your state department of conservation and wildlife. For example, here is the listing for laws related to pet ownership in the state of Connecticut: https://www.jud.ct.gov/lawlib/law/dogs.htm. If you are a new pet owner, you could also ask the veterinarian during your initial visit about what laws and regulations you need to follow in your particular state.

If you need the services of a local animal shelter that accepts stray dogs, search for any of the following: Society for the Prevention of Cruelty to Animals, Humane Society or Association, Animal Welfare League or Society, Animal Rescue League, Animal Protective Association or League, Animal Shelter, Animal Refuge, League for Animals or Animal League, Animal Havens League, Dumb Friends League, Animal Friends, Bide-a-Wee Home Association, and Animal Aid Association.

As noted before, if you are interested in a discussion about whether or not to eat animals for food, you will find organizations, associations, and publications related to that age-old debate in Chapter 18, Food, Hunger, Nutrition, and Eating Disorders.

Organizations and agencies that help with pet adoptions as well as helping you to deal with an unwanted pet in a more humane way than just abandoning it and other issues:

American Society for the Prevention of Cruelty to Animals (ASPCA)
424 E. 92nd Street
New York, NY 10128-6804
(https://www.aspca.org/)
Founded in 1866, the ASPCA offers low-cost hospital and clinic services for animals whose owners cannot afford to pay private veterinarian costs. Shelters for lost, strayed, or unwanted animals are maintained and an educational program for children and adults in the care of animals is available. It is also an advocacy organization championing for humane treatment of animals.

Animal Care Centers of New York City (ACC)
Administrative Office ONLY (No animals at this location)
11 Park Place, Suite 805
New York, NY 10007
https://www.nycacc.org/
info@nycacc.org
For adoption inquiries, write to adopt@nycacc.org. ACC wants to end homelessness for pets as it seeks to place abandoned dogs, cats, or rabbits in welcoming homes throughout the five boroughs of New York City.

Spay Neuter Project of Los Angeles
https://snpla.org/
Founded in 2007, SNPLA now has three locations as well as a mobile bus. Provides free spaying or neutering of pets in the Los Angeles area with the goal of eliminating euthanasia of pets by controlling the pet population.

Animal rights and care organizations with the broader mandate of preserving wildlife as well as humane animal treatment and dealing with pet abandonment:
Defenders of Wildlife
1130 17th Street NW
Washington, DC 20036
https://defenders.org/

Founded in 1925, this membership organization is composed of people who are dedicated to wildlife conservation and conducts public education and research programs to protect wildlife from inhumane treatment. Publishes *Defenders* magazine. One of their initiatives is the Center for Conservation Innovation.

For All Animals
www.forallanimals.org
From the website: "Mission: To inspire positive change on behalf of animals; to support those helping animals; and to document animals and the efforts being made on their behalf. Vision: A world where animals are respected, valued and protected."

Friends of Animals (FOA)
777 Post Road, Suite 205
Darien, CT 06820
https://friendsofanimals.org/
A national nonprofit membership organization formed in 1957 to try to reduce and eliminate the suffering of animals. Programs include activities to curb baby seal slaughter, hunting for sport, poisoning, bounties, and to promote saving porpoises and pet animal spaying. Their website lists vegan advocacy as one of their programs. From their website: "FoA has joined with the nation's original primate sanctuary, Primarily Primates, to help ensure that the non-human residents are well cared for in a safe, stable environment."

Fund for Animals
200 W 57th Street, #705
New York, NY 10019
www.fundforanimals.org
From their website: "The Fund for Animals was founded in 1967 by prominent author and animal advocate Cleveland Amory. For nearly 50 years, the Fund for Animals has spearheaded some of the most significant events in the history of the animal protection movement by employing hard-hitting advocacy campaigns and operating world-famous animal care facilities like the Cleveland Amory Black Beauty Ranch."

Greenpeace Foundation
Windward Environmental Center
1118 Maunawili Road
Kailua, HI 96734
http://greenpeacefoundation.com/
An international multipurpose environmental action organization, founded in 1971, concentrating on stopping the depletion and inhumane killing of seals

in Canada as well as the economics and activities of the worldwide whaling industry.

From their website: "Greenpeace Foundation is dedicated to solving and preventing environmental crises, preserving the ecosystem for future generations of people and animals to enjoy. As humans can speak for themselves, it is an unabashed advocate for species which cannot, upholding the founding ideals of the Greenpeace movement."

World Animal Protection
450 Seventh Avenue, 31st Floor
New York, NY 10123
https://www.worldanimalprotection.us
info@worldanimalprotection.us
World Animal Protection is a nonprofit organization that helps animals in disasters as well as in farming and in the wild.

American Humane
1400 16th Street NW, Suite 360
Washington, DC 20036
https://www.americanhumane.org
Founded more than a hundred years ago, this animal welfare organization has numerous services including rescuing animals and its "No Animals Were Harmed®" Hollywood program.

National Kitten Coalition
7371 Atlas Walk Way #212
Gainesville, VA 20155
Kittencoalition.org
info@kittencoalition.org
Their mission is to "increase survival rates of rescued kittens."

Other animal-related associations and advocacy groups:
American Pet Products Association
http://www.americanpetproducts.org/
A not-for-profit trade membership association for companies that service the pet industry.

Association for Animal Welfare Advancement
15508 W. Bell Road, Suite 101-613,
Surprise, AZ 85374
https://theaawa.org

From their website: "The Association for Animal Welfare Advancement members collaborate to rescue, shelter, rehabilitate and find good homes for animals." One of their projects is the National Council on Pet Population, http://www .petpopulation.org.

Beauty Without Cruelty (BWC)
PO Box 325
Twin Lakes, WI 53181
For customers in the United Kingdom or EU (European Union):
Beauty Without Cruelty
Unit 10 Gamma Terrace
West Road Ipswich, IP3 9SX, United Kingdom
https://www.beautywithoutcruelty.com/
Started in England in 1959 by the president of the National Anti-Vivisection Society, this group manufacturers cosmetics made without animal products or testing on animals. There are stores throughout the United States that stock their products.

American Veterinary Medical Association
931 North Meacham Road, Suite 100
Schaumburg, IL 60173-4360
http://www.avma.org
A professional membership association for veterinarians. In 1981, AVMA and the Auxiliary to the AVMA created National Pet Week, which is celebrated annually the first week in May.

Association for Pet Adoption (APAC)
http://www.myhappytail.org/about/
myhappytail@yahoo.com
Facebook page: https://www.facebook.com/groups/APACTempleTX/
Not-for-profit organization run by volunteers committed to helping people to adopt or foster pets.

Anti-vivisection organizations:
The National Anti-Vivisection Society (UK)
Millbank Tower, Millbank
London, SW1P 4QP
http://www.navs.org.uk/home/
From their UK website: "The National Anti-Vivisection Society, founded in 1875, is the world's first body to challenge the use of animals in research and continues to lead the campaign today. NAVS has spearheaded the adoption of advanced,

non-animal methods; exposed laboratory animal suffering and breaches of reg-ulations with our undercover investigations; funded non-animal scientific and medical research; educated public and media about the flaws of animal research and provided legislators detailed briefings to support the replacement of ani-mals in research with advanced methods." Their animal rescue work is described at http://www.navs.org.uk/animal_rescues/.

National Anti-Vivisection Society (US)
53 W. Jackson Boulevard, Suite 1552
Chicago, IL 60604
https://www.navs.org/us
Founded in 1929, NAVS supports alternatives to the use of animals in scientific research.

Animal Defenders International (USA)
953 Mission Street, Suite 200
San Francisco, CA 94103
http://www.ad-international.org
Advocacy organization for the treatment of animals in experiments, circuses, on the farm, and in other settings.

People for the Ethical Treatment of Animals (PETA)
501 Front Street
Norfolk, VA 23510
https://www.peta.org/
Founded in 1980, PETA is a nonprofit membership organization with the tagline "Animals are not ours to eat, wear, experiment on, use for entertainment, or abuse in any way." With a membership of 6.5 million, it claims to be the "largest animal rights organization in the world."

For listings related to vegetarianism and veganism, please go to Chapter 18, "Food, Hunger, Nutrition, and Eating Disorders."

Reading and Audiovisual Materials

Blackfish (documentary) (2013).

Charlotte's Web (1973) Starring Debbie Reynolds.

Gorillas in the Mist. (1988) Starring Sigourney Weaver as naturalist and mountain gorilla researcher Dian Fossey. Directed by Michael Apted.

Janet Barkas (a/k/a/ Jan Yager). *The Vegetable Passion: A History of the Vegetarian State of Mind.* Originally published by Scribner in 1975. Published in 2015 by Hanancroix Creek Books, Inc. with a new introduction and updated bibliography and resources.

Marley & Me. (2008) Starring Owen Wilson and Jennifer Aniston. Based on the book by John Grogan.

Peter Singer. *Animal Liberation.* New York: Harper Collins, 2009, 1975.

Rei Kimura. *My Name is Eric.* Stamford, CT: Hannacroix Creek Books, Inc., 2010.

CHAPTER 5

Arts

When unemployed and poverty-level groups are highlighted in the media, few include the often underpaid and out-of-work performers, visual artists, and writers. Yet complete reliance on writing, fine arts, or performing as a steady income is rare for all but the lucky few, and even then, it may only be for sporadic periods.

Although the rules of the competitive artistic professions do not change simply because there are unions (getting the assignment or the part may still depend upon talent, luck, and who you know), in those arts where rigid wage requirements are observed, the economic gains have been impressive. For example, the graduated scales and minimum weekly wages developed and enforced by such unions as the Newspaper Guild, Screen Actors Guild, and the Writers Guild have introduced the "living wage" for certain artistic pursuits. However, nonfiction and fiction writers, as well as painters, sculptors, and other artisans, still lack such uniform or unified wage standards. In light of that, it is even more important for artists to band together and, if they cannot officially and unanimously organize, to at least know what the going rates are and where they can turn to for public and private financial help as well as free or more affordable legal assistance.

Few would disagree that public support for the arts in the United States could be a lot more robust. But in some cities, such as New York, lower-cost housing for artists (such as Westbeth) or for performers (such as Manhattan Plaza) have helped those lucky enough to qualify. Private sources for financial aid are available, however, if you know where to look. For example, some writing organizations provide emergency loans, and there are artist colonies with low-cost or free residencies, as well as foundations offering grants and research funds. Some you can apply for, but others, like the mysterious MacArthur Foundation, which grants $625,000 "no-strings-attached" awards paid out in quarterly installments over five years to twenty-four men and women annually, are decided through nominations in a much more mysterious way or, as they put it at their website, "through a constantly changing pool of invited external nominators." One of the more famous recipients is Lin-Manuel Miranda, actor and creator of *Hamilton*, among other musicals, who won the award in 2015.

"Taking care of one's own" has a long history in the theater. For example, there is the Actors Fund (https://actorsfund.org/), which provides help to more than 17,000 men and women annually, and the Actors Fund Home (https://actorsfund.org/services-and-programs/actors-fund-home), an assisted living residence in New Jersey for actors. It includes a thirty-two-bed dementia care residence. There seems to be an attitude of camaraderie evolving in all the arts that is determined and pervasive.

Information sources for money in the arts. Please remember to also check out Chapter 17, Financial Assistance, for any listings that also apply, especially the section on crowdfunding:

Artwork Archive
PO Box 181185
Denver CO 80218
https://www.artworkarchive.com
Publishes "The Complete Guide to 2018 Grants and Opportunities": https://www.artworkarchive.com/blog/the-complete-guide-to-2018-artist -grants-and-opportunities.

Creative Capital
15 Maiden Lane, 18th Floor
New York, NY 10038
https://apply.creative-capital.org/contact-us
Forty-six awards of approximately $10,000 were made in 2018. The website has instructions on applying as well as deadlines for next year's awards. Basic eligibility requirements:

- A US citizen, permanent legal resident, or an O-1 visa holder
- At least twenty-five years old
- A working artist with at least five years of professional experience
- An applicant cannot be a full-time student

Dramatists Guild Foundation
356 W. 40th Street, 2nd Floor
New York, NY 10018

https://dgf.org
info@dgf.org
From their website: "Dramatists Guild Foundation (DGF) is a national charity that fuels the future of American theater by supporting the writers who create it. DGF fosters playwrights, composers, lyricists, and book writers at all stages of their careers. We sponsor educational programs; provides awards, grants, and stipends; offers free space to create new works; and gives emergency aid to writers in need."

Elizabeth Greenshields Foundation
https://www.elizabethgreenshieldsfoundation.org/
Created in 1955 by a Montreal lawyer and amateur artist in memory of his mother. Check the website for eligibility requirements.

Funds for Writers (FFW)
https://fundsforwriters.com/grants/
From their website: "FFW began in March 2000 after a women's writing group in Georgia opened my eyes to the fact that it's hard to write when you can't afford ink for the printer, postage for the manuscripts, or gas to the conferences." Founded by C. Hope Clark, a mystery writer, who says their newsletter reaches 35,000. Also offers the opportunity for a paid ad in her newsletter.

Government sources of information or funding:
National Endowment for the Arts
400 7th Street SW
Washington, DC 20506-0001
From their website: "The National Endowment for the Arts is an independent federal agency that funds, promotes, and strengthens the creative capacity of our communities by providing all Americans with diverse opportunities for arts participation." Funding available through NEA: https://www.arts.gov/publications /2020-guide-national-endowment-arts.
Grants for musicians: https://www.arts.gov/artistic-fields/music.

National Endowment for the Humanities (NEH)
400 7th Street SW
Washington, DC 20506
www.neh.gov
The NEH has fellowships and grants that writers, researchers, and scholars can apply for.

***The following federal agencies, international, and national organiza-
tions cover all the arts–performing arts, fine arts, and photography:***
United States Copyright Office, Library of Congress
101 Independence Avenue, SE
Washington, DC 20559-6000
https://www.copyright.gov
Founded in 1870 with the passage of the copyright bill, which took effect on
January 1, 1978. There is one system of statutory protection for all copyrightable
works, whether published or unpublished. However, registering unpublished
or published works does provide some additional legal and financial benefits
in the event of a copyright infringement suit. Contact an intellectual property
lawyer for professional advice about copyright matters.

Writers and writing:
American Society of Journalists and Authors, Inc. (ASJA)
355 Lexington Avenue, 15th floor
New York, NY 10017-6603
https://asja.org
Founded in 1948, this membership association of professional writers, focusing
on nonfiction, offers its members a range of services, from a monthly newsletter
to a writer referral service to an annual conference for members only. There is
also an annual all-day conference for aspiring writers. For its members, ASJA has
a useful section of their website and in their monthly newsletter where rates are
reported anonymously about various completed assignments. This is a way for
writers to see if any of the fees they are being offered, or that they want to quote,
are in the ballpark with what others are being paid for similar assignments or
even for the same publications, publishers, or other writing opportunities.

ASJA has established the Writers Emergency Assistance Fund (http://asja
.org/For-Writers/WEAF). Since 1982, it has given out 160 grants to writers in
emergency situations totaling an estimated $400,000. You do not have to be a
member of ASJA to apply.

Authors Guild, Inc.
31 West 32nd Street, 7th floor
New York, NY 10016
https://www.authorsguild.org
A membership organization founded in 1912 that represents more than 5,000
writers, especially regarding matters related to copyrights, fair contracts, and
censorship. Through the organization, writers can develop an author website
that is hosted for a reasonable quarterly fee. Dues are on a sliding scale based
on annual income from writing. Members are able to ask questions about their
specific contracts with the legal department of the Authors Guild.

The Drama Desk
www.dramadesk.org
A membership organization of New York drama critics, editors, and reporters. Since 1955, the Drama Desk Awards for excellence in the theater are presented annually.

Dramatists Guild
1501 Broadway, Suite 701
New York, NY 10036
https://www.dramatistsguild.com
A professional organization with initiation and yearly dues that sets professional policies and offers information about markets to its members. It now has an international conference for dramatists as well as online and in-person workshops. There are chapters throughout the country that regularly report in on local theater activities through the DG newsletter.

Newspaper Guild
501 Third Street NW, 6th floor
Washington, DC 20001-2797
www.newsguild.org
Founded in 1933 by Heywood Broun and affiliated with the International Federation of Journalists and the AFL-CIO, this membership organization represents journalists, especially those working for newspapers.

PEN American Center
588 Broadway, Suite 303
New York, NY 10012
https://www.pen.org
This is the US branch of International PEN—an association of writers with centers throughout the world. This membership organization is very concerned with the rights of writers who are doing their job as journalists but find themselves arrested and even imprisoned related to their work. To focus on these situations, they established the PEN/Barbey Freedom to Write Award.

Poetry Society of America
15 Gramercy Park
New York, NY 10003
https://www.poetrysociety.org
Established in 1910, this membership organization sponsors public poetry readings, contests, workshops, and maintains a poetry library.

Academy of American Poets
75 Maiden Lane
New York, NY 10038
https://www.poets.org
A national membership organization founded in 1934 "to encourage, stimulate and foster the production of American poetry by providing fellowships for poets of proven merit, by granting scholarships, awards and prizes for poetic achievement." There are affiliates throughout the United States.

Pen + Brush
29 East 22nd Street
New York, NY 10010
www.penandbrush.org
An international nonprofit organization of professional sculptors, writers, painters, and craftspersons. Founded in 1893 by painters Mary and Janet Lewis. Incorporated in 1912.

Writers Guild of America, East (WGAE)
250 Hudson Street, Suite 700
New York, NY 10013
https://www.wgaeast.org/
This is a labor union for those who write screenplays that are developed and broadcast in theaters, on TV, and on cable. Members pay dues based on their earnings. There are union scales for various aspects of the screenwriting business, from having a treatment option to selling a completed TV series. They also have a very popular script registration program that is open to non-members as well, at a somewhat higher rate than for members. Although registering your script with WGAE does not have the same protection as going through the copyright process with the Library of Congress, it's relatively inexpensive, easy to do, and better than no registration at all: https://www.wgaeast.org/script_registration.

Writers Guild of America West (WGAW)
7000 West 3rd Street
Los Angeles, CA 90048
https://www.wga.org/
See the listing for the Writers Guild East (above), since they offer similar benefits to union members from the West Coast part of the US. They also offer script registration services.

National Writers Union (NWU)
256 West 38th Street, Suite 703
New York, NY 10018
https://nwu.org

From their website: "The National Writers Union (NWU) represents all types of writers working in print, electronic, and multimedia formats." NWU is a member of UAW Local 1981. There are chapters in eight cities or states. Members have contract and grievance help as well as an Authors Network to help each other get the word out about new books. Dues are on a sliding scale based on annual writing income.

Performing arts:
Actors' Equity Association
165 West 46th Street
New York, NY 10036
https://www.actorsequity.org/
From their website: "Actors' Equity Association, founded in 1913, represents more than 51,000 professional Actors and Stage Managers nationwide. Equity seeks to foster the art of live theatre as an essential component of society and advances the careers of its members by negotiating wages, improving working conditions and providing a wide range of benefits, including health and pension plans. Actors' Equity is a member of the AFL-CIO and is affiliated with FIA, an international organization of performing arts unions."

SAG-AFTRA
5757 Wilshire Boulevard
Los Angeles, CA 90036
https://www.sagaftra.org/home
From their website: "SAG-AFTRA represents approximately 160,000 actors, announcers, broadcast journalists, dancers, DJs, news writers, news editors, program hosts, puppeteers, recording artists, singers, stunt performers, voice-over artists and other media professionals." There is an initiation fee as well as annual dues.

Directors Guild of America (DGA)
7920 Sunset Boulevard
Los Angeles, CA 90046
110 West 57th Street
New York, NY 10019
https://www.dga.org/
From their website: "Founded in 1936 when a small group of the best-known directors of the time joined together to protect the economic and creative rights of directors in motion pictures, the DGA is the world's preeminent organization representing directors and members of the directorial team, including Directors, Assistant Directors, Unit Production Managers, Associate Directors, Stage Managers and Production Associates—17,000 strong worldwide."

League of Resident Theatres (LORT)
1501 Broadway, Suite 1801
New York, NY 10036
http://lort.org/
From their website: "LORT is the largest professional theatre association of its kind in the United States, with 75 member Theatres located in every major market in the US, including 29 states and the District of Columbia."

Producers Guild of America
11150 West Olympic Blvd., Suite 980 Los Angeles, CA 90064

PGA East
1501 Broadway, Suite 1710 New York, NY 10036 https://www.producersguild.org/
PGA is a non-profit trade membership organization for those the production teams in film, television, and new media. Activities include an annual conference for networking and educational opportunities as well as publication of a related magazine entitled Produced By. One of their key functions, as stated at their website, is "creating fair and impartial standards for the awarding of producing credits."

Visual and fine arts:
Indian Arts and Crafts Board (IACB), Department of the Interior
1849 C Street, NW
Washington, DC 20240
https://www.doi.gov/iacb
A federal agency established in 1935 to promote the development of Native American fine arts and handicrafts—the creative work of Indian, Eskimo, and Aleut people. The headquarters acts as an information clearinghouse.

National Gallery of Art
6th and Constitution Avenue, NW (National Mall)
Washington, DC 20565
https://nga.gov
Called "the nation's museum," all the art given to the museum has been privately donated. The collection is housed in two buildings, East and West. There are self-guided and other tours available. From their website: "From a beginning [75 years ago] with a selection of 126 paintings and 26 sculptures given by the Gallery's founder Andrew W. Mellon, the collection has grown to more than 145,000 works today."

National Arts Club
15 Gramercy Park South
New York, NY 10003

www.nationalartsclub.org
Founded in 1898 by art and literary critic Charles DeKay, this private membership club relocated to the Samuel Tilden Mansion in 1906. Membership, with
dues ranging from $1,000 to $5,000 a year, needs to be proposed by two current members in good standing–one to propose and another to second the
membership.

National Museum of the American Indian
1 Bowling Green
New York, NY 10004
Free museum in downtown Manhattan that is part of the Washington,
DC-based Smithsonian. There are artifacts on display reflecting various tribes
of Native Americans. The museum also sponsors free events throughout the
year such as an expert discussion about the real foods that were eaten at the
first Thanksgiving.

Reading and Audiovisual Materials

Anne Lamott. *Bird by Bird: Some Instructions on Writing and Life*. NY:
    Anchor, 1995.

Genius (2016). Starring Colin Firth and Jude Law. About the complicated
    relationship between F. Scott Fitzgerald and his Scribner editor,
    Maxwell Perkins.

Jennifer Raiser. *Burning Man: Art on Fire*. Revised and updated.
    Photography by Sidney Erthal and Scott London, et. al. Race Point
    Publishing, 2016.

Julia Cameron. *The Artist's Way*. 25th Anniversary Edition. NY:
    TarcherPerigee, 2016.

Marilyn Horowitz. *How to Write a Screenplay in 10 Weeks*. NY, 2011.

Stephen King. *On Writing: A Memoir of the Craft*. 10th Anniversary
    Edition. NY: Scribner, 2010.

Steven Pressfield. *The War of Art: Break Through the Blocks and Win Your
    Inner Creative Battles*. NY: Black Irish Entertainment LLC, 2002.

Susan Granger. *150 Timeless Movies*. Stamford, CT: Hannacroix Creek
    Books, 2017.

Syd Field. *Screenplay: The Foundations of Screenwriting*. NY: Delta, 2007.

CHAPTER 6

Business, Entrepreneurship, and Employment

It used to be that you could search "how to start your own business." Now, however, you might instead find the wording has switched to "entrepreneurship." The concept is still pretty much the same thing: How to start your own business versus finding a job where you will be working for others.

I put business/entrepreneurship and employment in one chapter because many businesses that start out with just one owner, or entrepreneur, soon grow to employ others. Alternatively, if you run a business, you might ultimately decide this is not the right career path for you, or you might even decide you want or need a job "on the side" until your business becomes more lucrative.

Every business, unless you inherited it from your family, has to start somewhere! Look at the first company to become a trillion-dollar company: Apple. The inventors of technology equipment that has changed the way people communicate or interact, especially with the groundbreaking iPhone, started out in April 1976 when it was cofounded by Steve Jobs and Steven Wozniak, both college dropouts, and Ronald Wayne. They began the company in the garage of Jobs's childhood home in Los Altos, California.

Craig Newmark, founder of craigslist and Craig Newmark Philanthropies, shared about his own startup experience: "When I started craigslist, I had no specific vision, no expectations. However, for maybe tens of millions, craigslist became a place where you could put food on the table, where you could find a table, where you could find a roof to put that table under. That feels really good and really surreal."

Billionaire Jeff Bezos quit his Wall Street job to start Amazon.com in 1994 when he was thirty years old. He also initially ran his fledgling company out of his garage, but Bezos stated in an interview with the Academy of

Achievement, quoted at Fundable, that his parents helped him get his start by investing their life's savings of a couple hundred thousand dollars in his internet venture. The rest, as they say, is history.

Okay, so you want to start a business and your parents are unable or unwilling to give you a couple hundred thousand dollars for your venture. What can you do to get started? Today, more than ever before, there are options for those who want to start a company. Crowdfunding is an option that has become even more popular since the granddaddy of crowdfunding, Kickstarter, was founded in Brooklyn in 2009. In this chapter, you will find listings of various crowdfunding sites and options. (More detailed descriptions are included in the "Crowdfunding" section of Chapter 17, Financial Assistance.)

A newer version of crowdfunding was introduced within the last few years that enables you to offer an investment option in your company. It is a very different model than the traditional crowdfunding platform, which usually offers a perk or reward for the financial expenditure but is a one-time purchase or option rather than an ongoing relationship. For this business-oriented type of crowdfunding option, see the annotated listings below.

Yes, you usually need money to start a new company. How much money will vary greatly depending upon what you plan to sell; whether you plan to work from home or in an outside office, with rent and related additional overhead; and whether you are offering a service, selling other people's products, or manufacturing your own products. Keep in mind all the expenses that go into research, development, and manufacturing will incur costs.

Before you even start your company, however, you will have to call it something. What you name your company is not just a key decision for the identity of the company but has importance locally and even nationally or internationally, since you cannot reuse the name of another company for several reasons: first, because it would create confusion in the marketplace, and second, many companies trademark their names, so it would be a trademark violation if you used the same name.

You will probably have to register the name of your company with the local town hall as a DBA—Doing Business As.

In addition to your DBA, you have to decide if you are going to do business as an individual (also called sole proprietor), using your personal social security number to pay local, state, and federal taxes related to your business, or if you will set up an LLC or a corporation for your business.

There is free advice available from SCORE, the Service Corps of Retired Executives, listed below. This national organization, sponsored by the SBA (Small Business Administration), has more than 10,000 volunteer business executives who provide free business advice as well as workshops and seminars for new or current small business owners.

If you have an accountant, you could ask him or her for suggestions about setting up your business. If this is outside your accountant's area of expertise, ask for a recommendation for a trusted business consultant to help you set up your company.

If you do decide to become a corporation or an LLC, you will have to file certain forms and pay certain fees to register your company. There are some protections that being a corporation or LLC offers you versus remaining a sole proprietor. These issues are too important and too technical for me to advise what is best in your particular situation. Best to consult a business consultant.

In addition to hiring a lawyer, there are services you can use on your own to complete the paperwork: LegalZoom and Incorporate.com, described below.

If you become a corporation, you will have to get a Federal tax identification number, which is separate from your social security number. That will be the number that you use related to your business. You can obtain that tax ID number, known as an Employer Identification Number (EIN) from the government. (https://www.irs.gov)

You might also contact the trade association for whatever type of business you want to start. You will probably want to consider joining that trade association once you are up and running as a business anyway. They will more than likely be happy to answer your questions about how to get started.

These are some of the technical aspects of starting a business or becoming an entrepreneur. Here is a short self-quiz to help you decide if you have what it takes to start and make a go of your own business:

Should you start your own business/become an entrepreneur?
Answer each question with "Yes" or "No."

1. Are you passionate about the business you want to start?
2. Do you have enough money to pay your rent/mortgage and all your other bills until your business becomes profitable, which might take as long as 1–5 years?
3. Have you figured out how much money you need to launch your business?
4. Are you able to raise the money necessary to launch your business?
5. Are you good with money or, if you have money challenges, are you able to employ someone to handle the money part of things for you?
6. Are you detail-oriented?
7. Do you prefer to give orders rather than to take orders?
8. Do you have a business plan?
9. Have you done market research to know that your product, service, or store (online or brick-and-mortar) is something that seems to be in demand?
10. Do you have the necessary background or knowledge to successfully run the business you are planning or, if you do not, are you prepared to learn or to partner with someone who possesses that information?
11. Do you have a marketing plan for telling potential customers about your product/service/store?
12. Is your family supportive of your new business venture?

If you answered "yes" to all of the above twelve questions, you are in a good position to begin launching your new business. If you answered "no" to one or more questions, look over those "nos." What do they say about any roadblocks to launching your business? Are they surmountable challenges that you are able to deal with so you can turn those "nos" into "yeses" before you start a business that will take up so many resources including time, emotion, and especially money?

Funding sources for businesses:
Amber Grants
https://ambergrantsforwomen.com/get-an-amber-grant/apply-now/
Sponsored by WomensNet.net. From their website: "The Amber Grants began in 1998. It was launched by Womensnet to honor the memory of a young woman (Amber) who died at the age of 19—unable to fulfill her entrepreneurial dreams. Today the Amber Grant helps women like you achieve the dreams that Amber could not."

The grant is $2,000 each month to a woman business owner. Once a year, the annual recipients are all eligible to get one $25,000 grant. There is a $15 application fee, and a short form to complete, to apply for the monthly grant.

Dare to Dream Grant (Ann Bancroft Foundation)
211 N 1st Street, #480
Minneapolis, MN 55401
https://www.annbancroftfoundation.org/programs/grants/daretodream
From their website: "Fund Art, Cultural, Leadership, Educational, & Outdoors/ Wilderness Experiences for girls in grades 4 through 12, allowing them to begin exploring the outside world and begin recognizing their own abilities, values and strengths in the process."

Eligibility: Applicant must reside in Minnesota; requests cannot exceed $500.

Deadlines: Spring, April 1; fall, October 1.

Awesome Foundation
contact@awesomefoundation.org
Every month, a $1,000 grant is awarded. There are chapters of this foundation throughout the US and internationally.

From their website: "The Awesome Foundation is a global community advancing the interest of awesome in the universe, $1000 at a time. Each fully autonomous chapter supports awesome projects through micro-grants, usually given out monthly. These micro-grants, $1000 or the local equivalent, come out of pockets of the chapter's "trustees" and are given on a no-strings-attached basis to people and groups working on awesome projects."

Apply at https://www.awesomefoundation.org/en/submissions/new.

EquityNet
945 Liberty Avenue, Suite 500
Pittsburgh, PA 15222
https://www.equitynet.com
From their website: "EquityNet is a recognized pioneer and innovator of crowd-funding and marketplace finance, operating one of the largest business funding

platforms since 2005. EquityNet maintains many patents in the space and has helped over 100,000 individual entrepreneurs connect with investors, lenders, incubators, government support entities, and other members of the entrepreneurial community to plan, analyze, and fund privately-held businesses."

Girl Boss Foundation

2046 Hillhurst Avenue, #112

Los Angeles, CA 90027

https://www.girlboss.com/foundation

From their website: "The Girlboss Foundation awards one grant biannually to female entrepreneurs pursuing creative endeavors. Each grant beneficiary will receive project funding of $15,000, in addition to exposure through the Girlboss platform and community."

Eligibility: "Grants are exclusive to female business owners in the worlds of design, fashion, music, and the arts. To be eligible, applicants must identify as female, be US residents, and be 18 years or older by the close of the submission window. Unfortunately, we are currently unable to accept international applications."

Henry T. Nicholas III Foundation

https://www.htnfoundation.org/

info@htnfoundation.org

Offers grants to 501(c)(3) nonprofit organizations in their various focus areas, including the rights of crime victims.

MicroVentures

11601 Alterra Parkway, Suite 100

Austin, TX 78758

https://microventures.com/

From their website: "Founded in 2009, MicroVentures built a platform that gives both accredited and non-accredited investors access to invest in startups. Over $85M has been raised on our platform to date. MicroVentures is one of the financial industry's first organizations which merges crowdfunding with the venture capital industry. The San Francisco, CA and Austin, TX based firm provides an opportunity for angel investors to invest in startups alongside Venture Capitalists, often at the same terms. We conduct detailed due diligence on startups and if approved we help them raise capital from angel investors."

Walmart Foundation

http://giving.walmart.com/apply-for-grants/

Sam Walton opened his first store in 1950. Grants are given to nonprofit organizations and businesses. The three key areas that the foundation awards grants in are opportunity, sustainability, and community. The financial range for the grants is from $250 to $250,000 or more.

Government, nonprofit, and private sector resources for those who want to start or run a business including becoming an entrepreneur:

Entrepreneur Media, Inc
18061 Fitch
Irvine, CA 92614
https://www.entrepreneur.com
This company is devoted to educating entrepreneurs through its podcasts, videos, magazine (*Entrepeneur*), books, and online articles. Through the website, you can subscribe to the magazine on a print, digital, or print + digital basis. The website also features franchise businesses that are for sale.

Entrepreneurs' Organization (EO)
500 Montgomery Street, Suite 700
Alexandria, VA 22314
https://www.eonetwork.org
Founded in 1987, this is a global networking membership association with 186 chapters in 58 countries.

FoundersCard
Founders Card LLC
73 Spring Street, # 502
New York, NY 10012
https://founderscard.com/
Membership organization with over 15,000 entrepreneurs who get invited to members-only global networking events in large cities such as New York City, Los Angeles, and Miami, as well as offering discounts on travel and business products and services.

Network For Teaching Entrepreneurship (NFTE)
120 Wall Street, 18th Floor
New York, NY 10005
https://www.nfte.com/
From their website: "NFTE partners with schools where at least 50% of students qualify for free or reduced price lunch."

SCORE Association
1175 Herndon Parkway, Suite 900
Herndon, VA 20170
https://www.score.org/
From their website: "SCORE is volunteer business people helping small business people solve business problems. Volunteers give freely of their time, energy and knowledge to help others. SCORE volunteers donate over 1 million hours of their time each year to support their communities."

Find local SCOREs at https://www.score.org/find-location
To request a mentor, go to https://core.score.org/mentoring/request

SKI Charities
New York, NY
http://skicharities.org
A nonprofit organization that was started by Shyam K. Iyer in 2010 to empower women and their families in Zimbabwe and southern Chile through microfinancing to help them to become entrepreneurs.

US Small Business Administration (SBA)
409 3rd Street SW
Washington, DC 20416
https://www.sba.gov
An independent federal agency created by Congress in 1953, the SBA offers help to business owners through its regional offices. SCORE, listed above, is one of their initiatives. For information about SBA loans and funding, go to https://www.sba.gov/funding-programs/loans or https://www.sba.gov/funding-programs.

Please note (from their website): "The SBA doesn't give grants to start or expand most businesses. Limited grants are available for exporting, as well as research and development."

Learn more about this at https://www.sba.gov/funding-programs/grants.

Incorporate.com
https://www.incorporate.com
Online fee-based service offering direct help with incorporating or LLCs. Since they are not able to offer legal or financial advice, although there are articles at their site about what your incorporation options are, you should consider consulting with a lawyer or business consultant about your best option before using the site for the nuts and bolts of the process.

Legal Zoom
101 N. Brand Boulevard
Glendale, CA 91203
https://www.legalzoom.com/
Started in 1999, this online fee-based service can help with incorporating or LLCs and other legal issues that businesses or entrepreneurs have to deal with.

American Management Association (AMA)
1601 Broadway
New York, NY 120010
http://www.ama.org

Membership association for managers. Offers online and in-person seminars and training as well as newsletters.

CEO Club (Chief Executive Officer's Club, Inc.)

333 West 86th Street, #204
New York, NY 10024
www.ceoclubs.org
Founded in 1977, this is a networking membership association for CEOs. The website boasts over 10,000 members worldwide. Organizes international trips to learn about doing business with peers in other countries.

National Association of Female Executives (NAFE)

https://www.nafe.com/
Founded in 1972, NAFE is a part of the Working Mother Network, part of the Bonnier Corporation. This membership and educational association has networking and leadership summits. There are local affiliates in several states, including California and New York. Check the website for a complete list.

National Association of Women Business Owners (NAWBO)

601 Pennsylvania Ave NW, South Building, Suite 900
Washington, DC 20004
https://www.nawbo.org/
Founded in 1975, NAWBO is a networking and educational membership association for women business owners. It has local chapters as well as a national conference. Advocating for legislation to help women business owners and entrepreneurs is part of their mission. Its website states that they have more than 10 million members. Benefits include an annual educational and networking conference that is held in a different US city each year. They have created the NAWBO Institute for Entrepreneurial Development, an online learning platform.

Startup Professionals, Inc.

1950 Ventnor Circle
Prescott, AZ 86301
https://www.startupprofessionals.com/
Founder and CEO Martin Zwilling and Founder and Chairman Ernst H. Gemassmer provide advice to startups through coaching, blogs, books, and related published articles. Zwilling's related books include *Do YOU Have What It Takes to Be an Entrepreneur?*

Vistage
Vistage Worldwide
4840 Eastgate Mall
San Diego, CA 92121
https://www.vistage.com/
An educational membership organization, started in 1957, that helps businesses to grow through participation in a Peer Advisory Group, which is a group that meets monthly consisting of 12-16 successful CEOs and business leaders. Monthly executive one-to-one coaching is also available. There are 23,000 Vintage members in 20 countries.

Women's Media Group
PO Box 2119
Grand Central Station
New York, NY 10163-2119
http://www.womensmediagroup.org
Invitation-only membership association for women in the media including books, magazines, agents, film, TV, radio, and new media. Sponsors monthly luncheons, with guest speakers, as well as smaller lunches or dinners with six to eight members at restaurants or in members' apartments or homes in the tri-state area. Sponsors a college summer internship program.

This program teaches teens to become entrepreneurs and even offers them six college credits through UCSC (University of California San Diego) when they complete the 34-week courses:
Whatever It Takes (WIT)
550 West B Street, 4th Floor
San Diego, CA 92101
www.doingwit.org
info@doingwit.org
The tagline for this nonprofit organization is "Launching Teen Entrepreneurs." From their website: "Based in San Diego with locations in St. Louis, Austin, and New York City, WIT is the only six-unit college credit social entrepreneur and leadership program in the country. Founded in 2009 by Sarah Hernholm, a retired teacher."

For more organizations and programs that are helping children, teens, and young adults to become entrepreneurs, see the listings in Chapter 15, Education, under "Business or Entrepreneurship."

These organizations or services provide referrals to publicists or free daily listings of potential publicity opportunities that businessmen and women or entrepreneurs might find useful:

HARO

https://www.helpareporter.com/

Started by Peter Shankman and now part of Cision, HARO sends out three lists of potential media opportunities every day during the work week. You then have to pitch yourself or your company or product using the email address that is provided. Sign-up is free and then you will automatically get the daily announcements. Competition to get the attention of the media is fierce, however, considering there are more than 800,000 subscribers to the service. You can also sign up to create a pitch if you are a source or member of the media looking for publicity. Your request will be reviewed and if it is acceptable, it will be posted on the day and time that you requested or at the discretion of HARO.

PitchRate

www.pitchrate.com

Free subscription service through Wasabi Publicity that sends out available publicity opportunities that you can pitch yourself or your product to, if it seems like a good fit.

Public Relations Society of America (PRSA)

120 Wall Street, 21st Floor

New York, NY 10005-4024

https://www.prsa.org/

Membership organization for the US of this international association whose members work in the field of public relations. Provides information about the field, job openings and events at local chapters, and a national annual convention.

EMPLOYMENT

For some, it is only because you have a job that you are able to start a business "on the side," running the business and doing your job until your business is successful enough to quit your job. For others, being a business owner or entrepreneur is not something you dream of doing. Having a job is important to most adults, and even to teens who want or need to work. Work of course provides money to survive, but it's actually more than that. It can be a source of pride and satisfaction, a place where you learn and grow as much as you give to others. Whether your employment lasts months, years, or a lifetime, many people become identified with the company, nonprofit organization, or government agency where they are employed.

How to Deal With Losing Your Job, Whatever the Reason

Losing a job can be devastating on many levels: economically it can really hurt your wallet, especially if you lack a big emergency savings account. But it can also cause loss of self-esteem and routine and pattern to your weekdays, especially if you do not have any hobbies or other interests to keep you busy.

Finding a new job if you have lost your job, whether you were downsized, fired, or you quit, should become your new job. You have to put as much time and energy into looking for a job as you were putting into working. If you go about your job search haphazardly, you may not get the results you need and want. The longer you are out of work, in general, the harder it is to get back into the groove of working, so brush off your resume and get going on your job search.

Getting downsized or fired can be a very frightening experience, but there are things you can do to handle many of the problems that may arise.

1. How to Deal with Your Anxiety

Even if you know it's coming, when it actually happens, a job loss can rock even the most secure worker. What reactions might you expect when you find out you've been fired? I remember when I was fired on the spot for asking my former boss to talk to me with more respect. I was shocked. I naively thought he was going to thank me for pointing out that his behavior should change. After the shock wore off, my next thought was anxiety related to finances. Fortunately, my husband had a job, but we also relied on my income, which stopped all at once, with just the rest of that week paid, no severance. I was a consultant and the job spanned six months, so it was definitely a jolt financially.

Avoid feeling bad about yourself just because you were fired. Occasionally it might be related to something you actually did wrong, but often, especially in the private sector, it is related to:

- An economic downturn at the company that causes management to cut back
- A personality clash between you and your immediate boss, the senior executives, coworkers, or subordinates
- A change in the marketplace that is causing the company to tighten its belt

- A change in direction; the reason you were initially hired may no longer be valid, and they may not see a place for you at the company in another capacity

Getting fired or downsized is so common that it no longer has the stigma it used to have. Many years ago, during a lunch with a well-respected publishing executive who was then publisher of one of the major houses, he told me that getting fired when he was younger was one of the best things that ever happened to him. He learned so much from that experience and it made him stronger.

There are also unusual circumstances that impact not just you or hundreds or thousands but even millions, as in what happened in March 2020 in the United States, and in previous months around the world, because of the Coronavirus pandemic. Rebecca Rainey and Quint Forgey, writing in POLITICO, reported that in the three-week period ending on April 4, 2020, 17 million unemployment claims had been filed. In February, just two months before, the country had its *lowest* unemployment rate in fifty years. So much changed in such a short period of time; changes impacted every sector of the world's economy and lifestyle in a way that will be remembered for generations.

But you may feel stressed from what has just happened, so find a way to cope with it. Consider joining a job-loss support group or beginning or increasing your exercise regime—take a walk, jog, or work out at a gym—to cope with your anxiety.

2. Handling Your Finances

This is when having a nest egg or an emergency fund really comes in handy. If you have such a fund, pat yourself on the back because you will be able to handle the change in your financial circumstances, with or without a severance package, a lot better than someone who lacks such a fund.

What? No rainy day funds? No worries. You can and will get through this period until you find a new job. Here are some tips for making whatever funds you do have last:

- Cut back on all nonessentials. That means watching TV rather than going out to the movies. If you live in a big city and you're used to taking a cab, Uber, or even public transportation between relatively short distances, as long as the weather is okay and it's safe, try walking instead. Make your money stretch when it comes to food costs, including cutting back on eating out. Instead of buying books for your job hunt, go to the library and borrow them for free.

- Check your eligibility for state unemployment insurance. Eligibility varies from state to state, as well as what benefits you might receive, and for how long. You may be able to file your claim over the phone or online.
- If you own your home or your apartment and have equity in it, you may be able to apply for a home equity loan, which could be at a much lower interest rate (currently in the 5 percent range) than a credit card advance for immediate cash (which could be at a zero APR for a certain period of time, if you get a special offer, or as high as 15–28 percent if it is at a regular credit card interest rate). However, be aware that it will be much harder to convince lenders that you are a good risk for repayment of the loan since you have lost your job. You may need to show that you have some savings, unemployment insurance benefits, or other revenue streams so the monthly interest payments on the loan will be covered.
- If you have any possessions that you always considered selling but never got around to it, now might be the time to do that. You can sell jewelry or old coins at a local vendor or even online. You may also be able to sell books, vintage vinyl records, unopened toys, or other collectibles through online sites such as eBay, or you could even have a yard sale.
- If things are really tough, consider selling your apartment or home and, at least temporarily, renting or even moving in with friends or relatives who will help you out in your time of need.

3. The Smart Way to Look for a New Job

The internet has made it easier than ever to at least learn about available jobs. You can use free job engines to set up alerts for what you are looking for and the geographic area that you prefer to work in, and they will send you new job openings that meet your basic criteria. After that, you have to apply. The downside of this approach is that it has increased the number of applicants for each opening, which means that your resume has to be outstanding and targeted to that particular job. If possible, rewrite your resume with an emphasis on the skills that a specific job opening is looking for. You may have a better outcome than if you use the same resume for all job openings without customizing it.

In addition to free job search engines, like Indeed.com, you can look for a job through LinkedIn.com, the social media site. If you answer a job opening through LinkedIn, be aware that the potential employer may use your LinkedIn profile as a source of information about you as well as your resume, so make sure your profile is as up-to-date and as compelling as possible. Of course, make sure there are no typos or grammatical errors anywhere in your profile.

You can still use an agency or headhunter to help you find a job. Just make sure you know in advance who is paying the agent's fee—will it be you or the future employer? Since you have just lost your job and you may not have the funds to pay an employment agency, try to stick with applying for jobs where the future employer is paying the fee.

4. Boost Your Chances for Success

With so many competing for every job, how can you increase the likelihood that you (or your resume) will stand out?

Whether you attend an online event through Zoom, Microsoft Teams, Google Hangouts, Skype, or any other videoconferencing platforms, or you can go to meetings in person, the principle is the same: connect, connect, connect. That means you need to attend as many functions as possible where you will meet people who are hiring in the field or industry that you want to work in. Whether that means attending workshops, seminars, or conferences, or private parties that you can get yourself invited to, get out there and meet and greet. You may also want to attend breakfasts, lunches, or after-work networking events sponsored by the local Chamber of Commerce where you live, as well as similar events by any associations you belong to whose members are in your industry. If you are not a member, since this might not be the right time financially for you to join up, consider attending one or more events, such as the monthly meeting of an association, as a paying guest. It will also give you the chance to see if you might want to become a member when your situation changes and it is financially feasible for you to join.

Use this time as an opportunity to take some courses that might help you to sharpen or update your skills. Fortunately, today there are numerous courses available online so you do not have to worry about making the time, or spending the money to travel, to get to a course that meets in person. In addition to skills training, consider going for a certificate in your field, or even a new field, if you can afford it, to help you stand out from the competition.

Write an article or a blog and post it to your own or another website, whether for a fee or just for the prestige and visibility. That might help to get potential employers noticing you and coming to you with a job offer.

5. Thinking of a Career Change?

Getting downsized or fired can be an opportunity to take stock and ask yourself if you are doing what you really want to do. It can be the catalyst to giving a different answer to the question "What's next?" than the career path that you have been on. This might be a chance to go back to school, or to go for a graduate degree, if this is something you have put off. There might be scholarships or fellowships available to you, depending upon what field of study you want to pursue. Check at the schools, colleges, or graduate programs that you might want to apply to for any financial assistance that they might offer. Also check with any groups that you might be part of, such as if you are a veteran, where money might be available for school.

Consider the skills that you have and the times in your life when you felt most fulfilled at work. Is that the work you find yourself doing now? If not, is it possible for you to find that type of work again? If you have skills that you have not pursued for a career, can you find a career that will more closely match your skills? Richard N. Bolles's classic book, *What Color Is Your Parachute? A Practical Manual for Job-Hunters and Career-Changers*, updated annually, is still a worthwhile tool to rethinking your career goals and finding a job that is right for you.

Over the years, many entrepreneurs and freelancers have told me that the catalyst to self-employment was losing a job. If you think you have what it takes to start your own business, read or review the first part of this chapter, "Business/Entrepreneurship." See if that is the career path that you want to take at this point in your life and career.

6. Keep a Positive Attitude!

The worst thing someone who has lost his or her job—whether through downsizing, being fired, or even quitting—can do is to become negative and disgruntled. That may push potential employers away faster than anything else. So, as hard as it might be to do, try to stay positive and optimistic. So many terrific people have lost jobs, for a whole range of reasons, that you should know that you are not alone. Of course, if you know in your heart of hearts that you did something that led to you being let go, use this as a learning experience so things will go better at your next job. If you are finding negativity is too hard to combat on your own, consider joining a support group for those who have lost their jobs, or even seeing a therapist. You need to go about your job search, as well as any interviews that you do, in person or by phone, with your best foot forward. Sharing how you feel about what happened to you, as well as working on developing or reinforcing a positive mental attitude, may make all the difference in your job search.

Good luck!

Note: The previous section is a revised, edited, and updated version of the article I wrote entitled, "What to Do If You're Fired," that was published in *Parade Magazine*, 5/31/1992. Revised and reprinted by the copyright holder, Jan Yager.

Federal Government Jobs

Many may not immediately think of the federal government as a potential employer, but it is one of the biggest ones in the US with more than two million employees.

USA.gov

https://www.usa.gov/find-a-job

This is where you will find out all kinds of information about working in the US, for citizens as well as immigrants, including foreign workers. To search for specific job openings: https://www.usajobs.gov/Search?.

Look over the site carefully. There are many ways to customize your search according to the category of employee you fit into covering everything from "Veterans," "Senior Executives," and "Students" to various categories of federal employees.

You can also go to the website for the US government agency that you are especially interested in, such as the FBI (Federal Bureau of Investigation). Their eligibility requirements: https://www.fbiagentedu.org/fbi-requirements/

Armed forces of the United States:
US Air Force
https://www.airforce.com/apply-now

US Army
https://www.goarmy.com

Coast Guard
https://www.gocoastguard.com/apply-now

Marines
https://www.marines.com/becoming-a-marine/overview.html

US Navy
https://www.navy.com/careers

US Space Force
www.spaceforce.mil

Even though military service is now voluntary in the US, all males between the ages of 18 and 25 are required to register with the Selective Service System (SSS):
Selective Service System (SSS)
https://www.sss.gov/register/
All male US citizens and even undocumented male immigrants who are 18 through 25 are required to register with Selective Service. Visit the website for more detailed information about who needs to register and who is exempt, including, at this point, females.

State government jobs:
Remember that every state has a need for employees as well. Each state will have job openings posted on their website. In Tennessee, for example: https://www.tn.gov/hr/js1/employment-opportunities.html.

Local government jobs:
In addition to finding the website for your local community, you can look for government jobs at every level through LinkedIn or other free job search portals such as Indeed.com (listed below).
Follow the same process to find jobs that are available at the city level. If you live in a suburb or a rural area, you may have local government jobs through your county as well.

Running for Office
Democratic National Committee
430 South Capitol Street Southeast
Washington, DC 20003
https://democrats.org/

Emily's List
1800 M Street NW, Suite 375N
Washington, DC 20036
www.emilyslist.org
From the website: "Created by Ellen R. Malcolm in 1985 to fund campaigns for pro-choice Democratic women, and strategically torch-light the balance of power in our government.

"The name 'EMILY's List' was an acronym for 'Early Money Is Like Yeast' (i.e., it makes the dough rise)."

Independent Voting

CUIP, 417 Fifth Avenue, Ste 811
New York, NY 10016-2204
https://independentvoting.org
Representing the approximately 40 percent of Americans who identify themselves as independent, not belonging exclusively to either the Democratic or the Republican parties.

National Women's Political Caucus (NWPC)

PO Box 65010
Washington, DC 20035
http://www.nwpc.org/
Mission statement from the website: "NWPC is a national, pro-choice, multipartisan, grassroots membership organization dedicated to identifying, recruiting, training and supporting women candidates for elected and appointed office."

New Politics

https://www.newpolitics.org
From the website: "New Politics was founded in 2013 by City Year alumna Emily Cherniack, who saw during her service and subsequent political experience both the lack of support for national service alumni trying to re-enter public service and the transformational impact they could have if elected."

Republican National Committee

310 First St SE
Washington, DC 20003
https://www.gop.com/

Run for Something

https://runforsomething.net
From the website (by Amanda Litman): "On January 20, 2017, Inauguration Day, we launched Run for Something, a political action committee dedicated to helping young people run for office by lowering the barriers to entry."

She Should Run

80 M St SE, Floor 1
Washington, DC 20003
https://www.sheshouldrun.org/

From the website: "She Should Run is a non-partisan 501(c)3 with the mission to expand the talent pool of women running for office in the United States."

Private sector jobs (although some sites also post government job openings):
Bookjobs
www.bookjobs.com
Created and maintained by the AAP (Association of American Publishers). You can search jobs at http://www.bookjobs.com/search-jobs.

Career Builder
http://www.careerbuilder.com
Search for available jobs at https://www.careerbuilder.com/browse.

Chronicle of Higher Education
https://www.chronicle.com/
Job search portal for jobs in academia as well as related consulting jobs. You can put in job alerts and you'll get email notifications as jobs in those categories are posted.

Indeed
https://www.indeed.com/
Started in 2004, Indeed has headquarters in Austin, Texas and Stamford, Connecticut with additional offices throughout the US and internationally. You can create alerts by job category and location so you will get targeted new job openings emailed to you.

Jobspider
http://www.jobspider.com/
From their website: "My name is Chris McGarry and I designed it because I was looking for a network administrator and it was frustrating to not see an intuitive and nicely organized free job board. The response has obviously been overwhelming and my 'small project' has blossomed into a very popular job board that, in many ways, rivals the big boys (i.e. Monster, HotJobs, etc.)."

Jobvertise, Inc.
2280 Woodland Lane North
Riverwoods, IL 60015
www.jobvertise.com/
From the letter from the CEO, Samuel A. Rosenman, at their website: "Jobvertise's mission is to provide top tier recruiting and career tools at little or no cost. Our philosophy is simple: provide great tools, a fast web site, and a simple yet powerful interface for a fraction of the cost of the other major job boards."

LinkedIn
https://www.linkedin.com
You can search for jobs for free through LinkedIn. Make sure your profile is well-written and up-to-date, because that may be the first thing someone accesses if you apply for a job there, even before they consider your resume.

Mediabistro
https://www.mediabistro.com/
Jobs in the publishing and media fields including advertising, books, marketing, and production.

Monster
https://www.monster.com/
From their website: "Monster is a global online employment solution for people seeking jobs and the employers who need great people. We've been doing this for more than 20 years and have expanded from our roots as a 'job board' to a global provider of a full array of job seeking, career management, recruitment and talent management products and services."

Upwork
https://www.upwork.com/
Freelancers post their job qualifications and companies or individuals looking to hire someone can access their profiles.

You can search for a wide range of film/tv/radio career jobs at this site, by job title as well as location (New York, California, etc.):
EntertainmentCareers.net
https://www.entertainmentcareers.net/
Extensive job site for those in the film industry including paid jobs as well as internships. Jobs are organized by several geographic territories, such as Southern California, the Tri-State area (NY, NJ, CT), Chicago, and also by job category, from acting, film & TV production, to crew jobs, writing, and lots more.

Mandy
https://www.mandy.com/
Job site for cast and crew in the entertainment industry including actors, voice-over artists, crew, dancers, music, and theatre professionals.

Internships are often an excellent way to get a head start on a career. During college, you can apply for paid or for-credit internships. Even after college, or during graduate school, you can apply for paid internships as a way to learn a new career or get on-the-job training till you get a salaried job.

Internships or jobs in accounting:
Big4Bound
www.big4bound.com
Offers help to students and experienced professionals who are looking to land an internship or a job with one of the "Big 4" accounting firms.

Internships in the publishing industry:
Bookjobs.com
http://www.bookjobs.com/search-internships

This free site covers internships in a wide range of industries and fields:
Internships.com
A Chegg service
http://www.internships.com/
Searches can be conducted by location, job category, or even by company.

One of the many nonprofit organizations that offer internships:
Children's Defense Fund (CDF)
25 E Street, NW
Washington, DC 20001
https://www.childrensdefense.org/
cdfinfo@childrensdefense.org
Offers college internships at their headquarters and all the other CDF offices in California, Minnesota, Mississippi, New York, Ohio, South Carolina, and Texas for the fall, spring, and summer terms. Apply at https://www.childrensdefense .org/connect/join-our-team/internships-at-cdf/.

Employee rights and relationship issues
Society of Human Resource Management (SHRM)
https://www.shrm.org
Washington, DC-based professional organization with an estimated 300,000 HR professionals as members. Their website provides information on related human resource or personnel issues such as Tamara Lytle's July 13, 2015, article, "How to Resolve Workplace Conflicts."

Working Conversations, LLC
PO Box 19453
Minneapolis, MN 55419
http://janelanderson.com/
Janel Anderson, who holds a PhD in Organizational Communication, is a speaker and author (*Head On: How to Approach Difficult Conversations Directly*) who also consults on work-related issues.

Workplace Fairness
8121 Georgia Avenue, Suite 600
Silver Spring, MD 20910
https://www.workplacefairness.org
A nonprofit organization founded in 1994 as the National Employee Rights Institute (NERI) with a name change of the organization in 2001 to Workplace Fairness. From their website: "Workplace Fairness is a non-profit organization working to preserve and promote employee rights. This site provides comprehensive information about job rights and employment issues nationally and in all 50 states. It is for workers, employers, advocates, policymakers, journalists, and anyone else who wants to understand, protect, and strengthen workers' rights." At the website you can use their directory to search for an employment attorney by practice area, zip code, or state: https://www.workplacefairness.org/find-attorney.

See also related listings in Chapter 26, Relationships in the "Work Relationships" section.

Reading and Audiovisual Materials

Alex Masters. "What to do if a complaint is made against you?" Published January 19, 2016 in The Optimus Blog at Optimus Education, part of the Prospects Group, in the UK, http://blog.optimus-education.com/what-do-you-do-if-complaint-made-against-you

Eliyahu M. Goldratt and Jeff Cox. *The Goal: A Process of Ongoing Improvement.* Second Revised Edition. Great Barrington, MA: North River Press, Inc., 1992.

Ford R. Myers. *Get the Job You Want, Even When No One's Hiring.* Hoboken, NJ: Wiley, 2009.

Fred Yager and Jan Yager. *Career Opportunities in the Film Industry.* Second edition. Foreword by David Carradine. NY: Facts on File, Infobase, 2009.

—. *Career Opportunities in the Publishing Industry.* Second edition. Foreword by Laurel Touby, founder of Mediabistro. NY: Facts on File, Infobase, 2009.

George Will, "Big Government is Ever Growing, on the Sly," *National Review,* February 25, 2017. https://www.nationalreview.com/2017/02/federal-government-growth-continues-while-federal-employee-numbers-hold/

Jan Yager. *Grow Global.* Narrated by Lee Strayer. Stamford, CT: Hannacroix Creek Books, 2011. Audiobook version, 2014.

—. *Who's That Sitting at My Desk? Workship, Friendship, or Foe?* Stamford, CT: Hannacroix Creek Books, Inc., 2004.

Janel Anderson. *Head On: How to Approach Difficult Conversations Directly.* Gale House, 2018.

Jennifer Bobrow Burns. *Career Opportunities in the Travel and Hospitality Industry.* NY: Facts on File, Infobase, 2010.

Jill Lublin. *The Profit of Kindness.* Wayne, NJ: Career Press, 2017.

Marsha Sinetar. *Do What You Love, The Money Will Follow: Discovering Your Right Livelihood.* New York: Dell Publishing, 1987.

Martin C. Zwilling. *Do YOU Have What It Takes to Be an Entrepreneur?* La Vergne, TN: Ingram Publisher Services, 2010.

Nicolas Lore. *The Pathfinder: How to Choose or Change Your Career for a Lifetime of Satisfaction and Success.* New York: Touchstone, Simon & Schuster, 2012.

Nicolas Rapp and Clifton Leaf. "How Many People Work for the US Federal Government?" *Fortune,* March 21, 2019, posted at https://fortune.com/longform/government-employee-count-2019/

Rebecca Rainey and Quint Forgey. "Unemployment claims near 17 million in three weeks as coronavirus ravages economy" *Politico.* Posted on April 9, 2020 at https://www.politico.com/news/2020/04/09/coronavirus-unemployment-claims-numbers-176794

Richard Bolles. *What Color Is My Parachute?* Updated annually. New York: Ten Speed Press, 2018.

Tamara Monosoff. "So You Want to Be Your Own Boss . . ." Posted at Entreprener.com (no date).

Teddy Nykiel. "Small-Business Grants for Women: 11 Go-To Spots." Nerd Wallet, September 4, 2018. https://www.nerdwallet.com/blog/small-business/small-business-grants-for-women/

WomensNet.net, "20 Terrific Grants for Women Business Owners." Available for free at WomensNet.net by providing your email address.

CHAPTER 7

Children and Teens

- A twenty-five-year-old Illinois woman, who was supposed to be babysitting nine children, instead went to a local bar. While she was gone, a house fire broke out. By the time the fire department arrived, toxic levels of carbon monoxide had killed seven of the children between the ages of five months and seven years.
- An eleven-year-old Connecticut boy was left home alone for just forty-five minutes. Unfortunately, while his parents were away, he got pinned under fifteen panels of plasterboard in the hallway of his home, which was being renovated. He died the next day from his injuries.

These are just two examples of the countless tragedies that have occurred when children are left home alone before they are ready to handle the responsibility. Death and injury are of course the worst consequences of leaving a child home alone. A less horrific outcome is the stress that some children report if they are left home at age twelve or younger, especially if they are left in charge of younger siblings.

Is thirteen a reasonable age to leave your child home alone? It turns out that there is no one easy answer, since the legal age that it is permissible to leave a child home alone varies from state to state. As Karen Allen points out in her article, "When is it OK to Leave Your Child Home Alone?" published in the *Charlotte (NC) Parent*, in Illinois a child must be fourteen, but only eight in Maryland and ten in Oregon. It seems that in North Carolina, it is considered a more arbitrary situation, with parents making the decision, since legally only children eight and under still require adult supervision. "After that, it's up to the parent's discretion." There are, however, many considerations that parents have to address such as whether the child knows how to contact emergency services and how long will the child be left alone, among other key questions. In New York, the Office of Children and Family Services indicates that it depends on the child's maturity. Some children are responsible enough by twelve or thirteen, while some teenagers are too immature to be home in an unsupervised situation. They suggest parents use their judgment about when a child is ready for that responsibility.

But parents might like some guidelines. There are considerations at various ages and stages, from when it is okay to leave a sleeping infant in a crib while the parent runs down to the laundry room for twenty minutes (never if there is no one else in the house or apartment!), or if a four-year-old could be left alone for twenty minutes while his mother picks his sister up at the corner where the school bus drops her off. (It is not recommended, since tragedy can strike in a matter of seconds!).

There is little agreement if twelve is the ideal age that a child can handle some home-alone time, since it depends on the individual child's maturity level, if there will also be other minors in the apartment or house, and if a safe environment has been created that includes educating the child about what to do in an emergency.

How do you know if your child is ready to stay home alone? It is probably easier to answer the opposite question: How do you know a child should *not* be left home alone? That includes children, or even teenagers, regardless of their age, who have previously played with matches, been aggressive or abusive to their siblings, who lie or steal, who have a drinking or drug problem, or who might invite over other friends or friends of friends without getting permission.

I was a latchkey kid two days a week beginning at the age of ten because my mother went back to work, full time, as a kindergarten teacher and we only had someone in the house to clean and cook three out of five work/school days. I learned how to be alone at an early age and to do productive things with my time. I wrote my first novel at the age of ten and grew up to become a writer, so that is the positive side of that experience. But I can still remember that I hated being home alone, although I never shared those feelings with my mother. My older sister and brother preferred to hang out with their friends after school, not coming home until my mother was back from work at around 6 or 7 o'clock.

If you do feel your child is old enough and mature enough to spend some time home alone, and you are within the legal guidelines for your state, you still must take some precautions to make this as positive a situation as possible. That means teaching your child how to dial 911 in an emergency, what to do if the phone rings and you are not the caller, who to call if your child gets scared or has a question if you are not reachable and it is not a 911-type of emergency, how to contact the nearest fire or police stations, what to do if someone rings the front doorbell, and even how to administer basic first aid. One of the most important lessons you need to teach your child is what to do if someone knocks. Obviously, you do not want your child opening the door to anyone, but how do you teach a child to check if someone claiming to be the police is legitimate? Suggestion: They can ask for the police officer to state or show, through the peephole or front door camera, his or her name and badge number, and the child could call the local precinct to check if that person is legitimate. (This applies if your child is old enough to call the phone number for your local precinct, rather than 911, since this is technically not an emergency situation.) The child should let the police department know that someone who says he/she is a police officer is at the door, and ask the police to verify that badge number.

If all the potential things that could happen to your child when he/she is left home alone are making your head spin, that's okay. The good news is that more than ever today, there are alternatives to staying home alone. More and more communities are offering supervised after-school programs so that children need not stay home alone even for a few hours or even for one day. They can learn new skills, make friends, or even get a head start on their homework. The first place to start is at your child's school; they may have an after-school program so transportation to the activities is not a concern. You probably know about many of the outside organizations offering after-school programs already, but this chapter lists contact information and short descriptions for options such as the Boys and Girls Club of America, Big Brothers and Big Sisters of America, the Boy Scouts of America, the Girl Scouts of America, and an exemplary local program like New York's PAL (Police Athletic League), providing free after-school activities since 1914.

There is, of course, more expensive private care as an option. You could hire a trusted babysitter, even for a short time, especially if they live in your apartment building or nearby. I know of one woman who quit her job and turned her basement into a game room and play area so that her seventh grader and several of his friends had somewhere to go to after school. Since practically all the other mothers were working, the middle schoolers had been going home to empty houses—and some were getting into trouble. (If all the mothers pooled their resources and together shared the cost of hiring a caregiver to supervise the teens for a few hours a day, that mother could have continued working, if she needed to.)

Perhaps you and other parents could alternate watching each other's children or middle schoolers, one day a week each? Alternatively, grandparents or even aunts and uncles or trusted family friends who live within commuting distance might welcome spending time with your child or children so they are not home alone?

If you do think your child or teenager is old enough and mature enough to have some time home alone, consider creating a list of home rules that need to be followed as well as a second list of key telephone numbers for calling or texting if any questions or problems arise. The first home/apartment rule might be: "Never ever open the door to a stranger."

Home/Apartment Rules

1. _____

2. _____

3. _____

4. _____

Key Telephone Numbers

In an Emergency, Dial 911

Local police precinct # _____

Mom's work # _____

Dad's work # _____

Neighbor's Name and Phone # _____

Doctor's Name and Phone # _____

Dentist's Name and Phone #_____

Grandparent _____

Nearest hospital _____

For a commercial option, this is a company with a possible software solution:
Database Systems Corp. (DSC)
Latchkey-Kids.com (also accessible through CallingCare.com)
16841 N. 31st Avenue, Suite 160
Phoenix, AZ 85053
http://www.latchkey-kids.com/
From their website: "Since 1978, Database Systems Corp. (DSC) has been a leading provider of computer software solutions. Recently, DSC has been providing call center technology including home alone children (latchkey kids) and senior calling programs." Please note that this is a fee service starting at $14.95/month.
  They offer an automatic calling system to check in on the latchkey child.
  For educational purposes, they have a chart, "Latchkey Children Age Restrictions by State," at http://www.latchkey-kids.com/latchkey-kids-age-limits.htm.

There is parenting help available through classes taught in community centers, schools, women's centers, and the local YMCA or YWCA in your area. What to do about leaving your child home alone is just one of the many parenting challenges that may be addressed. Sibling rivalry, discipline issues, children who are reluctant to do their homework, and bullying at school or online are just some of the many parenting concerns that you might want to discuss with other parents. You could also start your own parenting group, through your neighborhood or church or synagogue.

CHILDREN

How to find the best childcare for your child:
Child Care Aware
1515 N. Courthouse Road, 2nd Floor
Arlington, VA 22201
http://www.childcareaware.org/
From their website: "At Child Care Aware, we work with over 400 Child Care Resource and Referral agencies (or CCR&Rs) all across the country. We partner with these local agencies to help you get the local child care information that you need no matter where you live or work." They offer a useful portal of information about local childcare resources at http://www.childcareaware.org/resources/map/.

Many programs offer local and online parenting classes, weekend boot camps, and monthly webinars:
Parent Encouragement Program (at Kensington Baptist Church)
10100 Connecticut Avenue
Kensington, MD 20895
http://pepparent.org
Office@PEPparent.org
From their website: "PEP was founded in 1982 by Linda Jessup, RN, MPH, FNP, who taught the first classes in her home. Incorporated as a nonprofit 501(c)3 organization in 1984, PEP expanded its classes into nearby schools and established its headquarters in 1990 in Kensington, where it remains today." Core classes cover parenting preschoolers, children five to twelve, and teenagers. The course "Why Don't My Children Listen To Me?" is available for free at https://pepparent.teachable.com/p/why-dont-my-kids-listen-to-me.

Information and services from the US government related to children:
Children's Bureau, Administration for Children and Families
330 C Street, SW
Washington, DC 20201
www.acf.hhs.gov/cb
From their website: "The Children's Bureau (CB) partners with federal, state, tribal and local agencies to improve the overall health and well-being of our nation's children and families. With an annual budget of almost $8 billion, the Children's Bureau provides support and guidance to programs that focus on: Strengthening families and preventing child abuse and neglect; Protecting children when abuse or neglect has occurred; Ensuring that every child and youth has a permanent family or family connection."

Education is handled at the local or state level. For more information on education for children and teens, go to Chapter 15, Education. This website is the US government site for education, but it has very specific mandates:
https://www.usa.gov/education
This site focuses on government information about primary, secondary, and higher education including collecting data on schools. You can also find out information about how to apply for federal student aid (FAFSA for college or career schools).
https://www.cdc.gov
Certain childhood diseases that used to be completely eradicated are coming back because more and more parents are choosing not to vaccinate their infants and children. To help parents learn more about immunization, the CDC (Centers for Disease Control and Prevention) has made several short videos addressing dif-

ference vaccines, available at: https://www.cdc.gov/cdctv/diseaseandconditions/vaccination/get-picture-childhood-immunization.html.

Stop Bullying
https://www.stopbullying.gov/
US government program to help kids and teens develop the skills they need to stop bullying. Information portal covering bullying at school and in person, as well as cyberbullying.

Other government help for children:
For information about Supplemental Nutrition Assistance Program (SNAP), what used to be called food stamps, go to Chapter 17, Financial Assistance.

International, national, or exemplary local nonprofits, associations, or companies:
Big Brothers Big Sisters of America
2502 N. Rocky Point Drive, Suite 550
Tampa, FL 33607
http://www.bbbs.org/
Started in 1904, this national organization with local affiliates pairs at-risk children with a big brother or big sister to mentor them. They call adult volunteers "Bigs" and the children, ages 6 to 18, "Littles."

American Academy of Pediatrics
345 Park Boulevard
Itasca, IL 60143
https://www.aap.org
This professional membership association for pediatricians has information about child-related issues at their website.

CHADD (Children and Adults with Attention-Deficit/Hyperactivity Disorder)
Lanham, MD 20706
Founded in 1987, this organization offers education and advocacy regarding ADHD in children and adults. It maintains a National Resource Center on ADHD (NRC).

National Children's Advocacy Center (NCAC)
210 Pratt Ave NE
Huntsville, AL 35801
https://www.nationalcac.org/
From their website: "The NCAC models, promotes, and delivers excellence in child abuse response and prevention through service, education, and leadership."
NCAC offers local services in their vicinity as well as online training in victim advocacy and how to recognize and treat child abuse.

National Parent Teacher Association (PTA)
1250 N. Pitt Street
Alexandria, VA 22314
https://www.pta.org
Founded in 1897, this national organization is dedicated to child advocacy
including improvement of public education for all children. Some of their concerns over the years have included nutritional lunches, school safety, and the
creation of kindergarten classes.

Boy Scouts of America (BSA)
PO Box 152079
Irving, TX 75015-2079
https://www.scouting.org
Founded in 1910, there are various groups, depending on age, that are avail-
able to children through teens to develop camping as well as interactive skills.
Beginning in 2018 and 2019, various groups and programs have been opened
up to girls.

Girl Scouts of the USA
420 Fifth Avenue
New York, NY 10018
https://www.girlscouts.org/
Started in 1912 in Savannah, Georgia, by Juliette Gordon Low. Girl Scouts, a
membership organization, considers the experiences that girls get by joining
their local affiliate of Girl Scouts to be a training ground for future leadership
positions. They have created the acronym G.I.R.L. to emphasize that focus:
Go-getter, Innovator, Risk-taker, Leader.

Boys and Girls Clubs of America
https://bgca.org
Started in Hartford, Connecticut, in 1860 by three women—Mary Goodwin, Alice
Goodwin and Elizabeth Hammersley. Then, in 1906, several Boys Clubs joined
affiliating with the Federated Boys Clubs in Boston. In 1990, the name was
changed to reflect that girls were a part of their mission as well. You can find a
local club at https://www.bgca.org/get-involved/find-a-club. The most important feature of the clubs is providing a safe out-of-school place for kids to go if
parents are unavailable because of work or other reasons. They have clubs in
public housing, on military bases, in schools, and other locations.

Books for Treats
https://booksfortreats.org/
Started on Halloween in 2001 by Rebecca Morgan, a speaker and author, Books
for Treats distributes books instead of candy to children to encourage reading

and making healthier choices. Events are now held in several states including California, Texas, Illinois, Massachusetts, Michigan, and Nebraska as well as in Canada. You can tweet about them @BooksForTreats or contact the organizer through the website.

Campaign for Tobacco-Free Kids
1400 I Street NW, Suite 1200
Washington, DC 20005
https://www.tobaccofreekids.org/
Started more than twenty years ago, this international nonprofit organization does not take any money from the tobacco industry or government sources. It is focused on stopping kids' smoking. They have several related websites, including kickbuttsday.org, tobaccofreebaseball.org, and takingdowntobacco.org.

Canines for Disabled Kids (CDK)
65 James Street, Suite 210
Worcester MA 01603
https://caninesforkids.org/
From their website: "At Canines for Disabled Kids, we operate under one guiding mission: Increasing independence for children with disabilities and their families by promoting service dog partnerships, understanding and awareness throughout the community." Started in 1998 as an outgrowth of NEADS, the National Education for Assistance Dog Services training program.

Children's Defense Fund (CDF)
25 E Street, NW
Washington, DC 20001
https://www.childrensdefense.org/
cdfinfo@childrensdefense.org
CDF has five state offices and is concerned with after-school and summer programs for children, health insurance, and leadership development. Founded in 1973 by Marian Wright Edelman, the first black woman admitted to the Mississippi bar. Their mission is to "Leave No Child Behind." Headquartered in Washington, DC, there are offices in other states including California, Minnesota, Mississippi, New York, Ohio, South Carolina, and Texas. Offers college internships at their headquarters and all the other CDF offices for the fall, spring, and summer terms. For more information and to apply, go to https://www.childrensdefense.org/connect/join-our-team/internships-at-cdf/.

D.A.R.E. (Drug Abuse Resistance Education) America
PO Box 512090
Los Angeles, CA 90051-0090

https://dare.org
From their website: "D.A.R.E. is a police officer-led series of classroom lessons that teaches children from kindergarten through 12th grade how to resist peer pressure and live productive drug and violence-free lives."

It began in 1983 in Los Angeles as a drug prevention program for children and teens by going into the schools to educate them, but soon spread nationwide and eventually to fifty-two countries globally.

D.A.R.E. has an online opioid use lesson they developed for students to educate them about this growing, life-threatening drug epidemic: https://dare.org/d-a-r-e-online-opioid-lesson/.

KaBoom!
4301 Connecticut Avenue NW, Suite ML-1
Washington, DC 20008
www.kaboom.org
Offers grants and other help to build playgrounds for those who need a safe place to play, especially in underprivileged areas or areas that have been hurt by natural disasters such as hurricanes.

Make-a-Wish Foundation
1702 E. Highland Avenue, Suite 400
Phoenix, AZ 85016
www.wish.org
Started in 1980, when the wish to become a police officer was granted to seven-year-old Chris Greicius, who had leukemia, this foundation grants wishes to children with serious or terminal illnesses. Read the moving story of how the Make-a-Wish Foundation came about on its website. There are local affiliates throughout the country. According to the website, in 2018, more than 300,000 children have been granted wishes since the organization's founding.

National Center for Missing and Exploited Children (NCMEC)
Charles B. Wang International Children's Building
699 Prince Street
Alexandria, VA 22314-3175
www.missingkids.com
24-hour call center: 1-800-THE-LOST (1-800-843-5678)
Started by an act of Congress in 1984, NCMEC is a private, nonprofit foundation that receives funding from the US government as well as private donations. They deal with runaways as well as stranger and family abductions. They are also concerned with online child exploitation.

New York Society for the Prevention of Cruelty to Children (NYSPCC)
https://nyspcc.org
Founded in 1875, this child protection agency has been dedicated to research, reporting, and advocating against child abuse and neglect.

Partnership for Drug-Free Kids
https://drugfree.org
Previously known as the Partnership for a Drug-Free America, this organization has been around since the mid-1980s, when the focus was on the crack epidemic. At the website, there is a lot of information related to drug use in children and teens, including an entire section devoted to the opioid epidemic: https://drugfree.org/heroin-opioid-epidemic/.

Reach Out and Read
89 South Street, Suite 201
Boston, MA 02111
www.reachoutandread.org
info@reachoutandread.org
A program to encourage parents to read to their children, especially from the ages of six months to five years, including a gift of a new children's book.

Save the Children
501 Kings Highway East, Suite 400
Fairfield, CT 06825
www.savethechildren.org
International nonprofit that offers food, health care, and education to children in more than fifty countries.

UNICEF (United Nations Children Fund)
125 Maiden Lane, 11th Floor
New York, NY 10038
https://www.unicef.org/
From their website: "UNICEF works in 190 countries and territories to protect the rights of every child. UNICEF has spent 70 years working to improve the lives of children and their families." The US fund for UNICEF was founded in 1947. They rely heavily on the help of volunteers.

For developmental, intellectual, and physical disabilities issues, go to Chapter 13, Disabilities

For health issues, go to Chapter 19, Health and Wellness.

TEENS

A majority of the agencies or organizations in this book may provide information or services for teens along with adult populations, so do not limit yourself to just these listings. However, if you are looking for separate teen help, here are some places to start:

Big Brothers Big Sisters of America
http://www.bbbs.org/
Since 1904 they've been matching up children and teens with adult mentors for guidance, making a connection, and support.
    See complete listing above under Children.

Boys and Girls Clubs of America
Has its roots in 1860 in Hartford, Connecticut, and in 1906 in Boston, with the national organization changing its name in 1990 to the Boys & Girls Clubs of America.
https://bgca.org
See complete listing above under Children.

Boy Scouts of America (BSA)
https://www.scouting.org
See complete listing in "Children" section of this chapter.

Girl Scouts of the USA
https://www.girlscouts.org/
Their mission, as stated at their website, is that the Girl Scouts of the USA "unleashes the G.I.R.L. (Go-getter, Innovator, Risk-taker, Leader)™ in every girl, preparing her for a lifetime of leadership . . ."
    See complete listing in "Children" section of this chapter.

Girlstart
1400 W. Anderson Lane
Austin, TX 78757
https://girlstart.org
Empowering and inspiring girls to go into STEM (Science, Technology, Engineering, and Math) with locations currently in Boston and Texas (Central Texas, North Texas, and Houston).

Do Something
Dosomething.org
An international initiative to get young people throughout the US and in more than 130 countries to do something to make the world a better place, like clean up cigarette butts or organize clothing drives for the homeless.
    See complete listing in Chapter 30, Volunteerism.

Girls Inc.
https://girlsinc.org
From their website: "The network of local Girls Inc. nonprofit organizations serves girls ages 6-18 at more than 1,400 sites in 400 cities across the United States and Canada."

HelpGuide
https://www.helpguide.org
This is a non-profit source of information on wellness and mental health. A publication entitled "Help for Parents of Troubled Teens," subtitled "Dealing with Anger, Violence, Delinquency, and Other Teen Behavior Problems" is at https://www.helpguide.org/articles/parenting-family/helping-troubled-teens.htm.

It Gets Better Project
https://itgetsbetter.org
From their website: "In 2010, Dan Savage and his partner, Terry Miller, uttered three words that would give rise to a global movement focused on empowerment of LGBTQ+ youth–*it gets better*."
See complete listing in Chapter 22, LGBTQ.

Jed Foundation
6 East 39th Street, Suite 1204
New York, NY 10016
https://www.jedfoundation.org
Text "START" to 741-741 or call 1-800-273-TALK (8255) (This is the phone number for the National Suicide Prevention Helpline.)
This is a mental health resource center and nonprofit organization with the goal of helping teens and young adults to deal with the challenges that they face with the goal of preventing suicides. A useful information sheet entitled "Help a Friend in Need" is at https://www.jedfoundation.org/wp-content/uploads/2016/07/help-a-friend-in-need-jed-facebook-instagram-guide-NEW.pdf.

Jason Foundation
jasonfoundation.com
Dedicated to preventing teen suicide.
See complete listing in Chapter 27, Suicide.

Johnny's Ambassadors
www.JohnnysAmbassadors.org
A nonprofit organization founded by speaker and productivity expert Laura Stack in 2020 after her 19-year-old son Johnny died from suicide on November

20th, 2019. Laura shared with me the organization's objective: "Our mission is to educate parents and teens about the dangers of dabbing high-THC marijuana wax and extracts."

My Brother's Keeper Alliance (MBK Alliance)

https://www.obama.org/mbka/

From the website: "President Obama launched My Brother's Keeper at the White House in February 2014 to address persistent opportunity gaps facing boys and young men of color. To scale and sustain its mission, the My Brother's Keeper Alliance was launched as a private sector entity in 2015."

National Teen Dating Abuse Helpline

https://www.loveisrespect.org/

24-hour hotline: 1-800-799-7233

This hotline is part of the National Domestic Violence Hotline initiative out of Texas, but it is geared to teens ages 13–18 who are experiencing dating abuse.

National Runaway Safeline

https://www.1800runaway.org

Helpline: 1-800-RUNAWAY

Offers help to teen runaways related to problems they have to deal with, including prostitution and bullying. There's a part of the website for parents as well.

Police Athletic League of New York City (PAL)

34 1/2 East 12th Street

New York, NY 10003

https://www.palnyc.org

This is a designated charity of the New York Police Department. It is supported by private and public funding. Started in 1914 by Police Commissioner Arthur Woods, its teen programs are for ages 13 to 19 and cover life skills as well as helping teens to find summer employment and after-school activities throughout the school year, usually three to five days a week, from 6:30–9:30 p.m. There is an acting program and other specialized activities, including short summer trips. The PAL programs are in each of the five boroughs of New York City. All activities are free to the teen participants.

Safe Place

https://www.nationalsafeplace.org

Makes referrals for teens who are in need of immediate free and confidential help.

From their website: "Along with accessing Safe Place in person, youth may also **TXT 4 HELP** to receive information about the closest Safe Place location and chat with a professional for more help. TXT 4 HELP is a nationwide, 24-hour text-for-support service for youth in crisis."

If you prefer calling rather than texting, call the National Runaway Safeline (1-800-RUNAWAY/ 1-800-786-2929).

Stand Up for Kids
200 Nelson Ferry Road, Suite B
Decatur, GA 30030
http://www.standupforkids.org/
staff@standupforkids.org
Their goal is "getting kids off the street." See complete listing in Chapter 20, Housing and Homelessness.

Student Safety Month
6 Azel Road
http://www.tellcarole.com/student-safety-month.html
Founded by Carole Copeland Thomas, a professional speaker, event organizer, and author, whose son, Mickarl D. Thomas, Jr. (known as Mickey), died on June 14, 1997 in a single occupancy car accident. That tragedy, and similar ones that same year, losses by three other mothers that Carole knew—one teen died by drowning trying to save another teen and two college sophomores died in a car accident—motivated her to start Student Safety Month. Although originally designed for June, the traditional month for proms, graduation parties, and increased driving and merriment once school is out, Student Safety Month could be celebrated during any month. For a free downloadable and printable 11-page guide by Carole Copeland Thomas, which includes an alcohol fact sheet and best practices, go to: http://www.tellcarole.com/uploads/7/6/8/2/7682161/6:2:15_student_safety_month_kit.pdf

Teen Line
PO Box 48750
Los Angeles, CA 90048-0750
https://teenlineonline.org/get-help/
They are open from 6 p.m. to 10 p.m. Pacific Time, every night.
(310) 855-HOPE (4673) or (800) TLC-TEEN (852-8336) (US & Canada only)

Teens are helping teens by offering to talk to them. There are also videos at the website and downloads that can be accessed. There are message boards where teens seeking help can post on topics such as eating disorders, health and fitness, homework, and relationships.

The Trevor Project
http://www.TheTrevorProject.org
Helpline: 866-4-U-TREVOR
This is a national 24/7 crisis and suicide prevention helpline for lesbian, gay, bisexual, and transgender youth. From their website: "Founded in 1998 by the creators of the Academy Award-winning short film TREVOR, The Trevor Project is the leading national organization providing crisis intervention and suicide prevention services to lesbian, gay, bisexual, transgender, queer & questioning (LGBTQ) young people under 25."

ULifeline
http://www.ulifeline.org/main/Home.html
Text "START" to 741-741 or call 1-800-273-TALK (8255)
Tagline: "Your online resource for college mental health."
From their website: "ULifeline is an anonymous, confidential, online resource center, where college students can be comfortable searching for the information they need and want regarding emotional health. ULifeline is a project of The Jed Foundation [see listing above], a leading organization working to protect the emotional health of America's college students, and was developed with input from leading experts in mental health and higher education."

Young Men's Christian Association (YMCA)
http://www.ymca.int/
Started in 1844, the YMCA–often referred to only as the "Y"–operates in 119 countries and, according to their website, reaches 58 million members. In addition to sports, educational, and cultural activities at the local Y, check with your facility to see what additional services they offer, from short- or longer-term lower-cost housing to summer day or sleepaway camps.

For developmental, intellectual, and physical disabilities issues, go to Chapter 13, Disabilities

For health issues, go to Chapter 19, Health and Wellness.

Reading and Audiovisual Materials

Adele Farber and Elaine Mazlish. *Siblings Without Rivalry.* New York: W.W. Norton, 2012.

Alex Berenson. *Tell Your Children: The Truth About Marijuana, Mental Illness, and Violence.* NY: Free Press, 2019.

Allison Klein. "When Is It Safe to Start Leaving Kids Home Alone?" *Washington Post*, August 29, 2017.

Anne Frank. *The Diary of a Young Girl*. New York: Doubleday, 1991.

Cindy Blankenship. "List of Teenage Help Organizations." Posted at https://oureverydaylife.com/.

Constance Stapleton. "Could the State Take Your Child?" *Woman's Day*, May 18, 1993, pages 54, 56, and 58.

Dr. Seuss and Roy McKie. *My Book about Me*. New York: Random House, 1969.

Dr. Seuss (Theodor Seuss "Ted" Geisel). *Oh, the Places You'll Go!* New York: Random House, 2013.

Frances E. Jensen, MD with Amy Ellis Nutt. *The Teenage Brain: A Neuroscientist's Survival Guide to Raising Adolescents and Young Adults*. New York: HarperCollins Publisher, 2015.

Haley Kilpatrick. *The Drama Years: Real Girls Talk About Surviving Middle School—Bullies, Brands, Body Image, and More*. NY: Free Press, 2012.

J. D. Salinger. *Catcher in the Rye*. Boston, MA: Little, Brown & Company, 1951.

J. Rajalakshmi and P. Thanasekaran. "The Effects and Behaviours of Home Alone Situation by Latchkey Children." *American Journal of Nursing Science*, Vol. 4, No. 4, 2015, pages 207-211. Posted online on July 21, 2015 at http://article.sciencepublishinggroup.com/pdf/10.11648.j.ajns.20150404.19.pdf

Jan Yager, PhD. *Road Signs on Life's Journey: Sayings and Insights to Help You Find Your Way*. Stamford, CT: Hannacroix Creek Books, Inc., 2003. Audiobook version, read by Sanford Orkin, 2013. Ebook, 2016.

Jay Asher. *13 Reasons Why*. New York: Razorbill, division of Penguin Random House, 2007. (A controversial Netflix series about suicide based on the book, produced by Anonymous Content and Paramount TV, had its first season in 2017 and its second season in 2018.)

John Green. *The Fault in Our Stars*. New York: Dutton, 2012. Also, a 2014 hit movie starring Shailene Woodley.

Karen Alley. "When is it OK to Leave Your Child Home Alone?" *Charlotte Parent*, July 31, 2017. http://www.charlotteparent.com/CLT/When-is-it-OK-to-Leave-Your-Child-Home-Alone/

More4kids, "25 Top Children's Charities." June 10 n.d. http://www.more4kids.info/652/top-childrens-charities/

Pat Harvey and Britt H. Rathbone. *Parenting a Teen Who Has Intense Emotions: DBT Skills to Help Your Teen Navigate Emotional and Behavioral Challenges*. Oakland, CA: New Harbinger, 2015.

Pegine Echevarria, MSW. *For All Our Daughters: How Mentoring Helps Young Women and Girls Master the Art of Growing Up.* Worchester, MA: Chandler House Press, 1998.

William Golding. *Lord of the Flies.* New York: Putnam, 1959.

CHAPTER 8

Consumer Affairs and Safety

GETTING HELP TO RESOLVE YOUR CONSUMER CONCERNS

It has become easier than ever to get help if you have a problem with a product or service. You can email a company and often get a response within 24 to 48 hours. Some companies still have phone customer service so you can talk to a live person about your consumer complaint. You may be offered the option to stay on the line on hold or provide your phone number to get a call back without losing your position in the queue. I have found that those call-backs are often quite efficient and reliable. Of course, if you don't mind being put on hold, you can still wait to speak to someone.

Another option today is a live online chat with someone from the company, usually either from customer service or tech support. There is a real person at the other end of the communications, and you do ask and answer questions just like a back-and-forth phone conversation. An added benefit of this approach is that you will have a text history of your conversation in case you need to refer to it later.

In addition to trying to get resolution for a problem by phone or online, you can bring a product back to the company where you bought it, if it was purchased locally. Although most require that you have a receipt for the purchase, a few may take your word for it (although without a receipt, you are usually only issued a store credit rather than a cash refund).

If the company does not resolve the situation in a reasonable way, you can take your complaint to the trade or professional association whose members are those companies, including the one that you are complaining about. One function of those trade and professional associations is to deal with disputes of that nature on behalf of their member companies.

You can search online for the association for the type of company that you want to complain about, from cleaning and moving and storage to funerals or automotive services. Another way to find a trade association is from the annual free report, *Consumer Action Handbook*, issued by the Federal Citizen Information Center of the Office of Citizen Services and Innovative Technologies, part of the General Services Administration. You can order a print copy, or you can download the 140+-page PDF for free: https://www.usa.gov/handbook.

If you're complaining:

- Getting angry is usually counterproductive.
- Stay as calm as possible.
- Explain the situation in a clear and detailed way.
- If you have a food product you want to return, but you did not bring it along, at least get the product code that is usually printed on the label and bring that information with you.
- Be openminded about how this could be resolved amicably, whether that means a refund, a gift card, or a store credit.

If you work in customer service and are hearing the complaint:

- Remember the old adage, "The customer is always right"? That's still a good concept to keep in mind and an approach to practice, if possible.
- If there are clear store policies about returns, have those rules printed out and available so you can show it to your disgruntled customer, or read it to him/her, so there is less ambiguity about what the guidelines say.
- Be understanding about your customer's situation. Do you really want to lose a customer over this one transaction?
- Remember that today, because of social media, including review sites like Yelp as well as Twitter, Facebook, and LinkedIn, where customers can post their experiences with a company, be as polite as possible. Reach a quick and mutually agreeable resolution as often as possible.
- Praise may not always be remembered but criticism and negative experiences usually endure.

Other suggestions about dealing with consumer affairs:
You can also start with local or state consumer agencies. Most states have at least one consumer agency. Some have even more than that.

- Here's an example for the state of Illinois: https://www.usa.gov/state-consumer/illinois
- For the city of Chicago: https://www.cityofchicago.org/city/en/depts/bacp.html

You can contact your local Better Business Bureau. They will look into disagreements between consumers and businesses: www.bbb.org/consumer-complaints/file-a-complaint/get-started.

You will find similar listings for your city or state. New York has their consumer complaint online forms posted at the Attorney General's office: https://ag.ny.gov/consumer-frauds/Filing-a-Consumer-Complaint. You are advised, however, to find a lawyer to represent you if you need to go court or for legal guidance, since the AG's office is unable to offer those services in individual cases.

There is also federal government help with consumer concerns. You will find those listings in the *Consumer Action Handbook*, described earlier.

Federal agencies that you can contact with consumer complaints:
Commodity Futures Trading Commission (CFTC)
https://www.cftc.gov/
From their website: "The mission of the Commodity Futures Trading Commission (CFTC) is to foster open, transparent, competitive, and financially sound markets."

US Consumer Product Safety Commission (CPSC)
https://www.cpsc.gov/
Concerned with protecting children and adults from injury, death, or property damage because of unsafe products.

Saferproducts.gov
https://saferproducts.gov
A place to report to the US government about an unsafe product.

US Department of Transportation (DOT)
www.transportation.gov
For complaints about airlines unrelated to security or safety.

Federal Communications Commission (FCC)
Deals with telecommunications issues. The FCC will not resolve the complaint for you but will tell you the steps to take to deal with it.
https://consumercomplaints.fcc.gov/hc/en-us

US Food and Drug Administration (FDA)
https://www.fda.gov
You can let the FDA know that there is a problem with one of the products that it regulates.

National Highway Traffic Safety Administration (NHTSA)
https://www.nhtsa.gov
If there is a safety issue with something related to your car such as tires, car seats, or other equipment, you can file a complaint with the NHTSA.

Organizations concerned with the rights of consumers and gathering objective consumer information:
Consumer Federation of America (CFA)
1620 I Street NW, Suite 200
Washington, DC 20006
https://consumerfed.org/
Founded in 1968, CFA is an education, research, and advocacy organization. It does not handle individual complaints.

Consumer Reports
101 Truman Avenue
Yonkers, NY 10703
https://www.consumerreports.org
Started in 1936, Consumer Reports is a nonprofit membership organization dedicated to testing products and sharing that information through its monthy magazine, *Consumer Reports*, as well as its annual product guide published in book format. Educating the public about the best products, from bike helmets and dishwashers to airlines and luggage, as well as advocacy, are part of its mission. Their website also has 9,000+ reviews.

Trade association for those involved in the consumer affairs profession:
Society of Consumer Affairs Professionals International (SOCAP)
625 N. Washington Street, Suite 304
Alexandria, VA 22314
www.socap.org
A membership organization founded in 1973 for those who deal with consumer care issues.

SAFETY

The public is now aware of the estimated 480,000 preventable deaths per year because of smoking cigarettes, but what about the number of unintentional deaths? You can see that safety is truly a matter of life and death. According to the National Center for Health Statistics, part of the CDC (Centers for Diseases Control and Prevention, according to their statistics, reviewed on October 30, 2020, the accidental or unintentional deaths in the U.S. were the following: unintentional injury deaths (167,127); deaths from unintentional falls (37,455); deaths from unintentional poisonings (62,399); and deaths from motor vehicle accidents (37,991).

Your home, the place where you and your family should feel safest, may actually be a dangerous place for everyone if it is not designed and maintained in an accident-free way. What we have to define, however, is what we mean by "safety." Home security is a key concern but a different issue than home safety. By home safety I am referring to the day-to-day issues like whether or not a dresser is sturdy enough that it won't fall over and possibly injure or kill a small child, which accounted for 195 deaths between 2000 and 2016, according to an article published in *People* quoting data from the Consumer Product Safety Commission. Another type of preventable safety-related death is infants and children being left in hot cars. Just in 2017, 43 children died in hot cars. According to the article "Kids in Hot Cars: One Child Is Too Many," published by the National Safety Council, it takes only ten minutes for the temperature in a hot car to rise twenty degrees, which is enough to lead to a child's death. Here are five suggestions, taken from the Safe Kids Worldwide tip sheet, about how to avoid such a tragedy:

- Never leave your child alone in a car, not even for a minute.
- Keep your car locked when you are not in it so kids don't gain access.
- Create reminders by putting something important in the back seat next to your child, such as a briefcase, purse, cell phone or your left shoe.
- If you see a child alone in a car, call 911.
- Set a calendar reminder on your electronic device to make sure you dropped your child off at daycare; develop a plan so you will be alerted if your child is late or a no-show.

Federal agencies concerned with safety:
National Highway Traffic Safety Administration
1200 New Jersey Avenue, SE
Washington, DC 20590
https://www.nhtsa.gov/
Additional sites that the NHTSA developed and oversees:

- trafficsafetymarketing.gov
- ems.gov
- 911.gov
- Safercar.gov

Report a car safety problem at https://www-odi.nhtsa.dot.gov/VehicleComplaint/.

Distracted driving has become a real problem because of cell phones and texting while driving. It is estimated that 3,450 died in 2016 in the US from distracted driving: https://www.nhtsa.gov/risky-driving/distracted-driving .

Another important issue is drowsy driving, accidents and vehicle deaths caused by falling asleep at the wheel due to exhaustion. This preventable cause of vehicle deaths is estimated to have claimed more than 800 lives in 2016: https://www.nhtsa.gov/risky-driving/drowsy-driving .

US Coast Guard Boating Safety Division
2703 Martin Luther King Jr. Avenue SE
Washington, DC 20593-7501
http://www.uscgboating.org/
From their website: "The US Coast Guard's Boating Safety Division (CG-BSX-2) is dedicated to reducing loss of life, injuries, and property damage that occur on US waterways by improving the knowledge, skills, and abilities of recreational boaters."

Occupational Safety and Health Administration (OSHA)
200 Constitution Avenue NW
Washington, DC 20210
https://www.osha.gov/
OSHA covers a wide range of safety issues in the workplace, including standards that employers must comply with so that their workers are in a safe and healthy environment. If a worker feels a workplace is in violation of the standards, a complaint may be filed at https://www.osha.gov/workers/file_complaint.html. It should be filed promptly, because citations may only be issued for violations that occur within the previous six months.

National and international organizations and trade associations addressing a wide range of safety concerns:

A.C.T.S. (Arts, Crafts & Theater Safety)
181 Thompson Street, #23
New York, NY 10012-2586
http://www.artscraftstheatersafety.org/
ACTSNYC@cs.com
From their website: "ACTS is a not-for-profit corporation that provides health, safety, industrial hygiene, technical services, and safety publications to the arts, crafts, museums, and theater communities. A part of the fees from our consulting services goes to support our free and low-cost services for artists."

Center for Auto Safety
1825 Connecticut Avenue NW, Suite 330
Washington, DC 20009-5708
https://www.autosafety.org
contact@autosafety.org
A nonprofit public interest research organization established by Ralph Nader and the Consumers Union in 1970 that became independent of its founders in 1973. To submit a complaint about a vehicle: https://www.autosafety.org/contact-cas/.

Kidpower
https://www.kidpower.org
See complete listing below under "Social and Social Media Safety."

Kids and Cars
https://www.kidsandcars.org
Founded by Janette Fennell, whose family's carjacking was the impetus to her car safety initiatives and the founding of Kids and Cars. You can read about her story at https://www.kidsandcars.org/wp-content/uploads/pdfupload/SFC-Baby-Survives-Pacific-Heights-Carjacking.pdf. To learn how to prevent heat-related car deaths of infants or children, go to https://www.kidsandcars.org/how-kids-get-hurt/heat-stroke/.

National Safety Council (NSC)
1121 Spring Lake Drive
Itasca, IL 60143-3201
https://www.nsc.org
A nonprofit public service membership organization, founded in 1913, that is an information clearinghouse with educational and training programs in all safety matters including child safety, fire protection, poisoning, defensive driving, road and work safety, and transportation safety. It was granted a congressional

charter in 1953. They also provide safety training around the world through their global partners: https://www.nsc.org/safety-training/international.

Safe Kids Worldwide
1255 23rd Street, NW, Suite 400
Washington, DC 20037-1151
https://www.safekids.org
Founded in 1988 by Dr. Marty Eichelberger, a pediatric trauma surgeon, and Herta Feely, a public relations professional, of Children's National Health System with support by funding sponsor Johnson & Johnson. Sponsors the annual Safe Kids Day worldwide. Offers free safety checklists at its website that can be downloaded, including safety checklists for home, medicine, pedestrian, play, water, fire, and child passengers: https://www.safekids.org/safe-kids-day/my-high-5/ready-made-checklists.

Student Safety Month
http://www.tellcarole.com/student-safety-month.html
See complete listing in Chapter 7, Children and Teens, under "Teens."

Toy Association
1375 Broadway,10th Floor
New York, NY 10018
https://www.toyassociation.org
info@toyassociation.org
Founded in 1916, this is the trade association for 950+ toy manufacturers. Safety is one of their initiatives. Visit http://www.playsafe.org/, which was created by the Toy Association to educate the public about toy safety.

Social and social media safety:
Google Safety Center
https://www.google.com/safetycenter/web/roadshow/
This is the Online Safety Roadshow, a 45-minute digital citizenship assembly for teens that strives to be like a Drivers Ed for the web." They offer five tips as part of their online safety advice are:

- Think Before You Share.
- Protect Your Stuff.
- Know and Use Your Settings.
- Avoid Scams.
- Be Positive.

There are also handouts for teachers that can be downloaded.

Kidpower
PO Box 1212
Santa Cruz, CA 95061
https://www.kidpower.org
safety@kidpower.org
Their mission, from their website: "To teach people of all ages and abilities how to use their power to stay safe, act wisely, and believe in themselves." Their kid safety training is available on six continents. They also deal with anti-bullying, anti-violence in schools, and sexual assault prevention. "We are the global non-profit leader in 'People Safety' education—an international movement of leaders reaching millions of people of all ages, abilities, genders, identities, and walks of life with effective, culturally-competent interpersonal and social safety skills."

Safety Net Kids
http://www.safetynetkids.org.uk/
info@safety-net.org.uk
A UK-based site with information for children on staying safe, including online: http://www.safetynetkids.org.uk/personal-safety/online-safety/. Some of the other issues they cover are friendship, school safety, and well-being.

Infant safety:
US Consumer Product Safety Commission (CPSC)
www.cpsc.gov
Consumer Hotline and General Information Phone: (800) 638-2772
From their website: "CPSC is charged with protecting the public from unreasonable risks of injury or death associated with the use of the thousands of types of consumer products under the agency's jurisdiction. Deaths, injuries, and property damage from consumer product incidents cost the nation more than $1 trillion annually."

The CPSC recommends that new parents become familiar with any product concerns before they buy products for their newborn and before their infant is born and in their care. Use the above CPSC hotline number to report a potential or real product hazard or a product-related injury or death.

You can learn more about their Safe to Sleep initiative, entitled "Crib Information Center," which includes written information as well as a three-minute sleep safe video: https://www.cpsc.gov/Safety-Education/Safety-Education-Centers/cribs

Safe to Sleep
https://safetosleep.nichd.nih.gov/
This is a public education campaign led by the National Institute of Health and other government initiatives to educate parents, especially new parents, about safe sleep practices for their newborns and infants.

Juvenile Products Manufacturers Association
https://www.jpma.org/
Membership trade association of manufacturers of juvenile products dedicated to the safety of products for infants and children. According to the association's website, they certify 2,000 products in twenty-four categories.

Public safety:
Center for Public Safety Innovation at SPC
3200 34th Street South
St. Petersburg, FL 33711
From their website: "The Center for Public Safety Innovation's (CPSI's) mission is to develop and deliver high-quality training for emergency and first responders, military personnel, and the general public, in a variety of formats—Web-based, video, broadcast, and face-to-face—using state-of-the-art technology and best practices in education and training. CPSI training focuses on public safety, the disaster preparedness cycle, illegal drug interdiction, community engagement, and enhanced quality of life for all."

Water safety:
Teaching your child how to swim at the earliest recommended age can be an effective tool in reducing the number of preventable injuries or deaths related to the water, which includes natural bodies of water, such as lakes and oceans, as well as in-ground or above-ground pools. We all know that infants and children are at risk for water-related tragedies, but adults have to be careful as well. Rip currents can make it hazardous to swim in the ocean at certain times, especially alone. If someone is intoxicated, it can even be dangerous to take a bath, since drownings at home can happen. One of the most famous ones in recent memory is singer Whitney Houston, who died at age forty-nine in 2012. Tragically, her twenty-two-year-old daughter, Bobbi Kristina Brown, three years later, was found unconscious in her bathtub; she died several months later.

ARAG legal insurance offers this useful article highlighting the guidelines someone with a pool in his/her backyard must follow to avoid any pool-related drownings: https://www.araglegal.com/individuals/learning-center/topics/home-and-property/pool-safety-tips-if-you-have-a-backyard-pool.

American Red Cross
https://www.redcross.org
Water safety information: https://www.redcross.org/get-help/how-to-prepare-for-emergencies/types-of-emergencies/water-safety.html .

The Red Cross also gives swimming lessons. For more on this, go to https://www.redcross.org/take-a-class/swimming/swim-lessons/kids-swim-lessons. Contact your local Red Cross for details on the schedule in your community.

In addition to private swimming lessons, your local YMCA or YWCA may offer lower-cost swimming lessons if they have a pool on their premises. (They may also use the pool at a nearby facility.)

Most suburbs or cities have public pools or free after-school or summer programs that offer swimming lessons to participants. Check the website for your town, city, or state to see what is offered, when, and what it costs, if anything.

Stew Leonard III Water Safety Foundation
100 Westport Avenue
Norwalk, CT 06851
https://stewietheduck.org/
The tragic drowning accidental death of twenty-one-month old toddler Stew Leonard III on January 1, 1989, was the catalyst to the formation of the Stew Leonard III Water Safety Foundation. Since that time, the foundation has raised $2 million, offering free or low-cost swimming lessons to 10,000 children a year. Kim and Stew Leonard Jr. wrote a book for ages 2–6, *Stewie the Duck Learns to Swim*, with all proceeds going to water safety and education. The book is available as a free download on iTunes or Google Play.

Reading and Video Materials

American Red Cross. "Beach Safety Tips." Narrated by Dr. Peter Wernicki of the American Red Cross Science Advisory Council. 3 minutes 21 seconds. https://www.youtube.com/watch?v=Xh-xXYpjDWY

ARAG. "Eight Rules for Having a Pool in Your Backyard." https://www.araglegal.com/individuals/learning-center/topics/home-and-property/pool-safety-tips-if-you-have-a-backyard-pool

Barbara A. Glanz. *Care Packages for Your Customers: An Idea a Week to Enhance Customer Service*. NY: McGraw-Hill, 2007.

CDC (Centers for Disease Control and Prevention). "Accidents or Unintentional Injuries." Data for 2015. Source: National Hospital Ambulatory Medical Care Survey: 2015 Emergency Department Summary Tables, Table 17. https://www.cdc.gov/nchs/fastats/accidental-injury.htm

Christopher Mele. "How to Complain and Get Results." *The New York Times*, June 15, 2017. https://www.nytimes.com/2017/06/15/smarter-living/consumer-complaint-writing-letter.html

Harvard Business Review. "'Sorry' Is Not Enough." Reprinted at the website for the *Harvard Business Review* from the January-February 2018 issue, pages 20-22.

Joe Tacopino. "Bode Miller's Young Daughter Dies in Tragic Pool Accident." *New York Post*, June 11, 2018. https://pagesix.com/2018/06/11/bode-millers-daughter-dies-in-tragic-pool-accident/

Linda Swindling. *Stop Complainers and Energy Drainers: How to Negotiate Work Drama to Get More Done*. Hoboken, NJ: Wiley, 2013.

Megan Stein. "Furniture Tip-Over Deaths Are on the Rise for Children: Here's How to Keep Your Family Safe." *People*, March 23, 2018. https://people.com/home/report-finds-furniture-tip-overs-cause-injuries-every-17-minutes/

National Safety Council, "Kids in Hot Cars: One Child Is Too Many." 2018. https://www.nsc.org/road-safety/safety-topics/child-passenger-safety/kids-hot-cars

US Consumer Product Safety Commission, "Learn How to Put Your Baby to Sleep Safely." https://www.cpsc.gov/Newsroom/Multimedia/?vid=61784

CHAPTER 9

Counseling, Depression, and Mental Health

These three topics go together:

- counseling, or seeking out help
- depression, one of the major reasons that help is sought
- and mental health, which is the much larger category of psychological concerns, beyond just depression

These three topics are often also tied to issues explored in other chapters in *Help Yourself Now*, including Chapter 1, Addiction; Chapter 11, Crime, Victims, Witnesses, and Prevention; and Chapter 27, Suicide: Prevention and Related Issues, to name just a few.

SELF-CARE FOR HELP PROVIDERS

The rest of this chapter is about getting help, but in this section I am addressing help for those who offer help. Several help providers asked me to include suggestions for how help providers can avoid burnout. Based on a survey of providers, here are some suggestions:

1. Get counseling, if needed.
2. Take a vacation.
3. Make time for "me time." For example, one help provider who responded to my survey shared that she is in a drumming group.
4. Practice self-care (which could include everything from meditating, reading a book, eating properly, and exercising to getting regular massages, listening to self-hypnosis recordings, and prioritizing sleep).

5. Connect with others who provide similar help to share and support each other's efforts.
6. Set boundaries. Yes, it's important to be empathetic but also to avoid making your client's, customer's, or case's problems your own.
7. Make time for friends and family. As New Jersey-based Julio Briones, a personal crisis manager, puts it, "It can get overwhelming at times [so] I make it a point to make sure I can have sufficient time with my family. Because time with them is how I relax and remember there are still good and beautiful things in the world."

For those who provide help in disasters, there is even an organization that offers them support. It's called the Antares Foundation (www.antaresfoundation.org), and it is a nonprofit organization based in the Netherlands that provides stress management training and psychosocial support for humanitarian aid workers worldwide. Even if you are not dealing with overwhelming natural disasters, you still might need some help so you can continue to offer help.

The staff of GoodTherapy.org terms it "compassion fatigue," rather than the older term of burnout, but the concept is similar. As they note in their article, "The Cost of Caring: 10 Ways to Prevent Compassion Fatigue": "Compassion fatigue can be a serious occupational hazard for those in any kind of helping profession." In addition to the seven ways listed above, the GoodTherapy.org staff suggests these:

1. Getting educated (to the symptoms and signs of burnout or compassion fatigue)
2. Keeping a journal
3. Boosting your resiliency, the ability to recover from stress—a skill that GoodTherapy.org and others believe can be learned

Psychoanalyst Herbert J. Freudenberger, PhD, wrote a book entitled *Burn-Out*, published in 1980, that is still relevant today. In the section on "Burn-Out and the Helping Professions" Freudenberger shares these cautionary words and a related suggestion:

If you are in one of these taxing [helping] professions, you have to learn to be on the lookout for your own symptoms. Watch yourself for tiredness before it becomes extreme exhaustion. Don't fall into the trap of considering yourself a superbeing who doesn't require rest. Everyone requires rest, and your need for it isn't a sign of weakness. Pay attention to physical symptoms like colds or headaches or nagging pains in the back. Your physical system is a good barometer of whether or not you're overdoing, and a day off early may save you weeks later.

Help providers, take note! You are a very important part of the getting-help equation, so remember to take care of yourself so you can continue to help others. As the flight attendants remind us, if it ever happens that there is a need for oxygen onboard, put the mask on yourself first before helping your family members or others who need assistance.

COUNSELING

What type of counseling is right for you? Although "psychiatrist" or "psychologist" usually come to mind, there are a wide range of trained and licensed professionals who may be able to provide one-on-one or group counseling that is right for you and whatever challenge you are facing. To name just a few:

- Clinical social worker (CSW)
- Pastoral counselor
- Psychotherapist
- Psychoanalyst
- Psychologist (PhD or PsyD)
- Psychiatrist
- Substance abuse counselor
- Marriage and family therapist (MFT)
- Grief counselor
- Mental health counselor (MHC)

In addition to a variety of types of counselors, there is a wide range of approaches to counseling:

- Art therapy
- Cognitive-behavioral therapy (CBT)
- Family therapy
- Gestalt psychology/therapy

- Hypnotherapy
- Neuro-linguistic programming (NLP)
- Psychoanalysis
- Behavioral therapy
- Psychodynamic counseling
- Rational emotive therapy

When looking for the right counselor for yourself or your loved one, there are many factors that you need to consider. Cost, of course, is a concern for most people. If you have health insurance, you could check for counselors in your local area that are considered "in network" and find out how many sessions your policy will cover and to what extent. If a counselor does not take your insurance, you have to decide if you are able to pick up the tab on your own. If you find a therapist through an association, or even through the therapist's website, they usually list their hourly rate, although it might be in a range, from $100 to $200 an hour or even higher.

In addition to cost, you need to consider the type of therapy a specific counselor offers. This may take some research on your part. If you want to focus on the present and changing behaviors or beliefs that seem to be sabotaging you, you might want to consider cognitive-behavioral therapy (CBT). If you want to delve into your earliest relationship with your parents, as well as explore the meaning of your dreams and your unconscious, the long-term and more traditional psychoanalysis that started with Sigmund Freud might be the approach for you.

Once you choose a therapist based on cost, approach, location, and perhaps a recommendation from a current or past satisfied patient, you will want to have an initial meeting to see what kind of rapport you have. Your potential therapist will be listening to you, but you should also be paying attention to this possible counselor. Do you feel like this is someone you can open up to? Do you have a connection in this initial meeting? Of course, relationships, even with a counselor, take time to develop, so you cannot expect too much in this first session. But you do have to listen to your gut about whether or not this is someone you want to work with on a weekly basis for months or possibly even years.

If you are in crisis, immediate danger, and/or a life-and-death situation, you may not have time to search for a counselor, although that may be your goal once the crisis is dealt with.

If you or a loved one are in crisis, call 911.

That is usually the first option and the fastest and easiest one.

You or your loved one could also call one of the crisis lines listed below. However, you are usually not getting someone to immediately respond to your premises such as a police officer, EMT, or firefighter.

For these crisis helplines, you will find those phone numbers through-out Help Yourself Now, but here are a few of those numbers again, for your convenience:

Crisis Chat
Contact Community Services
6311 Court Street Road
East Syracuse, NY 13057
1-315-251-0600 (Please note: This is not a free call)
http://contactsyracuse.org/
contact@contactsyracuse.org
Hours: 24/7

National Suicide Prevention Lifeline
1-800-273-8255
Suicidepreventionlifeline.org
Hours: 24/7
Started in 2004, this hotline represents a network of more than 150 crisis centers throughout the US. A project of SAMHSA (Substance Abuse and Mental Health Services Administration).

National Hopeline Network, Suicide & Crisis Hotline
1-800-442-HOPE (4673)
https://nationaltoolkit.csw.fsu.edu/resource/national-hopeline-network-suicide
-crisis-hotline-1-800-442-hope4673/
Hours: 24/7
A program of the Kristin Brooks Hope Center offering help in suicide prevention through talking on the phone to trained counselors.

RAINN (Rape, Abuse, and Incest National Network)
National Sexual Assault Hotline
1-800-656-HOPE (4673)
www.rainn.org
Hours: 24/7

Founded in 1994 by Scott Berkowitz, who serves as its CEO. RAINN works with 1,000 affiliated anti-sexual assault organizations providing services.

National Center for Missing & Exploited Children
699 Prince Street
Alexandria, VA 22314
1-800-843-5678
www.missingkids.org
Hours: 24/7
If you think you have seen a missing child, contact the above number. However, as they state at their website, "If you or someone else are in immediate danger, please call 911 or your local police."

National Tragedy Assistance Program for Survivors (TAPS)
(Caring for the Families of America's Fallen Heroes)
1-800-959-TAPS (8277)
www.taps.org
Hours: 24/7
Started in 1994. At the website you will find links to information for survivors, including available resources for direct help or for those who want to help.

National Runaway Switchboard (NRS)
3141B N. Lincoln
Chicago, IL 60657
1-800-RUNAWAY (1-800-786-2929)
www.1800runaway.org
Hours: 24/7
Point of communication and help for runaway or homeless children and teens.

Lines for Life
National Veterans Crisis Line
1-800-273-8255 Press 1
https://www.linesforlife.org
Hours: 24/7
Offers crisis intervention and someone to listen related to substance abuse and suicidal ideation issues that is confidential and independent of any branch of the military.

Self-Harm Text
Text HOME to 741741
See listing for Crisis Text Line below.

Crisis Text Line
https://www.crisistextline.org
Text "START" TO 741-741
Launched in 2013 by CEO Nancy Lublin. Allows someone needing help from a counselor to get it completely via text messaging. It is free and confidential.

National Helpline
SAMHSA (Substance Abuse and Mental Health Services Administration)
800-622-4387 (HELP)
https://www.samhsa.gov

National Domestic Violence Hotline
800-799-7233
https://www.thehotline.org/
Hours: 24/7
Advocates are available to talk and make referrals.

LGBT Hotline
LGBT National Help Center
Also has separate helplines for youths through age twenty-five and seniors.
888-843-4564 (This is the number for the national free hotline for gay, lesbian, bisexual, and transgender individuals.)
https://www.glbthotline.org/
HOURS: M–F 1pm to 9pm, *Pacific time*
(M–F from 4pm to midnight, *eastern time*)
Saturday (9am to 2pm, *Pacific time)*
(Saturday (noon to 5pm, *eastern time)*
Email: help@LGBThotline.org

Here is an international referral source for those needing help with suicide prevention and related mental health issues:
YLC (Your Life Counts)
https://yourlifecounts.org/
Founded in 2000 and dedicated to suicide prevention. YLC is an international effort to combat suicide. It is affiliated with referring those at risk to help in many countries besides the United States including the United Kingdom, Canada, New Zealand, Japan, France, and others. (See the complete list at this URL where you will find help by country: https://yourlifecounts.org/find-help/.

TEXT, EMAIL, PHONE, OR VIDEO COUNSELING

A newer development is online-only counseling, using email, Skype or other forms of video chatting such as FaceTime, and text messaging to communicate. You do not have the advantage of meeting with a counselor face-to-face, but it could definitely be more convenient for those who are unable to travel because of disability, shyness, family or work obligations, or even just a preference for online or phone interaction. Please note that unlike the above helplines or crisis phones for immediate help, these online counseling services are not free, although some may be covered by insurance plans. Check out each website and/or therapist that you are interested in to see what the cost will be.

Better Help

440 N. Wolfe Rd
Sunnyvale, CA 94085
https://www.betterhelp.com/
contact@betterhelp.com
Costs for working with a licensed therapist start at $40 to $70 per week, billed monthly. Over 2,000 therapists are listed at their site; therapists have a page with a photo, synopsis of their training, specialties, and even some reviews from satisfied patients.

ReGain

https://www.regain.us
contact@regain.us
Focuses on couples therapy with an average weekly cost $40 to $70, billed monthly, with approximately 1,000 licensed and credentialed therapists available through their site. In answer to the question of whether this online service can substitute for one-on-one, face-to-face traditional counseling: "The professionals who work through Regain are licensed and credentialed therapists who were certified by their state's board to provide therapy and counseling. However, while the service may have similar benefits, it's not able to substitute traditional face-to-face therapy in every case. Please note that your counselor won't be able to make an official diagnosis, fulfill any court order, or prescribe medication." They have a useful list of resources to contact for immediate help if someone is going through a crisis: https://www.regain.us/gethelpnow/.

My Therapist

https://www.mytherapist.com
contact@mytherapist.com
There are 1,000 licensed therapists with an average cost of $40 to $70 per week, billed monthly. From their website: "You can get counseling in four ways:

- Exchanging messages with your counselor
- Chatting live with your counselor
- Speaking over the phone with your counselor
- Video conferencing with your counselor"

TalkSpace
Headquartered in New York City
https://lp.talkspace.com
Started in 2012. On October 25, 2018, TalkSpace added teens to the populations that they serve. Talk Space helps individuals directly; they are also affiliated with more than seventy companies through their human resource departments. Over 2,000 licensed therapists with an average cost of $65 to $100 a week (it is a subscription service), depending upon the type of service you choose, from unlimited text, video, and audio messaging. This service has new clients fill out a questionnaire that is used to match with three potential therapists; the client chooses one. The service is available through its website or on iOS or Android.

Please note: Telemedicine also offers the opportunity to have videoconferencing with psychiatrists who are signed up with a service. See those listings in Chapter 19, Health and Wellness.

The following professional organizations and information referral services will provide referrals to counselors who are members and who offer help in-person and by phone, although some may offer online help. Check out each counselor's credentials, what services are offered, cost, what insurance is accepted, if any, and any posted reader reviews:
American Association for Marriage and Family Therapy (AAMFT)
112 South Alfred Street
Alexandria, VA 22314
www.aamft.org
Professional membership association for marriage and family therapists offering "Find a Therapist" through their website. There is an annual conference for members as well as ongoing educational webinars.

American Association of Pastoral Counselors (AAPC)
PO Box 3030
Oakton, VA 22124
https://www.aapc.org
Started in 1963, this is a national association of clergy of all faiths who have special counseling training.

American Psychiatric Association
800 Maine Avenue, SW, Suite 900

Washington, DC 20024
www.psychiatry.org
A professional association of psychiatrists whose main assistance to the public is through its membership directory, information at their website, and publications.

CONTACT USA, Inc.
6339 Charlotte Pike, #551
Nashville, TN 37209
A national organization which started in 1963 with centers throughout the United States of lay trained counselors. From their website: "CONTACT USA is a crisis helpline membership organization and the only accrediting entity in the US devoted solely to establishing best practice standards of service for crisis helplines. Our mission is to inspire, educate and accredit community-based emotional support programs with the vision of everyone having access to thriving, effective emotional support." At their website you will find a list of member crisis centers, listed alphabetically by state.

American Psychological Association (APA)
750 First Street, NE
Washington, DC 20002-4242
www.apa.org
A professional association of psychologists that has a psychologist locator referral service: https://locator.apa.org/.

GoodTherapy.org
Anchorage, AL
www.goodtherapy.org
Started in 2007, this association of mental health providers offers visitors an internet directory of therapists from more than 30 countries plus treatment and rehab centers across the United States. At the website the public will also find information on such topics as what therapy is, types of therapy, warning signs in therapy, and more. According to their website, GoodTherapy.org gets more than 1.5 million therapist searches monthly.

Peer Counseling (Self-Help Groups):
National Mental Health Consumers' Self-Help Clearinghouse
https://www.mhselfhelp.org/
selfhelpclearinghouse@gmail.com
Founded by Joseph Rogers in 1986. From their website: "The National Mental Health Consumers' Self-Help Clearinghouse is a peer-run national technical assistance and resource center that fosters recovery, self-determination, and community inclusion. The Clearinghouse serves individuals with lived

experience of a mental health condition, peer-run service and advocacy organizations, family members, mental health professionals and service providers, policy makers, and the public."

The following national self-help organizations have local affiliates throughout the country; the headquarters act as information clearinghouses and will refer you to your nearest local chapters or meetings. A growing number of national and international self-help organizations also offer phone or online help in addition to face-to-face weekly meetings, so location need not be a deterrent to getting the help you want or need. Also, most of these self-help groups are completely run by peers and/or volunteers rather than professionals. For a referral to a group run by a trained or licensed therapist, contact a therapist through the associations listed in the above section under "Counseling."

Compassionate Friends

1000 Jorie Boulevard, Suite 140
Oak Brook, IL 60523
https://www.compassionatefriends.org
Coping with grief through local self-help groups. At their website you will find referrals to chapters as well as information on coping with grief for those who have lost someone and others who want to know how to act toward someone who is grieving, including employees/coworkers.

Emotions Anonymous (EA)

PO Box 4245
St. Paul, MN 55104-0245
www.emotionsanonymous.org
Started in 1966 in Minneapolis by Marion Flesch. Uses the Twelve Steps of AA (Alcoholics Anonymous) as the basis of its self-help groups for recovery from mental and emotional illness. According to their website, there are now more than 600 groups, including Skype and phone meetings, in more than 30 countries.

Workaholics Anonymous (WA)

Post Office Box 289
Menlo Park, CA 94026-0289
http://www.workaholics-anonymous.org/
A confidential 12-step program in the AA (Alcoholics Anonymous) tradition for those who are addicted to work.

Alcoholics Anonymous (AA)

https://www.aa.org/
The original confidential 12-step program for those who have a drinking problem. See complete listing in Chapter 1, Addiction.

Narcotics Anonymous (NA)
https://www.na.org/
A confidential 12-step program in the AA (Alcoholics Anonymous) tradition adapted for drug addicts.
See complete listing in Chapter 1, Addiction.

Gamblers Anonymous (GA)
www.gamblersanonymous.org
A confidential 12-step program in the AA (Alcoholics Anonymous) tradition adapted for those who have a gambling addiction.
See complete listing in Chapter 1, Addiction.

Debtors Anonymous (DA)
https://debtorsanonymous.org/
An international confidential self-help support group approach, founded on the principles of AA (Alcoholics Anonymous), with in-person and phone sessions for those dealing with money challenges. Getting and staying out of debt as well as avoiding compulsive spending.

Spenders Anonymous
http://www.spenders.org/
The list of selected meetings throughout the US and internationally was updated on August 2, 2017: http://www.spenders.org/list.html. There are also useful materials that could be printed out and used to start your own local self-help group.

Supportiv
2222 Harold Way
Berkeley, CA 94704
http://www.supportiv.com/
info@supportiv.com
This is an anonymous peer support platform that matches individuals with others who are dealing with a similar issue. Those who moderate groups around a particular issue are trained by the site's developer and administrators. As the co-founder, Helena Plater-Zyberk, notes, "Every group chat is moderated by a human to keep the discussion safe and supportive." Although based in California, since the service is completely online, the site has users from around the world. After the first free 24 hours of unlimited access, you can get credits to keep your use of the site free by sharing about it on social media. If you prefer not to do that, the charge is 15 cents per minute (or less).

Newport Academy
https://www.newportacademy.com/
help@newportacademy.com
Outpatient and resident treatment for teens and adults who are dealing with eating disorders, trauma, mental health, and/or substance abuse issues.

Overeaters Anonymous (OA)
https://oa.org/
A confidential 12-step program in the AA (Alcoholics Anonymous) tradition adapted for those who are compulsive overeaters. The goal for OA participants is to achieve abstinence, although that can have a variety of meanings. For one member, it can mean adhering to a food plan. To another, it can mean avoiding eating compulsively or when someone is not hungry.
   See complete listing in Chapter 18, Food, Hunger, Nutrition, and Eating Disorders.

Information clearinghouses:
HelpGuide.org International
1250 6th Street, Suite 400
Santa Monica, CA 90401
HelpGuide.org
This comprehensive educational website was launched in 1999 by Robert Segal and his late wife, Jeanne Segal. Helpguide.org is a nonprofit organization providing information for dealing with all these issues: mental health, healthy living, children & family, aging, and relationships. The site provides material on a wide range of topics, from coronavirus, ADHD, depression, and eating disorders to relationships, stress, and suicide prevention. Through a collaboration with Harvard Health Publishing, the consumer health publishing division of Harvard Medical School, they are now reprinting their previously published articles related to HelpGuide's areas of concern.

DEPRESSION

Here is an excerpt from the National Institute of Mental Health website, "Depression," that may help you know if you or a loved one is clinically depressed and not just in a bad mood that will pass:

"If you have been experiencing some of the following signs and symptoms most of the day, nearly every day, for at least two weeks, you may be suffering from depression:

- Persistent sad, anxious, or 'empty' mood

- Feelings of hopelessness, or pessimism
- Irritability
- Feelings of guilt, worthlessness, or helplessness
- Loss of interest or pleasure in hobbies and activities
- Decreased energy or fatigue
- Moving or talking more slowly
- Feeling restless or having trouble sitting still
- Difficulty concentrating, remembering, or making decisions
- Difficulty sleeping, early-morning awakening, or oversleeping
- Appetite and/or weight changes
- Thoughts of death or suicide, or suicide attempts
- Aches or pains, headaches, cramps, or digestive problems without a clear physical cause and/or that do not ease even with treatment

You may experience just one of the above symptoms, several, or many. You may feel depressed just once in a while or regularly."

Still unsure if you or your loved one is depressed? You could watch this short video, "Signs, Symptoms, and Treatment of Depression,"—under 4 minutes—developed by NIMH and posted at https://www.youtube.com/watch?v=mlNCavst2EU.

What are some of the causes of episodic or chronic depression? According to a WebMD article, "Dysthymia (Mild, Chronic Depression)," revised by Jennifer Casarella, here are some of the causes of chronic depression, although the impact of any of these potential origins will vary from person to person such as a family history of depression: "abnormal functioning in brain circuits or nerve cells pathways that connect different brain regions…"; chronic illness; medications; and problems at work or in relationships.

Depression is a complex mental condition that usually needs professional treatment. What treatments are available? Working with a therapist is one option. There is a wide range of therapists who can treat depression, everything from social workers with clinical training, psychiatric nurses with clinical training, or psychologists, to physicians who specialize in psychiatry. Help could consist of individual or group therapy, including cognitive-behavioral therapy (CBT). It might also include being prescribed antidepressants, although that would require being under the care of a doctor, possibly working together with a psychologist or another therapist, who is able to prescribe and monitor the medication.

To find a therapist, ask a family physician for a referral. If you have a friend or family member who lives nearby who you know has depression, and you have seen a dramatic positive change in their behavior, you might ask them for a recommendation as well. The Anxiety and Depression Association of America (ADAA) also has a referral directory: https://members .adaa.org/page/FATMain. You will also find therapist referral directories at the websites for the American Psychological Association (https://locator .apa.org/) and the American Psychiatric Association (http://finder.psychiatry .org/).

As the NIMH video mentioned above notes at the very beginning of the overview on depression, the brains of those with depression tend to be different from those not suffering from it. This has led some researchers to look to brain-related treatments. One such innovative approach is being practiced by Dr. Mark George, who is trained as both a psychiatrist and a neurologist. Dr. George, who is Distinguished Professor of Psychiatry, Radiology, and Neuroscience, and Director of the Brain Stimulation Laboratory at the Medical University of South Carolina, has been doing research into repetitive transcranial magnetic stimulation research (rTMSR) through a grant from the National Institute of Mental Health. The process involves making an electric current without causing a seizure by putting an electromagnet on the brain for approximately thirty to forty minutes. In comparing those resistant to other treatment for depression who received the treatment to those who did not, there was a 14 percent improvement with the treatment compared to just 5 percent without.

Self-help groups are not a substitute for professional counseling, especially if it is decided that taking prescription drugs to treatment the depression is recommended. But peer groups may be useful in dealing with depression. To find a local support group, ask your physician or therapist for a referral or look online at the resources mentioned above.

In its extreme form, depression can lead to suicidal thoughts (discussed further in Chapter 27, Suicide). That is why it is so crucial to get help for depression. You do not have to suffer silently or alone. There is a light at the end of what may seem like an endless tunnel of darkness. Get help for your depression because life is precious. There are competent and caring professionals and even peers who want to aid you in your search for a happier and more joyful existence.

In addition to the organizations and sources of information listed above for "Counseling," here are organizations focused on depression:
Depression and Bipolar Support Alliance (DBSA)
55 E. Jackson Boulevard, Suite 490
Chicago, IL 60604
www.dbsalliance.org
From their website: "DBSA provides hope, help, support, and education to improve the lives of people who have mood disorders." Do a search at the website for local support groups.

Please also consult additional listings and sources of help for Suicide Prevention in Chapter 27, Suicide.

MENTAL HEALTH

I have focused on depression in this chapter, but mental health encompasses a much wider number of conditions, as listed by NAMI (National Alliance on Mental Illness) in the "Mental Health Conditions" at their website, including:

- ADHD (Attention deficit hyperactivity disorder)
- Anxiety disorders
- Autism
- Bipolar disorder
- Borderline personality disorder (BPD)
- Dissociative disorders
- Early psychosis
- Psychosis
- Eating disorders (discussed in Chapter 18, Food, Hunger, Nutrition, and Eating Disorders)
- Obsessive-compulsive disorder (OCD)
- Post-Traumatic Stress Disorder (PTSD)
- Schizoaffective Disorder
- Schizophrenia

Government agencies with information on depression, counseling, and mental health issues:
National Institute of Mental Health (NIMH)
National Institutes of Health (NIH)
6001 Executive Boulevard, Room 6200, MSC 9663
Bethesda, MD 20892-9663
https://www.nimh.nih.gov
One of the twenty-seven Institutes of NIH, NIMH is a research funding agency. It also has information on mental health issues but it is not a direct care provider.

Mentalhealth.gov
This is the government's public site about mental health. From their website: "MentalHealth.gov provides one-stop access to US government mental health and mental health problems information. MentalHealth.gov aims to educate and guide:

- The general public
- Health and emergency preparedness professionals
- Policy makers
- Government and business leaders
- School systems
- Local communities

Content for this website is provided by:

- Centers for Disease Control and Prevention
- MedlinePlus and National Institutes of Health
- National Institute of Mental Health (NIMH)
- Substance Abuse and Mental Health Services Administration (SAMHSA)
- Youth.gov"

You will also find information about mental health help for US veterans: https://www.mentalhealth.gov/get-help/veterans

Non-governmental organizations related to mental health:
Anxiety and Depression Association of America (ADAA)
8701 Georgia Avenue, Suite 412
Silver Spring, MD 20910
https://adaa.org/
Founded in 1979, ADAA is a nonprofit membership association focused on educating the public about anxiety and depression conditions. They also are concerned with the prevention, treatment, and cure of anxiety, depression, and

related conditions. It is not a direct service organization, but there are referrals to therapists and support groups at their website.

Mental Health America (MHA)
500 Montgomery Street, Suite 820
Alexandria, VA 22314
www.mentalhealthamerica.net
From their website: "Mental Health America (MHA)–founded in 1909–is the nation's leading community-based nonprofit dedicated to addressing the needs of those living with mental illness and to promoting the overall mental health of all Americans." Sponsors an annual conference for those concerned about the state of mental health in America.

National Alliance on Mental Illness (NAMI)
3803 N. Fairfax Drive, Suite 100
Arlington, VA 22203
https://www.nami.org/
Helpline: 800-950-6264
Founded in 1979, this advocacy, educational, and nonprofit association is concerned with the range of mental illnesses listed in this chapter. Their slogan is "You are not alone." There is an annual convention at a different US city each year.

See also these related chapters in **Help Yourself Now:**
> Chapter 1, Addiction: Alcohol, Drugs, Nictoine, and Gambling
> Chapter 3, Aging
> Chapter 11, Crime: Victims, Witnesses, and Prevention
> Chapter 14, Dying, Death, and Dealing with Grief
> Chapter 19, Health and Wellness
> Chapter 21, Legal Services
> Chapter 27, Suicide: Prevention and Related Issues
> Chapter 29, Veterans

Reading and Audiovisual Materials

Alice Gregory. "RU There?" The New Yorker, February 9, 2015, posted at www.thenewyorker.com. (The story of the way that the text-only crisis helpline, Crisis Text Line, came about.)

Anxiety and Depression. Mango, 2018.

Carol R. Ray, PhD. *Ph.D.s Have Bipolar Too: My Story.* Tate Publishing, LLC, 2017.

David A. Clark and Aaron T. Beck. *The Anxiety & Worry Workbook.* NY: Guilford Press, 2011.

Erik H. Erikson. *Childhood and Society.* Second edition. NY: Norton, 1963.

Erving Goffman. *Asylums: Essays on the Social Situation of Mental Patients and Other Inmates.* Garden City, NY: Doubleday, 1961.

Flora Rheta Schreiber. *Sybil.* NY: Warner Books, 1974.

Hannah Green. *I Never Promised You a Rose Garden.* HR&W, 1964.

Herbert J. Freudenberger, PhD with Geraldine Richelson. *Burn-Out: The High Cost of High Achievement.* Garden City, NY: Anchor Press, Doubleday & Company, Inc., 1980.

Jeanne Segal, PhD. *Feeling Loved: The Science of Nurturing Meaningful Connections and Building Lasting Happiness.* Dallas, TX: BenBella Books, 2015.

Kate Allan. *You Can Do All Things: Drawings, Affirmations and Mindfulness to Help With Anxiety and Depression.*

Ken Kesey. *One Flew Over the Cuckoo's Nest.* NY: New American Library, 1962, 1975.

Lisa Marshall. "Early birds less prone to depression." University of Colorado Boulder. June 15, 2018. https://www.colorado.edu/today/2018/06/15/early-birds-less-prone-depression (reporting on a study published that week in the *Journal of Psychiatric Research*)

Maxwell Maltz. *Psycho-Cybernetics.* NY: Pocket Books, 1969.

Mayo Clinic staff. "Depression (major depressive disorder)." https://www.mayoclinic.org/diseases-conditions/depression/symptoms-causes/syc-20356007

Nancy Lublin. CEO, dosomething.org. "How data from a crisis text line is saving lives." TED Women 2015. 8:21 minutes. Posted at https://www.ted.com/talks/nancy_lublin_how_data_from_a_crisis_text_line_is_saving_lives.

National Alliance on Mental Illness (NAMI). "Mental Health Conditions." https://www.nami.org/Learn-More/Mental-Health-Conditions

National Institute for Mental Health. "Depression." https://www.nimh.nih .gov/health/topics/depression/index.shtml

—. "Signs, Symptoms, and Treatment of Depression." 4-minute video. https://www.youtube.com/watch?v=mlNCavst2EU

Silver Linings Playbook (2012).Starring Bradley Cooper, Jennifer Lawrence, and Robert DeNiro. Written and directed by David O. Russell. Based on the novel by Matthew Quick.

Sylvia Nasar. *A Beautiful Mind.* (A biography of her husband John Forbes Nash Jr.) Starring Jennifer Connelly and Russell Crowe. Directed by Ron Howard. 2001.

Sonja Lyubomirsky. *The How of Happiness: A New Approach to Getting the Life You Want.* NY: Penguin, 2007.

Tina H. Boogren. *Take Time for You: Self-Care Action Plans for Educators (Using Maslow's Hierarchy of Needs and Positive Psychology).* Bloomington, IN: Solution Tree, 2018.

Viktor E. Frankl. *Man's Search for Meaning: An Introduction to Logotherapy.* Preface by Gordon W. Allport. Original title: *From Death-Camp to Existentialism.* Part One translated by Ilse Lasch. NY: Pocket Books, 1963, 1946.

CHAPTER 10

Courts and Dispute Resolution

The best time to go to court is when you do not have to—as an educational experience for you and your family. Understanding how the judicial system in the United States operates, or fails to, is a key to building a more effective and representative system. A good way to begin learning about the courts is to volunteer in a court-watching or monitoring project in your area. To find out what court-watching activities there are where you live, contact your local District Attorney's Office, citizen's crime commission, bar association, or those national organizations listed in this chapter's directory.

The most dramatic court encounters are seen on television or found in the real-life experiences of crime victims or those accused or found guilty of a crime. But even if none of these extreme real-life situations happens to you, you may find yourself in court for a more everyday reason, such as:

- serving on a jury
- appearing as a witness
- suing someone or defending yourself in a suit
- solving problems such as divorce, child custody or support, adoption, inheritances, or such minor offenses as traffic violations

The American system of justice is difficult to understand because of its dualistic nature—the federal courts and the state courts operate independently—and entire books have been written to explain the complex differences. In addition, since each state has its own criminal code, few generalities can be made. Some basic information on two key common experiences—being a juror and appearing as a witness—follows.

BEING CALLED TO SERVE ON A JURY

When you are called to serve on a jury, you probably will receive a form letter asking you to report to the court clerk's office. You will then fill out a questionnaire, and if you are later called to serve—unless you have legitimate and serious extenuating excuses—you are expected to report back to the court for the duration of your jury duty. You either receive a daily fee or, if your employer is paying you during your jury duty, you do not receive a fee or are asked to pass the fee on to your employer.

The process by which potential jurors are questioned is known as *voir dire*, and it can be harrowing for you if you feel the questions are intended to violate your privacy. But this procedure is a safeguard for both sides to see whether a juror has any biases or previous knowledge that would cause him or her to prejudge that case. Many jurors are also unaware that they are permitted to ask questions at any time during the trial proceedings. Lawyers and judges might not like a particular juror's interruptions, but it is better to get a point of law or evidence cleared up than to let it go unanswered until the deliberations.

Most important of all is the requirement that you treat the jury summons as a mandatory request that you report for jury duty, provide a valid reason why you should be excused, or ask for a new date, usually within one year of the initial jury duty date, rather than ignoring the notice. If you ignore it, after a period of time, you will be told that there will be grave consequences for your silence. For starters, a judge could issue a bench warrant to summon you or, if you ignore that follow-up direct request, you could even be ordered to your local jail.

When you receive your jury duty summons, there is usually a phone number or a website on the mailed request for follow-up information or questions.

If you do serve on a jury, you will get a written confirmation of your service. Usually you are not required to serve again for another three years. If you are contacted before the three years are up, just indicate that you provided service recently. Keep the written confirmation of your service in a safe place so you can enter the exact information or number assigned to you as proof of your previous service.

CRIME WITNESSES

Witnesses are the backbone of our judicial system, and a recognition of the poor treatment they once received in the courts has led to the establishment of witness information bureaus around the country—attached to district attorneys' offices, police departments, or privately run independent community services. They will answer your questions about your rights and any available compensation that you might be eligible to receive.

If you are asked to be a witness, if you volunteer to become one, or if you are subpoenaed to be one, you should receive financial compensation for any time you spend as a witness. (This varies from court to court, but some pay transportation, lunch, and a daily fee rate. Expert witnesses may receive much higher fees. As with being a juror, if your employer is also paying you, you are generally not allowed to keep both fees.)

Various pamphlets and leaflets are available for witnesses at the courthouse or from the website for your state. As a witness, you have rights, such as the ones listed below that were included in a witness rights card distributed in Colorado:

- To be free from intimidation
- To be assisted by your criminal justice agencies
- To be told about available compensation for court appearances
- To be told about all available help from social service or volunteer agencies

STATE COURTS

Based solely on the number of cases handled each year, the state courts are where most of the legal action is in the United States, though the federal courts get much of the publicity. It is also at the state level that the court system in the United States becomes confusing, even to some lawyers. What is legal in California might be illegal in Delaware. In some states, civil and criminal cases are handled in separate courts; in others, they are handled by one court. State systems may also include other local courts, such as the justice of the peace or small claims courts. But there is one generality—every state has one court as the highest court of appeals, although the name might vary from "Supreme Court" to "Court of Appeals" to "Supreme Court of Errors."

Since no generalities about state civil or criminal law are possible, it is important to know what the laws are *in your own state*. (Youth, for example, are quick to become familiar with differing marijuana legalization laws, but most other legal differences between states are far more complicated.) You cannot obey the law unless you know what it is. Perhaps the trend, observed in some states like New York, of having court decisions and contracts written in conventional English rather than "legalese" will help popularize laws that are now obscure.

For direct assistance with the courts, search the internet for your particular state under "Courts" or a specific court, such as Municipal, Civil, County, Criminal, Family or Domestic Relations, Small Claims, etc.

For example: State of Connecticut, Judicial Branch, https://www.jud.ct.gov/.

At that website, there is a wealth of information related to the state of Connecticut:

- Supreme Court
- Superior Court
- Appellate Court
- Probate Court

There is also information for jurors, victims, attorneys, and a lot more.

This national organization is involved in projects designed to modernize and standardize procedures in the state courts:
National Center for State Courts (NCSC)
300 Newport Avenue
Williamsburg, VA 23185
https://www.ncsc.org/
An information clearinghouse, but primarily a research center studying the modernization of court operations and the improvement of justice at the state and local levels. It functions as an extension of the state court systems, working for them at their direction. Related websites, associations, and partners of the NCSC: https://www.ncsc.org/About-us/Associations-and-partners.aspx.

CIVIL COURT

If civil and criminal matters are divided into two court jurisdictions in your state, it is advisable to know precisely what is available to you locally at the civil level. For example, is there a housing court within civil court where you can bring about a tenant-initiated action? What's the financial award limit if you are considering filing a claim with your state's small claims court?

    The major difference between a civil and a criminal suit is that in a civil case, the plaintiff (the one bringing suit) can be you; in a criminal case, the plaintiff is always the state, not an individual. Some crimes are also civil wrongs and since damages are awarded to persons in civil suits, many victims may decide to sue civilly, whether or not a criminal action was taken by the state. (For example, your "friend" hit you on the head and you had to be hospitalized; therefore, you sue him for a civil wrong of assault and battery so that you can use the judgment money to pay medical bills.) Another major difference between a civil and criminal case is that in a civil case, the jury must usually believe one side more than the other by "a preponderance of evidence." In a criminal case, to be convicted, the defendant must be found guilty "beyond a reasonable doubt," a much higher standard.

Unless you are taking a case to small claims court (where a lawyer is not necessary), you will want to consult an attorney before going into any civil court (see "How to Find a Lawyer" in Chapter 21, Legal Services).

SMALL CLAIMS COURT

Any person who feels that he or she has received unfair treatment from a business or individual can file a suit, without hiring a lawyer, in the small claims court in your area. (As pointed out in the "How Do I File a Small Claims Court Lawsuit?" article posted at www.findlaw.com, small claims court might also go by any of these names: pro se court, magistrate court, or justice of the peace court.) This court is usually part of the civil division of the municipal court of your county or city.

Here are examples of typical cases that might be brought to small claims court:

- Your landlord failed to fix a leak in your bedroom, causing you to awaken in a bed soaked with water, get pneumonia, and incur a $2,000 doctor's bill (not covered by your insurance).
- You advanced your floor polisher $150 for a job he never returned to do.
- You bought a computer for $1,250 that does not work, and the company will not repair it or refund your money.
- The dry cleaners ruined your clothing, valued at $300, but will not reimburse you.

The procedure for filing a small claims case will vary, but generally you must go to the clerk's office and fill out a form stating who it is you wish to sue, why, and for how much. Some courts will allow you to file a claim by fax or online. To avoid later problems, be sure you have the exact name of the person or firm you are suing. If you have doubts, stop at the county clerk's office and check the business filing name of the person or firm you are suing.

After completing the form, you will pay a filing fee and a notice will be delivered to the person you are filing against. There may be another small fee for delivery of the notice. When your case is called (it may take about a month), the judge will hear both sides of the story. Be sure to bring any evidence and witnesses you have (receipts, damaged clothing, sales tickets) along with you.

If you win your case, you will receive a judgment for the amount of damages listed on your claim plus the fees you paid to bring the case to court. In some states, if the defendant does not pay you within thirty days of receiving notification of the court's decision, you will be allowed to go back to court and sue the defendant for three times the amount of the original award, plus legal costs. If you lose the case, and the defendant had a lawyer, you will be charged court costs. Otherwise, "you just lose the case," as one clerk explained it.

Since all states now have a small claims court, you should know what the limit is for a claim in your state. Popular limits are $5,000, for example, for New York, Connecticut, Missouri, and Maryland, or as high as $10,000 in Illinois, District of Columbia, or North Carolina. But other states, like Tennessee, have a limit as high as $25,000, or, by contrast, as low as $2,500 in the state of Rhode Island or $3,500 in Mississippi. Those limits might influence your decision about whether it is worth the time and effort to pursue a small claims court case. (For a state-by-state listing of small claims courts maximums, go to https://www.nolo.com/legal-encyclopedia/small-claims-suits-how-much-30031.html.)

For information on how to file in your area, contact the small claims court or information office of the municipal court. There may also be useful information at the websites of your local consumer groups. The Consumer Affairs Bureau of your county or city government may also be able to help you (see listings in Chapter 8, Consumer Affairs and Safety).

FAMILY COURT

What situations will appear in family court? All legal matters concerning family life: divorce and annulment, paternity actions, child custody, adoption, delinquency, child neglect, child support, and assault offenses in which victim and offender are members of the same family (although there has been a movement to take assault cases out of family court and into criminal court).

In family court, the judge acts as both judge and jury, relying heavily on police and victim/witness testimony and investigations by probation and court liaison officers to make a judgment. There are generally four procedures in the family court process: probation intake (which has the discretion to adjust the case and throw it out, if necessary); intake (which is similar to arraignment in adult criminal court); fact-finding hearing; and disposition of the case. The disposition might be ACD (Adjournment and Contemplation of Dismissal), which usually gives a six-month period to see how the accused performs; probation; placement in a group home; prison; training school; private placement in another type of institution or with other relatives; a fine; or a dismissal.

CRIMINAL COURT

If someone is arrested and accused of a crime, that person usually will go to criminal court, although in recent years, there has been a push to resolve more and more criminal acts in alternative ways. (See the section on Dispute Resolution that follows.)

As you may know, the types of laws that someone can be accused of breaking and the potential punishment, if found guilty, depend on the type of crime and a number of other factors. First and foremost is whether the act is considered a misdemeanor, which is a less serious offense. If found guilty, and time in jail is part of the punishment, a misdemeanor charge will result in a sentence of no longer than one year in the county or local jail.

More serious crimes are known as felonies. If convicted of a felony, and prison time is part of the punishment, the time will be served in a state prison.

In a criminal court case, it is the state, not the victim, who is filing a charge against the accused. The defendant must be found guilty "beyond a reasonable doubt."

In TV shows like the long-running *Law & Order: Special Victims Unit*, which started its twenty-first season in Fall 2019, practically every case in each week's episode leads to a quick trial. But the reality in the United States criminal justice system is far from that Hollywood myth. The actuality is that over 90 percent of all criminal cases result in a plea bargain so that a court case is avoided. That means that if a defendant has been indicted for a crime, the assistant district attorney offers him or her a plea in lieu of going to trial. The defendant waives his or her right to a jury trial.

If a defendant is guilty, the rewards for taking the plea can be great. For example, instead of going to trial and facing a potential sentence of twenty-five years to life, a much shorter sentence of three to six years may be offered.

The plea-bargaining option saves the court time and money and may spare the crime victim from testifying if he or she prefers to avoid that trauma. But when it becomes complicated is if the defendant is really innocent but counsel has advised his or her client that there is a likelihood that he or she will be found guilty anyway. Agree to the plea and take the shorter sentence, or roll the dice and go to trial and risk a much longer sentence?

For more on criminal courts and the criminal justice system, please refer to Chapter 12, Criminal Justice or to Chapter 21, Legal Services.

DRUG COURTS

In an effort to reduce the number of Americans who are imprisoned for drug-related offenses, there has been a trend toward Drug Court as an alternative to incarceration. Although most Drug Courts are for non-violent offenders, especially first-time offenders, whereby the offender has to plead guilty to the offense and agree to participate in a drug rehabilitation program or else jail or prison is a very real possibility, some programs even take violent offenders if the offender's drug addiction was a major factor in the crime, the victim agrees with the court's decision to offer drug court, and the offender complies with the strict requirements that he stop using drugs. According to the National Institute of Justice (NIJ), in 2018 there were more than 3,100 drug courts throughout the United States; half were adult treatment drug courts.

Drug court resources:
National Drug Court Resource Center (NDCRC)
Justice Programs at American University
4801 Massachusetts Avenue, NW, Suite 508
Washington, DC, 20016-8159
https://ndcrc.org/
NDCRC provides information and resources about drug courts to those working in this field. You can find a drug court by visiting the site's map: https://ndcrc .org/database/

Court resources:
National Criminal Justice Reference Service
Law Enforcement Assistance Administration
US Department of Justice Washington, DC 20530
https://www.ncjrs.gov/
This service will answer a specialized inquiry on the criminal justice system—courts, corrections, police—by providing a search; registered users will receive information; copies of available documentation on request; on-site library use open to qualified persons.

US Department of Justice (DOJ)
Office of Public Affairs
Constitution Avenue and 10th Street, NW
Washington, DC 20530
https://www.justice.gov/opa
Will answer inquiries about activities of the Justice Department and its subordinate agencies, such as Drug Enforcement Administration (DEA), Bureau of Prisons, and Federal Bureau of Investigation (FBI), and about federal criminal and civil cases. Some information requests will be forwarded to other agencies.

FEDERAL COURTS

When someone mentions "federal courts," many people think of the Supreme Court with its nine justices. The Supreme Court has been on the minds of more Americans than ever before because of the media attention on the replacement of one or more judges because of death (Justice Antonin Scalia died suddenly on February 13, 2016) or retirement (Justice Anthony Kennedy retired on June 27, 2018) and how their replacements might shift the Supreme Court because of the political leanings of those replacements.

Of course, a justice's personal, political, or religious views should not affect his or her judicial decisions since their mandate is to interpret and uphold the Constitution of the United States. The power of the Supreme Court is undeniable, however. Its ruling that abortion should be legal (the landmark *Roe v. Wade* decision in 1973), that gay marriage should be legal (*Obergefell v. Hodges* in 2015), and, earlier, the ruling on desegregation of schools in the historic *Brown v. Board of Education of Topeka* in 1954 emphasize the importance and power of the Supreme Court.

But although the Supreme Court is the highest court (or court of last resort) to which state or federal cases can appeal, it is not the only federal court. The federal justice system is also composed of ninety-four US district courts and thirteen circuit courts.

Which matters will come up in federal district courts? Crimes such as tax evasion, drug dealing, robbery of banks insured by the federal government (FDIC), conflicts between people in two different states where more than $75,000 is involved, cases involving matters of federal civil or criminal law, and cases involving maritime law, bankruptcy, copyright, or patent infringement.

Information on the federal courts, including the Supreme Court:
Administrative Office of the United States Courts
Washington, DC 20544
http://www.uscourts.gov/
Founded in 1939, this office answers inquiries on the federal court system and makes referrals to those individual courts when a specific case is not handled directly by the Administrative Office. It is concerned with the administration, operation, budget, and maintenance of the federal court system. It also administers the Public Defender Program, the Criminal Justice Act, the US magistrate's system, the Bankruptcy Act, and the federal probation system. It publishes *Federal Probation*, a free journal published in June, September, and December, with articles, book reviews, reports, and statistical data on the business of the federal courts.

Federal Judicial Center
Thurgood Marshall Federal Judiciary Building
One Columbus Circle NE
Washington DC 20002-8003
https://www.fjc.gov

Created by an act of Congress in 1967, this center's goal is to further the development and adoption of improved judicial administration in the US courts. Although court personnel are favored, all requests for information on any judicial administration area will be answered or referred to other sources.

Supreme Court of the United States
1 First Street, NE
Washington, DC 20543
https://www.supremecourt.gov/
You will find a wealth of information here; everything from the history of the Supreme Court to judicial opinions. For any other questions, you may email the Public Information Office at https://www.supremecourt.gov/contact/contact_pio.aspx.

OUT-OF-COURT DISPUTE RESOLUTION

Because settling a dispute in a court of law is often time consuming, expensive, and formal, voluntary private solutions have become a more common way of handling grievances in civil and minor criminal matters. Two procedures—arbitration and mediation—are followed. In arbitration, the parties agree beforehand to accept the arbiter's decision. In mediation, there is an agreement to "consider" the mediator's opinion.

The most extensive service for settling disputes out of court is the National Center for Dispute Settlement. It seeks to keep lesser complaints from coming to trial. It is, however, strictly voluntary, and if the accused party does not agree to arbitration, the victim may still prosecute the original charge through the courts. The most common grievances handled by the program are neighbors' squabbles, simple assaults, and invasion of privacy. A lawyer may be present at the hearings if desired. The mediator at the hearings can only advise the parties to moderate their demands so that they may reach an equitable solution.

For business-related grievances that you do not wish to take to court, you may consult your local Better Business Bureau to find out if they offer a free arbitration service (see listings in Chapter 8, Consumer Affairs and Safety). Similar problems, as well as landlord-tenant and agency complaints, may be resolved through the intervention of a local consumer affairs program (see the listings in Chapter 8). Many colleges, universities, and law schools are forming "clinics" where volunteers, who have been through a training program, will also act as arbitrators or mediators.

Look for community dispute centers staffed by non-court personnel and run outside the court system in your town, suburb, or city. The goal of these centers is to refer certain offenses away from the overcrowded municipal courts and have the disputes resolved through mediation. Since compliance is voluntary, the courts are still a resort if this step fails.

Dispute settlement information and services:
American Arbitration Association
International Center for Dispute Resolution
120 Broadway, Floor 21
New York, NY 10271
https://www.icdr.org/
A national organization with regional offices throughout the US resolving disputes though arbitration and mediation, including matrimonial and family matters, community disputes, and social problems.

American Bar Association (ABA)
Section of Dispute Resolution
https://www.americanbar.org/groups/dispute_resolution.html
From their website: "The Section of Dispute Resolution provides members with accessible, relevant and cutting-edge information, practice tips, and skill-building opportunities. We are a vibrant forum for networking, professional development, and research that bridges together unique and diverse perspectives."

National Center for Dispute Settlement (NCDS)
12400 Coit Rd, Suite 1230
Dallas, TX 75251
www.ncdsusa.org
The NCDS focuses on these three types of disputes: automotive warranties, real property disclosures, and financial dispute settlements. Its clients are automotive, insurance, and real estate companies or associations.

Federal Mediation and Conciliation Service (FMCS)
250 E Street, SW
Washington, DC 20427
https://www.fmcs.gov/
Founded in 1947, FMCS is an independent agency established by law to assist in the settlement of labor and management disputes and to prevent or shorten work stoppages. Headquartered in Washington, DC, there are sixty field offices throughout the US. Federal law requires formal written notices to be filed regarding anticipated contract expirations.

NYC-DR listserv and NYC-DR Monthly Roundtable Breakfast
John Jay College of Criminal Justice, City University of New York
CUNY Dispute Resolution Center
524 West 59th Street, Room 520HH
New York, NY 10019
The CUNY Dispute Resolution Center at John Jay College began two initiatives for those interested and involved in the dispute resolution field after the terrorist attacks on the World Trade Center in New York City on September 11, 2001: a monthly breakfast and a listserv.

The NYC-DR monthly breakfast, which is free and open to all, features timely topics and well known dispute resolution experts on the first Thursday of each month. Since June 2007, the Association for Conflict Resolution of Greater New York has been a co-sponsor of the breakfasts with the CUNY DRC. From 8:00 a.m. to 8:30 a.m., participants may network over continental breakfast; the program runs from 8:30 a.m. to 10 a.m and is followed by informal networking with the speaker. Announcements for the breakfast are posted on the NYC-DR listserv and the websites of the co-sponsors: www.jjay.cuny.edu/disputeresolution and www.acrgny.org.

The NYC-DR listserv was started on Sept 27, 2001, for the purpose of facilitating information exchange and discussion among all those interested in dispute and conflict resolution, peacemaking, facilitation, dialogue, restorative justice, violence prevention, social justice, and related fields. To join or unsubscribe from the free listserv: http://listserver.jjay.cuny.edu/scripts/WA.exe?SUBED1=NYC-DR&A=1.

Many training programs in dispute resolution are available through colleges, universities, and mediation and dispute resolution centers. Here are a few of the many quality programs available for in-person training; inquire if an online version is also offered:
American Bar Association (ABA)
www.americanbar.org
This professional membership association for lawyers and law students provides a directory of alternative to dispute resolution training programs by state as well as for Canada, Australia and Bermuda at https://www.americanbar.org/groups/dispute_resolution/resources/adr_training_providers.html.

Center for Conflict Resolution (CCR)
11 E. Adams Street, Suite 500
Chicago, IL 60603
https://www.ccrchicago.org
Since 1979, this nonprofit organization based in Chicago has offered free mediation services as well as mediation training.

CPR Institute for Dispute Resolution
366 Madison Avenue
New York, NY 10017-3122
www.cpradr.org
Started in 1977.

New York State Dispute Resolution Association (NYSDRA)
255 River Street
Troy, NY 12180
www.nysdra.org
A professional membership organization founded in 1985 for those in the mediation and arbitration fields.

The Negotiation Institute (TNI)
101 Park Avenue, 27th Floor
New York, NY 10017
www.negotiation.com/
Started in 1966 and dedicated to training negotiators.

This is a certificate program offered through John Jay College of Criminal Justice, part of CUNY (City University of New York):
Dispute Resolution Certificate, John Jay College of Criminal Justice
Department of Sociology
524 West 59th Street, Room 520HH
New York, NY, 10019
https://www.jjay.cuny.edu/dispute-resolution-certificate
John Jay College provides matriculated students with an opportunity to learn about the causes of conflict, how to analyze it, and ways to resolve it. The coursework includes skillbuilding as well as an opportunity to do a practicum.

From the website: "Matriculated students who complete this certificate program receive a certificate in dispute resolution from John Jay College, authorized by the Board of Trustees of The City University of New York and the New York State Department of Education upon successful completion of coursework and a practicum. 21 credits are required for the certificate. Soc 101 (Introduction to Sociology) is a requirement to enter the program."

The college also offers a Dispute Resolution Minor for those who are not able to complete the Dispute Resolution Certificate. 18 credits are required for the Minor.

Programs dedicated to peace alternatives:
American Friends Service Committee
https://www.afsc.org/

From their website: "Founded in 1917, the American Friends Service Committee (AFSC) is a Quaker organization that promotes lasting peace with justice, as a practical expression of faith in action."

Amnesty International

International Headquarters
1 Easton Street
London WC1X 0DW, United Kingdom
https://www.amnesty.org/en/
USA Headquarters
5 Penn Plaza, 16th Floor
New York, NY 10001
https://www.amnestyusa.org
This international organization campaigns against the use of torture, capital punishment, and gun violence, and for refugee and migrant rights and other human rights issues. Funded through memberships and donations.

Conflict Resolution Program

The Carter Center
One Copenhill, 453 Freedom Parkway
Atlanta, GA 30307
https://www.cartercenter.org/peace/conflict_resolution/index.html
Former President Jimmy Carter and former First Lady Rosalynn Carter founded the Carter Center in 1982. Their mission: "The Carter Center, in partnership with Emory University, is guided by a fundamental commitment to human rights and the alleviation of human suffering. It seeks to prevent and resolve conflicts, enhance freedom and democracy, and improve health."

United Nations

www.un.org/
Representatives of fifty countries met in San Francisco in 1945 and the United Nations charter was created. There are now 193 members. The UN addresses peace, security, victims of terrorism, human rights, gender equality, violence against children, preventing sexual exploitation and abuse, global health crises, and other concerns through a variety of initiatives.

Reading and Video Materials

Anthony Leis and David W. Rintels. *Gideon's Trumpet*. Starring Henry Fonda, Jose Ferrer. TV movie. 1980. Directed by Robert L. Collins.

Howard Zehr. *The Little Book of Restorative Justice*. Good Books, 2014.

"Introduction to the Federal Court System." Offices of the United States Attorneys, US Department of Justice. https://www.justice.gov/usao /justice-101/federal-courts

Jennifer E. Beer and Caroline C. Packard. *The Mediator's Handbook*. Revised and expanded 4th edition. Gabriola Island, BC, Canada: New Society Publishers, 2012.

Jerome Roberts and Robert E. Lee, authors of the play upon which the movie *First Monday in October* was based. 1981. Starring Walter Matthau and Jill Clayburgh.

Linda Greenhouse. *The US Supreme Court: A Very Short Introduction*. NY: Oxford University Press, 2012.

Melvyn Bernard Zerman, *Call the Final Witness: The People v. Darrell R. Mathes, as seen by the eleventh juror*. New York: Harper & Row, 1977.

National Institute of Justice (NIJ), Office of Justice Programs, US Department of Justice. "Drug Courts." May 2018. 2-page overview.

RBG. 2018. Directed and produced by Betsy West and Julie Cohen. Documentary about Supreme Court Justice Ruth Bader Ginsburg, who celebrated twenty-five years on the bench of the US Supreme Court in 2018.

Roger Fisher and William L. Ury. Revised edition with Bruce Patton. *Getting to Yes: Negotiating Agreement Without Giving In*. Revised edition. NY: Penguin, 2011.

Twelve Angry Men. Starring Henry Fonda. 1957. Directed by Sidney Lumet.

CHAPTER 11

Crime: Victims, Witnesses, and Prevention

Someone who has been the victim of a crime is known as the primary victim. If a family member is killed, the survivors are known as secondary victims. In the case of sexual assault or rape, the victim's spouse could also be considered a secondary victim, since this is a crime that may affect the couple's relationship.

In this chapter, you will learn about a representative sample of government, nonprofit, and fee-based services that are available for those who are victims of the so-called street crimes—murder, rape, robbery, burglary, aggravated assault, or motor vehicle theft—as well as property crimes including larceny-theft, identity theft, and white-collar crimes including Ponzi schemes and embezzlement. According to the FBI 2016 crime statistics, there were an estimated 1,248,185 violent crimes including murder and nonnegligent manslaughter as well as an estimated 7,919,035 property crimes which covers burglaries, larceny-thefts, and motor vehicle thefts. Remember that the FBI statistics are based only on crimes that are reported to the approximately 18,000 local police precincts that then report their data to the FBI for annual tabulation. The number of actual crime victims may be much higher especially since certain crimes, such as rape, are underreported. According to RAINN (Rape, Abuse & Incest National Network), only 230 out of 1,000 rapes are reported, or, stated another way, 3 out of 4 rapes go unreported. The majority of organizations and services that follow will help a crime victim whether or not the crime is reported. You can find out if a particular government agency or private company, such as insurance, requires a victim to report the crime to get help or benefits.

These national organizations and federal agencies offer information on all types of violent and property crimes:
National Organization for Victim Assistance (NOVA)
510 King Street, Suite 424
Alexandria, VA 22314
http://www.trynova.org/
Founded in 1975, NOVA is a nonprofit membership association that offers information on crime victimization as well as training for those who want to help victims recover from their experience. They are also an advocacy organization, championing the rights of crime victims. They can send in a crisis response team (CRT) when there is a school shooting or a similar mass crime victim situation. They sponsor an annual training event, usually in August, that lasts several days with numerous workshops on all aspects of crime victimization.

National Center for Victims of Crime
2000 M Street NW, Suite 480
Washington, DC 20036
https://victimsofcrime.org
In 1985, Ala Isham and Alexander Auersperg, the children of heiress Sunny von Bulow, started a not-for-profit organization to offer information and help to crime victims. A membership organization, some of their programs include the Stalking Resource Center, the DNA Resource Center, a list of national helplines, and the Victim Connect Resource Center (http://victimconnect.org/), which offers confidential referrals for victims of domestic violence, elder abuse, homicide and grief, human trafficking, sexual assault, and stalking.

Office for Victims of Crime, US Department of Justice
810 Seventh Street NW
Washington, DC 20531
https://www.ovc.gov
For the Office for Victims of Crime Online Directory of Crime Victim Services, go to https://ovc.ncjrs.gov/findvictimservices/. They also offer free online training for those who want to help victims. Go to www.ovcttac.gov/VATOnline for more information and to register for a course. Established by President Ronald Reagan in 1981, every April, the Office for Victims of Crime sponsors National Crime Victims Rights Week (NCVRW) which increases public awareness about victims of all crimes, and their needs, including the families and friends of those whose loved ones died because of crime. For more information on crime victims, and NCVRW, go to: https://ovc.ncjrs.gov/ncvrw/

National Network for Safe Communities (NNSC)
John Jay College of Criminal Justice
524 W. 59th Street, Suite #031W
New York, NY 10019
https://www.nnscommunities.org/
The National Network for Safe Communities (formerly the Center for Crime Prevention and Control) at John Jay College of Criminal Justice is a research and educational center using evidence-based violence reduction approaches to lower homicide and gun violence throughout the US and internationally. Founded 10 years ago by David M. Kennedy, NNSC sponsors a biannual conference that brings law enforcement, other criminal justice professionals, and academics to share their local successes. The June 2019 "The Emerging Science of Violence Prevention" highlighted many successes in violence reduction including Oakland, California, a city previously included as one of the ten most violent cities in America, then in 2017 recording its lowest homicide rate in 47 years.

GETTING DIRECT HELP

When someone is the victim of a crime, the key impacts are if there are physical, emotional, legal, or financial effects; if property is stolen; or if work is missed for medical, emotional, or legal reasons.

If you or someone you know is the victim of a crime, you will want to call 911 to report it to the police if it is an emergency including a crime in progress. If it is not an emergency, such as a burglary that previously occurred, to keep 911 for crisis situations, call the local police precinct. Even if it was dark, or you didn't see the assailant, reporting the crime could give the police valuable information to help catch the criminal, especially if this is part of a pattern of similar crimes.

If you are injured, you will want to go to the emergency room or to your own doctor to be checked out.

Most communities today have a local crime victim advocacy service that offers free or low-cost help on a sliding scale for payment. Each city, suburb, or rural area is different in where it offers this help, but you should usually look for these services through the local police department, the district attorney's office, a woman's center, a hospital, the State Attorney's Office in the state capital, or a dedicated crime victims or victim-witness assistance program.

What each program offers is also different, but it usually provides short-term counseling services and, if a suspect was caught, someone to accompany the victim to the police station or to court.

Gift From Within

16 Cobb Hill Rd. Camden, Maine 04843 https://www.giftfromwithin.org/
This non-profit organization's mission is to help those suffering from PTSD (Post Traumatic Stress Disorder), or at risk of developing PTSD, caused by trauma and victimization. Do a search at the website for links to local and international support group and information for survivors and caregivers on retreats and related books.

Victim Connect Resource Center

National Center for Victims of Crime
Washington, DC 20036
http://victimconnect.org/
1-855-4-VICTIM (1-855-484-2846)
This is the confidential referral arm of the National Center for Victims of Crime, focusing on these types of victimizations: domestic violence, elder abuse, homicide and grief, human trafficking, sexual assault, and stalking. You can talk to a victim assistance specialist at the above number.

Crime Victim Compensation:

Each state has a crime victim compensation program offering financial aid to crime victims. Although what is covered and the maximum amount varies, in general the funds cover medical expenses and, in the case of homicide, funeral costs and a lump-sum payment. For a link to each state's compensation board, maintained by the National Association of Crime Victim Compensation Boards, go to http://www.nacvcb.org/index.asp?sid=6.

Each state may offer different compensation and benefits. For example, in Florida, property crime victims who are disabled or over the age of 60 may get reimbursed for their stolen goods if the theft was reported to the authorities within 72 hours. There are guidelines on what tangible goods will be reimbursed.

Here are some of the benefits that New York State offers its crime victims:

- Medical and counseling expenses
- Loss or damage of essential personal property (up to $500)
- Burial/funeral expenses (up to $6,000)
- Lost wages or lost support including lost wages of parents if a child victim is hospitalized (up to $30,000)
- Transportation (necessary court appearances for prosecution)
- Occupational/vocational rehabilitation
- Use of shelters by domestic violence victims and their children
- Crime scene clean-up (up to $2,500)
- Good Samaritan property losses (up to $5,000)
- Moving expenses (up to $2,500)

Contact ovs.ny.gov for more information on New York state or search for your own state to find similar lists of benefits for crime victims.

Victims of Violence, Violent Crimes, and Murder

In addition to financial and legal issues related to homicide or murder, dealing with the grief of having lost a family member or close friend can require outside help. Here are some of the key national associations offering information or, through their local chapters, weekly support groups as well as advocacy groups:

Jennifer Ann's Group
2554 Drew Valley Rd NE
Atlanta, GA 30319 https://jenniferann.org/
A non-profit organization educating teens, their parents, and the public on teen dating violence. It was founded by Drew Crecente, in memory of his daughter, Jennifer Crecente, a high school honors student, who was murdered by her ex-boyfriend on February 15, 2006.

Alliance for Hope International
101 W. Broadway, Suite 1770
San Diego, CA 92101
https://www.allianceforhope.com/
From their website: "Developing innovative ways to end violence against women, children, and families at home and around the world." Their programs include Camp Hope America, Training Institute on Strangulation Prevention, and Family Justice Center Alliance.

MADD (Mothers Against Drunk Driving)
511 E. John Carpenter Freeway
Irving, TX 75062
https://www.madd.org
Founded in 1980 by Candace Lightner, a mother whose thirteen-year-old daughter, Cari Lightner, was killed by a drunk driver.
See expanded listings in Chapter 28, Transportation, Travel, and Recreation and Chapter 30, Volunteerism.

National Coalition of Anti-Violence Programs
https://avp.org/ncavp/
24-hour bilingual (English/Spanish) Hotline: 1-212-714-1141
This program offers national advocacy for local LGBT communities.

National Indigenous Women's Resource Center (NIWRC)
P.O. Box 99

Lame Deer, MT 59043
https://www.niwrc.org/
1-406-477-3896
Includes information on violence against American Indian and Alaska Native women and children. Sponsors related webinars and conferences. The staff and board members are Native women from throughout the United States.

The National Organization of Parents of Murdered Children (POMC)
635 West 7th Street, Suite 104
Cincinnati, OH 45203
http://www.pomc.com
Founded in 1978 by Robert and Charlotte Hullinger after the murder of their 19-year-old daughter, Lisa, a college student who was killed by her ex-boyfriend when they were both exchange students in Germany. There are chapters throughout the US offering support through regular meetings. There is also an annual conference held during the summer: http://www.pomc.com/chapters.html.

Justice for Homicide Victims
PO Box 4202
Cerritos, CA 90703
https://justiceforhomicidevictims.org/
JHVinfo@gmail.com
From their website: "Justice for Homicide Victims is dedicated to helping survivors of homicide victims deal with the pain and suffering associated with a violent death of a loved one. We provide support through monthly meetings, help in coping with legal issues and ensure that survivors know their rights within the legal system. We help with court support, parole hearings, and provide knowledgeable advice and/or referral information." In September 2018, JHV held their first National Day of Remembrance of Murder Victims event, a 5K run/walk fundraiser in Long Beach, California. Contact JHV for information if you want to participate in next year's event.

Help for victims of various kinds of abuse:
National Center on Elder Abuse (NCEA)
https://ncea.acl.gov/
This government agency is part of the US Administration on Aging. They offer direct links to state and tribal sources of help for victims of elder abuse. They also conduct research and have free related information.

Childhelp National Child Abuse Hotline
4350 E. Camelback Road, Bldg. F250
Phoenix, AZ 85018

https://www.childhelp.org/hotline/
1-800-422-4453
This 24/7 helpline is run by Childhelp, founded in 1959 by Sara O'Meara and Yvonne Fedderson to prevent and treat child abuse. At their site you can find a list of local child advocacy centers.

National Domestic Violence Hotline
24-hour-hotline: 1-800-799-7233
See complete listing below under domestic violence.

National Teen Dating Abuse Helpline
1-866-331-9474
This 24/7 hotline is part of the National Domestic Violence Hotline initiative out of Texas, but it is geared to teens who are experiencing dating abuse.

Safe Horizon
2 Lafayette Street
New York, NY 10007
https://www.safehorizon.org/
Founded in 1978. During National Crime Victims Week in April, Safe Horizon holds a candlelight vigil for New York City crime victims and for the families of homicide. Safe Horizon operates three hotlines:
- Domestic violence hotline: 800-621-HOPE (4673)
- Rape and sexual assault hotline: (212) 227-3000. In an emergency, call 911 or NYC's 311.
- All crime victims, including support for family members of homicide victims: 866-689-HELP (3457)

Stalking Resource Center
The National Center for Victims of Crime
https://victimsofcrime.org/stalking-resource-center/
Started in 2000, this initiative provides information to agencies, the media, and the public related to the crime of stalking.

These are organizations that provides help to those who are the victims of IPV (intimate partner violence), also known as domestic violence:
Urban Resource Institute (URI)
Central Office
75 Broad Street, Suite 505
New York, NY 10004
https://urinyc.org
info@urinyc.org
Contact URI to find out about the domestic violence services that they offer.

Childhood Domestic Violence Association (CDV)
261 Madison Avenue, 8th floor
New York, NY 10016
https://cdv.org
Brian F. Martin founded CDV in 2007. This is an educational and advocacy organization helping to educate the public about the way that growing up in a domestic violence situation impacts children and teens as well as adult survivors of this type of trauma.

Childhood Domestic Violence Association–Georgia Chapter
5605 Glenridge Drive NE, Suite 620
Atlanta, GA 30342
https://cdv.org/about-us/georgia-cdv/
Founded in 2016, the Georgia Chapter is the first regional chapter of the Childhood Domestic Violence Association. Founded by Dr. Linda Olson, licensed psychologist, who is also the president of the chapter. The chapter offers educational tools, as well as training, for those who are helping those impacted by childhood domestic violence, those dealing with it now, or the adult survivors of childhood domestic violence.

National Center on Domestic Violence, Trauma & Mental Health
www.nationalcenterdvtraumamh.org
From their website: "The Center is one of four national Special Issue Resource Centers funded by the US Department of Health and Human Services; Administration on Children, Youth and Families; Family Violence Prevention and Services Program and is a member of the Domestic Violence Resource Network (DVRN)."

National Domestic Violence Hotline
PO Box 161810
Austin, TX 78716
http://www.thehotline.org/
24-hour hotline: 1-800-799-7233
Founded in 1996, this free 24/7 hotline offers information on what abuse is as well as where and how to get help. There are materials on what a healthy relationship is and videos and links to information on domestic violence. The hotline is funded through a government grant.

National Network to End Domestic Violence (NNEDV)
Founded in 1990 as an advocacy training and information effort with the goal of ending domestic violence.

Safe Horizon
2 Lafayette Street
New York, NY 10007
https://www.safehorizon.org/
Founded in 1978. During National Crime Victims Rights Week in April, Safe Horizon holds a candlelight vigil for New York City crime victims and for the families of homicide victims. From their website: "Our mission is to provide support, prevent violence, and promote justice for victims of crime and abuse, their families and communities. We offer assistance to victims that includes shelter, advocacy, counseling, legal services and more. Our programs and services touch the lives of more than 250,000 children, adults and families throughout New York City each year." Safe Horizon operates these hotlines:
Domestic violence: 800-621-HOPE (4673)
All crime victims, including support for family members of homicide victims: 866-689-HELP (3457)

Women's Law
https://www.womenslaw.org/ https://hotline.womenslaw.org/ (Warning: Make sure your e-mail and/or cell phone is not being monitored before you use the e-mail hotline)
Offering help to women and men who are dealing with domestic violence. Founded in Brooklyn, New York in 2000 by Elizabeth Martin and others including lawyers, educators, teachers, and advocates. The e-mail hotline at the website offers referrals and information.

Human trafficking
The Danish Center against Human Trafficking
Socialstyrelsen
Edisonsvej 1.
5000 Odense C
Denmark
https://www.cmm.dk/english/the-danish-centre-against-human-trafficking
Founded in 2007. From their website: "The Danish Centre against Human Trafficking is responsible for coordinating and developing the nationwide social efforts for victims of trafficking and of involved parties." Check the website for information on the international agreements and protocols that this anti-trafficking organization has agreed to.

World Hope International
1330 Braddock Place, Suite 301
Alexandria, VA 22314
https://www.worldhope.org

This nonprofit organization includes ending human trafficking and gender-based violence as two of their core concerns, along with clean water, sanitation, and education.

These organizations offer help to victims of sexual assault, rape, and harassment:
1in6
https://1in6.org/
Founded in 2007, 1in6 offers information and support for men who experienced sexual abuse as a child or as adults.

Center for Changing Our Campus Culture
http://changingourcampus.org/
Includes the "Not Alone" initiative to increase awareness about sexual violence on campus, how to get help, and how to reduce or eliminate it.

Lean In
855 El Camino Real
Building 5, Suite 307
Palo Alto, CA 94301
https://leanin.org
Founded by Sheryl Sandberg, the organization now has more than 40,000 Lean In Circles that are dedicated to empowering women. One of their initiatives is helping survivors of sexual harassment: https://leanin.org/sexual-harassment

MaleSurvivor
PO Box 276
Long Valley, NJ 07853
http://www.malesurvivor.org
Since 1994, this organization has been offering resources helping male victims of sexual assault find therapists and local support groups.

Rape, Abuse & Incest National Network (RAINN)
National sexual assault hotline, available 24 hours: 1-800-656-4673
https://www.rainn.org
https://www.rainn.org/about-national-sexual-assault-online-hotline
RAINN runs this hotline and is affiliated with more than 1,000 local centers to help sexual assault victims. They also have a training program for those who want to offer sexual assault victim advocacy services. At the site, there is also information on sexual harassment, and a referral to local help: https://centers.rainn.org/

National Sexual Violence Resource Center (NSVRC)
2101 N Front Street
Governor's Plaza North, Building #2
Harrisburg, PA 17110
https://www.nsvrc.org
Started in 2000, a national nonprofit organization offering information and advocacy related to sexual violence.

Promoting Awareness/Victim Empowerment (PAVE)
233 S Wacker Drive, 84th floor
Chicago, IL 60606
www.ShatteringTheSilence.org
Founded in February 2001 by Angela Rose, who had been kidnapped from a shopping mall when she was seventeen years old. Her abductor took her to an isolated location and sexually assaulted her. Her national nonprofit organization is concerned with educating students on how to be less likely victims. They also help survivors to heal. There are more than fifty chapters and affiliates throughout the country.

Safe Horizon
https://www.safehorizon.org/
Rape and sexual assault: 212-227-3000 (In an emergency, call 911 or call NYC's 311)
See complete listing above under domestic violence.

SNAP (Survivors Network of those Abused by Priests)
PO Box 56539
Saint Louis MO 63156
http://www.snapnetwork.org/
Founded in 1988 by Barbara Blaine as a network of self-help groups for sex abuse victims of the clergy whether the assault was by a minister, nun, rabbi, or priest.

Terrorism
US Department of Homeland Security
Washington, DC.
https://www.dhs.gov/
This US government agency was founded in 2002, in the aftermath of the September 11, 2001, terrorist attacks on US soil, integrating 22 federal agencies and departments into one central Cabinet. Two of its many programs include Ready .gov, a public awareness service related to preparing for natural disasters or possible terrorism attacks, and #BeCyberSmart, an educational campaign to heighten individual awareness of the online security precautions that everyone needs to take.

International Crisis Group (ICC)
708 3rd Ave
New York, NY 10017
https://www.crisisgroup.org/
Founded in 1995 as a non-governmental, international organization respond-ing to the conflicts in Somalia, Rwanda and Bosnia. From their website: "Crisis Group today is generally regarded as the world's leading source of information, analysis and policy advice to prevent and resolve deadly conflict."

National Counterterrorism Center (NCTC)
Washington, DC 20511
https://www.dni.gov
Founded in the aftermath of the September 11, 2001, terrorist attacks on the United States. The five missions of the NCTC are: threat analysis; identity man-agement; information sharing; strategic operational planning; and national intelligence management. Some of the key partners of the NCTC are the Central Intelligence Agency (http://www.cia.gov); Department of Homeland Security (http://www.dhs.gov); Drug Enforcement Administration (http://www.jus-tice.gov/dea); Federal Bureau of Investigation (http://www.fbi.gov); National Security Agency (http://www.nsa.gov); and others.

Property Crimes

Unfortunately, the federal crime insurance program that provided some protec-tion to residents in twenty-five states against losses from burglary and robbery was discontinued in the 1980s. Now any losses you experience may be reim-bursed through your private homeowner's or renter's insurance (if you already have a policy) or, depending upon what your state crime victim compensation board has decided, through their benefits program. (See the above listing on the state crime victim compensation boards for how to get more information on your state.) Reporting the crime to the police is usually a requirement to put in a claim, so if you are a victim of a property crime, consider reporting it, whether or not you are optimistic that the assailant might be caught. If it is not an urgent situation, you could call the local precinct to report the crime. If it is an urgent situation, especially if the assailant is still on the premises or you are in fear for your life, call 911. (Remember, if you arrive at your apartment or home and the door or window is ajar, and you remember closing the window or locking your door, police officers and crime prevention experts will advise you *not* to enter. Go to a safe location and call 911.

Financial Crime Resource Center

The National Center for Victims of Crime
http://victimsofcrime.org/our-programs/financial-crime-resource-center

This initiative of the National Center for Victims of Crime helps to train those working with victims of financial crimes such as identity theft, investment fraud, cyber crime, and financial exploitation.

National White-Collar Crime Center (US)
https://www.nw3c.org/
Founded in 1978 as the Leviticus Project. From their website: "NW3C is a non-profit, membership-affiliated organization comprised of state, local, federal and tribal law enforcement and prosecutorial and regulatory agencies. NW3C provides a nationwide support system for law enforcement and regulatory agencies involved in the prevention, investigation and prosecution of economic and high-tech crime. We deliver training in computer forensics, cyber and financial crime investigations and intelligence analysis."

Stolen 911
https://stolen911.com/
Started in 2007. This is a California-based website that helps victims find their stolen property throughout the US and Canada. It was started by twenty-year veteran police detective Marc Hinch, now retired, initially to help him with his own cases, but he expanded it to include anyone who wants to list their stolen property. Some of the listings offer a reward to try to encourage the return of their stolen property.

Cybercrime and Identity Theft
This tipsheet was prepared by the National Cyber Security Alliance, a partnership started in 2011 with nonprofit organizations as well as companies and the US Department of Homeland Security. It covers cybercrime, including cyberbullying:

Federal Trade Commission (FTC)
https://www.identitytheft.gov/
Those who have been the victim of identity theft can report that here and create a recovery plan.

Internet Crime Complaint Center
Federal Bureau of Investigation (FBI) https://www.ic3.gov/
At this page, you may file a complaint as well as find out consumer and industry alerts related to internet crime.

Identity Theft Resource Center (ITRC)
https://www.idtheftcenter.org/
A nonprofit California-based organization providing direct help to victims of identity theft in resolving their cases as well as information about identity theft. Offers a toll-free Victim Assistance Call Center (1-888-400-5530).

https://staysafeonline.org/wp-content/uploads/2017/09/What-To-Do-If-You-Are-a-Victim-of-Cybercrime.pdf

NortonLifelock Inc.®
60 East Rio Salado Parkway, Suite 400
Tempe, AZ 85281
https://www.lifelock.com
This is a private company that helps to prevent identity theft by monitoring the accounts of its subscribers. There is an annual charge for their service but some online services, such as aol.com, have been offering NortonLifelock as a free benefit for their subscribers. Check to see if you qualify. It now includes Norton 360 anti-virus software with your membership subscription.

US Federal Bureau of Investigation, Intellectual Property Theft/Piracy
935 Pennsylvania Avenue, NW
Washington, DC 20535-0001
http://www.fbi.gov/ipr
This government agency investigates intellectual property theft/piracy, which robs the legitimate creators of everything from books to films of some earnings, if pirated illegal versions are available online for free.

CRIME WITNESSES

The criminal justice system can be somewhat confusing because a witness to a crime may or may not also be a victim of the crime. If you are only a witness, and not the victim, you still have rights. The most important right is that you will not be intimidated by the offender or his/her family or friends to either modify your testimony or even to drop the charges, if that is an option.

This excerpt from a booklet provided by the state of New Jersey may prove informative, since other states and/or federal cases would be quite similar:

The Victim-Witness Program
Each United States Attorney's office has a Victim-Witness program which is staffed by at least one Victim-Witness Coordinator or Victim Advocate. The goal of the Federal Victim-Witness Program is to ensure that victims and witnesses of federal crimes are treated

fairly, that their privacy is respected, and that they are treated with dignity and respect. Victim-Witness Coordinators and Victim Advocates work to make sure victims are kept informed of the status of a case and help victims find services to assist them in recovering from the crime.

Witness

A person who has information or evidence concerning a crime and provides information regarding his/her knowledge to a law enforcement agency.

(Source: The United States Attorney's Office, District of New Jersey, "Victims and Witnesses: Understanding Your Rights and the Federal Court System" https://www.justice.gov/usao-nj/victim-witness/handbook#Program)

Beginning in the 1970s, there was a movement to create a victim-witness advocacy office in every major city and state to handle the rights of crime victims and witnesses. There are now more than 10,000 victim-witness programs in the US. A milestone occurred in 1982 with the passage of the federal Victim and Witness Protection Act, which pertained to fair treatment of victims and witnesses in the federal criminal justice system. One of the rights that witnesses were granted was to be kept in a separate waiting area from the defendant while waiting to give testimony. Ideally, the witness's privacy is to be kept. Being free of intimidation is one of the most important rights.

If you are a crime victim, as well as a witness, please look at the listings related to the specific crime noted in this chapter as well as the national crime victim organizations that offer help for all crime victims.

This describes the rights of a witness to a crime in Illinois:

Witnesses of crime

If you saw a crime happen, and have been asked to testify in court for the State of Illinois, you are a **witness**, and you also have certain rights. These rights include:

- Notifications of the time, date, and place of all court proceedings, including cancellations, that you are expected to be at
- Assistance with your employer to minimize loss of pay and benefits

- Secure waiting area at court, away from the accused person and
- Bringing a translator

As a witness, you also have the right to be notified if the accused person has filed a request to have their conviction overturned, has been put on parole, or has escaped. However, you must **make a written request** to get these notifications.

To be notified if the accused person has filed a request to overturn their conviction, contact the State's Attorney's office in your county. To get their contact information, you can call your local Circuit Clerk.

To be notified if the accused person has been put on parole or has escaped, contact the Prisoner Review Board.

(Source: Illinois Legal Aid Online, https://www.illinoislegalaid .org/legal-information/rights-crime-victims-and-witnesses)

CRIME PREVENTION

This is advice provided to this author by Robert D. Sollars, security expert (www.robertdsollars.com) and author of *Murder in the Classroom: A Practical Guide for Prevention* and *One Is Too Many: Recognizing and Preventing Workplace Violence*, on how to avoid workplace or school violence:

We can either choose to act upon or ignore the warning signs
If you act upon the warning signs, all twenty-four (listed below) of them, then you may prevent an incident. [But] no guarantees of this . . .

Warning signs
If you see as many as four of the warning signs in another individual then you probably don't have to worry. But if you begin to see five or more it may be time to worry and take action. That action could have innumerable remedies attached to it, including seeing a therapist, suspension, a conference between schools and parents or an employee and company (a long one), and in some cases termination from the company or school.

Some of these signs are subtle and others such as threats and attendance problems will be readily seen. Of the twenty-four I have, one of them ties each one of them together . . . a slow or sudden—possibly drastic—change in their behavior.

In this instance, [you need to have] a HR department, supervisor, educator, friends (who may not be willing to "snitch"), and others who must step in and assist the individual with whatever is at hand. Nearly every business and school have an assistance plan of counselors, therapists, and so on within a phone call's reach. They need to take advantage of this and no zero tolerance or ignorance; we are not two-year-olds. The warning signs that I have collected are not meant to be all-inclusive because some people have different definitions:

1. Attendance problems
2. Bullying
3. Concentration problems
4. Continual excuses
5. Cruelty to animals
6. Disciplinary issues
7. Domestic violence
8. Drug and alcohol abuse
9. Fascination with weapons
10. Free expression
11. Impact on supervisory/instructor time
12. Inconsistent work habits/decreased productivity
13. Known mental illness
14. New religious/political fervor
15. Obsession with military/police tactics
16. Poor health and hygiene
17. Poor relationship skills
18. Safety
19. Serious stress
20. Simmering or uncontrollable anger
21. Threats both open and veiled
22. Unshakable depression
23. Unusual or changed behavior
24. Violent music, movies and video games

Resources for crime prevention information and direct help:
International Centre for the Prevention of Crime (IPC)
United Nations Office on Drugs and Crime (UNODC)
Vienna International Centre
Wagramer Strasse 5
A 1400 Vienna
Austria
http://www.unodc.org/
http://www.crime-prevention-intl.org/
https://www.unodc.org/unodc/en/commissions/CCPCJ/PNI/institutes-ICPC.html
     Founded in 1994. Covers a wide range of crime-related topics such as cor-
ruption, firearms, drug trafficking, terrorism prevention, human trafficking,
money laundering, and more. Launches campaigns to spread awareness as well
as creating UN commissions that create or modify policies.

National Crime Prevention Council
https://www.ncpc.org
In 1979, nineteen organizations banded together to fight crime. Their slogan is
the well-known "Take a bite out of crime." McGruff the Crime Dog became the
mascot for the program.

National Neighborhood Watch
https://www.nnw.org/
Sponsored by the National Sheriffs' Association, which started it in 1972. For
more information, go to: https://www.sheriffs.org/programs/crime-prevention
Office of Juvenile Justice and Delinquency Prevention
https://www.ojjdp.gov/
Provides information on the various programs that the government has started
to try to deal with the juvenile crime problem, including the 2003 creation of the
National Gang Center: https://www.nationalgangcenter.gov/

Gun control and gun violence prevention organizations and initiatives:
Giffords
https:giffords.org
In 2016, two organizations—the Americans for Responsible Solutions and the Law
Center to Prevent Gun Violence—joined together to become known as Giffords.
Gabby Giffords is a former US congresswoman who was shot in 2011 at a meet-
and-greet with the public in Arizona in 2011; she is married to astronaut Mark
Kelly. The organization is dedicated to getting new laws passed to ensure gun
safety. Check out the list of key issues that they are addressing at their website.

Everytown for Gun Safety
Manhattan, NY
https://everytown.org/
Founded in 2014 by former New York mayor Michael Bloomberg. Educational and political action organization dedicated to ending gun violence.

The Joyce Foundation
321 N. Clark Street, Suite 1500
Chicago, IL 60654
http://www.joycefdn.org/programs/gun-violence
This private foundation, established in 1948 by Beatrice Joyce Kean invests in Gun Violence Prevention & Justice Reform as one of its five policy research, advocacy, and development areas.

Sandy Hook Promise
PO Box 3489
Newtown, CT 06470
https://www.sandyhookpromise.org/
Started after the December 2012 mass shooting tragedy that claimed the lives of elementary school children, teachers, and staff. Their mission, from their website: "Prevent gun-related deaths due to crime, suicide and accidental discharge so that no other parent experiences the senseless, horrific loss of their child."

Reading and Audiovisual Materials

Annie E. Clarkand Andrea L. Pino. *We Believe You: Survivors of Campus Sexual Assault Speak Out*. New York: Holt, 2016.

Beth M. Sipe and Evelyn H. Hall. *I Am Not Your Victim: Anatomy of Domestic Violence* (SAGE Series on Violence Against Women), 2nd edition. Thousand Oaks, CA, 1996.

Beverly Engel. "Why Don't Victims of Sexual Harrassment Come Forward Sooner?" Posted at PsychologyToday.com on November 16, 2017.

Butch Losey. *Bullying, Suicide, and Homicide: Understanding, Assessing, and Preventing Threats to Self and Others for Victims of Bullying*. New York: Routledge, 2011.

Catherine Dolan. *The Not So Sexy Truth: Women, Men, and Sexual Harassment in the Workplace*. CA: Motivational Press, 2018.

Deborah Spungen. *Homicide: The Hidden Victims: A Resource for Professionals*. Thousand Oaks, CA: Sage, 1997.

Debra Puglisi Sharp. *Shattered: Reclaiming a Life Torn Apart by Violence.* NY: Atria, 2004.

Ellen Bass and Laura Davis. *The Courage to Heal: A Guide for Women Survivors of Child Sexual Abuse.* NY: HarperAudio, 2013.

Jan Yager. *The Pretty One: A Novel.* Stamford, CT: Hannacroix Creek Books, 2011. Audiobook narrated by Staci Anderson.

—. *Victims.* With a new introduction. New York: Scribner's, 1975; updated version, Stamford, CT: Hannacroix Creek Books, Inc., 2020, 2015.

Janine Latus. *If I Am Missing or Dead: A Sister's Story of Love, Murder, and Liberation.* NY: Simon & Schuster, 2008.

Jessie. *Please Tell: A Child's Story About Sexual Abuse (Early Steps).* Hazelton Publishing, 1991.

John Macdonald. *Armed Robbery: Offenders and Their Victims.* Charles Thomas, 1975.

Leigh Byrne. *Call Me Tuesday.* North Charleston, SC: CreateSpace, 2013.

Newtown (2016). Documentary about the aftermath of the Sandy Hook Elementary School massacre in 2012 on the parents of the children who died and the families of the slain staff members. For more information, go to http://newtownfilm.com/

Office for Victims of Crime. "Landmarks in Victim's Rights and Services." 32-page PDF. Posted in 2018. "NCVRW Resource Guide." https://ovc.ncjrs.gov/ncvrw2018/info_flyers/2018NCVRW_Landmarks_508.pdf

Patriot's Day (released in January 2017). Dramatization of the 2013 Boston Marathon bombing and its impact on the first responders and some of the victims. Starring Mark Wahlberg.

Peter Grabosky. *Cybercrime.* New York: Oxford University Press, 2016.

Louise Shelley. *Human Trafficking: A Global Perspective.* NY: Cambridge University Press, 2010.

Robert D. Sollars, *Murder in the Classroom: A Practical Guide for Prevention.* Createspace, 2018.

—. *One is Too Many: Recognizing and Preventing Workplace Violence.* BookBaby, 2018.

Steve Kardian with A. Clara Pistek. *The New Super Power for Women: Trust Your Intuition, Predict Danger Situations, and Defend Yourself from the Unthinkable.* NY: Touchstone, Simon & Schuster, Inc., 2017.

Susan Brownmiller. *Against Our Will: Men, Women, and Rape.* NY: Ballantine, 1993.

Susan Opotow and Zachary Baron Shemtob, editors. *New York After 9/11*. New York, NY: Empire State Editions, Fordham University Press, 2018.

Tower. Documentary with animation about the mass school shooting fifty years ago at the University of Texas, with the emphasis on the victims of the crime rather than the perpetrator.

United Nations Office on Drugs and Crime (UNODC). "Global Study on Homicide: Gender-related killing of women and girls." Vienna, Austria: UNODC, 2018.

Witness. Documentary made by the brother of Kitty Genovese, who was killed fifty years ago and inspired research into bystander behavior, 2015.

CHAPTER 12

Criminal Justice: Law Enforcement, Corrections, and Alternatives to Prison

The criminal justice system includes law enforcement personnel, prosecutors and defense attorneys, courts, and corrections. Prosecutors and defense attorneys are the subject of Chapter 21, "Legal Services." The courts are explored in Chapter 10, "Courts and Dispute Resolution." This chapter addresses police (law enforcement), prison (corrections), and alternatives to prison (community service, restorative justice).

The United States is a vast country of an estimated 325.7 million people. The criminal justice system is large as well. Although it was not until 1838 that Boston became the first American city to start a police force, there are now an estimated 18,000 local law enforcement agencies. The National Law Enforcement Officers Memorial Fund estimates that there are 900,000 law enforcement officers, today; 12 percent are women.

The Prison Project estimates that there a 2.3 million people in federal and state prisons and local jails in the US with 840,000 people on parole.

Alternatives to incarceration includes the 3.7 million people on probation. There is also the trend toward restorative justice programs in conflicts and minor offenses as an alternative to incarceration. In some cases even violent offenders go to Drug Court because they agree to participate in a drug rehab program, along with other conditions.

The call for reform in the criminal justice system is being heard from many corners of society, from those who are part of the system to its victims, witnesses, and even the general public who want to know that the system is "fair." The reality is that unfortunately too few are concerned about the criminal justice system unless it impacts them personally because either that individual, a family member, or a friend is arrested, or, the opposite occurs, and they find themselves the victim or witness to a crime, pulled into dealing with the system because of that experience. If you are interested in learning about the criminal justice system, one of the most efficient ways to keep up with related developments is by getting a free subscription to The Marshall Project. This is site written by journalists who are focused on the criminal justice system. The Marshall Project has a staff doing original reporting related to criminal justice such as interviews with exonerated ex-offenders, the decline of the death penalty, what prisons are like in other countries, and more. For more information, see the listing below.

Information on the criminal justice system:
National Institute of Justice (NIJ)
810 7th Street NW
Washington, DC 20531
https://www.nij.gov
Established in 1968 under the Omnibus Crime Control and Safe Streets Act of 1968 as part of the LEAA (Law Enforcement Assistance Administration), it was renamed the National Institute of Justice in 1978. The NIJ is the evaluation, research, and development agency of the US Department of Juice. Part of its research is its activities related to DNA.

The Marshall Project
156 West 56th Street, Suite 701
New York, NY 10019
https://www.themarshallproject.org
As the tagline says at their website: "Nonprofit journalism about criminal justice." At the website you can search by name of journalist or topic to read articles related to criminal justice. Here is the link to sign up to get the free daily newsfeed and articles sent to you via email daily: https://www.themarshallproject.org /subscribe.

Summer college internships are available; the application deadline is January 31.

Organizations for those in law enforcement:
International Association of Chiefs of Police (IACP)
44 Canal Center Plaza #200
Alexandria, VA 22314
http://www.theiacp.org
Founded in 1893, it now has more than 30,000 members around the world.

National Sheriffs' Association
1450 Duke Street
Alexandria, VA 22314
http://www.sheriffs.org
Founded in 1940.

Federal Law Enforcement Officers Association (FLEOA)
http://www.fleoa.org
A voluntary organization founded in 1977 whose membership consists of those in federal law enforcement.

Crime Science Investigation
American Academy of Forensic Sciences (AAFS)
http://www.aafs.org
Founded in 1948.

American Society of Crime Laboratory Directors (ASCLD)
http://www.ascld.org
Founded in 1974, ASCLD is a nonprofit professional association whose members include forensic scientists and crime lab directors.

Blue Lives Matter NYC
https://bluelivesmatternyc.org/
bluelivesmatternyc@gmail.com
Advocacy and educational association founded to raise money and awareness about the losses that police officers and their families experience when one of them is killed in the line of duty. Founded in December 2014 by NYPD Sgt. Joseph Imperatrice.

International Crime Scene Investigators Association (ICSIA)
5774 S. La Grange Road, PMB 385
Orland Park, IL 60462
http://www.icsia.org
icsia@icsia.org
An internet-based nonprofit association for those in the field of crime scene investigation.

GoLawEnforcement.com
https://golawenforcement.com/

JAN (Job Accommodation Network)
https://askjan.org/ JAN is funded by a contract from the U.S. Department of Labor, Office of Disability Employment Policy (ODEP). It offers phone and online

assistance about issues related to work and disabilities including accommodations and the Americans with Disabilities Act (ADA).

Started in 2008 to offer information for those interested in pursuing a law enforcement career. Maintains an extensive list of websites (https://golawenforcement.com/law-enforcement-associations-and-organizations/) related to law enforcement, divided into categories: police/sheriff organizations; federal law enforcement organizations; crime scene investigation organizations; women in law enforcement organizations; ethnic organizations including Asian, black, and Latino; narcotic officers associations; and criminal justice student organizations.

These organizations are concerned with police accountability:
Mothers Against Police Brutality (MAPB)
1910 Pacific Avenue, Suite #9550
Dallas, TX 75210
http://mothersagainstpolicebrutality.org/
mothersagainstpolicebrutality@gmail.com
Co-founded by Collette Flanagan, Sara Mokuria, and John Fullinwider to advocate for policy reform and increase police accountability.

National Police Accountability Project
A Project of the National Lawyers Guild
2022 St. Bernard Avenue Suite 124A
New Orleans, LA 70116
https://www.nlg-npap.org/
From their website: "Founded in 1999, the National Police Accountability Project (NPAP) is a nonprofit public interest organization dedicated to protecting the human and civil rights of individuals in their encounters with law enforcement and detention facility personnel. The central mission of NPAP is to promote the accountability of law enforcement officers and their employers for violations of the Constitution and the laws of the United States."

Corrections (Prisons)
As is often mentioned, the United States has 5% of the world's population yet it has 25% of the world's prison population. The last decade has seen a concerted push toward reforms in the criminal justice system including who is sent to prison, and for how long. Non-violent drug offenders who were in possession of just a small amount of marijuana are even being released from prison, especially in states where marijuana has been legalized, and even having their criminal records related to the conviction and incarceration expunged. Other prison reforms are being championed including eliminating mass incarceration, any instances of disparity in sentencing due to race or ethnicity, and better reentry services for the formerly incarcerated upon their release so the risk of recidivism—being rearrested or returned to prison—is decreased.

American Correction Association (ACA)
206 N. Washington Street, Suite 200
Alexandria, VA 22314
www.aca.org
Professional membership association for those working in the prison industry, founded in 1870. Holds an annual conference in alternating US cities.

American Probation and Parole Association (APPA)
c/o The Council of State Governments
701 E. 22nd Street, Suite 110
Lombard, IL 60148
https://www.appa-net.org
A professional association for those in the fields of probation and parole offering on-site and online training.

Women's Prison Association
110 Second Avenue
New York, NY 10003
http://www.wpaonline.org/
From their website: "WPA works with women at all stages of criminal justice involvement. We promote alternatives to incarceration and help women living in the community to avoid arrest or incarceration by making positive changes in their lives. Inside prison and jail, we are a source of support to women and a resource to them as they plan for release. After incarceration, women come to WPA for help to build the lives they want for themselves and their families in the community."

Alternatives to Prisons
National Association of Community and Restorative Justice (NACRJ)
https://www.nacrj.org
A membership association. From their website: "On June 19, 2013 the NACRJ was publicly presented to the attendees at the 4th National Conference on Restorative Justice hosted by the University of Toledo and the Lourdes University, Toledo, OH. The National Association of Community and Restorative Justice was created to serve as the parent organization for the biannual 'National Conference on Restorative Justice.'"

Osborne Association
Bronx, NY
www.osborneny.org
Founded more than ninety years ago, this innovative organization is dedicated to alternatives to prison including probation and parole with the overall goal of reducing crime.

Vera Institute of Justice
233 Broadway, 12th Floor
New York, NY 10279
https://www.vera.org
Founded in 1961 by philanthropist Louis Schweitzer and dedicated to improving the criminal justice system, especially a bail system that incarcerates too many people only because they are too poor to pay their bail. Their three key priorities are: ending mass incarceration; ending any injustice in the justice system based on the race or ethnicity of the accused; and improving the conditions of confinement especially reducing the use of solitary confinement.

These are considered exemplary local probation programs as an alternative to incarceration for drug offenders:
HOPE
https://www.courts.state.hi.us/special_projects/hope/about_hope_probation
From their website: "In 2004, First Circuit Judge Steven Alm launched a pilot program to reduce probation violations by drug offenders and others at high risk of recidivism. This high-intensity supervision program, called HOPE Probation (Hawaii's Opportunity Probation with Enforcement), is the first and only of its kind in the nation. Probationers in HOPE Probation receive swift, predictable, and immediate sanctions—typically resulting in several days in jail—for each detected violation, such as detected drug use or missed appointments with a probation officer."

Brooklyn Treatment Court
Brooklyn, NY
https://www.nycourts.gov/courts/2jd/brooklyntreatment/about.shtml
From their website: "The Brooklyn Treatment Court (BTC) opened in Kings County Supreme Court in 1996 and offers substance abuse treatment as an alternative to incarceration for nonviolent defendants. The Court aims to reduce crime by recognizing the role that substance abuse plays in criminal behavior."

These research and advocacy organizations are dedicated to improving the criminal Justice system, including reevaluating the frequency and situations in which incarceration is used:
Center for American Progress
1333 H Street NW, 10th Floor
Washington, DC 20005
https://www.americanprogress.org
Their mission, from their website: "The Center for American Progress is an independent nonpartisan policy institute that is dedicated to improving the lives of all Americans, through bold, progressive ideas, as well as strong leadership and concerted action. Our aim is not just to change the conversation, but to change

the country." Key issues of research and concern include criminal justice; courts; disability; gun violence; and others. (See their website for a complete listing and related articles.)

Justice Policy Institute
1012 14th Street, NW, Suite 600
Washington, DC 20005
www.justicepolicy.org
From the website: "We envision a society with safe, equitable and healthy communities; just and effective solutions to social problems; and the use of incarceration only as a last resort."

Smart on Crime
https://www.smartoncrime.us
From the website: "This project was created with support from the John D. and Catherine T. MacArthur Foundation as part of the Safety and Justice Challenge which seeks to reduce over-incarceration by changing the way American thinks about and uses jails."

The Smart on Crime Innovation Conference, held at John Jay College of Criminal Justice in New York City, brings together men and women throughout the United States, including lawyers, mayors, researchers, and others, who are involved in groundbreaking approaches to dealing with crime and violence at the grassroots and national levels. On their website, the "Resources" section has various reports on innovations related to dealing with crime.

Reading and Audiovideo Materials

Alisa Roth. *Insane: America's Criminal Treatment of Mental Illness*. NY: Basic Books, 2018.

Angela Y. Davis. *Are Prisons Obsolete?* NY: Seven Stories Press, 2003.

Coy H. Johnston. *Careers in Criminal Justice*. Thousand Oaks, CA: SAGE, 2018.

John Oliver. "Prison: Last Week Tonight with John Oliver (HBO17:42 (length)" Posted at https://www.youtube.com/watch?v=_Pz3syET3DY

John S. Dempsey, et.al. *An Introduction to Policing*. Boston: Cengage Learning, 2018.

Peter Wagner and Wendy Sawyer. "Mass Incarceration: The Whole Pie 2018." March 14, 2018. https://www.prisonpolicy.org/reports/pie2018.html

Robert Johnson, et. al. *Hard Time*. Hoboken, NJ: Wiley-Blackwell, 2016.

CHAPTER 13

Disabilities: Developmental, Intellectual, and Physical

We have come a long way from the days, just a few decades ago, when those who had disabilities were called "handicapped." Individuals who had intellectual, physical, or developmental issues might have been put into an institution so that they were out of sight, out of mind.

Fortunately, today there is more help for those with disabilities as well as less of a stigma or even fear from the public if they encounter, or even find themselves dealing with, the wide range of issues that are considered disabilities. Where to get help for these disabilities will be addressed in this chapter (in alphabetical order):

- Asperger syndrome
- Autism and autism spectrum
- Brain injury
- Cerebral palsy
- Developmental disabilities
- Down syndrome
- Fetal alcohol spectrum disorders (FASD)
- Hearing impairments including deafness
- Intellectual disabilities (previously known as mental retardation)
- Spina bifida

US government agency concerned with protecting employment rights for the disabled:
US Department of Labor
200 Constitution Avenue NW
Washington, DC 20210
https://www.dol.gov/

Those who are disabled are protected under Section 501 of the Rehabilitation Act, which stops federal agencies from discriminating against both those who are applying for a job and existing employees based on having a disability.

These organizations offer information on a range of disabilities, including information and/or referrals for direct help:
American Association on Intellectual and Developmental Disabilities (AAIDD)
501 3rd Street NW, Suite 200
Washington, DC 20001
http://www.aamr.org/
AAIDD, formerly AAMR–American Association on Mental Retardation–was founded in 1876.

The Arc
Headquarters
1825 K Street NW, Suite 1200
Washington, DC 20006
https://www.thearc.org
Started in 1950, this organization offers information, advocacy, and referrals to local chapters. From their website: "With nearly 700 state and local chapters nationwide serving more than a million individuals with I/DD (intellectual and developmental disabilities) and their family members, we are on the front lines to ensure that people with intellectual and developmental disabilities and their families have the support they need to be members of the community."

American Association of People with Disabilities
2013 H Street NW, 5th Floor
Washington, DC 20006
https://www.aapd.com/
An advocacy organization on behalf of those with disabilities.

InterAgency Council of Developmental Disabilities Agencies, Inc. (IAC)
150 W. 30th Street, 15th Floor
New York, NY 10001
https://www.iacny.org/
This New York region nonfiction organization has more than 150 agency members providing direct services to those with intellectual and developmental disabilities.

Dreamscape Foundation
5629 Strand Boulevard, #404
Naples, FL 34110
https://dreamscapefoundation.org
Nonprofit foundation and advocacy group raising awareness about those with disabilities, especially vision impairment. Started by Joseph Sehwani, who lost his eyesight to a hereditary disease, Leber's Hereditary Optic Neuropathy (LHON).

National Ability Center
www.discovernac.org
From their website: "The National Ability Center empowers individuals of all abilities by building self-esteem, confidence and lifetime skills through sport, recreation and educational programs."

Jim Lubin's disABILITY Information and Resources
www.makoa.org
This directory was created by Jim Lubin, who is a C2 quadriplegic.

Special Olympics
1133 19th Street NW
Washington, DC 20036-3604
https://www.specialolympics.org
An international athletic competition program since 1968.

Sprout
270 West 96th Street
New York, NY 10025
https://gosprout.org
Started in 1979. From their website: "Through our vacation program we have taken thousands of groups on supervised vacations to over half the states in the US and more than a dozen countries throughout the world–providing community-based experiences to more than 2,000 individuals with developmental disabilities annually." They also have a film program. Their mission statement/ motto is "Making the invisible visible."

Council for Exceptional Children
2900 Crystal Drive, Suite 100
Arlington, VA 22202-3557
https://www.cec.sped.org/
A nonprofit professional membership organization founded in 1922 and concerned with advancing the educational opportunities for gifted and/or disabled children.

President's Committee for People with Intellectual Disabilities (PCPID)
https://www.acl.gov/programs/empowering-advocacy/presidents-committee
-people
Established in 1966 by President Lyndon B. Johnson under the previous name
of the President's Committee on Mental Retardation, the committee advises the
president on matters related to those with intellectual disabilities.

Yesterday's Children
360 Main Street
Ellsworth, ME 04605
https://www.ycimaine.org
From their website: "The foundation of our organization is the belief that when
people with intellectual and developmental disabilities are provided with care
that meets their unique needs it enriches their lives and employers them to participate in the world around them."

Here is a list of help for specific challenges, listed in alphabetical order:

Autism
Autism Research Institute (ARI)
4182 Adams Avenue
San Diego, CA 92116
https://www.autism.com/

Autism Speaks
1 East 33rd Street, 4th Floor
New York, NY 10016
https://www.autismspeaks.org/

Autism Spectrum Connection
PO Box 524
Crown Point, IN 46308
http://www.aspergersyndrome.org/

National Autism Association
One Park Avenue, Suite 1
Portsmouth, RI 02871
http://nationalautismassociation.org
naa@nationalautism.org

Cerebral Palsy
Cerebral Palsy Guidance
https://www.cerebralpalsyguidance.com/

Down Syndrome

Down Syndrome Education USA
18023 Sky Park Circle, Suite F
Irvine, CA 92614
https://www.dseusa.org/en-us/

Down Syndrome Education International
6 Underley Business Centre
Kirkby Lonsdale
Cumbria, LA6 2DY, UK
https://www.down-syndrome.org
Helping to globally improve the education of children with Down Syndrome.

Down Syndrome: Health Issues
http://www.ds-health.com/
This site is developed and maintained by Len Leshin, MD, FAAP, a physician who has a son with Down Syndrome.

Fetal Alcohol Syndrome

National Organization on Fetal Alcohol Syndrome (NOFAS)
1200 Eton Court, NW, Third Floor
Washington, DC 20007
https://www.nofas.org

Hearing issues

Alexander Graham Bell Association for the Deaf and Hard of Hearing
3417 Volta Place NW
Washington, DC 20007
www.agbell.org
info@agbell.org

American Academy of Audiology
11730 Plaza America Drive, Suite 300
Reston, VA 20190
www.audiology.org
info@audiology.org

American Association of the Deaf-Blind (AADB)
8630 Fenton Street, Suite 121
Silver Spring, MD 20910-3803
www.aadb.org
AADB-Info@aadb.org

American Sign Language Teachers Association (ASLTA)
PO Box 92445
Rochester, NY 14692-9998
www.aslta.org
info@aslta.org

American Society for Deaf Children (ASDC)
3820 Hartzdale Drive
Camp Hill, PA 17011
www.deafchildren.org
asdc1@aol.com

American Tinnitus Association
522 SW Fifth Avenue, Suite 825
PO Box 5
Portland, OR 97207-0005
www.ata.org
tinnitus@ata.org

Gallaudet University
800 Florida Avenue NE
Washington, DC 20002
www.gallaudet.edu

National Association of the Deaf (NAD)
8630 Fenton Street, Suite 820
Silver Spring, MD 20910
www.nad.org
They have an extensive list of organizations: https://www.nad.org/resources/directories/deaf-and-hard-of-hearing-organizations/

Spina Bifida
Philip A. Keelty Center for Spina Bifida and Related Conditions
707 North Broadway
Baltimore, MD 21205
https://www.kennedykrieger.org

Spina Bifida Association (SBA)
1600 Wilson Boulevard, Suite 800
Arlington, VA 22209
spinabifidaassociation.org

National membership and education organization with chapters throughout the US. Sponsors a conference and fund-raising events. The association is also committed to research, reducing the risks, and public awareness.

Local program concerned with employment for the disabled:
The Arc Westchester
The Gleeson-Israel Gateway Center
265 Saw Mill River Road
Hawthorne, NY 10532
https://www.arcwestchester.org
From their website: "Since 1949, The Arc Westchester has been connecting people with intellectual and developmental disabilities, as well as those with autism spectrum disorder, to the Westchester employment community." Extensive list of links and short descriptions of related organizations: https://www.arcwest chester.org/about/disability-links.

Training program for those who work with individuals with intellectual and developmental disabilities:
Friendship & Dating Program
UAA Center for Human Development
University of Alaska at Anchorage
2702 Gambell Street, Suite 103
Anchorage, AK 99503
https://www.uaa.alaska.edu/academics/college-of-health/departments/center
-for-human-development/friendships-and-dating/
Designed as a two-day distance-based training program, there are also related videos and online materials to supplement the program. The program is designed so that a trainer who takes the course can go back and implement it in small groups of 8–10.

Publishing company that focuses on books about disabilities:
Disabilities Books Press
PO Box 322
Exeter, NH 03833
https://www.disabilitiesbookspress.com

Reading and Audiovisual Materials

Annette Hames and Monica McCaffrey. *Special Brothers and Sisters: Stories and Tips for Siblings of Children with Special Needs, Disability or Serious Illness.* Jessica Kingsley, 2005.

Bobbi Kates. *We're Different, We're the Same.* Illustrated by Joe Mathieu. Sesame Street Books, 2017.

CDC. "Facts About Developmental Disabilities." Content source: National Center on Birth Defects and Developmental Disabilities. Last reviewed: April 17, 2018.

"Coach with No Arms or Legs Is the Soul of the Team." Published on January 4, 2017 by USA Today at https://www.youtube.com /watch?v=JtyWwtqgp-o (1:13)

Jessica Miller-Merrell. "27 Companies Who Hire Adults with Autism." April 12, 2016. https://workology.com/companies-hiring-adults -with-autism/

Kathryn W. Heller, et. al. *Understanding Physical, Health, and Multiple Disabilities.* 2nd edition. Pearson, 2008.

Nancy D. Rich Wiseman. *Could It Be Autism? A Parent's Guide to the First Signs and Next Steps.* NY: Broadway Books, 2006.

Samuel L. Odom, editor. *Handbook of Developmental Disabilities.* NY: Guilford Press, 2007.

Wehmeyer, Michael L. *A Comprehensive Guide to Intellectual and Developmental Disabilities.* Second edition. Baltimore, MD: Brookes Publishing, 2017.

CHAPTER 14

Dying, Death, and Dealing with Grief

This chapter covers help for the three key issues related to death: dying, death itself, and dealing with grief. What are some sources of help as you deal with the myriad of physical, financial, and emotional issues that you have to face? But you might also be interested in considering these two concerns if you are the one who is dying or, if you are currently in perfectly fine health, if you want to plan for the future.

The dealing with grief part of this chapter is for those left behind, whether a widow who has lost her beloved spouse of forty-one years; a parent who has lost a child to illness, suicide, or an accident; a sibling who has lost a brother or a sister; or a friend who is mourning a pal's passing.

If the death is sudden, some of the information in this section on "Dying" will be irrelevant. If you like, you can skip ahead to the section on "Death."

DYING

Except for sudden death due to a traumatic event, like an accident or a crime, in health-related situations, there is a period of time from diagnosis until death actually occurs. It could be years, months, weeks, days, or even hours. When a patient sees a physician and the news is not good, the cliché has been that the doctor would say, "You had better get your affairs in order," which is code for "You are dying."

So, there is that very practical aspect if you or someone you love have received this news. "Getting your affairs in order" usually means making sure you have a will and that those you love and that depend on you are made aware of all your financial information, even the passwords to your computer and financial, social media, and other important accounts.

Of course, it is best if a will and all of this planning has been done months or even years ahead of time, because when someone receives a terminal diagnosis, it can be hard to think clearly about such matters. In Chapter 16, Emergencies, Disasters, and Preparedness, I include a section in "Preparedness" that encourages readers to put all their key information together in case of an emergency or a disaster. By having all that information available so you are prepared for anything, you and your family will be ready if you find out that someone is dying.

There has been a trend toward hospice care in the United States so that someone who has been told that he/she will probably die within six months or less can get hospice care to help the family and loved ones deal with the ending and, depending upon religious and medical perspectives, with the physical part of dying as well. But not all hospice care takes place at home or in a dedicated hospice facility. Hospice care may also take place in a hospital, nursing home, or at an assisted living facility. It is designed to improve the quality of life for the person and their family in the remaining time.

Information on hospice and hospice care:
Hospice Association of America
228 Seventh Street SE
Washington, DC 20003
http://hospice.nahc.org/
From their website: "The Hospice Association of America (HAA) is an affiliate of the National Association for Home Care & Hospice (NAHC) that represents thousands of hospice organizations, caregivers, and volunteers who serve terminally ill patients and their families. HAA advocates on behalf of the industry's interests before Congress and regulatory agencies, as well as with other national organizations, the courts, the media, and the public."

National Hospice and Palliative Care Organization
1731 King Street
Alexandria, VA 22314
https://www.nhpco.org/
Membership organization offering education about hospice and palliative care issues as well as conducting research and advocacy activities.

Share the Care
New York, NY
http://www.sharethecare.org

Nonprofit organization started by Shelia Warnock to help those who are dealing with the seriously ill to best handle the caregiving responsibilities. Warnock is also coauthor, with the late Cappy Caposella, of *Share the Care: How to Organize a Group to Care for Someone Who Is Seriously Ill*, a self-help book for caregivers. The book and the nonprofit are an outgrowth of Warnock's firsthand experience in the late 1980s being part of a group of twelve women, ten friends plus her friend's two daughters, which was called Susan Farrow's Funny Family. After she was diagnosed with a brain tumor , they shared taking care of their friend over the next three and a half years until she passed.

DEATH

When death happens, there are so many decisions to be made. Should there be a burial or a cremation? Who should be called to take care of the arrangements? Should there be a traditional funeral or should it be more like a memorial service or a celebration of life? Who should speak at the service? Will there be food served? Should photos of the deceased be put on display? Who will create a program for the service and what should it include? Should there be music? Singing? If the family wants donations to a cause in lieu of flowers, what should that charity be and is the information about it up to date? To help the family with these details, some are putting their wishes in writing, even going so far as to prepay a particular place where they want their funeral to be held, or at least putting the funds aside to cover the costs of the service.

In March and April 2020, the restrictions in the United States and other countries around the world because of the coronavirus pandemic completely changed what a funeral and burial would be like, at least while the crisis continued. Some communities and states recommended, while others required, that gatherings include no more than ten people, and they remain six feet apart from each other. One family member might be chosen to go with the coffin to the cemetery and the rest of the family and friends would be viewing the event over a smartphone or videoconferencing. These decisions needed to be considered as well.

Associations, organizations, agencies, and companies that deal with dying, death, or grief:

Amnesty International
https://www.amnestyusa.org/
Abolishing the death penalty in the US and internationally is one of their priority issues.

See the complete listing in Chapter 10, Courts and Dispute Resolution.

Association for Death Education and Counseling (ADEC)
The Thanatology Association
400 S. 4th Street, Suite 754E
Minneapolis, MN 55415 USA
https://www.adec.org
A nonprofit interdisciplinary membership association for those working in the field of death, dying, and bereavement, started in 1976. In the Resources section of the website, there is an extensive list of related organizations with links to their websites.

Death with Dignity National Center
520 SW 6th Avenue, Suite 1220
Portland, OR 97204
https://www.deathwithdignity.org
From their website: "The mission of the Death with Dignity National Center is to promote death with dignity laws based on our model legislation, the Oregon Death with Dignity Act, both to provide an option for dying individuals and to stimulate nationwide improvements in end-of-life care."

Death Penalty Information Center
1701 K Street NW, Suite 205
Washington, DC 20006
https://deathpenaltyinfo.org
From their website: "A national non-profit organization serving the media and the public with analysis and information on issues concerning capital punishment. Founded in 1990, the Center promotes informed discussion of the death penalty by preparing in-depth reports, conducting briefings for journalists, and serving as a resource to those working on this issue."

National Center for Death Education at Mount Ida College
www.programsforelderly.com
This site researches and lists programs and documentaries related to aging including end of life, stopping elder abuse, dementia, and memory loss.

National Funeral Directors Association (NFDA)
13625 Bishop's Drive
Brookfield, WI 53005
http://www.nfda.org/
Professional association for funeral directors providing education, networking, and mentoring.

US Social Security Administration
https://www.ssa.gov/planners/survivors/ifyou.html
Information about the one-time lump sum payment of $255 that is given to eligible surviving spouses. The required form to submit is available online as well.

DEALING WITH GRIEF

Grief or bereavement is such a personal state. Some find it helpful to join a grief support group to be surrounded by others who are going through the same situation. Others prefer to throw themselves into their work and push down the grief, at least temporarily. Still others prefer to cry quietly or talk to a few choice relatives or friends about their feelings.

Since I am a writer, I turned to writing to help me cope when my parents died. I even wrote a poem that I read at my mother's funeral. But that was a different kind of poem. That was tied to my immediate thoughts about her death at age ninety, related to the Lewy Body Dementia that she was struggling with for the previous five years.

A few weeks later, however, I found myself still dealing with grief. I even wrote a new poem about it entitled "Grief." I'll share the first three stanzas; hopefully you will agree that it captures the way that grief is a feeling that you have to deal with, but you suddenly know when the cloud is starting to lift and you are ready to move on.

> **"Grief" by Jan Yager**
> Intellectually I was ready to get back to work after a few days of
> mourning.
> I told myself that Shiva* was a wise concept
> Because it meant that when I stopped sitting Shiva*
> I would be ready to rejoin the world.

---

* In the Jewish religion, Shiva is the seven days of mourning that begins after the funeral where you "sit Shiva" after a close relative dies.

But that's not what my mind and body told me.
It's been a few weeks and I'm still in a bathrobe.
My concentration is very poor
I've watched more mindless TV in a few weeks
Than in a few years.

But I know, just today, I'm turning the corner
On this grief thing.
I washed the sink full of dishes.
No one had to tell me to do that
I just did it
Because suddenly the dirty dishes were annoying me.

Writing helped me to cope with my grief after the deaths of my parents and brother but also when my beloved cat died. Here are some other ways to cope with grief that you may find effective:

- Reading poetry
- Reading a book about grief
- Listening to music
- Going to a concert
- Becoming part of a support group
- Starting a support group if there are none nearby
- Working out/exercising
- Talking a walk/jogging
- Joining a new group unrelated to grief
- Getting together with friends or family even if through video-conferencing or through your phone
- Talking to friends or family on the phone
- Texting loved ones
- Finding a therapist to talk to
- Getting enough sleep
- Eating healthy
- Allowing yourself to feel the grief
- Interacting more with your pet
- Doing volunteer work
- Traveling to a new destination
- Praying or attending a place of worship, virtually or in person

In the section below, I share organizations and sources of help for the grief you may be experiencing. It may be for a recent loss or it may be unresolved grief for a loss that happened months, years, or even decades before that you realize you have to finally deal with so you can go on.

Please also refer to the listings in Chapter 9, Counseling, Depression, and Mental Health. Grief help is available from self-help support groups, in person, by phone, by text, or even online, as well as from trained therapists including clinical social workers, psychotherapists, psychologists, psychiatrists, and other mental health professionals.

Getting Help for Grief
AARP
https://www.aarp.org
If you are a member of AARP and have a local group that you get together with, see if there is a grief support group as well or, if not, consider starting one.
Here is an article related to dealing with grief: https://www.aarp.org/caregiving/basics/info-2017/grieving-death-bereavement.html.

Betterhelp.com
https://www.betterhelp.com/
See the complete listing in Chapter 9 for this online counseling option.

Camp Widow
2828 Cochran Street, #194
Simi Valley, CA 93065
https://www.campwidow.org
contact@soaringspirits.org
Camp Widow is a fee-based weeklong event that happens three times a year, bringing together those who are widowed to make new friends and to celebrate the past while moving forward to a new future. Upcoming dates, rates, and various locations, such as Toronto, San Diego, Australia, and Denver, are listed at the website.

A Caring Hand–The Billy Esposito Foundation Bereavement Program
303 Fifth Avenue, Room 806
New York, NY 10016
www.acaringhand.org
info@acaringhand.org
Offers an eleven-week support group program and other services to help children and teens who have lost a loved one. The organization was established by the children of Billy Esposito after their father, who worked at Cantor Fitzgerald in the World Trade Center, lost his life in the September 11, 2001, terrorist attacks.

Center for Loss and Life Transition
3735 Broken Bow Road
Fort Collins, CO 80526
http://www.centerforloss.com
Founded in 1984 by grief counselor Dr. Alan Wolfelt. Offers training for those who help others with their grief as well as educational materials related to bereavement. Through its publishing company, Companion Press, the Center publishes extensively in this field. Free online database of grief counselors for you or your loved one: https://www.centerforloss.com/grief/find-a-grief-counselor/.

Compassionate Friends
https://www.compassionatefriends.org
Self-help groups for those who have lost a child.
See complete listing in Chapter 9, Counseling, Depression, and Mental Health in the section on peer self-help support groups.

First Candle
49 Locust Avenue, Suite 104
New Canaan, CT 06840
http://firstcandle.org/
Help for those who have lost an infant to Sudden Infant Death Syndrome.

Grief.com
Founded by David Kessler, a grief expert and author of several books about grief including *Finding Meaning: The Sixth Stage of Grief.* The website is an information portal of articles, links to resources, and to directories of grief counselors and support groups. In addition to his extensive work in the field, Kessler personally had to deal with grief after his twenty-one-year-old son's sudden death.

Griefnet.org
PO Box 3272
Ann Arbor, MI, 48106-3272
http://www.griefnet.org/
Support groups through email. Here is what they state about the fee for participating in a grief group: "We request $10 per month per group for membership in our support groups, but no one is turned away if they suffer financial hardship." Founded and directed by Cendra Lynn, there are numerous email support groups for a range of losses from the loss of a spouse or partner to loss due to a miscarriage to loss of a parent, loss of a sibling, loss of a friend, and more. Description of all the available email grief support groups: http://www.griefnet.org/support/groups.html

Modern Loss
https://www.modernloss.com
A website, started in 2013, which has essays on all types of grief, including the loss of a parent, friend, grandparent, child, pet, or sibling because of suicide, murder, car accidents, cancer, or any type of sudden or prolonger issue.

National Widowers Organization
https://nationalwidowers.org
A nonprofit organization founded by Sam Feldman after his wife of fifty-three years passed away following a one-year battle with cancer. At the website there is information focused on men's grief as well as a listing of men's grief support groups in several states, and related educational materials.

University of Texas at Austin
Counseling and Mental Health Center
Austin, TX 78712
https://cmhc.utexas.edu/griefloss.html
Has a lot of useful information covering many key topics related to grief, including a list of normal reactions and a reading list.

W Connection
https://widowsconnection.org
Membership organization founded in 2009. From their website: "While dealing with their own personal tragedies, the co-founders of The W Connection, Ellen Kamp and Dawn Nargi, experienced firsthand the difficulty widows face in locating appropriate support services and guidance to assist women going through one of the most traumatic episodes in their lives. This revelation provided the genesis for The W Connection. The organization was founded with the simple yet challenging goal of making life easier for women who have lost a spouse."

There are chapters in Long Island; Westchester, Pennsylvania; and California, as well as a virtual chapter.

Reading and Video Materials

Alan Wolfelt. *When Your Soulmate Dies: A Guide to Healing Through Heroic Mourning*. Fort Collins, CO: Companion Press, 2016.

Brook Noel and Pamela Blair, PhD. *I Wasn't Ready to Say Goodbye: Surviving, Coping and Healing After the Sudden Death of a Loved One*. Naperville, IL: Sourcebooks, 2008.

Cappy Capossela and Sheila Warnock. *Share the Care: How to Organize a Group to Care for Someone Who Is Seriously Ill*. Revised and updated.

Foreword by Sukie Miller, PhD. NY: Simon & Schuster, Fireside, 2004, 1995.

Carole Brody Fleet with Syd Harriet, PhD, PsyD. *Widows Wear Stilettos: A Practical and Emotional Guide for the Young Widow.* Far Hills, NJ: New Horizon Press, 2009.

David Kessler. *Finding Meaning: The Sixth Stage of Grief.* NY: Simon and Schuster, 2019.

Elisabeth Kubler-Ross. *On Death and Dying: What the Dying Have to Teach Doctors, Nurses, Clergy, and Their Own Families.* New York: Simon & Schuster, Inc., Scribner, 1969.

Fred Yager, Jan Yager, Priscilla Orr, Scott Yager, and Seth Alan Barkas. *The Healing Power of Creative Mourning: Poems.* Stamford, CT: Hannacroix Creek Books, Inc., 2001.

Harold Kushner. *When Bad Things Happen to Good People.* NY: Schocken Books, 1981.

"How Do You Help a Grieving Friend?" 3:59 video narrated by Megan Devine. http://www.refugeingrief.com/2018/07/19/help-a-friend-video/

Jan Yager, *Friendgevity.* Stamford, CT: Hannacroix Creek Books, Inc., 2021.

_____, *Friendshifts.* 2nd edition, In Chapter 10, "How to Handle Friendships That End," see the section entitled, "Coping with Endings Because of Death." Stamford, CT: Hannacroix Creek Books, Inc., 1997, 2014.

Maggie Callanan and Patricia Kelley. *Final Gifts: Understanding the Special Awareness, Needs, and Communications of the Dying.* New York: Simon & Schuster, reprint edition, 2012.

Megan Devine. *It's Okay That You're Not Okay.* Foreword by Mark Nepo. Boulder, CO: Sounds True, 2017.

Philippe Aries. *Western Attitudes Toward Death from the Middle Ages to the Present.* Baltimore, MD: John Hopkins University Press, 1974.

Stacy Julien, AARP. "What to Do When a Loved One Dies." Article and checklist. https://www.aarp.org/home-family/friends-family/info-06-2012/when-loved-one-dies-checklist.html

CHAPTER 15

Education

There is an exciting transformation going on in public and private schools throughout the United States and even internationally. Call it active learning or interactive learning, students are taking more of a role in their education. They are no longer considered the passive recipients of the knowledge that their teachers or professors are imparting. They are learning by doing—whether that means traveling, doing an internship, or creating a project from scratch—in science, business, or the arts. Many criticize the internet, and yes, it can be addicting, but if it is used properly, it can open up the world to students who before did not even have a textbook or the ability to read. You can compose music or watch or create movies on a computer. You can study with a teacher online or you can attend class in the traditional way, but you can be connected through a computer with a professor or students in countries 10,000 miles away.

It is a wonderful time to be a student because there are so many options. Free homeschool programs are available to parents who prefer to teach their children at home. College courses that do not rely on textbooks is a trend for some. But textbooks are still a viable option and there have been advancements in this area with a wealth of materials being made available for professors to enhance the classroom experience as well as making the textbook available on a subscription model, rental, or even ebook basis, in addition to a print version.

Continuing education, whether required or not, is becoming the norm in practically every field. Information keeps changing and no one wants to be out of date. Webinars enable you to take a course in the comfort of your home or office. These webinars can be live or recorded and archived so you can access them at your convenience.

There are many more options for learning because of the internet and such useful sources of free videos, including Ted and TedX talks, on YouTube.

As the Department of Education website states, it is really at the state and local level that you will find out more about education: "Please note that in the US, the federal role in education is limited. Because of the Tenth Amendment, most education policy is decided at the state and local levels. So, if you have a question about a policy or issue, you may want to check with the relevant organization in your state or school district."

Federal agency for education:
US Department of Education
400 Maryland Avenue SW
Washington, DC 20202
https://www.ed.gov/
Functions of the federal education department: to provide information about federal student aid funds; administer grant programs such as the Pell Grants; collect data and statistics; and more.

From their website: "Our mission is to promote student achievement and preparation for global competitiveness by fostering educational excellence and ensuring equal access."

National organizations or companies related to education, from pre-school through secondary education.

Homeschooling:
Homeschool.com
https://www.homeschool.com/
Originally founded by Rebecca Kochenderfer, this website offers information on homeschooling for K-12 including free materials that parents or educators can download and print out for their use.

K12
Herndon, VA
https://www.k12.com/
This is a free online for-profit school that provides full-time instruction, started in 1999/2000. To find availability by state, go to their website. Make sure you read through all the information about the program including if there are any costs you need to know about to affirm that this is the best option for your child.

National Home School Association (NHSA)
9249 S. Broadway, #200-368
Highlands Ranch, CO 80129
https://nationalhomeschoolassociation.com/
Membership organization for those who are homeschooling their children.

United States Distance Learning Association (USDLA)
10 G Street, NE
Suite 600
Washington, DC 20002
https://usdla.org/
A nonprofit membership organization founded in 1987 and dedicated to distance learning in K-12, higher education, as well as in companies and government agencies.

National and global associations or organizations for education, including higher education:
2U, Inc.
Headquarters:
7900 Harkins Road
Lanham, MD 20706
https://2u.com/
2U, partnered with universities, helps to build and deliver undergraduate, graduate, and certificate online degree programs as well as offering in-person and virtual short courses and boot camps. The company's goal is to use education technology to transform higher education.

American Association for Higher Education (AAHE)
12110 Grandview Road
Grandview, MO 64030
https://www.aahea.org/
This nonprofit organization started in 1870. Mission statement: "AAHEA is the individual membership organization that promotes research, collaboration, scholarship, best practices, evidence-based research to move together into the era of increasingly digitized education. A leader in the transition from old norms to new standards for a new age. The association equips individuals and institutions committed to such changes with the knowledge they need to bring those changes about."

Association of American Colleges (AAC)
1818 R Street NW
Washington, DC 20009
https://www.aacu.org
From their website: "The mission of the Association of American Colleges & Universities is to advance the vitality and public standing of liberal education by making quality and equity the foundations for excellence in undergraduate education in service to democracy." Founded in 1915.

CLEP (College-Level Examination Program)
https://clep.collegeboard.org

From their website: "The College-Level Examination Program (CLEP) helps you receive college credit for what you already know, for a fraction of the cost of a college course."

NAFSA: Association of International Educators (NAFSA)
https://nnedv.org/
International nonprofit membership organization concerned with global education. Offers related educational materials as well as regional and worldwide conferences. One of its many accomplishments was to help get the Violence Against Women Act (VAWA) passed in 1994.

National Education Association
www.nea.org
Membership organization. Tagline: "Great public schools for every student."

College Selection and Funding
American Association of University Women (AAUW)
1310 L Street NW, Suite 1000
Washington, DC 20005
https://www.aauw.org/what-we-do/educational-funding-and-awards/career-development-grants/
Offers grants to female college graduates who want to do postgraduate work to advance their careers.

The College Board
250 Vesey Street
New York, NY 10281
https://www.collegeboard.org/
From their website: "The College Board is a mission-driven not-for-profit organization that connects students to college success and opportunity. Founded in 1900, the College Board was created to expand access to higher education. Today, the membership association is made up of over 6,000 of the world's leading educational institutions and is dedicated to promoting excellence and equity in education."

Peterson's
8740 Lucent Boulevard, Suite 400
Highlands Ranch, CO 80129
https://www.petersons.com
From their website: "The Peterson's databases include over 50,000 accredited Schools and Programs, and over 5,000 Scholarships. Use our search tools to find the school, program, or scholarship that's right for you."

Soroptimist International of the Americas
1709 Spruce Street
Philadelphia, PA 19103-6103
https://www.soroptimist.org
You can apply for a Live Your Dream Award. From their website: "Soroptimist's *Live Your Dream: Education and Training Awards for Women* assist women who provide the primary financial support for their families. *Live Your Dream Awards* give women the resources they need to improve their education, skills and employment prospects."

Apprenticeships:
US Department of Labor
https://www.apprenticeship.gov/
Government-developed and-run website with information for employers, educators, and career seekers who are interested in apprenticeship opportunities. Sponsors the National Apprenticeship Week every November.

Information and education materials on all types of adult education:
Adult Education Association of the United States of America (AAACE)
https://www.aaace.org/
From their website: "is dedicated to the belief that lifelong learning contributes to human fulfillment and positive social change."

Council for Adult and Experiential Learning (CAEL)
https://www.cael.org/
Their concept is "linking learning and work." Their members are colleges and universities throughout the US.

Canvas Network
https://www.canvas.net/
Free online courses provided by colleges and universities. A sample of course offerings includes "Engaged Thinking," "Aviation 101," and "College Readiness: Reading, Writing, and Math."

ThoughtCo.
https://www.thoughtco.com
An information portal of free articles related to adult learning covering these three main areas: students and parents, educators, and adult learners. Their tagline is "Lifelong Learning."

Organizations offering education on business or entrepreneurship for children, teens, or young adults:
Acton Children's Business Fair
2201 Alexander Avenue
Austin, TX 78722
https://www.childrensbusinessfair.org
From their website: "The Acton Children's Business Fair is a free program offered to entrepreneurial families by the growing network of Acton Academy schools and the Acton MBA program." To sign up for a free launch kit, go to https://www.childrensbusinessfair.org/start. The Acton Children's Business Fair program is part of the philanthropic activities of the Acton Academy.

Junior Achievement USA
One Education Way
Colorado Springs, CO 80906
https://www.juniorachievement.org
From their website (history): "Junior Achievement was founded in 1919 by Theodore Vail, president of American Telephone & Telegraph; Horace Moses, president of Strathmore Paper Co.; and Senator Murray Crane of Massachusetts. Its first program, 'JA Company Program,' was offered to high school students on an after-school basis. In 1975, the organization entered the classroom with the introduction of Project Business for the middle grades. Over the last 39 years, Junior Achievement has expanded its activities and broadened its scope to include in-school and after-school students." See also https://www.jaworldwide.org/.

Lemonade Day
https://lemonadeday.org
Founded in 2007 in Houston, Texas, by Michael Holthouse.
From their website: "Our mission is to help prepare youth for life through fun, proactive and experiential programs infused with life skills, character education, and entrepreneurship. The foremost objective is to help today's youth become the business leaders, social advocates, community volunteers and forward-thinking citizens of tomorrow. We want to build self-esteem and new mindsets that can propel youth to success they likely would not have pursued otherwise." For more information, and to see what cities have a program in place already, go to https://lemonadeday.org/raisingcanes.

Uncharted Learning
234 James St.
Barrington, IL 60010
www.incubatoredu.org

From their website: "Uncharted Learning is a 501(c)3, not for profit organization. Our mission is to bring authentic, rigorous, and experiential education to all students to foster the development of real-world skills." Offers several programs for elementary, middle, and high school students: INCubatoredu, ACCELeratoredu, freshINCedu, and mxINCedu.

Internships

Bookjobs.com

Site created and maintained by the AAP–Association of American Publishers. Lists available internships at book publishers as well as paid jobs.

US Department of Labor

https://www.dol.gov/whd/regs/compliance/whdfs71.htm

Fact Sheet #71: Internship Programs Under the Fair Labor Standards Act. This provides detailed information about whether interns or students working for a "for-profit" company are entitled to minimum wages and overtime pay under the Fair Labor Standards Act.

Internships.com, a Chegg service

https://www.internships.com/

Information about available internship for college students. Potential internship providers create a free account and then post internship announcements. Potential interns follow up and apply. It is up to the internship provider to log on and contact any potential candidates for follow-up.

Children's Defense Fund (CDF)

840 First Street NE
Suite 300
Washington, DC 20002
https://www.childrensdefense.org/
cdfinfo@childrensdefense.org

Offers college internships at their headquarters and all the other CDF offices in California, Minnesota, Mississippi, New York, Ohio, South Carolina, and Texas for the fall, spring, and summer terms. For more information and to apply: https://www.childrensdefense.org/connect/join-our-team/internships-at-cdf/.

For more information on internships, go to Chapter 6, Business, Entrepreneurship, and Employment.

For information on study abroad, go to the listings pertaining to study abroad in Chapter 28, Transportation, Travel, and Recreation.

Computer skills for girls
Girls Who Code
https://girlswhocode.com
Founded by Reshma Saujani, whose goal is to see the gender gap in technology jobs no longer an issue. In the Summer of 2019, 80 different free seven-week coding courses were offered at locations throughout the US. The programs last all day (9 a.m. to 4 p.m.), Monday through Friday, and the girl must be going into 11th or 12th grade in high school to be eligible to apply. Check out their website for a list of the locations of the upcoming free courses.

Girls Inc
https://girlsinc.org
From their website: "Girls Inc. was founded in 1864. Across the decades, we adapted to meet the specific challenges facing young women. Although times have changed, Girls Inc. has always been and will always be about girls." A goal of Girls Inc. today is to help girls learn how to become leaders. Girls Inc. is in 400 cities throughout the US and Canada, servings girls in the 6–18-year-old age group and in more than 1,400 program locations.

Girls Who STEM
https://girlswhostem.com
Free information about resources, books, and organizations to encourage girls to go into the STEM (Science, Technology, Engineering, Math) fields. RKT Publishing owns and operates the Girls Who Stem site.

Environment organizations
4Oceans
https://4ocean.com/
Co-founded by Andrew Cooper and Alex Schultze to clean up the oceans and shorelines of plastics and other debris.

Greenpeace Foundation
http://greenpeacefoundation.com/
An international multipurpose environmental action organization, founded in 1971, concentrating on stopping the depletion and inhumane killing of seals in Canada as well as the economics and activities of the worldwide whaling industry.
For complete listing, go to Chapter 4, Animal Rights and Care.

National Wildlife Federation
11100 Wildlife Center Drive
Reston, VA 20190

https://www.nwf.org/
Their mission statement, from their website: "Uniting all Americans to ensure wildlife thrive in a rapidly changing world."

Sierra Club
2101 Webster Street, Suite 1300
Oakland, CA 94612
https://www.sierraclub.org
Membership club dedicated to enjoying the outdoors. Go to their website to see the wide range of programs they have done and are currently involved in with the goal of improving the earth and its resources.

Public speaking
National Speakers Association (NSA)
1500 South Priest Drive
Tempe, AZ 85281
https://www.nsaspeaker.org
Membership organization for professional speakers with local chapters and educational programs offered on a monthly basis as well as biannually and yearly for the entire membership.

Toastmasters International
9127 S. Jamaica Street, Suite 400
Englewood, CO 80112
https://www.toastmasters.org
International membership association with chapters that offers those who want to improve their public speaking skills opportunities to speak regularly at the local meetings.

These organizations, companies, and government agencies are concerned with discrimination related to race, ethnicity, or religion:
Anti-Defamation League (ADL)
(formerly known as the Anti-Defamation League of B'Nai B'Brith)
www.adl.org
Founded in 1913, dedicated to helping Jews around the world and to the fight against anti-Semitism.

Council on American-Islamic Relations (CAIR)
https://www.cair.com
Founded in 1994, a non-profit organization concerned with fostering a positive image of Islam and Muslims in America.

Dynamic Digital Advertising (DDA)
http://www.ddacorp.com
DDA has developed an extensive directory concerned with discrimination. "Prejudice Tracker" can be accessed at https://prejudicetracker.org.

Equal Justice Initiative (EJI)
Montgomery, AL
https://www.eji.org
Founded in 1989 by Bryan Stevenson. According to its website EJI "is committed to ending mass incarceration and excessive punishment in the United States, to challenging racial and economic injustice, and to protecting basic human rights for the most vulnerable people in American society."

National Association for the Advancement of Colored People (NAACP)
https://naacp.org
Founded in 1909, the NAACP's mission is advancing minority civil rights.

U.S. Equal Employment (EEOC)
https://www.eeoc.go
Title VII of the Civil Rights Act of 1964 prohibits employment discrimination based on race, color, religion, sex and national origin.

Reading and Audiovisual Materials

Carmine Gallo. *Talk Like TED: The 9 Public Speaking Secrets of the World's Top Minds*. NY: St. Martin's Press, 2015.

Christy Rakoczy. "Experts Reveal 19 Best Places to Find Free Money for College." November 22, 2017. https://studentloanhero.com/featured/free-money-for-college-grants-scholarships/

Daniel Coyle. *The Little Book of Talent: 52 Tips for Improving Your Skills*. NY: Bantam, 2012.

Frank Bruni, "How to Choose a College" January 5, 2013, *New York Times*, Posted at https://www.nytimes.com/2013/01/06/opinion/sunday/bruni-how-to-choose-a-college.html

Jan Yager. *The Fast Track to Speaking in Public*. Stamford, CT: Hannacroix Creek Books, Inc., 2011. Audiobook version narrated by Lee Strayer (2013).

John Holt. *How Children Learn*. NY: DaCapo, Hachette, 2017, 1967.

CHAPTER 16

Emergencies, Disasters, and Preparedness

Since most natural disasters (tornadoes, hurricanes, fires, earthquakes, blackouts, snowstorms) or medical emergencies (heart attacks, choking, cessation of breathing, wounds) come with little or no warning, BE PREPARED is the best advice. The tools, information, and supplies necessary to deal with an emergency or disaster need not be elaborate or expensive, but they must be readily available. Information can often minimize risks and reduce the time between the event and the arrival of help. A personal contact sheet, such as the one that follows, and some basic equipment can maximize the chances for a person's or family's survival, whether in an urban apartment, a suburban home, a car, or a rural cabin.

Make copies of the form or personal contact sheet and fill one out for yourself and one for each member of your family. Place copies of these detailed contact sheets in your residence or business. Up-to-date photographs are helpful in case a child or an adult is missing; this will save time hunting through albums and ensure that the likeness is a current one. Write in pencil or make copies of the blank record to be used later, since vital information may change.

If you have not already done so, consider taking a CPR and a first aid class taught by the American Red Cross, the American Heart Association, or other local or national organizations. It may prove useful to you if there is an emergency that requires quick action even before the medics or police can arrive. But make sure you get the necessary training and that you are confident that you can do the procedures correctly. You do not want to do more harm than good.

Stephanie Benjamin, MD, an emergency physician at a hospital in California, shared her top six tips for evaluating during a natural disaster or similar emergency:

1. **Focus:** Stop and take a deep breath. Focus on what your family needs and plan on where your family will be evacuating. A moment to collect one's thoughts will set the stage for a calmer and more organized packing process.

2. **Documents and Prescriptions:** Gather important documents first. This includes driver's license, birth certificates, passports, Social Security cards, prescriptions, insurance information, copies of utility bills, etc. Ideally these are already organized and stored in a fireproof waterproof safe in your home. Having digital copies on a password protected flash drive is beneficial as well. Add in prescriptions and glasses.

3. **Sentimental items:** Be sure to take sentimental such as wedding albums, photos, and jewelry and items that are irreplaceable.

4. **Gear:** Add three days of food, water, and clothing to your car. Even in summer, add in a warm jacket and several layers of clothing. Make sure to have a phone charger (or two). Consider adding camping gear such as sleeping bags and tents if you are unsure where you will be sleeping. Other items to grab are flashlights, a first aid kit, and self-defense items.

5. **Children and Pets:** Children may need additional comfort items to help during this period. Toys and games provide comfort and distraction from stressful events. Take your pets! Don't plan on an evacuation lasting for just the weekend. Don't forget to pack identification, adoption paperwork, carriers, and extra food and water for your pets as well.

6. **Be prepared:** Most importantly: be prepared ahead of time. Develop an evacuation plan with your family including where your family will go and what task each person will do to help with packing. Have the above items organized and readily available. Additionally, keep your gas tank greater than half full, and always have a phone charger and a vehicle road kit in your car. Being prepared ahead of time will make this process easier and less stressful.

Creating an Emergency Information Sheet

For certain information—such as blood type, allergies, and inoculations—do not guess. If you are unsure, have tests performed, find old records, or call your physicians so that the information contained in your personal contact sheet is accurate and readily usable.

Keep this contact sheet in an accessible place. An abbreviated version with just a few crucial numbers is also included. That form should be placed by the telephone or, if you no longer have a landline, by the refrigerator or a central place in your home. Parents should be careful to have a list of vital numbers available for babysitters or, for those caring for seniors, for caregivers; someone, perhaps a neighbor, especially someone who lives next door or nearby, could be listed in case parents (or, in the case of seniors, adult children), cannot be reached.

EMERGENCY INFORMATION SHEET

PERSONAL CONTACT SHEET

Name: _____

Date of birth: _____

Individual or Family (or Office Staff) Photograph

EMERGENCY TELEPHONE NUMBERS

Fire department: _____

Police Emergency Number: _____

Local Police Precinct Phone: _____

Ambulance service Phone: _____

Nearest hospital Phone: _____

Physicians: _____

Family physician Name: _____ Office After hours number: _____

Medical specialists:

_____ Phone: _____

_____ Phone: _____

Poison Control: _____

Psychiatrist or Therapist: _____ Phone: _____

Mental Health Clinic: _____ Phone: _____

Suicide Prevention Phone: _____

Crime Victims Assistance Phone: _____

Next of Kin

Name: _____ Relationship: _____

Phone: _____

Neighbor

Name: _____ Phone: _____

Address: _____

Neighbor

Name: _____ Phone: _____

Address: _____

OTHER SERVICES

Lawyer Name: _____ Phone: _____

Legal Aid—Phone: _____

Health Department—Phone: _____

Consumer Complaints—Phone: _____

Identity Theft Reporting Company or Agency: _____

    Phone: _____

Post this list, or a facsimile, in a central place, by the door, refrigerator, or your landline telephone (if you still have one):

IMPORTANT TELEPHONE NUMBERS

Fire emergency number: _____

Police emergency number: _____

Local police precinct: _____

Ambulance service: _____

Nearest hospital: _____ Phone: _____

Family physician: _____ Phone: _____

Veterinarian: _____ Phone: _____

Poison control: _____

Crisis Intervention Counseling: _____

Next-door Neighbor: _____ Phone: _____

Parents at work:

- Mother: _____
- Father: _____

Children's schools

- Teacher: _____ Phone: _____
- Teacher: _____ Phone: _____

Childcare: _____ Phone: _____

Recommended Items to Include in a Basic Emergency Supply Kit:*

☐ Water, one gallon of water per person per day for at least three days, for drinking and sanitation

☐ Food, at least a three-day supply of non-perishable food

☐ Battery-powered or hand crank radio and a NOAA Weather Radio with tone alert and extra batteries for both

☐ Flashlight and extra batteries

☐ First aid kit

☐ Whistle to signal for help

☐ Dust mask, to help filter contaminated air and plastic sheeting and duct tape to shelter-in-place

☐ Moist towelettes, garbage bags and plastic ties for personal sanitation

☐ Wrench or pliers to turn off utilities

☐ Can opener for food (if kit contains canned food)

☐ Local maps

*Source: FEMA Federal Emergency Management Agency Washington, DC 20472, https://www.ready.gov/build-a-kit.

HANDLING MEDICAL EMERGENCIES

CPR (Cardiopulmonary Resuscitation)

Although the best advice when faced with a medical emergency is usually to call 911, you may find yourself in a situation where there is just not enough time to wait for help to arrive. In cases of cardiac arrest, where breathing has stopped, the greatest chance of survival is for help to be administered immediately. After cardiac arrest, consciousness may be lost within 15 seconds, and breathing may stop within 30 to 60 seconds. Though the brain can survive another 6 minutes before irreversible brain damage will occur, you can see why CPR (cardiopulmonary resuscitation) may be required.

However, administering CPR is a responsibility not to be taken lightly. To prepare for this possibility, you will need to be trained in CPR. Today this may be required for caregivers. Your local community may offer free CPR courses taught by trained medical professionals. If not, there are national programs such as the ones listed below that can refer you to local training.

Organizations that offer CPR training:
American Heart Association (AHA)
http://www.heart.org/en/cpr
AHA trains in CPR. Check with your local AHA office for courses offered. At the website for the national headquarters click on "Find your local office" to search via zip code.

American Red Cross
https://www.redcross.org/take-a-class/bigred/learn
Your local American Red Cross offers online and in-person training in CPR.

National CPR Foundation (NCPRF)
https://www.nationalcprfoundation.com
What is CPR? From their website: "CPR is a combination of chest compressions and compression ventilation (mouth to mouth). Chest compressions manually pump the heart when it has stopped while compression ventilation inflates the victim's lungs." Their website provides information on the courses they offer, as well as the cost.

Choking and the Heimlich Maneuver

Another common medical emergency is choking. Once again, although calling 911 is the most logical thing to do, time may be of the essence, so consider if this is a life-or-death situation in which you or someone else may need to perform the Heimlich maneuver. As with CPR, training is necessary to do the Heimlich maneuver properly. Ideally, you would take courses in first-aid emergencies, administered through your local American Red Cross. There are also articles available online about how to help choking victims, such as this one entitled "Choking: First Aid" written by the staff of the Mayo Clinic: https://www.mayoclinic.org/first-aid/first-aid-choking/basics/art-20056637.

For a general introduction to helping a responsive choking victim who is at least one year of age or older, the following link will take you to a one-minute video entitled "How to Help Someone Who Is Choking - Heimlich Maneuver," posted by Online CPR Certification: https://www.youtube.com/watch?v=SYIwQNekj8I.

While you can study online articles and videos, actually learning the technique in a classroom setting would be preferable because you will have your technique reviewed by a trained professional.

Call 911 for help. Remember that every emergency situation is unique.

Organizations, agencies, companies, and associations related to medical emergencies and natural disasters:
FEMA (Federal Emergency Management Association)
https://www.fema.gov/
Started in 1979, FEMA is part of US Department of Homeland Security. Its mandate is to deal with preparing for disasters as well as supporting first responders, responding to damage, and helping citizens recover their homes and businesses from natural disasters such as hurricanes and floods. FEMA offers free distance learning online courses: https://training.fema.gov/is/crslist.aspx. From their website: "The primary audience for the Independent Study Program is first responders, EMS personnel and US citizens. The Independent Study Program has no requirements for instructors to teach our courses; however, we do suggest the instructor is familiar with the course materials before teaching the course."

Community Emergency Response Teams (CERT)
https://www.ready.gov/community-emergency-response-team
Educates volunteers about disaster preparedness such as basic disaster response skills including disaster medical operations and fire safety.

The Disaster Distress Helpline
SAMHSA
Substance Abuse and Mental Health Services Administration
1-800-985-5990
This is a hotline providing immediate crisis counseling to anyone impacted by the COVID-19 pandemic.

Federal Interagency Committee on Emergency Medical Services (FICEMS)
1200 New Jersey Avenue SE, West Building
Washington, DC 20590
https://www.ems.gov/ficems.html
From their website: "The Federal Interagency Committee on Emergency Medical Services was established by Congress in 2005 to ensure coordination among Federal agencies supporting local, regional, State, tribal, and territorial EMS and 911 systems. FICEMS was also created to improve the delivery of emergency medical services (EMS) throughout the nation."

American National Red Cross
430 17th Street, NW
Washington DC 20006

www.redcross.org/
Clara Barton founded the American Red Cross in 1881. In 1900, the American Red Cross received a congressional charter requesting that the organization provide services to American military and their families as well as disaster relief in the US and around the world. This global organization has more than 23,000 employees and 330,000 volunteers. Some of the services that the American National Red Cross provides:

- Training and certification in health and safety
- Organizing blood donation
- Disaster relief

The Halter Project
12099 Sonoma Highway
Glen Ellen, CA 95442
https://www.halterproject.org/
rescue@halterfund.org
Started by Julie Atwood, a rancher, equestrian, and philanthropist. Since 2012, she has hosted Ranch Readiness Day to help neighbors and even first responders from around the country to learn about emergency and disaster preparedness. From the website: "The HALTER Project provides first responders and their communities with information and resources for animal emergencies. In any situation: road accident, fire, flood, earthquake, landslide, or pasture, the best outcome for animals and humans is achieved through teamwork between trained first responders, veterinarians, and animal owners working safely together."

National Disaster Medical System (NDMS)
https://www.phe.gov/ndms
From their website: "When NDMS is called into action at the request of state, local, tribal or territorial authorities or by other federal departments, these medical professionals provide patient care, patient movement, and definitive care; contribute veterinary services; furnish fatality management support; and more."

The NDMS falls under the US Department for Health and Human Services. NDMS subgroups include disaster medical assistance teams; trauma and critical care teams; disaster mortuary operational response teams; victim information center teams; and the national veterinary response teams.

Salvation Army
615 Slaters Lane
PO Box 269
Alexandria, VA 22313
https://www.salvationarmyusa.org/usn/

Founded in 1865, the Salvation Army serves in 130 countries around the world. In the United States, the Salvation Army provides shelter for the homeless, fights against human trafficking, gives food or meal assistance to the hungry, and offers career coaching and advice to help those who have lost a job or are out of work to find employment.

Fire Emergencies and Prevention
National Fire Protection Association (NFPA)
1 Batterymarch Park
Quincy, MA 02169
https://www.nfpa.org/
Founded in 1896, NFPA "is a global nonprofit organization . . . devoted to eliminating death, injury, property and economic loss due to fire, electrical and related hazards." There are more than 50,000 members from around the world. Since 1922, they have officially sponsored the annual Fire Prevention Week, which is held annually in October. Go to https://www.nfpa.org/Public-Education/ By-topic/Smoke-alarms for more information on the value of smoke detectors.

National Safety Council (NSC)
1121 Spring Lake Drive
Itasca, IL 60143
https://www.nsc.org
NSC is a nonprofit membership organization dedicated to educating the public as well as safety teachers in the many wellbeing-related priority issues such as fire safety.

See complete listing in Chapter 8, Consumer Affairs and Safety.

Smokey the Bear Campaign
https://smokeybear.com/en/smokeys-history/about-the-campaign
From their website: "Created in 1944, the Smokey Bear Wildfire Prevention campaign is the longest-running public service advertising campaign in US history, educating generations of Americans about their role in preventing wildfires. As one of the world's most recognizable characters, Smokey's image is protected by US federal law and is administered by the USDA Forest Service, the National Association of State Foresters and the Ad Council."

Contaminated Food and/or Poisoning
Reprinted from the website for the National Capital Poison Center, https://www.poison.org/. In the US, there are two ways to get help for a poison emergency:
Contact Poison Control right away if you suspect a poisoning. Help is available online with webPOISONCONTROL® or by phone at 1-800-222-1222. Both options are free, expert, and confidential.

The National Capital Poison Center
https://www.poison.org/
From their website: "The National Capital Poison Center, founded in 1980, is an independent, private, not-for-profit 501(c)(3) organization. In recognition of its high quality, the Center is accredited by the American Association of Poison Control Centers. The Center is not a government agency."

Reading and Audiovisual Materials

Arthur T. Bradley. *Handbook to Practical Disaster: Preparedness for the Family.* 3rd edition. 2012.

Daniel Limmer and Michael F. *Emergency Care.* 13th edition. Pearson, 2015.

Gail Tuchman. *Hurricane Katrina.* Level 2 Reader. NY: Scholastic, 2015.

H. Norman Wright. *The Complete Guide to Crisis & Trauma Counseling: What to Do and Say When It Matters Most.* Revised Edition. Roosevelt, NY: Bethany House, 2011.

Joseph Alton and Amy Alton. *The Ultimate Survival Medicine Guide: Emergency Preparedness for ANY Disaster.* NY: Skyhorse, 2015.

Liz Szabo. "Medical emergencies occur on 1 in every 6 flights." *USA Today,* May 29, 2013. https://www.usatoday.com/story/news/nation/2013/05/29/medical-emergencies-airline-flights/2364159/

National Capital Poison Center. "Poison Statistics." https://www.poison.org/poison-statistics-national

CHAPTER 17

Financial Assistance

As I point out in my book, *21 Ways to Financial Freedom*, hard times can happen to almost anyone. It could start with losing a job, or even switching jobs or careers, with a dramatic decrease in pay; or a medical, legal, or even educational expense that is crucial but beyond your budget. If you take out a loan or use credit cards and incur debt rather than pay off your entire balance each month, before you know it, you might be in deeper than you ever imagined. If you are living paycheck to paycheck, without any backup savings, all you need is one or two paychecks to get withheld for whatever reason, and the wolf may be at the door in no time. Or you might just want to read this chapter because you want to learn about financial matters, from credit to investing, or even about how to find a financial manager.

The most important message of this chapter is that if you are having financial challenges, there is nothing to be ashamed of. Sadly, too many people are driven to despair by money problems. Even if you are having financial difficulties, and even if you have had such challenges for a while, there is help and hope.

International self-help support group that helps those with money problems, especially overreliance on credit cards:
Debtors Anonymous (DA)
General Service Office
PO Box 920888
Needham, MA 02492-0009
https://debtorsanonymous.org/
Based on the principles of Alcoholics Anonymous (AA), DA's only requirement is that members of this free self-help weekly support group be determined to stop incurring debt. To find a local meeting: https://debtorsanonymous.org/getting_started/index.php/find/findameeting.

Radio personality and author who is on a mission to help people get out of debt, and stay out of debt:
Ramsey Solutions
1011 Reams Fleming Boulevard
Franklin, TN 37064
https://www.daveramsey.com
At his website you will find a wealth of free information about Dave Ramsey's approach to getting out of debt and staying solvent. Dave's radio show, The Dave Ramsey Show, reaches more than 13 million listeners week. Check out his "7 Baby Steps" suggestions at his website.

Finding funding for a project you are proposing, or for yourself, is part of financial assistance. Government sources of funding:
National Endowment for the Arts
400 7th Street SW
Washington, DC 20506-0001
www.arts.gov
From their website: "The National Endowment for the Arts is an independent federal agency that funds, promotes, and strengthens the creative capacity of our communities by providing all Americans with diverse opportunities for arts participation." Funding available through NEA: https://www.arts.gov/sites/default/files/2018_NEA_Guide.pdf.

National Endowment for the Humanities (NEH)
400 7th Street, SW
Washington, DC 20506
http://www.neh.gov
The NEH has fellowships and grants that writers, researchers, and scholars can apply for.

Note on grants and crowdfunding:
Remember that the majority of grants available through philanthropic organizations, such as the Ford Foundation (https://www.fordfoundation.org) or the Bill and Melissa Gates Foundation (https://www.gatesfoundation.org) are awarded to nonprofit organizations, such as programs with a tax-exempt status. The good news for individuals is that the growth of the crowdfunding movement (with examples listed below) now offers artists, writers, small business owners, musicians, filmmakers, and those with a medical, educational, or financial need the opportunity to raise funds as well.

Resources that offer funding:
Candid
32 Old Slip, 24th Floor
New York, NY 10005-3500
https://candid.org
Founded in 1956 and after merging with Guide Star, the new organization is called Candid, an independent nonprofit educational organization with regional offices throughout the country. It collects, analyzes, and disseminates information about philanthropic foundations and the grants that they award. They offer a subscription to their online Foundation Directory at $49/month for the basic version; request a quote for the expanded Professional type. Candid also offers training through their Training Center to help those grant-seekers master the skills that will help them improve their chances of getting funded.

One of its initiatives is the Funding Information Network. From their website: "The Funding Information Network program is nonprofit outreach 'in-a-box,' enabling organizations to become local nonprofit funding experts. The program packages include access to our world-class database, Foundation Directory Online, product and training certification courses, and support materials to assist your local nonprofit community."

The Grantsmanship Center
350 South Bixel Street, Suite 110
Los Angeles, CA 90017
https://www.tgci.com, https://www.instagram.com/grantsmanship/
Founded in 1972 by Norton J. Kiritz to offer training in how to apply for a grant. Some of the services offered: 1–training , such as public workshops held around the country; 2–publication of their news; 3–information about getting a grant. Two popular training programs are the 2-day Essential Grant Skills ($495) and the 5-day Grantsmanship Training Program ($1,095). Go to their website for a schedule of upcoming trainings. There is a helpful free directory at their site that lists potential funding sources by state: https://www.tgci.com/funding-sources. Please note that the Grantsmanship Center does not give out funds. It is an educational and training organization.

GrantWatch
https://www.grantwatch.com
This is a fee-subscription service for information on available grants: Weekly: $18; Monthly: $45; 3 Months: $90; 6 Months: $150; 1 Year: $199. When recently accessed, Grant Watch claimed to have detailed information on "more than 13,864 current grants, funding opportunities, awards, contracts and archived grants (that will soon be available again)." Founder, president, and CEO Libby Hikind, who was a New York City school teacher for thirty years, raised

millions of dollars for educational efforts and started GrantWatch.com after she retired. There is a related site run by Grantwatch.com for those who are seeking grants for businesses: https://www.mwbezone.com/ They also offer a grant-writing fee service: https://www.grantwriterteam.com/ They have also developed a crowdfunding branch: https://www.youhelp.com/how-it-works

Nonprofits with several goals, including providing financial aid:
Jewish Federations of North America (JFNA)
25 Broadway, 17th Floor
New York, NY 10004
https://www.jewishfederations.org/
Offers help in times of crisis providing food, housing, and trauma counseling. Represents 147 Jewish Federations and over 300 network communities. From their website: "JFNA is the legal successor of United Jewish Appeal, Inc. (UJA) and The Council of Jewish Federations, Inc. (CJF)." JFNA is on the National Board of the Emergency Food and Shelter Program.

Stand Together
https://standtogether.org/
A nonprofit organization that is dedicated to helping in a range of issues and causes including education, poverty, criminal justice, immigration, free expression, economic opportunity, technology and innovation, and more. Founded by Charles Koch, a businessman, billionaire, and philanthropist, it was formerly known as the Seminar Network.

United Way
701 N. Fairfax Street
Alexandria, VA 22314
https://www.unitedway.org/
From their website: "In 1887, a Denver woman, a priest, two ministers and a rabbi got together . . . It sounds like the beginning of a bad joke, but they didn't walk into a bar; what they did do was recognize the need to work together in new ways to make Denver a better place."

Their mission: "We are the problem-solvers, the hand-raisers, the game-changers. We fight for the health, education and financial stability of every person in every community."

Please note that United Way does not offer direct financial assistance.

Other sources of funding:
Operation Homefront (OH)
1355 Central Parkway S, Suite 100
San Antonio, TX 78232
https://www.operationhomefront.org/

Info@OperationHomefront.org
This organization provides emergency funding and other help within 24 to 72 hours to the families of service members and warriors who are wounded.

The Pollination Project
1569 Solano Avenue, #643
Berkeley, CA 94707
https://thepollinationproject.org
From their website: "Our daily grant making began on January 1, 2013, and since then, we have funded a different project every single day. We also make larger impact grants of up to $5000 to projects that have demonstrated impact and success." Most grants are for $1,000. COVID-19 became a focus from March-August 2020.
    To apply: https://thepollinationproject.org/pre-screen-quiz/.

For more sources of funding in the arts, consult the listings in Chapter 5, Arts.

Money
Sapling.com
Leaf Group
1655 26th Street
Santa Monica, CA 90404
New York
24 Union Square East, 5th Floor
New York, NY 10003
https://www.leafgroup.com/brands/#sapling
Offers information on money, investing, and careers.

Suze Orman
https://www.suzeorman.com/
Bestselling finance writer and speaker Suze Orman has a wealth of information at her website dealing with a range of topics, from credit and debt to paying for college, student loans, and retirement planning. Her books include *The Money Class: How to Stand in Your Truth and Create the Future You Deserve* (Spiegel & Grau, 2012).

Crowdfunding
Crowdfunding is a phenomenon that has expanded in popularity over the last two decades, beginning with the enormously successful site Kickstarter, which began in 2009 in Brooklyn, New York. Being able to create a campaign and try to get funders (or "backers" as they are often called) by posting about the crowdfunding campaign on personal websites and social media sites (e.g., Facebook) or just sharing the link with friends, family, and acquaintances took the task of

finding support to a whole new level of efficiency and practicality. Some crowd-funding platforms expect the fundraising recipient to offer backers something in return (referred to as a "perk" or "reward"); it could be anything from an advance sample of the product being funded, like a book or invention, or something less tangible, like a simple thank you. Some crowdfunding platforms, like Gofundme.com, do not require any type of perk or reward. It is customary for backers to receive an email from the funding recipient as a thank you, as well as occasional progress reports related to whatever is being funded, though, this is optional.

FundRazr
Vancouver, Canada
https://fundrazr.com
This Canadian crowdfunding platform was started in 2009 by CEO Daryl Hatton. At the website, you can find more information or start a fundraising campaign in one of these three general categories: nonprofit, individual, or company. Fundrazr allows users to receive payments through PayPal. The commission to the site is 5 percent, plus some additional fees to cover the cost of processing payments.

Gofundme
https://www.gofundme.com/
Unlike Indiegogo or Kickstarter (see listings below), Gofundme is a different model that does not rely on perks or benefits, like books or samples of the new product that is being funded, to encourage financial help. Because of that, this model works very well for individual issues, especially medical concerns, like raising money for an operation or cancer treatment, or for funeral expenses, or emergency housing if someone has lost his or her home due to a natural disaster. You can create a Gofundme campaign for yourself or on behalf of a family member or friend. To start a campaign, you set a funding goal, share the story—this is where you are telling what happened to encourage people to donate—then add a picture or video. You then post the campaign on social media, like Facebook, or you can include it in emails or text messages. After you receive donations, you send out a thank-you to your donors, and then you get the funds. Note that Gofundme does not charge a platform fee to run your campaign but there is a standard payment processing fee deducted by that processing company from the amount donated.

Indiegogo
https://www.indiegogo.com/
Unlike Kickstarter (see listing below), this site lets you keep the funds you raise, whether or not you make your goal. Commission is 5 percent on whatever revenue you raise plus a 3 percent credit card processing fee. Like Kickstarter, what

you offer as perks for funding your project can be pivotal to getting the financial assistance that you seek.

Indiegogo Equity Model
https://equity.indiegogo.com/
This is a newer approach to crowdfunding. From their website: "Own a piece of your favorite companies and token sales. Brought to you by Indiegogo and Microventures."

Kickstarter
https://www.kickstarter.com
Started in 2009, 139 people now work for Kickstarter. They have successfully funded over 150,000 projects. What's important to know about this crowdfunding option is that the goal you set is very important. Unlike some of the other sites, if you miss making your goal, you will not be able to keep any of the money that you have raised. You need to create an account, ask for money for a specific project, offer perks for various levels of funding, and set an end date for your funding. If you meet your goal, Kickstarter will charge a percentage of your revenue as a fee for using their platform (5 percent commission plus 3–5 percent for credit card processing fees).

Patreon
https://www.patreon.com/
This crowdfunding platform has a different model whereby the funding is done on a continual basis unless someone cancels. You create your campaign and then set your levels of investment, which could range from free or $5/a month to $10 or $25 or even $500/month. You will probably want to have perks or rewards that your patrons will get for that investment. This seems to be popular with podcasts and internet video providers. The fee (or commission) is 5 percent of the revenue you generate. There are now reportedly over 100,000 creators on Patreon, including writers, illustrators, educators, animators, podcasters, and more. A project called "Crash Course," which provides short videos in a range of college disciplines including psychology, sociology, history, and biology, posted for free on YouTube, has 6,157 patrons with membership levels ranging from a low of $3 a month.

Pozible
Level 2, 108-112 Langridge Street
Collingwood, Victoria, Australia 3066
https://www.pozible.com
From the website: "Pozible is an Australian born, global crowdfunding platform that specialises in all-or-nothing, reward based crowdfunding. We are a small

and dedicated team that offers anyone the opportunity to launch an idea." A commission of 5% is taken from the total amount raised. It is dedicated to being a crowdfunding platform for artists of all kinds as well as communities in Australia.

Publishizer
297 Starr Street
Brooklyn, NY 11237
https://publishizer.com
This platform is based on putting a book proposal online through Publishizer, including a 1–2 minute video and putting the book out for pre-order. Based on the number of pre-orders and the proposal, there may be offers from a publisher to purchase the project. Considers itself the first "crowdfunding literary agency." Publishizer does get a 30 percent commission on pre-orders but not on future earnings after the book is published. To attract the "big five" major houses, aim for at least 500 pre-orders. For more information, visit: publishizer.com/live-big

Wishberry
102/103 Matharu Arcade, Subhash Road, Vile Parle (E)
Mumbai 400057 INDIA
https://www.wishberry.in
Modeled after Kickstarter, Wishberry started in 2012 in India. To see what they charge for advice and to participate in their crowdfunding platforms, geared to creative projects, such as films, music, and theater, go to: https://www.wishberry .in/pricing/#/pricing

Besides crowdfunding sources, like Gofundme, there are fund-raising programs to raise money for causes:
Alex's Lemonade Stand Foundation (ALSF)
111 Presidential Boulevard, Suite 203
Bala Cynwyd, PA 19004
https://www.alexslemonade.org
Many know the story of Alex Scott, diagnosed with neuroblastoma, a form of childhood cancer, before her first birthday. At just four years old, she decided to start fundraising by setting up a lemonade stand to use the money to find a cure for neuroblastoma and other types of childhood cancer. By the time Alex passed away in 2004 at the age of eight, she had raised more than $1 million. The Alex's Lemonade Stand Foundation, through her family, is committed to keeping Alex's legacy and commitment to raising money to find a cure for neuroblastoma and other childhood cancers going. Through products and donations, the foundation has raised $150 million that has gone to 800 cancer research projects as well as a travel program to help families children in cancer treatment.

Unbound (United Authors Publishing Limited)
London, United Kingdom
https://unbound.com/
From their website: "Pitch your idea to our commissioning editors—if it has the makings of a great book, we'll launch it on our site." This is a unique crowdfunding model in that you will actually be publishing with Unbound if they accept your manuscript and set up a crowdfunding platform for it at their site.

The following federal agencies provide financial assistance through their field or regional offices; the national headquarters will provide general background information on eligibility requirements:
USA.gov
https://www.usa.gov/benefits-grants-loans
Describes federal benefits available as well as the eligibility requirements.
Food assistance: https://www.usa.gov/food-help . If you meet the resource and income eligibility requirements, you apply at the state level. Here is the URL for information related to applying at your state: https://www.fns.usda.gov/snap/apply

Emergency Food Assistance Program (TEFAP)
https://www.fns.usda.gov/tefap/emergency-food-assistance-program
This program is administered by the US Department of Agriculture. "The Emergency Food Assistance Program (TEFAP) is a Federal program that helps supplement the diets of low-income Americans, including elderly people, by providing them with emergency food and nutrition assistance at no cost. It provides food and administrative funds to States to supplement the diets of these groups."

Temporary Assistance for Needy Families (TANF)
https://www.acf.hhs.gov/ofa/programs/tanf
TANF, "also known as welfare, is designed to help families recover from temporary difficulties and move forward." States have different names for their welfare programs, and since you apply at the state level, find your state's name here: https://aspe.hhs.gov/dataset/tanf-program-names [Note: In 1996, TANF replaced what used to be called Aid to Families with Dependent Children (AFDC)]

Federal Student Aid Office
830 First Street NE
Washington, DC 20002
https://studentaid.ed.gov/sa/fafsa
The FAFSA application is the necessary form to fill out to apply for student aid for college, professional/career school, or graduate school. See https://studentaid

.ed.gov/sa/1819/help/deadlines for an explanation of the schedule for filling out the application. As the site notes, there are probably state as well as federal deadlines and the college/school you are applying to may have its own deadline: https://studentaid.ed.gov/sa/fafsa#deadlines.

HUD's Public Housing Program
See the complete listing in Chapter 20, Housing and Homelessness.

US Social Security Administration Office of Public Inquiries
1100 West High Rise
6401 Security Boulevard
Baltimore, MD 21235
https://www.ssa.gov/
From their website: "Please do not send applications or documents needed to request a Social Security number or benefits to this address." Instead, contact your local Social Security office and/or try to find the information you need online.

On August 14, 1935, President Franklin D. Roosevelt signed the legislation that was to create the Social Security Board (SSB), which eventually became the Social Security Administration.

The basic benefits available through Social Security include retirement benefits, beginning at age 62, although the "full" retirement age is now 66 or 67, as well as disability benefits, supplemental security income, and survivors' benefits. (Medicare is administered through another agency. See the complete listing below.) To find your local Social Security office go to https://secure.ssa.gov/ICON/main.jsp.

Medicare
Centers for Medicare & Medicaid Services (CMS)
US Department of Health and Human Services (HHS)
200 Independence Ave SW
Washington, DC 20201
https://www.medicare.gov
If you are 65, you may be eligible for Medicare, a government-funded program that basically covers 80 percent of any Medicare-eligible health costs and a certain percentage of hospitalization costs. If you are still working and getting health insurance through your employer, you may prefer to only have the hospitalization part of Medicare and not the part that you have to pay for. (Depending upon your financial circumstances, you may pay the standard monthly premium for Part B of $135.50 or even higher if your income exceeds the maximum allowed for the basic premium.) For more information, go to https://www.medicare.gov/your-medicare-costs/medicare-costs-at-a-glance.

CREDIT

In the United States, your credit score is important for everything from applying for a loan to starting a business or buying a car. Your score determines if you are "credit worthy." There are three main credit reporting agencies in the US: Equifax, Experian, and Transunion.

Free Annual Credit Report

Every twelve months, you are entitled to a free credit report from each of the nationwide credit reporting companies. Go to www.annualcreditreport .com to obtain these records. If necessary, you may also call 1-877-322-8228.

You will be asked to provide your name, address, social security number, and date of birth so your identity can be verified.

Since you get a free credit report from each of the bureaus only once a year, you might want to space out your requests. That will enable you to review your first report, report any errors, and see if those corrections have been made when you request the second report. It will also give you a chance to improve your score in between reports if you think that certain positive credit-related actions could help you to improve your score.

Any corrections to a particular report should be reported directly to that credit reporting agency. Follow each agency's instructions for reporting any errors or providing any supporting documentation.

Here is the basic information about the three credit reporting agencies:
Equifax
PO Box 740256
Atlanta, GA 30374
www.equifax.com

Experian
475 Anton Boulevard
Costa Mesa, CA 92626
www.experian.com

TransUnion
PO Box 2000
Chester, PA 19016
www.transunion.com

Most banks now offer a free monthly credit score as part of their services. Scores may vary depending upon what credit reporting service they use. The two main scores are the VantageScore, which is used by CreditKarma (see below), and the FICO score (see below).

Credit Karma
www.creditkarma.com
A free service that enables you to find out what your credit score is. They also make recommendations for credit cards or loans that you might want to consider, based on your credit score information. The site provides tracking tools and tools for calculating ways to improve your credit score.

FICO
www.myfico.com
The website for Fair Isaac, the company that invented the FICO score, which is most often used to assess credit risk. MyFICO is their consumer division. It has a lot of information that will help you learn more about credit scores.

Government and private agencies or organizations offering information or direct help with credit and other financial matters:
Bankrate
http://www.bankrate.com
A financial site with thousands of archived articles on money and credit-related issues. Includes a series of calculators to assist consumers in computing everything from the cost of a car loan to how to expedite paying off a home equity loan.

Credit.com
http://wwww.credit.com
Started in 1995, this free site is a place to check your Experian credit score. It also offers calculators to tabulate your debt-to-income ratio and credit card payoffs.

Debtors Anonymous
www.debtorsanonymous.org
See full listing earlier in this chapter.

Financial Therapy Association
https://www.financialtherapyassociation.org
A membership association for financial coaches and psychotherapists who deal with individuals or couples experiencing money problems. Lists selected members offering paid help by phone or in person.

Consumer Financial Protection Bureau (CFPB)
http://www.consumerfinance.gov
The CFPB was established in 2010 to educate consumers about critical financial choices. The website provides information on everything from paying for college to purchasing a home, credit cards, credit card regulations, and dealing with debt.

Federal Trade Commission (FTC)
www.ftc.gov
This government agency has a separate website–www.identitytheft.gov–which provides a step-by-step plan if you are the victim of identity theft.

National Foundation for Credit Counseling®
https://www.nfc.org
This is a non-profit association that offers financial counseling through its member agencies. You could get advice for everything from debt management to bankruptcy, credit reports, or reverse mortgages. At the website you can put in your zip code and find a member credit counseling agency near where you live. They also offer small business financial counseling.

Reading and Audiovisual Materials

Charles H. Green. *The SBA Loan Book: The Complete Guide to Getting Financial Help Through the Small Business Administration*. NY: Adams Media, 2011.

Chonce. "Don't Let Your Financial Woes Turn into Suicidal Thoughts." My Debt Epiphany, September 18, 2018. https://www.mydebtepiphany.com/dont-commit-suicide-over-debt/

Christine Luken. *Money Is Emotional: Prevent Your Heart From Hijacking Your Wallet*. 2017.

Dave Ramsey. *The Total Money Makeover: Classic Edition: A Proven Plan for Financial Fitness*. Thomas Nelson, 2013.

Jamey Stegmaier. *A Crowdfunder's Strategy Guide: Build a Better Business by Building Community*. Berrett-Koehler, 2015.

Jan Yager, PhD. *21 Ways to Financial Freedom*. Stamford, CT: Hannacroix Creek Books, Inc., 2018. Audiobook version narrated by Al Moulliet. Available through ACX/Audible.

Joseph Hogue. *Step by Step Crowdfunding: Everything You Need to Raise Money from the Crowd for Small Business Crowdfunding and Fundraising*. Ebook edition. 2015.

Judy Robinett. *Crack the Funding Code: How Investors Think and What They Need to Hear to Fund Your Startup*. NY: AMACOM, 2019.

Katie Kindelan and Kelly McCarthy. "How to get financial help during coronavirus pandemic." *Good Morning America*. April 2, 2020. Posted at https://www.goodmorningamerica.com/living/story/financial -coronavirus-pandemic-69681482

Morrie Warshawski. *Shaking the Money Tree: The Art of Getting Grants and Donations for Film and Video*. 3rd edition. Los Angeles, CA: Michael Wiese Productions, 2010.

CHAPTER 18

Food, Hunger, Nutrition, and Eating Disorders

When I saw the hit movie *Crazy Rich Asians*, the line that got the biggest laugh was when the very rich men and women are having a meal together, sitting around the table in Singapore, trying to tell the little children that they shouldn't waste their food because children in America are starving. But unfortunately, in America it is no laughing matter that there are children who are going hungry. Not enough people talk about it or are even aware that it is actually occurring because the image of America is often of a land with obesity problems, associated with having enough money to consume too much food. While obesity is indeed a concern—and a growing problem among children—it is only one among many issues surrounding food. Further, obesity and hunger issues in the United States are not limited only to children; there are people in all age groups, including the elderly, who need help getting enough food and/or making healthy choices about their nutrition.

Food, hunger, nutrition, and eating disorders are not just American concerns either. This chapter shares help for all these pivotal issues, not just across American demographics, but worldwide as well.

Food and Nutrition
Academy of Nutrition and Dietetics (formerly the American Dietetic Association)
120 South Riverside Plaza, Suite 2000
Chicago, IL 60606-6995
http://www.eatright.org
Professional association of dietitians. Sponsors annual National Nutrition Month each March.

Online help/healthy eating/fitness communities:
SparkPeople®
www.sparkpeople.com
Online community offering information on diet and exercise as well as recipes and motivational tips.

Vegetarianism and veganism:
North American Vegetarian Society (NAVS)
PO Box 72
Dolgeville, NY 13329
https://navs-online.org/
Founded in 1974, NAVS is a nonprofit education association.

Vegetarian Society of the United Kingdom Limited
Parkdale, Dunham Road
Altrincham WA14 4QG, United Kingdom
https://www.vegsoc.org/
Local groups in the United Kingdom: https://www.vegsoc.org/localgroupsmap

Main Street Vegan Academy
New York, NY
https://mainstreetvegan.net
Started in 2012 by Victoria Moran, who serves as its Director. Mission statement from their website: "Main Street Vegan Academy is committed to training committed vegans to help others adopt and maintain a positive vegan lifestyle and health-promoting diet, geared to the needs and preferences of the individual. We endorse no particular iteration of vegan diet or animal rights ideology, trusting the conscience of our graduates to live up to their highest light in furthering the ethic of reverence for life."

VegFund
https://vegfund.org
From their website: "We exist to support you, a member of a global community of vegan advocates, in your efforts to inform the public about the benefits of vegan living. VegFund provides grant funding for food sampling, film screenings, vegfests and health fairs, conferences, and learning events. We can even help you bring your own ideas for innovative advocacy to life."

Hunger:
How many out of the more than seven billion people in the world are considered hungry? According to the World Hunger Organization, based in Washington, DC, an estimated 815 million people are hungry. In the United States, where there is

so much emphasis on the medical and psychological drawbacks of being overweight or obese, it can be more challenging to focus on the hunger problem,
but it is a very real one and a life-threatening concern. So what are the numbers
related to hunger in the United States? According to Why Hunger, there are an
estimated 6.1 million American households who are hungry, and millions more
are suffering from various levels of what is called "food insecurity," which means
that, due to economic hardship, people are forced to skip meals, limit how much
they eat per meal, or buy cheaper but less nutritious food.

Here are some organizations working to feed the hungry as well as reduce
hunger in general:

Feeding America
35 East Wacker Drive, Suite 2000
Chicago, IL 60601
www.feedingamerica.org
John Van Hengel, a retired businessman, established the nation's first food
bank at St. Mary's Food Bank in Phoenix, Arizona. Feeding America is now a
network of two hundred food banks throughout the United States making dis-
carded but not expired food available. For more information, visit: http://www
.feedingamerica.org/our-work/food-bank-network.html.

Feed the Children
PO Box 36
Oklahoma City, OK 73101-0036
www.feedthechildren.org
Started in 1979, an international organization dedicated to feeding hungry chil-
dren throughout the US and globally.

WhyHunger
505 Eighth Avenue, Suite 2100
New York, NY 10018
https://whyhunger.org
In 1975, singer Harry Chapin and radio DJ Bill Ayres co-founded WhyHunger, a
grassroots nonprofit organization dedicated to eliminating worldwide poverty
and hunger.

World Hunger Education Service
PO Box 29015
Washington, DC 20017
https://www.worldhunger.org

Local food programs:
Connecticut Food Bank
2 Research Parkway
Wallingford, CT 06492
www.ctfoodbank.org
From their website: "The Connecticut Food Bank distributes food products and resources through a network of partners and programs such as food pantries, soup kitchens, emergency shelters and day programs serving adults and children throughout Fairfield, Litchfield, Middlesex, New Haven, New London and Windham counties."

St. John's Bread & Life
795 Lexington Avenue
Brooklyn, NY 11221
https://www.breadandlife.org
From their website: "Since 1982, St. John's Bread & Life has worked to alleviate hunger and poverty in Brooklyn and Queens. We serve nearly 3,000 meals to hungry New Yorkers every day." Volunteers serve food, work in the pantry, and attend events.

Meals on Wheels America
1550 Crystal Drive, Suite 1004
Arlington, VA 22202
https://www.mealsonwheelsamerica.org/
Provides free meals to needy seniors through its local programs. At the website there is a search function that enables you to find a local program by zip code.

Eating Disorders
Occasionally eating disorders are thrust into the national spotlight; one such example was in 1982, when the hugely popular singer Karen Carpenter died at the young age of 32 from heart failure, which was said to be related to anorexia nervosa. When someone says the phrase "eating disorders," some may think of anorexia nervosa or bulimia, a related disorder which involves consuming a large number of calories and then inducing vomiting to avoid weight gain. Binge eating disorder is another kind which is little understood or discussed.

Newton-Wellesley Eating Disorders & Behavioral Medicine
1419 Beacon Street
Brookline, MA 02446
https://www.n-wedbmed.com/
Offers individual and family treatment for eating disorders including anorexia nervosa, bulimia, binge eating disorders, and related issues.

Academy for Eating Disorders (AED)
60 Revere Drive Suite 500
Northbrook, IL 60062-1577
www.aedweb.org
Professional association of therapists and researchers.

Eating Disorder Referral and Information Center (EDRIC)
International Eating Disorder Referral Organization
2923 Sandy Pointe, Suite 6
Del Mar, CA 92014-2052
http://www.edreferral.com

Eating Recovery Center
Denver, CO 80230
https://www.eatingrecoverycenter.com/
An international program headquartered in Colorado helping those with anorexia, bulimia, binge eating disorders, and other eating disorder issues. There are affiliated Eating Recovery Centers in Texas, Washington, Illinois, Ohio, California, and South Carolina.

Bulimia.com
https://www.bulimia.com/topics/find-a-therapist/
An education site with many articles on bulimia and related eating disorders that is a project of Recovery Brands, LLC, a subsidiary of American Addiction Centers, Inc. ("AAC").

National Association of Anorexia Nervosa & Associated Disorders (ANAD)
220 N. Green Street
Chicago, IL 60607
www.anad.org

National Center for Overcoming Overeating
PO Box 1257
Old Chelsea Station
New York, NY 10113-0920
www.overcomingovereating.com
The National Center for Overcoming Overeating was founded in 1990 and inaugurated The Women's Campaign to End Dieting and Body Hatred.

National Eating Disorders Association (NEDA)
1500 Broadway, Suite 1101
New York, NY 10036

http://www.nationaleatingdisorders.org
Sponsors NEDA walks as well as an annual conference.

Weight-control Information Network (WIN)
National Institutes of Health
NIDDK (National Institute of Diabetes and Digestive and Kidney Diseases)
US Department of Health & Human Services
1 Win Way
Bethesda, MD 20892-3665
https://www.niddk.nih.gov/health-information/communication-programs/win

Obesity and Overweight
American Society for Metabolic and Bariatric Surgery (ASMBS)
100 SW 75th Street, Suite 201
Gainesville, FL 32607
https://www.asmbs.org

International Association for the Study of Obesity (IASO)
Charles Darwin House
12 Roger Street
London WCIN 2JU, UK
http://www.iaso.org

Noom®
https://www.noom.com
This is an app to help monitor food consumption and exercise. From the website:
"On your smartphone, Noom uses cutting-edge technology to accurately monitor your progress and provide expert advice and analysis to keep you on track."
The website is available in four languages besides English: Korean, Japanese, German, and Spanish.

The Obesity Society
1110 Bonifant Street, Suite 500
Silver Spring, MD 20910
https://www.obesity.org/
Founded in 1982, this is a professional society concerned with the prevention and treatment of obesity.

Overeaters Anonymous (OA)
PO Box 44020
Rio Rancho, NM 87174-4020
www.oa.org

A twelve-step recovery program for compulsive overeating. It is not itself a weight loss program; participants are encouraged to be following a medically sound, supervised weight loss program in conjunction with OA meetings.

Weight Acceptance Associations
National Association to Advance Fat Acceptance (NAAFA)
P.O. Box 61586
Las Vegas, NV 89160
https://www.naafaonline.com/dev2/index.html
This advocacy and education association was founded in 1969 to raise public awareness about the discrimination that overweight and obese people may face at work and in their portrayal by the media.

Inpatient Treatment Facilities
Duke Diet & Fitness Center
501 Douglas Street
Durham, NC 27705
www.dukedietcenter.org
Offers world-renowned one-, two-, three-, or four-week residential treatment programs for the treatment of obesity.

Healthy Within
5665 Oberlin Drive, Suite 206
San Diego, CA 92121
www.healthywithin.com
Treatment facility offering inpatient and outpatient help. From their website: "Healthy Within provides a team of psychologists and therapists with extensive background in the treatment of depression, anxiety, PTSD, anorexia, bulimia, TBI, headaches, fibromyalgia, stroke, dementia, autism, and substance abuse."

Renfrew Center
www.renfrewcenter.com
A network of seven East Coast women's mental health centers specializing in eating disorders. Organizes a conference for eating disorder professionals each fall in the Philadelphia area.

Oliver-Pyatt® Centers
6100 SW 76th Street
Miami, FL 33143
http://www.oliverpyattcenters.com
Inpatient residential treatment center founded by eating disorder expert and psychiatrist Wendy Oliver-Pyatt, author of *Fed Up!* and the Academy of Eating Disorders' *Guidelines for Obesity Prevention Programs*.

Monte Nido
6100 SW 76th Street
Miami, FL 33143
http://www.montenido.com/
Founded in 1996 in Malibu, California, by Carolyn Costin, Monte Nido provides day and residential eating disorder treatment at locations in California, New York, Massachusetts, and Oregon.

Reading and Audiovisual Materials

Carolyn Costin and Gwen Schubert Grabb. *8 Keys to Recovery from an Eating Disorder Workbook.* NY: Norton, 2017.

Geneen Roth. *Breaking Free from Emotional Eating.* NY: Plume, 2003.

Glenn Levingston, PhD. *Never Binge Again.* Psy Tech Inc., 2015.

J. L. Barkas. *The Vegetable Passion: A History of the Vegetarian State of Mind.* NY: Scribner's, 1975; with new introduction, updated resources and bibliography, Stamford, CT: Hannacroix Creek Books, Inc., 2015.

Jan Yager. *365 Daily Affirmations for Creative Weight Management.* Stamford, CT: Hannacroix Creek Books, Inc., 2000.

—. *The Fast Track Guide to Losing Weight and Keeping It Off.* Stamford, CT: Hannacroix Creek Books, Inc., 2015. Audiobook version narrated by Dave Wright.

Jonathan Safran Foer. *Eating Animals.* NY: Little, Brown and Company, Hachette, 2009.

National Institute of Diabetes and Digestive Diseases and Kidney Diseases, National Institute of Health, US Department of Health & Human Services, "Overweight and Obesity Statistics," August 2017, https://www.niddk.nih.gov/health-information/health-statistics/overweight-obesity.

Peter Singer. *Animal Liberation.* NY: HarperCollins, 2009.

Roxane Gay. *Hunger: A Memoir of (My) Body.* NY: Harper Perennial, 2018.

Victoria Moran with Adair Moran. *Main Street Vegan: Everything You Need to Know to Eat Healthfully and Live Compassionately in the Real World.* New York: TarcherPerigee/Penguin, 2012.

Walter Willett. *Eat, Drink and Be Healthy: The Harvard Medical School Guide to Healthy Eating.* NY: Free Press, 2017.

CHAPTER 19

Health and Wellness

Today more than ever, information and direct help is available for all kinds of medical conditions, from allergies, cancer, or cataracts, to psoriasis, sexually transmitted diseases, or sleep disorders. But as scientific information and treatment improves, so does an individual's responsibility to get help, whether for himself or herself or for a dependent family member, as soon as possible. For decades, it was called "self-care." It's an important concept and attitude, now more than ever, because we know that early diagnosis can make all the difference in one's survival rate. Tied to early diagnosis is the concept of preventive medicine, which may offer the best opportunity for early diagnosis. Although there is a wealth of health and medical information available at your fingertips today through the internet from such sites as WebMD or the Mayo Clinic, that is not a substitute for consulting a physician.

Here is a self-quiz to help you see what your current "Health IQ" is:

Your Health IQ Factor

This "test" is intended for educational purposes only. Do not act upon any of these suggestions without first consulting your physician. Answer each question: Yes, No, or Sometimes.

1. Do you have a thorough physical checkup once a year, including any necessary blood tests?
2. Do you have your eyes examined by an optician or ophthalmologist every one to two years?
3. Do you have your teeth checked by a dentist at least annually?
4. Do you eat a balanced and varied diet that is nutritionally sound?
5. Are you at the ideal weight for your height and body frame/type?

---

6. Do you follow a regular exercise program of twenty minutes at least three or four times a week?

7. Are you a nonsmoker?

8. Do you limit the amount of alcohol, sugar, coffee, tea, or drugs that you consume?

9. Do you sleep at least 6–8 hours a night?

10. Are you able to function without drugs for either sleep or anxiety?

11. Do you have a family physician or internist that you are pleased with that you consult/visit as needed?

12. Do you know the names and contact information of specialists for any conditions you or your family members currently have or are may be likely to have in the future in case you have an emergency?

13. Do you have health insurance?

14. Is your insurance adequate for you and your family?

15. Are you properly treating any allergies, medical conditions, or disabilities that you have?

16. Have you gotten help–or are you getting help–for any emotional problems that are making you feel depressed, anxious, or stressed?

17. Do you take a one-week vacation at least once a year?

18. Do you feel like you are in good health?

If you are a woman:

19. Do you have a thorough checkup by a gynecologist once a year?

20. Do you examine your breasts at the same time each month and/or get a mammogram according to the recommendations for your age group and risk level for breast cancer?

If you answered *no* or *sometimes* to any of the previous twenty questions, especially 1 through 10, your health IQ needs improvement. Now is the time to change those habits and seek out the help and information that will give you an excellent health IQ score.

A family physician, or internist, can be crucial to your family's budget, as well as your health. That is because catching problems early, or even dealing proactively with certain conditions like obesity, can head off much more expensive procedures or conditions. You may also be reducing the likelihood of preventable surgeries or conditions that could cause you to miss some or even weeks or months of work. Since it is usually recommended that you stay with the same physician in your local area, since he or she will be most familiar with you and your history, choose your family physician wisely. A referral from trusted local friends is still the best way to start the process. Today, of course, there are online directories that provide extensive information about a potential doctor's credentials as well as their specialties. Many sites even have endorsements by current or former patients that you can read.

Your family physician may be the best place to start if you need a recommendation for a specialist. Today there is an increased awareness of the value of getting a second opinion when it comes to specialist treatment. Check with your insurance policy to see if it will cover a second opinion. If it does not, you can still pay for the second opinion out of pocket. Having at least two opinions about the best course of action may boost your confidence as you weigh your options about what is best for you or your loved one. As Yale Medicine, the clinical practice of the Yale School of Medicine, states at its website, "When confronted with a new diagnosis or treatment, a second opinion from a specialty physician can offer you peace of mind and self-assurance knowing that you are making well-informed decisions about your healthcare."

A personal example of this was when my father, at age seventy-two, was diagnosed with lung cancer. The first specialist said that the situation was hopeless. He basically suggested my father get his affairs in order. The second specialist said that he would take out the cancerous lobe. He could not guarantee the outcome, but he was optimistic that my father could beat his lung cancer. We went with the second oncologist's suggestion, and my father had another eight years, passing away at the age of eighty from a brain tumor that may or may not have been related to the lung cancer. Yes, it was hard to lose my dad at eighty, but it would have been much sadder to do so at seventy-two.

Of course, sometimes the two opinions are in total agreement. In that case, it will be a question of which specialist you prefer. It could be a question of having a specialist who is located closer to home, or it could be a cost concern.

Fortunately, most physicians are excellent, but what if you have an unsatisfactory outcome that you think constitutes negligence? How do you complain about a doctor? Contact your state medical board. Find yours at https://www.fsmb.org/contact-a-state-medical-board/ and if their credentials and all other factors seem equal, it might be a question of whose bedside manner makes that doctor a better choice for you or your family member.

Membership association for physicians:
American Medical Association (AMA)
AMA Plaza
330 N. Wabash Avenue, Suite 39300
Chicago, IL 60611-5885
http://www.ama-assn.org
Founded in 1847, this professional membership association of physicians has an annual meeting and also publishes the peer-reviewed journal, *JAMA (Journal of the American Medical Association).*

American Board of Medical Specialties (ABMS)
353 North Clark Street, Suite 1400
Chicago, IL 60654
https://www.abms.org/
A membership association, and source of education for the public, related to the 24 Member Specialty Boards. Complete contact information on those boards if you wish to follow-up on a particular specialty is available at: https://www.abms .org/member-boards/contact-an-abms-member-board/

This international organization covers a range of health concerns:
National Organization for Rare Disorders
https://rarediseases.org
You can search for a specific rare disease and see if they have information on it: https://rarediseases.org/for-patients-and-families/information-resources/ rare-disease-information/.

World Health Organization (WHO)
Headquartered in Switzerland
http://www.who.int/en
From their website: "WHO began when our Constitution came into force on 7 April 1948–a date we now celebrate every year as World Health Day. We are now more than 7000 people from more than 150 countries working in 150 country offices, in 6 regional offices and at our headquarters in Geneva."

VIRTUAL OR TELEMEDICINE

Even if someone would have never considered virtual or telemedicine appointments before the COVID-19 pandemic, when the requests to stay home became real for millions, so did a telemedicine option. Telemedicine or virtual doctors appointments does for medicine what distance learning did for college teaching. You are talking to a real person in real time, in this case, a physician, virtually, through a computer, a smartphone, or a tablet. You can do it from the comfort of your home or, if you are still working outside of your home, from your office or work site. Based on your initial virtual meeting, a recommendation might be made for you to go to a hospital or for medical procedures that require face to face interaction, such as surgery. But at least the initial consultation on medical procedures could be virtual. For behavioral and psychological issues, such as depression, anxiety, and grief especially in times when you or your loved ones might be apprehensive because of the potential of getting COVID-19 if you go to a session in person, virtual sessions, and even sessions via phone, e-mail, or texting, are options.

Once life returns to normal, and social distancing is not required, how many will continue to use virtual or telemedicine instead of always visiting a physician in person remains to be seen. But millions have been forced to learn about the benefits and possibilities of telemedicine, especially those who have to "see" a doctor in order to get approval for a prescription renewal.

Amwell
https://business.amwell.com/
Offers telemedicine care for urgent and chronic conditions including cardiology, pediatrics, women's health, therapy, menopause care, and more. Once you sign up, you could get connected to board certified physicians, 24/7, through your computer, smartphone, or tablet.

MDLive
https://www.mdlive.com/
This is a 24/7 resource for having a LIVE doctor visit via your computer, smartphone, or tablet. The first step is to register to become a member. (It's free). Then you do a search for a doctor and once the appointment is confirmed, you can start your visit. There is help available in more than 30 medical (cough, sneeze, pink eye), dermatological ($69 or less, depending on your insurance), and behavioral (depression, anxiety, grief) issues. The fees for a virtual visit with a psychiatrist is listed at their website: $259 for the first visit and $99 for follow-up visits.

Teladoc Health
https://teladochealth.com/
Offers appointments 24/7 and 365 days a year via computer, smartphone, or tablet in the areas of general medicine, pediatrics, dermatology, and behavioral health.

Telehealth
1100 Crescent Green Drive
Cary, NC 27518

https://www.telehealth.com/
As Telehealth states at their website, they are not a provider of telemedicine services. Instead, they supply the equipment to hospitals that makes it possible for physicians and patients to communicate virtually.

HEALTH INSURANCE

Although immigration and border security has become the more talked-about issue in the US in recent years, getting affordable health care and health insurance are still key concerns for the majority of Americans. The listings below can provide you with information as well as direct referrals to health insurance providers. Everyone's situation is unique based on family situation or size, income, age, physical and mental health, and wellness, so it is challenging to generalize. One generalization is possible, however: having some kind of coverage so you and your family will be able to handle medical emergencies as well as preventive care, as needed, is a challenge that everyone needs to consider and deal with on a regular basis.

Healthcare.com
https://www.healthcare.com
From their website: "We are an online healthcare company focused on improving how consumers shop for and enroll in health insurance coverage." Started in 2006, the company has a team of more than forty working in New York, Miami, and Guatemala City.

Children's Health Insurance Program (CHIP)
https://www.insurekidsnow.gov/
Information about qualifying for free or low-cost health insurance for children and teens through CHIP.

Centers for Medicare and Medicaid Services
US Department of Health and Human Services (HHS)
https://www.cms.gov
This is the main website for everything related to Medicare and Medicaid. At the website, you will find a link to more information about Medicare and Medicaid in each state, along with other information, such as the location of the ten regional offices.

Medicaid
https://www.medicaid.gov/
At this site you will find out about Medicaid, eligibility requirements, and how to apply if you qualify.

Medicare
https://www.medicare.gov/
For those who are turning 65, or retiring, so you will no longer have employer-based insurance, this site offers information about Medicare. At this site you can sign up for Medicare, change plans, and find out information about what Medicare Part A and Part B covers, among other essential topics.

US Department of Health & Human Services
https://www.healthcare.gov/
Open enrollment in a new health care insurance policy is from November 1 to December 15. At this government website, you will find links to information about the Affordable Care Act (ACA) and other related topics. An alternative US government site related to health insurance is: https://www.usa.gov/health-insurance.

These companies offer health insurance as well as details on what they offer and the cost:
Aetna
https://www.aetna.com/
Provides an article, "How health insurance works: The ultimate guide": https://www.aetna.com/health-guide/health-insurance-ultimate-guide.html.

Anthem
https://www.anthem.com/
Offers health, dental, and vision insurance.

Blue Shield of California
PO Box 272540
Chico, CA 95927-2540
https://www.blueshieldca.com/
From their website: "Blue Shield of California, an independent member of the Blue Shield Association, is a nonprofit health plan dedicated to providing Californians with access to high-quality health care at an affordable price."

Centene Corporation
7700 Forsyth Boulevard
St. Louis, MO 63105

https://www.centene.com
In thirty-one states and two international markets.

Cigna
https://www.cigna.com
Cigna and its predecessor, Insurance Company of North America, have been in the health insurance field since 1792.

Humana
https://www.humana.com/
Humana is a health insurance company based in Louisville, Kentucky, that was founded in 1961.

Kaiser Permanente
https://healthy.kaiserpermanente.org/
Founded in 1945. In 2018–2019, they will be opening the new Kaiser Permanente School of Medicine in Pasadena, California.

UnitedHealth Group
https://www.unitedhealthgroup.com/
This group combines UnitedHealthCare and Optum.

Information and Help for Health Concerns—from Allergies to Women's Health
In the listings below, listed alphabetically by health concern, you will find government and nonprofit sources of help including professional associations, information clearinghouses, and advocacy efforts.

Allergies
American Academy of Allergy, Asthma, and Immunology (AAAAI)
555 E. Wells Street, Suite 1100
Milwaukee, WI 53202-3823
https://www.aaaai.org/
To locate an allergist or immunologist, go to http://allergist.aaaai.org/find/.

National Institute of Allergy and Infectious Diseases (NIAID)
5601 Fishers Lane, MSC 9806
Bethesda, MD 20892-9806
https://www.niaid.nih.gov/
Federal agency founded in 1955.

Arthritis
Arthritis Foundation
1355 Peachtree St NE, Suite 600
Atlanta, GA 30309
https://www.arthritis.org
Membership organization publishing *Arthritis Today* and advocating on behalf of those who have arthritis, including children.

National Institute of Arthritis and Musculoskeletal and Skin Diseases (NIAMS)
1 AMS Circle Bethesda, MD 20892-3675
https://www.niams.nih.gov/
Federal agency conducting research into diseases in this area including arthritis, rheumatic diseases, bursitis, gout, juvenile arthritis, and more.

Back Pain
American Chronic Pain Association (ACPA)
https://www.theacpa.org/
See complete listing under Pain in this chapter.

Birth Control
Girls Health
https://www.girlshealth.gov/body/sexuality/birthcontrol.html
An informative site developed and maintained by the US Department of Health & Human Services.

Birth Defects
American Society of Human Genetics (ASHG)
6120 Executive Boulevard, #500
Rockville, MD 20852
www.ashg.org/
Professional membership association, founded in 1949, for human genetics specialists.

March of Dimes
https://www.marchofdimes.org
For a complete listing, go to Chapter 25, Pregnancy and Childbearing.

National Tay-Sachs & Allied Diseases, Inc.
2001 Beacon Street, Suite 204
Boston, MA 02135
https://www.ntsad.org/

Spina Bifida Association
1600 Wilson Boulevard Suite 800
Arlington, VA 22209
http://spinabifidaassociation.org/

Blood
American Association of Blood Banks (AABB)
www.aabb.org

American National Red Cross Blood Program
https://www.redcrossblood.org/
At the website you can put in your zip code to find out if there is a blood drive where you can donate blood scheduled in your vicinity.

National Hemophilia Foundation (NHF)
https://www.hemophilia.org/

Burns
American Burn Association (ABA)
311 S. Wacker Drive, Suite 4150
Chicago, IL 60606
https://ameriburn.site-ym.com/
Membership association for health care or first responders interested in the burn field including physicians, nurses, firefighters, fire prevention educators, burn patients, and others.

Shriners Hospitals for Children®–Cincinnati
3229 Burnet Avenue
Cincinnati, OH 45229
shrinershospitalcincinnati.org
Providing pediatric burn and plastic surgery care since its founding in 1968.

Cancer
American Cancer Society (ACS)
https://www.cancer.org/
Founded in 1913, there are now 900 offices throughout the US. The mission of the ACS is to find a cure for cancer through research but also to offer information and direct referrals for those who are dealing with cancer and their families.

BCAN (Bladder Cancer Advocacy Network)
4320 East West Highway, Suite 202
Bethesda, MD 20814
https://www.bcan.org/

Founded in 2005 by Diane and her husband John Quale, who was diagnosed with bladder cancer at the age of 53. BCAN raises money to fund bladder cancer research as well as providing support services for those with bladder cancer. Since 2011, annual fundraising walks have been sponsored throughout the US on behalf of BCAN. Its website also serves as an information clearinghouse on bladder cancer, its risk factors, diagnosis, and treatments.

Candelighters (Texas)
Childhood Family Cancer Alliance
https://candle.org/

Candelighters (New York City)
Childhood Cancer Foundation
http://candlelightersnyc.org/

The Judith A. Lese Breast Cancer Foundation
16012 Chester Mill Terrace
Silver Spring, MD 20906
www.judithalese.org
lesecancerfdn@aol.com
Mission statement from website: "The Judith A. Lese Breast Cancer Foundation is committed to educating individuals with updated, accurate knowledge; to empower individuals to become the strongest advocates for breast health care for selves and others, and to work to eradicate this insidious disease." This grassroots not-for-profit organization was founded in 2003 by Judith A. Lese, a cancer survivor. Among their many activities are publishing an annual newsletter and hosting an annual fundraising walk and dinner with a guest speaker. Their website offers information on key cancer publications and links to other organizations: http://www.judithalese.org/services.htm.

Susan G. Komen Breast Cancer Foundation
5005 LBJ Freeway, Suite 250
Dallas, TX 75244
www.komen.org
Founded in 1982, two years after Nancy G. Brinker promised her sister, who was dying from cancer, that she would devote herself to finding a cure for cancer. Provides a lot of information related to breast cancer at its website. Information about fundraising events is available at the companion site: https://ww5.komen.org/RaceForTheCure/

National Breast Cancer Foundation, Inc. (NBCF)
2600 Network Boulevard, Suite 300
Frisco, TX 75034
https://www.nationalbreastcancer.org
Founded in 1991 by breast cancer survivor Janelle Hail. NBCF provides information about breast cancer, the programs it offers, including its HOPE Kit, a box distributed to those undergoing cancer treatment that includes a HOPE Journal, socks, and an inspirational bracelet, and its National Mammography Program.

Reach to Recovery® Program
American Cancer Society
https://www.cancer.org/treatment/support-programs-and-services/reach-to-recovery.html
For breast cancer patients. From their website: "Our Reach To Recovery volunteers are specially trained to help people through their experience by offering a measure of comfort and an opportunity for emotional grounding and informed decision making."

St. Jude Children's Research Hospital
262 Danny Thomas Place
Memphis, TN 38105
https://www.stjude.org
Founded in 1962 by entertainer Danny Thomas, the hospital's mission is (from their website) "to advance cures, and means of prevention, for pediatric catastrophic diseases through research and treatment. Consistent with the vision of our founder Danny Thomas, no child is denied treatment based on race, religion or a family's ability to pay." There is an A to Z list of the diseases that St. Jude Children's Research Hospital treats including brain tumors, blood disorders, and leukemias and lymphomas: https://www.stjude.org/disease.html

Coronavirus
COVID-19
https://www.coronavirus.gov/
Government website providing up-to-date information about dealing with COVID-19 jointly developed and maintained by The White House, the CDC, and FEMA.
   Two key components of the site are the sections entitled: "How to protect yourself & others" and "If you are Sick or Caring for Someone."

Infectious Diseases Society of America (IDSA)
https://www.idsociety.org/

Founded in 1963, this is a membership community of over 12,000 physicians and public health experts specializing in infectious diseases. There is a resource center with short videos and articles discussing various issues related to COVID-19 such as social distancing. Here is the link to that part of their site: https://www.idsociety.org/public-health/COVID-19-Resource-Center/

National Foundation for Infectious Diseases (NFID)
https://www.nfid.org/
See complete listing for this educational non-profit under "Flu."

Cystic Fibrosis
Cystic Fibrosis Foundation
https://www.cff.org/

Dental
American Dental Association
https://www.ada.org/en
Professional membership association for dentists.

Diabetes
American Diabetes Association
http://www.diabetes.org/

JDRF (Juvenile Diabetes Research Foundation)
https://www2.jdrf.org

Digestive Diseases
National Institute of Diabetes and Digestive and Kidney Diseases
US Department of Health & Human Services
https://www.niddk.nih.gov/

Dementia
Alzheimer's
Alzheimer's Association
225 N. Michigan Avenue, Floor 17
Chicago, IL 60601
https://alz.org/

American Brain Foundation
201 Chicago Avenue
Minneapolis, MN 55415
https://www.americanbrainfoundation.org/
Founded in 1922 by the American Academy of Neurology.

Lewy Body Dementia
Lewy Body Dementia Association
https://www.lbda.org/

Eating Disorders
See listings in Chapter 17, Food, Hunger, Nutrition, and Eating Disorders

Epilepsy
Epilepsy Foundation
https://www.epilepsy.com/

Exercise
See listings in following "Wellness" section.

Eyes
American Macular Degeneration Foundation
https://www.macular.org

American Optometric Association
https://www.aoa.org/
Professional association.

National Eye Institute
https://nei.nih.gov/
Established by the government in 1983.

Foundation Fighting Blindness
https://www.blindness.org

National Society to Prevent Blindness
211 W. Wacker Drive
Chicago, IL 60606
https://www.preventblindness.org
info@preventblindness.org

Flu
National Foundation for Infectious Diseases
1629 K Street, NW
Suite 300
Washington, DC 20006
https://www.nfid.org/

Founded in 1973, this is a non-profit organization dedicated to helping the public as well as those working in the healthcare field to learn more about a wide range of infectious diseases including the flu (influenza), coronavirus, chicken pox, shingles, Ebola, HIV/AIDS, polio, and more. (See the complete list at their website.)

Foot Care
American Podiatry Medical Association
https://www.apma.org/
Professional membership association for doctors specializing in foot and ankle health.

Gynecology
See listings in the "Women's Health" section that follows.

Hearing
ASHA (American Speech-Language-Hearing Association)
https://www.asha.org/

Heart Conditions
Arrhythmia Alliance
(Atrial Fibrillation)
Unit 6B, Essex House
Cromwell Business Park
Chipping Norton
OX7 5SR
United Kingdom
https://www.heartrhythmalliance.org/

American Heart Association (AHA)
7272 Greenville Avenue
Dallas, TX 75231
www.heart.org
Founded in 1924, this educational and advocacy organization is also a leader in CPR training.

American Stroke Association
https://www.stroke.org
This is a division of the American Heart Association.

HIV/AIDS
Elton John AIDS Foundation
584 Broadway, Suite 906

New York, NY 10012
http://newyork.ejaf.org
Founded in the United States by Sir Elton John in 1992 and the following year in the United Kingdom. In addition to fighting AIDS discrimination, it is an advocacy initiative as well as providing treatment and assistance.

Huntington's Disease
Huntington's Disease Society of America
https://hdsa.org/

Hypoglycemia
Hypoglycemia Support Foundation
https://hypoglycemia.org/

Immunization
Immunization Action Coalition (IAC)
2550 University Avenue West, Suite 415 North
Saint Paul, MN 55114
www.vaccineinformation.org
In partnership with the CDC (Centers for Disease Control and Prevention), the IAC was started in 2002 to increase public awareness about preventable diseases through immunization.

Infectious Diseases
National Institute of Allergy and Infectious Diseases
https://www.niaid.nih.gov/
NIAID, which traces its origins to a laboratory started in 1887 at a hospital in Staten Island, New York, is a government medical agency whose mission is to achieve a better understanding of the treatment and prevention of infectious diseases.
    See additional listings under Coronavirus and Flu in this chapter.

Infertility
American Society for Reproductive Medicine
https://www.asrm.org

RESOLVE (National Infertility Association)
7918 Jones Branch Drive, Suite 300
McLean, VA 22102
https://resolve.org/
Founded in 1974, Resolve is an information clearinghouse on infertility as well as providing direct help through the affiliated local support groups. There is also

a professional directory at the website and a helpline that enables you to leave a message and get a return call from a volunteer within one to three days.

Kidney Disease
American Kidney Fund
www.kidneyfund.org

National Kidney Foundation
https://www.kidney.org/

Lyme Disease
Lyme Disease Association
https://www.lymediseaseassociation.org/

Multiple Sclerosis
National MS Society
https://www.nationalmssociety.org/

Muscular Dystrophy
Muscular Dystrophy Association
https://www.mda.org/

Myalgic Encephalomyelitis (ME)/Chronic Fatigue Syndrome (CFS)
Solve ME/CFS Initiative
5455 Wilshire Boulevard, Suite 1903
Los Angeles, CA 90036-0007
https://solvecfs.org/
National nonprofit organization dealing with myalgic encephalomyelitis (ME)/chronic fatigue syndrome (CFS).

Myasthenia Gravis
Myasthenia Gravis Foundation of America
http://myasthenia.org/

Pain
American Chronic Pain Association (ACPA)
PO Box 850
Rocklin, CA 95677
https://www.theacpa.org/
Founded in 1980, ACPA is a non-profit membership association dedicated to helping the public learn how to manage pain through education as well as peer support groups. Back pain, sciatica, and knee pain are some of the many pains that are addressed.

Parkinson Disease
American Parkinson Disease Association
https://www.apdaparkinson.org/

The Michael J. Fox Foundation for Parkinson Research
Grand Central Station
PO Box 4777
New York, NY 10163-4777
https://www.michaeljfox.org
To learn about clinical trials seeking those with Parkinson's and those without (the control group) and to sign up for voluntary participation, visit: https://fox trialfinder.michaeljfox.org.

Psoriasis
National Psoriasis Foundation
https://www.psoriasis.org

Respiratory and Lung Conditions
American Lung Association
https://www.lung.org/

Sciatica
American Chronic Pain Association (ACPA)
https://www.theacpa.org/
See complete listing under Pain.

Sexually Transmitted Diseases
American Sexual Health Association
www.ashasexualhealth.org

Herpes Virus Association
https://herpes.org.uk/

Skin
American Academy of Dermatology
https://www.aad.org/
Professional membership association of physicians specializing in the skin and skin disorders, founded in 1938.

Sleep and Sleep Disorders
American Academy of Sleep Medicine
https://aasm.org/
Professional association of physicians and other healthcare professionals specializing in sleep medicine.

National Sleep Foundation
http://www.sleepfoundation.org
nsf@sleepfoundation.org
Professional membership association of sleep experts. Sponsors Sleep Awareness Week every year, usually at the same time as the association's annual meeting. In November, it sponsors a separate Drowsy Driving Prevention Week to increase public awareness about the relationship between sleep deprivation and the increased risk of car and vehicle accidents and even death.

Thyroid
American Thyroid Association (ATA)
https://www.thyroid.org/
Professional membership association for doctors working in the thyroid field.

Tinnitus
American Tinnitus Association (ATA)
PO Box 424049
Washington, DC 20042-4049
https://www.ata.org
Information clearinghouse and membership association that raises awareness about tinnitus as well as trying to find a cure for this condition. Publishes a magazine entitled *Tinnitus Today*.

Women's Health
American College of Obstetricians and Gynecologists (ACOG)
https://www.acog.org/

Gennev
2033 6th Avenue, Suite 600
Seattle, WA 98121
https://gennev.com
Online help for women dealing with menopause.

Office on Women's Health
https://www.womenshealth.gov/

National Women's Health Network
https://www.nwhn.org

WELLNESS
Dealing with Stress

Taking care of your health, we now know, includes eating healthy, getting enough exercise, and scheduling an annual checkup. We now know that stress, especially chronic stress, can cause emotional issues like anxiety and depression, but it can also lead to physical problems, including tension headaches, insomnia, chronic pain, asthma, and heart-related issues like irregular heartbeat, stroke, or high blood pressure, among other health concerns.

Figuring out the causes of your stress is an important first step. Is the cause financial? Work-related? Related to a relationship in your personal or business life, such as a friend, partner, boss, or coworker?

Talking to a therapist, as discussed in Chapter 9, Counseling, Depression, and Mental Health, is a way to start coping better with the stress you are feeling. Another way to reduce stress, advocated by leading health providers, like Mayo Clinic, is to meditate. In "Meditation: A simple, fast way to reduce stress," Mayo Clinic staff recommend discussing ways of dealing with stress with your physician. I will echo that suggestion. If you do ultimately decide that meditation is the right step for you to deal with your stress, you will discover that meditation consists of three distinct phases: Phase 1 is preparation to meditate; Phase 2 is the meditation itself; and Phase 3 is what you do immediately afterward.

Meditation
Transcendental Meditation
https://www.tm.org
TM is a nonprofit organization that was founded by Maharishi Mahesh Yogi. The TM technique is taught in four sessions and on consecutive days by a certified TM teacher. You may find a referral to a local certified teacher through their website. There are more than 180 TM centers throughout the US as well as additional centers in many other countries.

David Lynch Foundation
228 E. 45th Street, 15th Floor
New York, NY 10017
https://www.davidlynchfoundation.org
Established by filmmaker David Lynch, this foundation's tagline is "Healing Traumatic Stress and Raising Performance in At-risk Populations." One of their

meditation/TM-related initiatives is Quiet Time in school. From their website: "Quiet Time provides students with two 15-minute periods of Transcendental Meditation each day to help balance their lives and improve their readiness to learn. This schoolwide program complements existing educational strategies by improving the physiological underpinnings of learning and behavior."

Exercise
American Council on Exercise (ACE)
4851 Paramount Drive
San Diego, CA 92123
http://www.acefitness.org
Nonprofit organization established in 1985 concerned with the quality of exercise trainers.

Road Runners Club of America
https://www.rrca.org
Membership association for runners since 1958.

Journaling
Center for Journal Therapy
https://journaltherapy.com/

International Association for Journal Writing
http://www.iajw.org/

Fitness Spas or Resorts
Canyon Ranch
http://www.canyonranch.com
Well-regarded spa resort offering nutrition and exercise opportunities along with classes related to healthy living, with locations in Tucson, Arizona; Lenox, Massachusetts; Las Vegas, Nevada; and Miami, Florida.

The Biggest Loser Resort at Fitness Ridge
Inspired by the hit NBC-TV fitness reality TV series *The Biggest Loser*, the resort started in 2012: Biggest Loser Resort Niagara in upstate New York.

Rancho La Puerta
Tecate, Baja California, Mexico
http://www.rancholapuerta.com
Started by Deborah Szekely, this well-regarded spa offers a week-long program of healthy eating and fitness activities.

Stress
Thrive Global
New York, NY
https://thriveglobal.com/
Founded by Ariana Huffington, who is also the CEO, Thrive Global, is dedicated to "ending the epidemic of stress and burnout." It plans to offer products to help visitors to the website to improve their performance as well as conducting related seminars and workshops especially related to the importance of sleep.

Reading and Audiovisual Materials

Avital Miller. *Healing Happens: Stories of Healing Against All Odds*. Seal Rock, OR: APG Publishing, 2018.

Beni Johnson. *Healthy and Free: A Journey to Wellness for Your Body, Soul, and Spirit*. Destiny Image, 2015.

Charles P. Pollak, MD, Michael J. Thorpy, MD and Jan Yager, PhD. *The Encyclopedia of Sleep and Sleep Disorders*. Third edition. NY: Facts on File, Inc., 2009.

Heidi Schauster. *Nourish: How to Heal Your Relationship with Food, Body, and Self*. Somerville, MA: Hummingbird Press, 2018.

Joe Petreycik, RN. Foreword by Stuart W. Zarich, MD. *Pump It Up! Exercising Your Heart to Health*. Stratford, CT: Take Exercise to Heart, LLC, 2014.

Kenneth G. Walton, PhD, Robert H. Schneider, MD and Sanford Nidich, EdD. "Review of Controlled Research on the Transcendental Meditation Program and Cardiovascular Disease: Risk Factors, Morbidity, and Mortality." *Cardiology Review*, 2004, Volume 12, Number 5, pages 262–266. https://www.ncbi.nlm.nih.gov/pmc/articles/PMC2211376/

Kilburn Gordon III, MD. *Med School 101 for Patients: A Patient's Guide to Creating an Exceptional Doctor Visit*. Bloomington, IN: Archway Publishing, 2017.

Lisa Genova. *Still Alice*. NY: Simon & Schuster, Gallery Books, 2009.

Marty Kaminsky. *Uncommon Champions. Fifteen Athletes Who Battled Back*. Honesdale, PA: Boyds Mills Press, 2000.

Matthew Edlund, MD. *The Power of Rest: Why Sleep Alone Is Not Enough*. NY: HarperOne, 2010.

Mayo Clinic Staff. "Meditation: A Simple, Fast Way to Reduce Stress."
     October 17, 2017. https://www.mayoclinic.org/tests-procedures
     /meditation/in-depth/meditation/art-20045858

Michael J. Thorpy, MD and Jan Yager, PhD. *Sleeping Well*. NY: Checkmark
     Books, 2001.

Phoebe Lapine. *The Wellness Project: How I Learned to Do Right by My
     Body, Without Giving Up My Life*. NY: Pam Kraus/Avery, 2017.

WebMD. "Stress Symptoms," reviewed by Varnada Karriem-Norwood,
     MD. July 11, 2017. https://www.webmd.com/balance/stress-
     management
     /stress-symptoms-effects_of_stress-on-the-body#1

Yale Medicine. "Get a Second Opinion." https://www.yalemedicine.org
     /patient_guide/second-opinion.html

CHAPTER 20
Housing and Homelessness

HOUSING

Help for housing covers everything from finding an apartment or house to live in to finding emergency housing because of a disaster or even a pandemic.

Rural, suburb, or city? These are some of the questions housing brings up. As Baby Boomers age, staying in a long-time home or relocating to be closer to children and grandchildren, or even to another country for financial or lifestyle reasons, becomes an issue of concern as well.

In the 1970s, and again recently, there has been a reconsideration of city life and a reevaluation of moving to the suburbs, the trend that characterized the postwar years. Many are reluctant to undertake longer or more expensive commutes that the suburbs or even more rural, but less expensive, areas would require.

Psychologist and author Jonathan Freedman, in his book *Crowding and Behavior: The Psychology of High-Density Living,* based on five years of research, showed that high-density living could be beneficial; it need not automatically cause stress or distress. Freedman concluded that crowding and pathology are not directly correlated to each other, nor does crowding automatically cause stress. He also emphasized that living in high-density areas offers social and intellectual stimulation, which anyone who has lived in a major city would verify.

However, the choice about where to live depends upon many factors, from where you work and how long a commute you are willing to deal with, to how much living space you can afford, how much greenery you need outside your window, or even if you're willing to give up having a terrace or backyard because there are other cultural or educational benefits.

If at all possible, start any search for a new home as early as possible. Research the community's schools if you have school-age children, closeness to public transportation or major roads if that is a factor, and even where the nearest supermarket might be. But even with a lot of time to do your research and look at as many options as possible, if you happen to find something that you think will be a great opportunity for you, even if it is one of the first options you see, whether on your own or through a real estate agent, be ready to jump on it. You just might be having beginner's luck, as they say!

These are a couple of commercial sites that might provide you with some basic information, but you might want to work with a realtor who has exclusive listings and detailed knowledge of the area:
Realtor.com
https://www.realtor.com
You can enter a particular address or do a search and see available houses or apartments to rent or buy.

Zillow
https://www.zillow.com/
Started in 2006 and headquartered in Seattle, Washington. Enter an address or a location to see what's available to buy or rent.

Professional associations for realtors:
National Association of Realtors (NAR)
430 N. Michigan Avenue
Chicago, IL 60611-4087
https://www.nar.realtor/
From their website: "The National Association of REALTORS® was founded as the National Association of Real Estate Exchanges on May 12, 1908, in Chicago. With 120 founding members, 19 Boards, and one state association, the National Association of Real Estate Exchanges' objective was 'to unite the real estate men of America for the purpose of effectively exerting a combined influence upon matters affecting real estate interests.'"

National Association of Real Estate Brokers, Inc. (NAREB)
9831 Greenbelt Road
Lanham, MD, 20706
http://www.nareb.com
From their website: "The National Association of Real Estate Brokers, Inc. (NAREB) was founded in Tampa, Florida, in 1947 as an equal opportunity and civil rights advocacy organization for African American real estate professionals, consumers, and communities in America."

Federal government housing help:
US Department of Health and Urban Development
451 7th Street SW
Washington, DC 20410
HUD.gov
Public housing program: https://www.hud.gov/topics/rental_assistance/phprog.
Information about rental assistance: https://www.hud.gov/topics/rental
_assistance.
    For information specific to your state, go to https://www.hud.gov/states.

National organizations providing information on affordable housing,
neighborhood redevelopment, and even some direct help:
Volunteers of America
1660 Duke Street
Alexandria, VA 22314
https://www.voa.org
From their website: "Volunteers of America has understood the power of housing as a foundation for life since its beginnings in 1896. And since those early days, Volunteers of America has grown into one of the largest and most effective nonprofit housing organizations in the nation. In its 2015 ranking, Affordable Housing Finance Magazine ranked Volunteers of America as the largest nonprofit affordable housing owner in the country in terms of total units owned. Our network of affordable housing facilities now includes 484 properties in 40 states and Puerto Rico and our nationwide portfolio has grown to 19,426 affordable housing units and includes large urban complexes, small rural developments, elderly housing, multifamily housing and housing for those with disabilities. We house more than 25,000 people each year."
VOA provides housing for these four groups:

- Seniors
- Low-income families
- Veterans
- Persons with disabilities

To check for available housing in your area, go to https://www.voa.org/housing.

Christian Church Homes
303 Hegenberger Road, Suite 201
Oakland, CA 94621-1419
(510) 632-6712
https://www.cchnc.org/housing-development

From their website: "Established in 1961, Christian Church Homes is a non-profit organization that has been building and managing affordable housing communities where seniors can live and thrive in the comfort of their own home. Having served over 100,000 seniors over 50 years, CCH has now grown to 57 caring communities that are More Than Home to residents in seven states." Those states are California, Texas, Pennsylvania, Colorado, Arizona, Georgia, Idaho, and Maryland. Waiting lists are at https://www.cchnc.org/list/waiting-lists/.

Habitat for Humanity International®
2865 Peachtree Street NW, Suite 2700
Atlanta, GA 30303
https://www.habitat.org
Their story (from their website): "The idea that became Habitat for Humanity first grew from the fertile soil of Koinonia Farm, a community farm outside of Americus, Georgia, founded by farmer and biblical scholar Clarence Jordan. On the farm, Jordan and Habitat's eventual founders Millard and Linda Fuller developed the concept of 'partnership housing.' The concept centered on those in need of adequate shelter working side by side with volunteers to build decent, affordable houses. The houses would be built at no profit. New homeowners' house payments would be combined with no-interest loans provided by supporters and money earned by fundraising to create "The Fund for Humanity," which would then be used to build more homes."

The Fullers took the idea to Zaire, now the Democratic Republic of Congo. After three years, they returned to the US and in 1976, Habitat for Humanity International was founded.

Two celebrity advocates for Habitat for Humanity who have been involved in building houses themselves are former President Jimmy Carter and his wife Rosalynn.

The Emergency Food and Shelter Program
https://www.efsp.unitedway.org/efsp/website/index.cfm
This program is governed by a National Board composed of representatives of the American Red Cross (see Chapter 16); Catholic Charities, USA; the Jewish Federations of North America (see Chapter 17); National Council of the Churches of Christ in the USA; the Salvation Army (see chapter 16); and United Way Worldwide (see chapter 17). The Board is chaired by a representative of the Federal Emergency Management Agency (FEMA).

Housing Assistance Council (HAC)
1025 Vermont Avenue NW, Suite 606
Washington, DC 20005
www.ruralhome.org

Started in 1971, HAC is a nonprofit corporation. Headquartered in Washington, DC, there are regional offices in New Mexico and Missouri. From their website: "a national nonprofit organization that helps build homes and communities across rural America." One of their initiatives is lending: "HAC makes short-term loans at below market interest rates to local nonprofits, for profits and government entities developing affordable housing for low-income, rural residents."

Temporary housing locally or far away:
Those who travel need temporary housing. There are more options than ever before since the controversial Airbnb website and app became widely available. Although privately renting out apartments or homes informally has always been around, Airbnb made it standardized and more accessible. Remember that you can always contact a hotel chain directly, such as the Marriott Hotels (https://www.marriott.com) or Hilton Worldwide (https://www3.hilton.com), other chains or even unique hotels, going to their websites, sending an email, or calling to find out about their rates or special offers and to do direct bookings.

Airbnb
https://www.airbnb.com/

Booking.com
https://www.booking.com/

Expedia.com
https://www.expedia.com/

Hotels.com
https://www.hotels.com /

Kayak.com
https://www.kayak.com/

Priceline.com
https://www.priceline.com/

Trip Advisor
https://www.tripadvisor.com

Trivago.com
https://www.trivago.com/

HOMELESSNESS

You may think of a homeless person as someone who has lost their home because of losing a job, is unable to keep up with the rent or mortgage payments, or lacks a place to stay with family or friends. But there are other reasons people become homeless, such as natural disasters or domestic violence.

According to a 2018 article by Kizley Benedict, homelessness is getting worse in the United States, with an estimated 554,000 homeless and 193,000 "unsheltered," or living on the streets. That is more than the population of the entire country of Iceland. Imagine if everyone in Iceland were homeless. Maybe putting the homeless problem in that context will help put more attention on the US homelessness problem. But more than half a million homeless with 193,000 estimated to be living on the streets are still startling numbers that Benedict's article suggests are rising.

A man or woman living on the street is not the only type of homelessness today. There are entire families living in shelters and some even in their cars. According to the National Alliance to End Homelessness (see listing below), in 2017, on a single night, almost 17,000 *families* were living on the street, in a car, "or in another place not meant for human habitation."

The nonprofit, government, and other initiatives that follow are dedicated to finding shelter for those who are homeless and to permanently ending this situation in America. Some even offer direct help for the homeless.

Organizations that are seeking to help end homelessness in America and internationally:
Coalition for the Homeless
129 Fulton Street
New York, NY 10038
www.coalitionforthehomeless.org/
This New York City-based program is working to end homelessness in New York City. In the meantime, it provides food and other direct services including job training. Their resource guide of emergency services: http://www.coalitionforthe homeless.org/resource-guide/.

Chrysalis
522 S. Main Street
Los Angeles, CA 90013
(Additional locations in Orange County, Santa Monica, and San Fernando Valley)
https://changelives.org/

This organization is dedicated to helping the homeless change their lives by getting a job. They operate The Bin, one of two storage facilities in Los Angeles where the homeless are able to store their belongings for free. This helps them in their job search since they can store the necessary items that they need without fear of having something stolen, whether they are living on the street or in a shelter. They rely on volunteers to instruct their clients on how to deal with the interview experience, writing a resume, and facilitating classes related to the job search.

Families Forward
8 Thomas
Irvine, CA 92618
https://www.families-forward.org/
This is a nonprofit organization in Orange County, California, helping families who are homeless or are at risk of becoming homeless to find housing. From their website: "Families Forward exists to help families in need achieve and maintain self-sufficiency through housing, food, counseling, education, and other support services."

Family Promise
71 Summit Avenue
Summit, NJ 07901
https://familypromise.org
Started by Karen Olson and celebrating their thirtieth year in October 2018. From their website: "Family Promise has come to represent not just the programs that touch the lives of more than 93,000 people in need annually and engage more than 200,000 volunteers. It represents a national movement that believes we can address family homelessness–right here in our own communities." Their programs include direct services through housing and education.

Jericho Project Administration
245 West 29th Street, Suite 902
New York, NY 10001

Jericho Project Veteran Program
210 East 43rd Street, Suite 314
New York, NY 10001
http://www.jerichoproject.org/
https://twitter.com/JerichoProject1
Founded in 1983, the Jericho Project has seven residences in the Bronx and Harlem for various homeless populations including young adults, veterans, men, women, and families. From their Twitter description: "Helping NYC's homeless find affordable housing, employment, and healthcare, w/special programs for veterans, families, young adults 18-25 and LGBTQ housing." Here is the

link for volunteer opportunities: http://www.jerichoproject.org/get-involved/
volunteer-opportunities/

LA Family Housing
7843 Lankershim Boulevard
North Hollywood, CA 91605
https://lafh.org/
From their website: "LA Family Housing helps people transition out of homelessness through a continuum of housing enriched with supportive services."
Started in 1983.

Institute of Global Homelessness (IGH)
1 East Jackson Boulevard
Chicago, IL 60604
https://www.ighomelessness.org
From their website: "The Institute of Global Homelessness (IGH) supports an
emerging global movement to end street homelessness. As a first step toward
achieving this goal, we are working with key global strategic partners to eradicate street homelessness in 150 cities around the world by 2030. Our vision is
that within a generation we will live in a world where everyone has a place to call
home–a home that offers security, safety, autonomy, and opportunity"

National Alliance to End Homelessness
1518 K Street NW, 2nd Floor
Washington, DC 20005
https://endhomelessness.org
Founded in 1983. It is an advocacy group. This map shows how many are estimated to be homeless by state: https://endhomelessness.org/homelessness
-in-america/homelessness-statistics/state-of-homelessness-report/.

Skid Row Housing Trust
1317 E. 7th Street
Los Angeles, CA 90021
skidrow.org
info@skidrow.org
From their website: "The Skid Row Housing Trust provides permanent supportive housing so that people who have experienced homelessness, prolonged
extreme poverty, poor health, disabilities, mental illness and/or addiction can
lead safe, stable lives in wellness."

*Please note: If homelessness is due to a domestic violence situation,
see the listings for free housing (shelters) for abused women and their
families in Chapter 11, Crime: Victims, Witnesses, and Prevention.*

Reading and Audiovisual Materials

Brenda Reeves Sturgis. *Still a Family: A Story about Homelessness.*
Illustrated by Jo-Shin Lee. INDPB Publisher, 2017.

Elliot Liebow. *Tell Them Who I Am: The Lives of Homeless Women.* NY:
Penguin, 1995.

Jonathan Kozol. *Rachel and Her Children: Homeless Families in America.*
NY: Penguin, 2006.

Kizley Benedict. "Estimating the Number of Homeless in America."
January 21, 2018. http://thedataface.com/2018/01/public-health/american
-homelessness

Matthew Desmond. *Evicted: Poverty and Profit in the American City.* NY:
Penguin Random House, 2017.

Melanie Pinol. "Top 10 Ways to Find the Best Place to Live." Posted at
Lifehacker.com, September 13, 2014.

Saul Gonzalez. "Inside LA's storage facility for homeless people." February
18, 2016. Posted at http://curious.kcrw.com/2016/02/storage-facility
-for-homeless

Steve Corbett and Brian Fikkert. *When Helping Hurts: How to Alleviate
Poverty Without Hurting the Poor . . . and Yourself.* Moody, 2014.

Zalman Velvel. *How to Get a Good Deal on a Mobile Home: or Even Get
One for Free!* Ft Myers, FL: Velvel, 2016.

CHAPTER 21

Legal Services

Legal services are usually sought when you, a family member, or friend have a legal problem, whether it is being accused of a crime or having to deal with a civil matter, such as getting a divorce, setting up a corporation, or securing a trademark. Obviously, the stakes may be quite different in each of these situations with criminal charges potentially leading to a dismissal, probation, jail or prison time, or, in some states, capital punishment, with the issues in civil matters generally involving "only" money.

To say that the best time to get a lawyer is when you don't need one is a cliché and also impractical. You may have a family member or friend who is an attorney, who can serve as a source of referrals, but for most, finding a lawyer will occur when you are in the thick of whatever situation has caused you to seek out legal services.

If you currently do not have any legal issues and see no need to find a lawyer, you still might want to review the general guidelines for finding and working with a lawyer in criminal cases, so you are prepared if the situation arises in the future. See "How to Find an Attorney" which follows the next section, contributed by Kevin Gres, a California-based attorney, who shares seven tips that you should review now and also have available to you later.

7 Tips to Review Now and/or to Pull Out and Reread if You Get Pulled Over
by California Criminal Defense Attorney Kevin Gres*

1. **Do not try to talk your way out of being arrested—it's a trap.**
   Most people think they are clever enough to avoid arrest. Men and

---

* **Note from Kevin Gres:** Nothing in this informational newsletter (published in May 2017 on a very limited basis) should be construed as legal advice. It is rather just the opinion of its author, Kevin Gres.

women alike believe if they can just argue their case to the officer, the officer will admit defeat, shake hands and leave. This rarely happens, not even in the movies. If you are being stopped for anything besides a traffic ticket, do not engage the officer with your version of events. You will invariably say something that incriminates you, even if you do not realize it. Officers are trained to get you to say incriminating things accidentally. A classic example of this is with DUI stops. One of the first questions officers ask is "How many drinks did you have tonight?" The question is not "Did you have any drinks?" but rather "How many?" The driver almost always answers "*Just* one or two a few hours ago." The driver thought she was saying the right thing, i.e. minimizing how much she drank, but all she did was give the officer probable cause to arrest her. This example is straightforward, but many crimes require technical facts that need to be proven if they are to hold up in court, such as identity, knowledge, and intent. Seemingly innocent statements often serve as the basis for the prosecutor being able to prove up these technicalities. Officers want you to talk. Don't, it's a trap.

2. **Don't consent to a search—there are no free lunches.** When officers pull over a car or stop someone on the street, they do not have carte blanche permission to search through the vehicle, wallets, phones, backpacks etc. To justify a search, police need probable cause. That means they need articulable facts that would lead a reasonable person to believe there is some type of contraband in the item to be searched. If police search a car, backpack or any other item absent the proper legal justification, anything the officer finds will be suppressed in court, which can likely lead to the case being dismissed. One of the easiest and most convenient exceptions to the probable cause requirement is consent. If officers get your consent to search an item, they don't need probable cause. Often, officers will ask someone for consent to search an item as an insurance policy if the probable cause is weak or absent. I have seen hundreds of cases where officers, with little or no probable cause get consent to search a vehicle, only to find illegal contraband. Had the person not consented, the likelihood of beating the case, or even avoiding arrest altogether, is infinitely higher. Expect officers to use the classic "If you got nothing to hide, can I search the car?" Do not be intimidated or pressured. If police are asking your permission to

search, it means they *want* your permission because it will make their case against you stronger. Lastly, if you see officers searching your belongings without your permission, make sure to tell officers, albeit politely, that you do not consent to a search. Don't give the officers a free lunch by giving them consent. Make them earn it.

3. **Be polite—your peers may be watching.** It seems like every week there is another video released of an arrest gone awry. Officers are recorded using excessive force, racial epithets, or in extreme situations, outright lying. Videos capture everything—including you. If you scream "Fuck the police!" or use racial slurs yourself, your case will be significantly weakened because the prosecutor and judge may treat your case more harshly, or worse, the jury will get a very poor image of you and won't sympathize with you. While it may feel good to get some choice words off your chest, it does no favors to your defense attorney. If you are stopped or if you are getting arrested, remember, a jury of your peers may be watching. Act appropriately.

4. **Interrogation—you don't stand a chance.** If you think for one second officers hauled you into the station just to get some information on someone, you have another thing coming. Officers are allowed by law to mislead and deceive you in interrogation. This is not an interview with Ellen DeGeneres. It is called an interrogation for a reason. On one side you are sitting there, anxious, nervous, tired, maybe hungry and thirsty, and most definitely ignorant of all the information the police know. On the other side of the table are hard-nosed detectives trained in the art of getting you to say things you don't even realize will hurt you. Officers will tell you they have the "whole thing on camera" or "your friends all pointed the finger at you" and all they want is "your side of the story" or "the truth so the prosecutor will take it easy on you." See tip number 1—it's a trap. Don't talk. Exercise your right to remain silent and request a lawyer immediately. Lastly, just remember, if the police had such a strong case against you and had the whole thing on video, they wouldn't waste their time hauling you into the station for an interrogation. If they are interrogating you, that means there is, likely, a factual or evidentiary weakness in the case they are trying to bolster. Don't play their game, because you don't stand a chance.

5. **No field sobriety or roadside breathalyzer—lose the battle, win the war.** An officer pulls someone over for a DUI investigation. The

driver's breath may smell like alcohol, but that doesn't necessarily mean the driver is drunk, and it certainly can't be determined how drunk. There are actually dozens of legitimate reasons why a sober person's breath may smell like alcohol. The officer also sees the driver's eyes are bloodshot, but that doesn't necessarily mean the driver is drunk. Again, there are dozens of legitimate medical reasons why a sober person's eyes may be bloodshot. The officer is at a crossroads. On one hand the officer observes objective signs of intoxication (breath and eyes) but those signs are certainly not conclusive enough to make the arrest. What does the officer do— enter the field sobriety tests and roadside breathalyzer test? These voluntary tests serve no other purpose than to build a stronger case for the prosecutor. Field sobriety tests, also referred to as roadside gymnastics, is subjective in interpretation. They are not pass/fail. No matter how well you do, officers can and will note that you struggled to complete them or properly follow instructions. For example, officers will ask you to close your eyes and estimate 30 seconds. This is no easy task for anybody. I have had cases where my client estimates 29 seconds only for the officer to conclude she "failed" the test. Officers are famous for saying "If you pass the breathalyzer, I won't arrest you, but if you don't take it, I will definitely arrest you." Don't get sucked into the trap. If not taking the breathalyzer will result in an arrest (which is not necessarily true) then at least you stand a much higher chance of beating your case in court because there is no quantifiable scientific data relating to your blood alcohol concentration at the time you were operating the vehicle. Just remember, lose the battle on the street, and win the war in the courtroom. Don't consent to voluntary field sobriety tests or the roadside breathalyzer tests.

6. **Jail house calls—this call may be recorded.** You failed to listen to tips 1 through 5 and you find yourself in custody. During the interrogation, you came up with some pretty clever excuses, or the more common scenario, you just played dumb. Officers allow you to use the phone, so you call a friend or family member to let them know you are in custody. You explain "I told the cops [insert your super clever story] but [the truth] is what really happened . . ." or "I didn't tell the cops anything. I didn't tell them anything about John being there with me." When in custody you

have no legitimate expectation of privacy. Calls made from custody are recorded. They are not private. If you say anything that contradicts your previous statements or incriminates you, a copy of the jail call will be downloaded and transcribed and put on the desk of the prosecutor the following day. I have had many clients with excellent defenses get completely undercut because of negligent and boneheaded statements they made on the jail phone. In case you are unclear, just be quiet. Your calls are being recorded.

7. **Obey all "minor" traffic violations—don't give police an excuse to pry.** Lastly, don't roll through that stop sign. Don't drive with expired plates or a busted tail light. Don't have your windows illegally tinted. Use your signal when making turns, and don't burn rubber. Pretextual stops are often found constitutional if there is an objective reason in addition to the pretext that justifies the stop. Don't give officers an excuse to stop you. Once you are stopped, things have a way of snowballing. If officers stop you, they start looking into your windows, center console, and if they see or smell something they don't like, it can turn into a full blown vehicle search. Keep your vehicle clean. Don't have an empty beer bottle on the floor. Don't have a pill box (even if lawfully prescribed) out in the open. Don't have a big switch blade (even if legal) hanging from your front visor. Keep things out of plain sight. Don't give the police an excuse to pry.

HOW TO FIND AN ATTORNEY

Law is divided into criminal and civil, although there are still what are called general practice lawyers, someone in a small firm or solo practice who might handle a wide range of legal matters. There are also law firms that specialize in a certain type of law, such as criminal law, civil litigation, business law, or family law, for example. Even within the broad areas of the law, such as criminal law, you may find a lawyer and firm that specializes in a type of case, such as DUIs (driving under the influence).

Matt Pinsker has been a prosecutor, a defense attorney, and a criminal justice professor working at the local, state, federal, and international level. Pinsker has suggestions for how to find and work with a lawyer who can help if you or a family member is arrested. Says Pinsker, "Over ninety percent of the people who end up in trouble in the criminal justice system are just ordinary people who made a bad decision but can get back on track."

Pinsker, an adjunct professor of homeland security and criminal justice in the L. Douglas Wilder School of Government and Public Affairs at Virginia Commonwealth University, says that looking for a lawyer to represent you is similar to shopping for a new car. "Just like cars, there's good ones, and there's bad ones. There are certain vehicles that are good for certain situation and not for others. The same thing is true for lawyers."

He suggests you apply the same logic to finding the right attorney. You could start by asking for referrals from any family or friends who have had a similar situation, or if they know someone to refer you to. Those connections could also steer you clear of lawyers you should avoid.

But you might not have those connections, or you might be embarrassed about admitting that you need help for a criminal charge, so here are some guidelines for finding a criminal defense attorney on your own. Whether the referral is through someone you know, an online search, or a referral from a national or local bar association, here are some questions to ask yourself to help you find the right lawyer for your case:

- Where did the charge happen?
- What court is it in?
- Does a particular lawyer have experience in this area? Is it in the right area of practice?
- How many cases of this type does the lawyer do?
- What percentage of their practice is handling your type of case?

Pinsker compares looking for a criminal lawyer with a particular area of expertise to searching for a doctor who focuses on a certain condition or disease. You would not go to a cardiologist if you needed to be treated for cancer. In the same way, a bankruptcy lawyer does not have the same skill set or experience as a criminal defense attorney.

Pinsker suggests finding a criminal defense attorney with at least five years of experience after law school. But, cautions Pinsker, "Experience is helpful to a point. Just because someone's been doing something longer doesn't mean they've been doing it right."

Pinsker continues, "Going back to the car analogy, what a lawyer charges may vary on many factors. Since most lawyers charge on the basis of time, how long a case may take will be a factor in the charge you are quoted."

Most criminal defense lawyers charge a flat fee. They may build a rider for additional costs into the projected charges if the case goes to trial, for example, but the flat fee may be more comforting to you since you will know what your cost for their services will be from the start, and can budget accordingly. If the lawyer underestimates how long a case will take and ends up undercharging you, they will just have to swallow the loss unless they made provisions for renegotiating their fee.

If you want to keep your fee as low as possible, avoid doing anything that might get you labeled a high maintenance client who will require more time or will be a pain to work with. If it looks like you're going to be calling three times a day, or you evidence the kind of personality that is difficult to deal with, your quoted fee might be higher than if you seem like a very reasonable client who will be pleasant to work with.

Avoid selecting a criminal defense attorney solely on the basis of the fee. Finding the right attorney is too important a decision for fee alone to be the deciding factor.

Try to meet the attorney in person.

Now that you have chosen the lawyer you or your family member will be working with, Pinsker's number one piece of advice is to be open and honest with your attorney. Do not lie, or it could backfire royally. For example, Pinsker had a new client who was accused of being in possession of stolen goods. But it's only a crime if the person knew the goods were stolen. Explains Pinsker, "It was a $14 tool from my client's retail shop. My client swore up and down that he did not know the item was stolen, and promised that he had not made any statements or confessions admitting to knowing the item was stolen. Without an admission to knowing the item was stolen, I was extremely confident I would win at trial and spent considerable time preparing for it, rather than working to negotiate a favorable plea deal. When I declined the plea offer and asked for a trial, the incredulous prosecutor asked me, 'What are you doing? Why don't you want to plead it out?' I told him we were going to take it to trial because he had zero evidence my client had any knowledge the tool was stolen, to which the prosecutor passed me a piece of paper in my client's handwriting and replied, 'How about your client's signed and written confession?'"

Pinsker explains, "In that case, because the client was preparing to go into the military, and the value of the item stolen was so minimal and someone else had given it to him, I was able to make a deal so that the client could plead guilty and still go into the military and not do any jail time. Still, a lot of time was wasted preparing for trial, I charged a higher rate because my client misled me into believing we'd go to trial, and most important of all, had the client not lied to me I would have spent the bulk of the work on the case not focused on a trial but instead negotiating a plea deal that would have likely led to an outright dismissal."

Once you find a criminal defense attorney, you will want to pay promptly and according to whatever agreement you have worked out. Be honest with your attorney, and be a pleasant client but not someone who is overly chatty. Only say what you need to say to establish and maintain a rapport with your attorney and/or sharing information you need to provide (or learn) pertaining to your case.

If You Are Accused of a Crime and Are Unable to Pay for an Attorney

The right to an attorney is guaranteed by the Sixth Amendment of the Constitution, originally written in 1789 and revised in 1992:

> In all criminal prosecutions, the accused shall enjoy the right to a speedy and public trial, by an impartial jury of the State and district wherein the crime shall have been committed, which district shall have been previously ascertained by law, and to be informed of the nature and cause of the accusation; to be confronted with the witnesses against him; to have compulsory process for obtaining witnesses in his favor, and to have the Assistance of Counsel for his defense.

The right to counsel was decided by the Supreme Court of the United States in the landmark *Gideon v. Wainwright* case, decided in favor of the plaintiff, Gideon, on March 18, 1963. This right is even part of the well-known Miranda warning that is required to be stated to anyone who is facing a criminal charge:

> You have the right to remain silent. Anything you say can and will be used against you in a court of law. *You have the right to an attorney. If you cannot afford an attorney, one will be appointed.*

Kevin Gres, the California-based criminal defense specialist whose tips began this chapter, even includes the right to remain silent right on his business card:

Client Advisement
If questioned by law enforcement state, "I exercise my right to remain silent. You may not question me further without my attorney present."

The court can appoint an attorney for you. A lot of public defenders get a bad reputation, which may not be deserved. Some court-appointed attorneys may be doing that work in addition to handling similar cases for clients who can pay their fees. The challenge with court-appointed attorneys is that they may have a humongous case load that might motivate them to "plea out" as many cases as possible, rather than take them to trial, which can be a long and drawn-out process, one requiring a lot of additional time for research, prepping witnesses and those who will testify, and numerous court appearances.

To find a public defender, search online for "public defender" and the name of your state. You might also go to the website for your state. For example, here is the website for the State Public Defender of Colorado:

Office of the Colorado State Public Defender
http://www.coloradodefenders.us/

Non-Criminal Legal Services
For help with civil legal matters for those unable to pay:
Legal Services Corporation (LSC)
3333 K Street NW
Washington, DC 20007
https://www.lsc.gov/
Established by an act of Congress in 1974, this independent nonprofit organization offers referrals to local participating legal services that provide free legal counsel to those who are eligible for assistance. LSC is also an information clearinghouse on poverty law in general available to attorneys or the general public.

National Legal Aid and Defender Association (NLADA)
1901 Pennsylvania Avenue NW, Suite 500
Washington, DC 20006
http://www.nlada.org/
A private, nonprofit national organization and information clearinghouse founded in 1911, devoting its resources to the support and development of

quality legal assistance for the poor. Membership includes attorneys, individuals, and legal services and defender programs around the country.

Southern Poverty Law Center (SPLC)

400 Washington Avenue
Montgomery, AL 36104
www.splcenter.org
Concerned with a range of issues from criminal justice reform and LGBT rights to immigrant rights and children's rights. Has a staff of more than 100 lawyers. From their website: "For more than four decades, we've won landmark cases that brought systemic reforms in the Deep South. We've toppled remnants of Jim Crow segregation and destroyed violent white supremacist groups. We've shattered barriers to equality for women, vulnerable children, the LGBT community and the disabled. We've protected migrant workers and immigrants from abuse, ensured the humane treatment of prisoners, reformed juvenile justice practices, and more."

Standing Committee on Lawyer Referral Service, American Bar Association (ABA)

321 North Clark Street
Chicago, IL 60654
https://www.americanbar.org/groups/lawyer_referral/
From their website: "The committee provides support and assistance to local public service lawyer referral programs that provide information on appropriate, quality legal services to the public. We offer a number of resources for local bar leaders and lawyer referral programs."

At the local level, there may be low-cost legal services available for those who would not meet the means test for free services. Do a search locally to see what your state offers. For example, in New York, there are three key programs for those who fall into the reduced fee category: Moderate Means Program; Civil Court Project; and Co-op and Condo Mediation. For more information, go to https://www.nycbar.org/for-the-public/low-cost-legal-services.

Additional sources of information on legal matters, including professional associations for lawyers and career-related material:
National Academy of Elder Law Attorneys (NAELA)

NAELA Foundation
1577 Spring Hill Road, Suite 310
Vienna, VA 22182
https://www.naela.org/

Professional association for attorneys who specialize in the legal issues related to the elderly such as wills and trusts. A directory of member lawyers is available at the website.

American Academy of Matrimonial Lawyers (AAML)
150 N. Michigan Avenue, Suite 1420
Chicago, IL 60601
aaml.org
Founded in 1962. Academy Fellows practice family law. There is a "Find a lawyer" function at the website.

Nolo
7031 Koll Center Parkway, Suite 260
Pleasanton, CA 94566
https://www.nolo.com
Established in the late 1960s, Nolo is a source of information originally started by two legal aid attorneys who wanted to make legal advice accessible to more people. Nolo publishes books about law for the layperson. They also have a lot of information at their website, including a directory of lawyers: https://www.nolo.com/lawyers.

American Bar Association (ABA)
321 North Clark Street
Chicago, IL 60654
Washington DC Office
1050 Connecticut Avenue NW, Suite 400
Washington, DC 20036
https://www.americanbar.org
Founded in 1878, this active professional membership association for lawyers sponsors an annual conference. The ABA is affiliated with no fewer than twenty-eight national legal organizations including the American Immigration Lawyers Association, the National Legal Aid and Defender Association, and the National LGBT Bar Association. Complete list of all affiliates: https://www.americanbar.org/about_the_aba/affiliated_related_organizations.html.

National Association of Criminal Defense Lawyers (NACDL)
1660 L Street, NW 12th floor
Washington, DC 20036
https://www.nacdl.org/
This is a professional membership association of criminal defense attorneys. At the website you will find a directory that enables you to search for member attorneys by name, city and state, and area of practice, among other factors.

National Bar Association
https://nationalbar.org/
Membership organization founded in 1925 with more than 65,000 lawyer, law school educators, and law student members.

National District Attorney's Association (NDAA)
https://ndaa.org/
Founded in 1950, NDAA's membership consists of state prosecutors and assistant district attorneys (ADAs). Offers training, e-learning, and continuing education courses.

Institute for Judicial Administration, New York University School of Law
40 Washington Square South
New York, NY 10012
Founded in 1952, this institute, under the sponsorship of NYU School of Law, is interested in court moderation as well as offering judicial education. It sponsors the annual William J. Brennan Jr. lecture series and coordinates bar association and judicial council activities.

National Lawyers Guild
132 Nassau Street, Suite 922
New York, NY 10038
https://www.nlg.org/
Founded in 1937, this multiracial and progressive membership association is concerned with immigration, gay rights, prisons, treatment of women, grand jury abuse, and other timely and controversial issues.

Also check out listings in other chapters related to Dispute Resolution including Arbitration or Mediation as an alternative to legal services.

IMMIGRATION

One of the most controversial issues in America today and around the world is immigration. In an ideal world, if someone wanted to relocate to another country, and there was nothing about that person, such as a criminal history that might make that individual a threat to the adopted country, why not let that person in and grant citizenship, either right away or after a probationary period? But it is not that simple. The application process can be long and complicated; the wish to immigrate can be desperate and immediate. This can lead to desperate actions culminating in entering a country illegally and in some cases fatally, such as boats that overturn in route from Syria to Turkey, or, as Daniel Gonzalez points out in his article, "Border crossers, and the desert that claims them," the increasing number of migrants who die in their attempts to cross into the US from Mexico. According to the article, by the end of June 2017, the remains of eighty-one migrants had been found in southern Arizona.

Both legal and illegal immigration are complicated issues that may require more than just immigration help. Some of the crossover issues could be everything from Education or Legal Services to Pregnancy and Childbirth to Crime Victims. (See pertinent chapters for these resources.)

American Civic Association
131 Front Street
Binghamton, NY, 13905-3101
https://www.americancivic.com/
From their website: "The American Civic Association has been dedicated to its mission of helping immigrants and refugees and building bridges of under-standing between foreign- and native-born communities since 1939. We are a registered 501(c)(3) nonprofit organization." They offer immigration services at reduced fees. In the Binghamton area, they offer free ESL (English as a Second Language) courses to anyone nineteen or older.

American Immigration Lawyers Association (AILA)
1331 G Street NW, Suite 300
Washington, DC 20005
https://www.aila.org/
Started in 1946, this professional membership organization is for approximately 15,000 lawyers who practice in the area of immigration law. There is a free refer-ral service: https://www.ailalawyer.com/. The site is available in English and Spanish. You will also find additional information, such as "Know Your Rights Handout: If ICE Visits a Home, Employer, or Public Space": https://www.aila.org/advo-media/tools/psas/know-your-rights-handouts-if-ice-visits and available in seven languages besides English including Punjabi, Arabic, Portuguese, Haitian Creole, Spanish, and Chinese.

Catholic Charities USA
2050 Ballenger Ave, Suite 400
Alexandria, VA 22314
https://www.catholiccharitiesusa.org
From their website: "Catholic Charities has been providing assistance to immi-grants and refugees for more than 100 years. Our agencies help them adjust to

life in the United States by offering a wide range of social and legal services that help them get established in the community. The services include housing and financial assistance, employment and training, language classes, adjustment of status, counseling, and other support. We advocate for just and compassionate migration and refugee policies that respect the life and dignity of each person."

Center for Immigration Studies
1629 K Street NW, Suite 600
Washington, DC 20006
https://cis.org
From their website: "The Center for Immigration Studies is an independent, non-partisan, non-profit research organization founded in 1985. It is the nation's only think tank devoted exclusively to research and policy analysis of the economic, social, demographic, fiscal, and other impacts of immigration on the United States."

Immigration Equality
https://www.immigrationequality.org/
From their website: "Immigration Equality is the nation's leading LGBTQ immigrant rights organization. We represent and advocate for people from around the world fleeing violence, abuse, and persecution because of their sexual orientation, gender identity, or HIV status." Check out the related Resources listed at the site.

Immigration and Ethnic History Society
https://iehs.org/
Publishes a quarterly journal. They offer a syllabus for teaching immigration at http://editions.lib.umn.edu/immigrationsyllabus/about/.

Nolo
https://www.nolo.com
Nolo is a source of information originally started by two legal aid attorneys who wanted to make legal advice accessible to more people. Immigration lawyers listed by state: https://www.nolo.com/lawyers/immigration-law

Government resources on immigration:
US Citizenship and Immigration Services
US Department of Homeland Security
https://www.uscis.gov/
Find your nearest field office at https://www.uscis.gov/about-us/find-uscis-office. "Path to Citizenship" is at https://www.uscis.gov/us-citizenship/citizenship-

through-naturalization/path-us-citizenship. "A Guide to Naturalization" is at https:
//www.uscis.gov/us-citizenship/citizenship-through-naturalization/guide
-naturalization, along with much more additional information.

Reading and Audiovisual Materials

Daniel Gonzalez, "Border Crossers, and the Desert that Claims Them." Posted at *USA Today* network, 2017.

Emily Doskow. *Nolo's Essential Guide to Divorce*. 7th edition. Pleasanton, CA: Nolo, 2018.

Helen Thorpe. *The Newcomers: Finding Refuge, Friendship, and Hope in America*. NY: Scribner, 2018.

Michael H. Roffer. *The Law Book: From Hammurabi to the International Criminal Court, 250 Milestones in the History of Law*. NY: Sterling, 2015.

Rene A. Wormser. *The Story of the Law and the Men Who Made It—From the Earliest Times to the Present*. Revised and Updated. NY: Simon & Schuster, 1962, 1949.

Sean Patrick. *The Know Your Bill of Rights Book: Don't Lose Your Constitutional Rights—Learn Them!* Oculus Publishers, 2012.

CHAPTER 22

LGBTQ (Lesbian, Gay, Bisexual, Transgender, and Questioning)

In September 2018, India overruled a 150-year ban on homosexuality. In 2015 the US Supreme Court ruled in *Obergefell v. Hodges* that same-sex couples couple can marry and have the same rights as heterosexual couples. These steps forward make it seem like discrimination against anyone who is LGBTQ (lesbian, gay, bisexual, transgender, and questioning) is over. But in some parts of the world, and in the hearts and minds of some individuals, being gay is still considered immoral even if it is legal. As *The Guardian* pointed out in a 2017 article, being gay is still illegal in seventy-two countries; it can result in the death penalty in eight.

This chapter highlights some of the resources that those in the LGBTQ community might find useful, especially in dealing with the bullying that may still occur at school, at work, or in communities because of someone's sexual orientation. Finding help for that type of prejudice and bullying is important, since we know from statistics released by organizations like the Trevor Project that LBGTQ youths are five times more likely to attempt suicide than heterosexual youths.

Ali Forney Center
224 West 35th Street, 15th Floor
New York, NY 10001
https://www.aliforneycenter.org/
Ali Forney was a homeless gender-nonconforming youth who liked helping others. Carl Siciliano met Ali when he was seventeen, when Carl was working at a drop-in center for homeless youths. Five years later, when Ali was only

twenty-two, he was murdered. That tragedy motivated Carl to start the Ali Forney Center, a place for homeless LGBT youths to stay and get food, medical care, and mental health services, as well as job readiness training.

Astraea Lesbian Foundation for Justice
116 East 16th Street, 7th Floor
New York, NY 10003
https://crm.astraeafoundation.org
Founded in 1977, a philanthropic foundation to support the cause of LGBT around the world.

Audre Lorde Project
85 South Oxford Street
Brooklyn, NY 11217-1607
https://alp.org/
From their website: "a Lesbian, Gay, Bisexual, Two Spirit, Trans and Gender Non-Conforming People of Color community organizing center, focusing on the New York City area."

GATE
http://transactivists.org/
gate@transactivists.org
From their website: "We are an international organization working on gender identity, sex characteristics and, more broadly, on bodily diversity issues."

Gay Men's Health Center (GMHC)
307 West 38th Street
New York, NY 10018
http://www.gmhc.org/
An organization concerned with HIV/AIDS prevention, cure, and advocacy. From their website: "In 1981, six gay men (and their friends) gathered in writer Larry Kramer's living room to address the 'gay cancer' and raise money for research. This informal meeting provided the foundation for what would soon become Gay Men's Health Crisis."

Human Rights Campaign (HRC)
1640 Rhode Island Avenue NW
Washington, DC 20036-3278
https://www.hrc.org/
A civil rights organization concerned with the gay community being treated fairly. Moved into its permanent building in Washington, DC in 2003.

Immigration Equality

https://www.immigrationequality.org/

This organization provides legal services to lesbian, gay, bisexual, transgender, and HIV-positive immigrants who seek asylum in the United States because they live in one of the 70+ countries where being LGBTQ is a crime.

See complete listing in Chapter 21, Legal Services, under "Immigration."

National Center for Lesbian Rights

870 Market Street, Suite 370

San Francisco, CA 94102

Washington, DC office

1776 K Street NW, Suite 852

Washington, DC 20006

http://www.nclrights.org/

Established in 1977, this is a nonprofit organization offering information, legal referrals, and advocacy: http://www.nclrights.org/legal-help/

National Center for Transgender Equality (NCTE)

1133 19th Street NW, Suite 302

Washington, DC 20036

https://transequality.org/

Founded in 2003. Covers a wide range of issues affecting transgender people including aging, race, employment, health and HIV, housing and homelessness, non-discrimination laws, and more.

National Resource Center on LGBT Aging

c/o SAGE

305 Seventh Avenue, 6th Floor

New York, NY 10001

https://www.lgbtagingcenter.org/

From their website: "Established in 2010 through a federal grant from the US Department of Health and Human Services, the National Resource Center on LGBT Aging provides training, technical assistance and educational resources to aging providers, LGBT organizations and LGBT older adults. The center is led by Services & Advocacy for GLBT Elders (SAGE) in collaboration with 18 leading organizations from around the country."

PFLAG

http://www.pflag.org/

An organization for parents and friends of LGBTQ people. To find a chapter: http://www.pflag.org/find-a-chapter.

Pride at Work
815 16th Street NW
Washington, DC 20006
https://www.prideatwork.org/
From their website: "We seek full equality for LGBTQ Workers in our workplaces and unions." Some of the issues that Pride at Work is concerned about include combating workplace discrimination and bathroom access.

Stonewall
192 St. John Street
London EC1V 4JY, UK
https://www.stonewall.org.uk
Founded in 1989, this organization, based in the United Kingdom, has the goal of helping those in the LBGTQ community to feel accepted.

Sylvia Rivera Law Project
147 W. 24th Street, 5th Floor
New York, NY 10011
https://srlp.org/
From their website: "The Sylvia Rivera Law Project works to guarantee that all people are free to self-determine gender identity and expression, regardless of income or race, and without facing harassment, discrimination or violence." SRLP offers legal help as well as trainings and workshops.

It Gets Better Project
Los Angeles, CA
https://itgetsbetter.org
info@itgetsbetter.org
From their website: "In 2010, Dan Savage and his partner, Terry Miller, uttered three words that would give rise to a global movement focused on empowerment of LGBTQ+ youth–*it gets better*." They have created over 60,000 videos of youths sharing their stories. Go to: https://itgetsbetter.org/stories/ Dan Savage founded It Gets Better Project because too many LGBTQ were being driven to suicide because of bullying.

The Trevor Project
PO Box 69232
West Hollywood, CA 90069
http://www.TheTrevorProject.org
info@thetrevorproject.org
Helpline: 866-4-U-TREVOR (24/7 help for LGBTQ youth having suicidal thoughts)

The founders are the creators of TREVOR, a short that won the Academy Award® in 1988. The Trevor Project is a national, 24/7 crisis and suicide prevention helpline for lesbian, gay, bisexual, and transgender youth, 25 and younger. They have The Lifeguard Workshop available for online training for middle and high school school teachers.

A sample of local programs for the LGBTQ community includes:
The Center
Lesbian, Gay, Bisexual, and Transgender Community Center
208 W. 13th Street
New York, NY 10011
https://gaycenter.org
The Center offers information and referrals; substance abuse treatment; free HIV testing; arts, entertainment, and cultural events; and other services. List of related resources: https://gaycenter.org/resources/.

SF LGBT Center
1800 Market Street
San Francisco, CA 94102
www.sfcenter.org
This center offers information and referrals to services including housing, health, wellness, immigration, small business, trans employment, and socializing concerns. Check out the events calendar the site for the extensive activities offered at the center. They are also always looking for volunteers.

Reading and Audiovisual Materials

Cathie Sheets. "10 Amazing LGBT Organizations to Donate to This Year (Part 1)." https://www.pride.com/lgbt/2016/4/22/10-amazing-lgbt-organizations-you-should-donate-year-part-1

Center for Disease Control and Prevention. "LGBT Youth." https://www.cdc.gov/lgbthealth/youth.htm

Kate Bornstein. *Gender Outlaw: On Men, Women, and the Rest of Us.* NY: Penguin Random House, 2016.

Merle Miller. *On Being Different: What It Means to Be a Homosexual.* Foreword by Dan Savage. NY: Penguin, 2012, 1971.

Pamela Duncan. "Gay relationships are still criminalised in 72 countries, report finds." *Guardian*, July 27, 2017. https://www.theguardian.com/world/2017/jul/27/gay-relationships-still-criminalised-countries-report

"Supporting Your LGBTQ Youth: A Guide for Foster Parents." https:
//www.childwelfare.gov/pubs/lgbtqyouth/

The Trevor Report. "Preventing Suicide: Facts About Suicide." https:
//www.thetrevorproject.org/resources/preventing-suicide/facts-about
-suicide/#sm.0000k854if12icwyx1b1mwa76fado

CHAPTER 23

Offenders, Inmates, and the Formerly Incarcerated

In the decades that I have been involved in the criminal justice system—as a researcher, author, volunteer, crime prevention resource center director, and full-time or adjunct college professor—I have seen a definite shift in the way the government, the public, and those who are incarcerated or formerly incarcerated are being treated as well as how they see themselves. There is a movement to reconsider the mass incarceration that led to the prison population multiplying from 200,000 just a few decades ago to the estimated 2.2 million or more men and women in prison at the local, state, and federal level today. As the Prison Policy Initiative and others point out, the United States has the highest incarceration rate in the world (https://www .prisonpolicy.org). Add in the number of Americans under the supervision of the criminal justice system for probation or parole, that number goes up to around 7 million. A quick way to get an overview of the number and type of offenders who are incarcerated in the United States is through the chart developed by the Prison Policy Initiative, "Mass Incarceration: The Whole Pie 2018," updated annually and posted online.

Alternatives to incarceration are being pursued more vigorously especially for non-violent and first offenders. Bail reform efforts are being pursued so fewer are jailed while awaiting a plea bargain or a trial. There is an increased use of drug court as an alternative to incarceration. But one of the most important takeaways from the two-day Smart on Crime Innovation Conference that I attended at John Jay College of Criminal Justice on September 25-26, 2018, was that there are hundreds of thousands who are sent to or returned to prison, not for new crimes, but for parole or probation violations. This is a serious situation that needs to be addressed.

After years characterized by the War on Drugs, which led to the incarceration of hundreds of thousands for drug offenses, as well as a decline in funding education for inmates, the twenty-first century has seen an advocacy for different and more progressive attitudes toward offenders, inmates, and the formerly incarcerated. An encouraging sign of change is the rise in educational opportunities for those incarcerated. For example, the Prison-to-College Pipeline (http://johnjaypri.org/educational-initiatives/prison-to-college-pipeline/) is an innovative program in New York State, which is administered by the Prison Reentry Institute at John Jay College of Criminal Justice. This program starts in prison and then, upon release, as long as certain criteria have been met, guarantees the formerly incarcerated a place at a college participating in the program (see listing below for more information).

In this chapter, you will find a selection of organizations and agencies that are helping offenders, inmates, and the formerly incarcerated, as well as their families, to deal with the impact of the criminal justice system on their lives. Although not listed as separate entries, there are countless examples of the formerly incarcerated doing productive things after their prison experiences. Some even use the experience to educate others, such as: Anthony Papa, who became an artist and an advocate for change in the drug laws, as well as the author of two books, including *15 to Life: How I Painted My Way to Freedom*; Randy Kearse, who used his prison experiences to write a self-help book entitled *Changin' Your Game Plan*; and Julio Briones, who used ten years of the twelve-year sentence he served to start his own company called Briones Consulting Group(https://www.thebrionesgroup.com/) based in New Jersey and offering workshops and seminars, as well as coaching on what to do if you are arrested and how to best deal with the incarceration experience.

Government resources that deal with prisons:
Federal Bureau of Prisons
320 First Street NW
Washington, DC 20534
https://www.bop.gov
Started by Herbert Hoover in 1940, this agency administers all the federal prisons in the United States: https://www.bop.gov/locations/list.jsp. You may find an inmate by name or number: https://www.bop.gov/inmateloc/.

There are 102 federal prisons, which operate at five security levels (although the 2016 Survey of Prison Inmates (see listing in Reading Materials) puts the number of federal prisons at 193). The federal prison population in 2017 was 185,617, down from a high in 2015 of 205,723: https://www.bop.gov/about/statistics/population_statistics.jsp#old_pops .

Prisons (Correctional Facilities) by State

Each state has its own correctional system. The 2016 Survey of Prison Inmates (SPI) conducted by BJS Statisticians (see listing in Reading Materials) listed the number of state correctional facilities at 1,808 state prisons. Local communities, such as cities and even suburbs, have their own local jails as well. You can find your local or state correctional facility by searching online or by visiting the website for your locality or state. The federal government also offers a portal that will direct you to your state's department of corrections: https://www.usa.gov/corrections.

These national organizations offer help to offenders and/or inmates:

American Civil Liberties Union (ACLU)
125 Broad Street, 18th Floor
New York, NY 10004
https://www.aclu.org
Founded in 1920, the ACLU is dedicated to preserving the rights of all Americans as protected by the Constitution. Some of its key issues are capital punishment, reforming the criminal justice system, and juvenile justice.

Drug Policy Alliance (DPA)
http://www.drugpolicy.org/
An advocacy nonprofit organization whose mission is the reform of harsh drug incarceration policies that were an outgrowth of the war on drugs.
See complete listing in Chapter 1, Addiction.

Extended Family
http://www.extendedfamilyhelp.org/
Tagline at website: "A support system for family of prisoners."
This organization, founded in 2003, helps those who have a family member in jail or prison to deal with the experience. Their site has an extensive database of helpful resources: http://www.extendedfamilyhelp.org/resource-database/.

The Last Mile (TLM)
San Francisco
https://thelastmile.org/
info@thelastmile.org

A nonprofit educational organization founded in 2010 after Chris Redlitz was invited to be a guest speaker at San Quentin State Prison because of his background in venture capital. He and his wife and business partner, Beverly Parenti, developed an education and career-training program which initially was a 6-month intensive entrepreneurial training program with a focus on technology. Since 2014, in partnership with the California Department of Corrections and Rehabilitation (CDCR) and CalPIA, they have been providing computer-coding training at the correctional facility.

The Lionheart Foundation
PO Box 170115
Boston, MA 02117
https://lionheart.org
questions@lionheart.org
Established in 1992, this nonprofit organization is "dedicated to providing social emotional learning (SEL) programs to incarcerated adults, youth at risk and teen parents in order to significantly alter their life course." From their website: "Houses of Healing. Lionheart's prison program provides education, rehabilitation and reentry support to incarcerated men and women in prisons and jails throughout the United States. At the heart of this initiative is a powerful emotional literacy program, Houses of Healing. This program offers prison inmates encouragement and the necessary support to take stock of the life experiences that have propelled them into criminal activity, take responsibility for their criminal behavior, change lifelong patterns of violence and addiction, and build productive lives."

Their teachings are based on the book, *Houses of Healing: A Prisoner's Guide to Inner Power and Freedom* by Robin Casarjian, who is Executive Director. In addition to their Prison Project they have a project for teens to help them make better choices than violence and crime: https://lionheart.org/youth_at_risk/the-power-source-program/.

National Lawyers Guild
132 Nassau Street, RM 922
New York, NY 10038
http://jailhouselaw.org/
Offers a free handbook that can be downloaded from their website for inmates who want to "file a Section 1983 lawsuit in federal court regarding poor conditions in prison and/or abuse by prison staff. It also contains limited information about legal research and the American legal system." (from the Prison Law Project online listing)

Prison Book Program
c/o Lucy Parsons Bookstore
1306 Hancock Street, Suite 100
Quincy, MA 02169
http://prisonbookprogram.org/
Mails books to prisons to help them with their educational and vocational pursuits with the hope that it will help reduce recidivism, or returning to prison after their release. To have a book sent to a loved one in prison: https://prison bookprogram.org/resources/request-books/. There is also a list of the books they most need to have donated, including dictionaries, business, and self-help books: https://prisonbookprogram.org/donatesection/donate-books/top -book-requests/.

Prison Fellowship
44180 Riverside Parkway
Lansdowne, VA 20176
https://www.prisonfellowship.org
Chuck Colson, former White House Counsel to President Richard Nixon, voluntarily pleaded guilty to obstruction of justice on a Watergate-related charge. He served seven months at the federal prison in Alabama. After that experience, he pledged to help those who were still incarcerated, founding the Prison Fellowship. From their website: "Prison Fellowship seeks to restore those affected by crime and incarceration by introducing prisoners, victims, and their families to a new hope available through Jesus Christ."

Prison Policy Initiative
PO Box 127
Northampton, MA 01061
https://www.prisonpolicy.org
From their website: "The non-profit, non-partisan Prison Policy Initiative produces cutting edge research to expose the broader harm of mass criminalization, and then sparks advocacy campaigns to create a more just society." Although they do not provide legal services to those who are incarcerated, they do provide a resource list, by state, of those providing such services: https://www.prison policy.org/resources/legal/. They state that they automatically remove from the database any entry that has not been confirmed by the organization within the last year.

Right on Crime
901 Congress Avenue
Austin, TX 78701
http://rightoncrime.com/

From their website: "Right on Crime is a national campaign to promote success-ful, conservative solutions on American criminal justice policy–reforming the system to ensure public safety, shrink government, and save taxpayers money. By sharing research and policy ideas and mobilizing strong conservative voices, we work to raise awareness of the growing support for effective reforms within the conservative movement. We are transforming the debate on criminal jus-tice in America." They are concerned with juvenile justice, victims, prisons, adult probation, law enforcement, the opioid crisis, parole and reentry, pretrial, fines and fees, substance abuse, overcriminalization, and more. Right on Crime is a project of the Texas Public Policy Foundation in partnership with the American Conservative Union Foundation and Prison Fellowship (see listing above).

TASC (Treatment Alternatives for Safe Communities)
700 S. Clinton Street
Chicago, IL 60607
www2.tasc.org
Started in Illinois in 1976, there are now TASC programs throughout the US. From the LinkedIn description for TASC of Illinois: "TASC, Inc. is a statewide, non-profit organization in Illinois that advocates for and serves people in courts, jails, prisons, and child welfare systems who have alcohol/drug and mental health problems." Priorities include alternatives to incarceration and reentry services.

Center for Health and Justice
700 S. Clinton St.
Chicago, IL 60607
http://www2.centerforhealthandjustice.org/
Services include consulting, training, research, and public policy initiatives such as Jail Diversion for Veterans: http://www2.centerforhealthandjustice.org/content/project/jail-diversion-veterans.

Voices From Within
https://www.voicesfromwithin.org
This is a multimedia project that started at Sing Sing Correctional Facility, a maximum security state prison in Ossining, New York. Superintendent Michael Capra got together several inmates who are doing hard time, some life sen-tences, because of gun violence. Together with Dateline producer Dan Slepian they produced a powerful six minute short film where the men share about the consequences of their choices with the hope they can inspire others, especially teens, to avoid gun violence. Their next project is on addiction.

The link to the video is included in the Resource section at the end of this chapter.

For those who believe they have been wrongly convicted:
Innocence Project
40 Worth Street, Suite 701
New York, NY 10013
https://www.innocenceproject.org/
From their website: "The Innocence Project, founded in 1992 by Peter Neufeld and Barry Scheck at Cardozo School of Law, exonerates the wrongly convicted through DNA testing and reforms the criminal justice system to prevent future injustice." Since its founding, The Innocence Project has exonerated 350 formerly incarcerated offenders due to DNA evidence.

Help for offenders and for the formerly incarcerated including reentry challenges
Exodus Transitional Community
2271 Third Avenue, Second Floor
New York, NY 10035
www.etcny.org
Three locations: East Harlem, Poughkeepsie, and Newburgh. In March 1999, Julio Medina founded Exodus Transitional Community after spending twelve years at Sing Sing Correctional Facility. Almost everyone working at Exodus, a nonprofit organization, has been affected by the justice system. They are there to help youths and others to gain employment and deal with substance abuse and mental health issues. They offer an individualized approach to the issues that those who are released from jail or prison have to face.

Federal Bureau of Prisons
The BOP provides resources for those who are formerly incarcerated, including information on how to obtain your GED and links to information on getting a job: https://www.bop.gov/resources/former_inmate_resources.jsp.
(See complete listing above)

US Social Security Administration
https://www.ssa.gov/reentry/
Offers information on obtaining Social Security or other benefits after incarceration: https://www.ssa.gov/reentry/benefits.htm.

Help for Felons
https://helpforfelons.org
Offers legal information, job leads, recommended books, and suggestions for financial help for those who were formerly incarcerated. They are also open to submissions and publication of articles at their website. Reentry programs by state: https://helpforfelons.org/reentry-programs-ex-offenders-state/.

The Osborne Association
809 Westchester Avenue
Bronx, NY 10455
www.osborneny.org

The history of The Osborne Association is a unique one in that its founder, Thomas Osborne, the former mayor of Auburn, New York, voluntarily spent a week inside a prison to learn, first-hand, what the experience was like for those who are incarcerated. Later, Osborne became warden at Sing Sing Correctional Facility, known for his reformed approach to managing a prison. In 1933, following Osborne's death, The Osborne Association was founded to perpetuate his innovative approach to incarceration and alternatives to prison.

From their website: "The Osborne Association offers opportunities for individuals who have been in conflict with the law to transform their lives through innovative, effective, and replicable programs that serve the community by reducing crime and its human and economic costs. We offer opportunities for reform and rehabilitation through public education, advocacy, and alternatives to incarceration that respect the dignity of people and honor their capacity to change." Direct services are offered in New York City (Bronx, Manhattan, and Brooklyn office) and Newburgh, New York.

Institute for Justice and Opportunity at John Jay College (formerly the Prisoner Reentry Institute)
524 W 59th Street
New York, NY 10019
https://justiceandopportunity.org

Founded in 2005. Conducts research and also provides direct help to the formerly incarcerated who are reentering society. One of their initiatives is offering a free, 10-week course, Tech 101, to help the formerly incarcerated to learn the computer skills that they probably missed out on during their time in prison to help them with life skills and enhanced job options.

One of their programs is the Prison-to-College Pipeline, which enables inmates in selected prisons in New York State to take college courses while incarcerated and, upon release, if they meet certain criteria, to continue their education at a cooperating college. For more information, go to: https://justice andopportunity.org/educational-pathways/prison-to-college-pipeline/.

Statewide programs that are helping offenders to reenter society and reduce recidivism (getting rearrested and/or sent back to prison):
Fortune Society
29-76 Northern Boulevard
Long Island City, NY 11101
https://fortunesociety.org

In 1967, David Rothenberg produced the off-Broadway play, *Fortune and Men's Eyes*. The play led to audience discussions which were the catalyst for starting the Fortune Society. They now serve 7,000 individuals annually through their self-help support groups, housing through the residences in Manhattan, and help with finding a job, mental health treatment, substance abuse treatment, and other aids to help in reentry. Approximately 50 percent of the staff at the Fortune Society were formerly incarcerated.

The Fortune Society is looking for volunteers. See complete details in Chapter 33, Volunteerism.

Hope House
Bronx, NY
https://hopehouse.nyc/
info@hopehouse.nyc
Hope House NYC is a project of The Ladies of Hope Ministries. It is a free place for formerly incarcerated single women to stay for up to one year after their release providing a positive re-entry experience. Plans are underway to expand the Hope House model to other cities and states including New Orleans and Detroit.

Open Doors
485 Plainfield Street
Providence, RI 02909
www.opendoorsri.org
admin@opendoorsri.org
Helps those released from prison to find housing, register to vote, find a job, apply for food stamps, and pay their taxes. Their Reentry Case Management program works with those in the Men's Minimum-Security Facility at the Department of Corrections for up to six months before their release to set things up for their reentry.

Pioneer Human Services
7440 West Marginal Way S.
Seattle, WA 98108
https://pioneerhumanservices.org/
Jack Dalton opened one half-way house in Seattle in 1963. Since that time, Pioneer Human Services has grown to more than 50 locations throughout the state of Washington. Their advocacy and direct services for the formerly incarcerated revolve around housing, employment, vacating criminal records, and other issues.

Reading and Other Materials

Ann Edenfield. *Family Arrested: How to Survive the Incarceration of a Loved One*. Americana Publishing, 2002.

Anthony Papa, *15 to Life: How I Painted My Way to Freedom*. NY: Feral House, 2004.

—. *This Side of Freedom: Life After Clemency*. CreateSpace, 2016.

Bernard B. Kerik. *From Jailer to Jailed: My Journey from Correction and Police Commissioner to Inmate #84888-054*. NY: Threshold Editions, Simon & Schuster, Inc., 2015.

Dan Slepian, producre, Michael Capra, Superintendent. *Voices from Within*. Six minute documentary about gun violence. Produced at Sing Sing Correctional Facility and filed with inmates serving sentences for gun violence. Available at: https://www.youtube.com/watch?v=unSvcD7xnsY.

Eric Mayo. *From Jail to a Job: Get the Edge and Get Hired*. Pleasantville, NJ: Believe Publications, 2005, 2012.

Gordon Hawkins. *The Prison: Policy and Practice*. Chicago, IL: University of Chicago Press, 1976.

H. Bruce Franklin, editor. Foreword by Tom Wicker. *Prison Writing in 20th-Century America*. NY: Penguin, 1998.

John Grisham. *The Innocent Man: Murder and Injustice in a Small Town*. NY: Dell, 2012.

Julio Briones. *Surviving Arrest: The Complete Guide*. NJ, 2018.

Kirk Blackard. *Nurturing Peace: How Families Can Help Incarcerated Loved Ones Change Their Lives*. Bridges to Life Books, 2014.

Mariel Alper and Lauren Glaze. "Data Collection: Survey of Prison Inmates (SPI), BJS (Bureau of Justice Statistics), 2016, posted at https://www.bjs.gov/index.cfm?ty=dcdetail&iid=488

Megan Comfort. *Doing Time Together: Love and Family in the Shadow of the Prison*. Chicago, IL: University of Chicago Press, 2008.

Michelle Alexander. *The New Jim Crow*. NY: The New Press, 2012.

Peter Wagner and Wendy Sawyer. "Mass Incarceration: The Whole Pie 2018" Posted Mrach 14, 2018 at the Prison Policy Initiative. https://www.prisonpolicy.org/reports/pie2018.htm

Randy Kearse. *Changin' Your Game Plan: How I Used Incarceration as a Stepping-stone for SUCCESS*. NY: Positive Urban Literature Inc., 4th edition, 2015.

Ronald L. Krannich, PhD. *Best Jobs for Ex-Offenders: 101 Opportunities to Jump-Start Your New Life*. Second edition. Manassas, VA: Impact Publications, 2015.

—. *The Ex-Offender's Re-Entry Success guide: Smart Choices for Making It on the Outside*. Manassas, VA: Impact Publications, 2016.

Ronald Stefanski. *Jobs for Felons: The Past Is Behind You, Now It's Time to Get to Work*. Amazon Digital Services, 2015.

Valdez, Rudy, filmmaker and director. *The Sentence*. Documentary distributed by HBO. 2018.

Wes Denham. *Arrested: What to Do When Your Loved One's in Jail*. Chicago, IL: Chicago Review Press, 2010.

CHAPTER 24

Parenting, Stepparenting, Grandparenting, and Family

The parent-child relationships, both mother-child and father-child, are the first and most fundamental relationships that each and every one of us experience. The parent-child relationship starts long before birth. From the moment of conception, through pregnancy, childbirth, and those first minutes, hours, days, weeks, months, and even years of parent-child interaction, not only one's relationship to one's parent is being formed, but the infant's and then the child's relationships to others are being shaped by those parent-child connections.

Some of the anecdotes we hear about how our mother or father did or did not connect to us right at birth, or what our mother's pregnancy was like, can tell a lot about the bonding we did or did not receive from the beginning. There's the bonding that happens between parent and child during those pregnancy months and soon after birth and the bonding that hopefully happens throughout the child's formative years.

No two childhoods are the same, even if siblings share the same parents. Since parents can interact differently with each child, and the personality of each child is unique, the parent-child connection that each child experiences is special. So it doesn't really help if your sibling tells you that her view of your childhood is radically different, whether better or worse, from your view. Your view is your view and dealing with your parent-child relationship is the work of a lifetime.

Probably the most important insight I can share about parent-child relationships is that if you lacked the optimal relationship with your own parents that you wanted growing up, you can still try to get along better with them once you are an adult yourself. It may take literally years of work to try to achieve that goal. I've observed that too many give up before they achieve those changes, but if you can keep trying, you may be pleasantly surprised, even in a small way, when your parent or parents shift their behavior toward you.

Even if they do not, you still have a chance with your own children to be the parent you always wanted your parents to be. By being that good parent to your own children, you internalize the good parent, even if you feel what you received from your parents was less than ideal.

There are few generalizations you can make today about the typical family in the United States or even internationally. As divorce and as single parenting have become more acceptable, you will still of course find examples of the traditional nuclear family—married father, mother, and one or more biological children—but variations are more common than ever before. There are families with stepparents or what is now called a blended family, because of divorce, widowhood, or remarriage. Single parenting including the increase in single adoptions is common, as is living together before or in lieu of marriage, single by choice, couples or singles that are childfree by choice, as well as same-sex couples. Grandparenting today may mean seeing your grandchildren occasionally, helping out by babysitting, or even full-time parenting. What is considered a family today is definitely varied, but the goal for parents, stepparents, grandparents, and families in general has remained consistent: to love, educate, and discipline one's children as you prepare them to take flight and become independent. Families, whether nuclear or extended, usually share the goal of wanting to get along and stay connected, especially if they are living far apart.

Some parenting or family issues are just a matter of style, like whether you eat together as a family every night during your children's formative years, or at what age you feel your child is old enough to have his or her own cell phone. But other issues, like making sure you never leave an infant or child alone in a car especially if it could get overheated, are a matter of life and death. As the website Kids and Cars (https://www.kidsandcars.org) notes, 39 children died in the United States from being left in a hot car in 2016; in 2017 there were 43; and 51 in 2018.

The impact of a new child on a couple or a single person is a huge issue that today's new parents are faced with. One of the most controversial issues that all parents have to deal with is how they will discipline an unruly child. How do you discipline with love, avoiding the potential immediate or long-term damage that being overly punitive can cause a child or teen?

Getting help with parenting, stepparenting, and even grandparenting may be just what you need if your friends are not going through what you are experiencing or are at a different stage in life, or your own parents are busy, are too far away, or have passed on. Also, if there are ways that you were parented that you do not want to follow with your own children, this could be the perfect time to seek out better alternatives for your own family.

Sometimes help finds you in unique ways. When my older sister Eileen, who lives in Washington, DC, had her daughter Vanessa in 1984, her pediatrician suggested that my sister contact some of the other mothers in his practice who had given birth around the same time. So began her mother's group that still gets together even now for a monthly dinner. By contrast, when my son Scott was born six months later and I told my pediatrician about that idea, he said that was not something he was prepared to do. But I was determined, however, and got the word out through local newspapers and newsletters that I was looking to connect with other new mothers, and for at least the next six months a few of us got together with our infants on a regular basis.

Information or direct help related to parenting:
American College of Obstetricians and Gynecologists (ACOG)
409 Twelfth Street SW
Washington, DC 20024-2188
http://www.acog.org
This is the professional membership association of obstetricians and gynecologists that publishes lots of information on women's health issues, including postpartum depression and employment issues: https://www.acog.org/Womens-Health/Employment-Considerations-During-Pregnancy .

Care.com
Headquarters
201 Jones Road, Suite 500
Waltham, MA 02451
www.care.com
Company founded in 2006 that matches caregivers with a range of individuals and families needing care including parents and their children, seniors with health issues, as well as those needing tutoring and housekeeping.

Center for Parent Information and Resources (CPIR)
c/o Statewide Parent Advocacy Network (SPAN)
35 Halsey Street, 4th Floor

Newark, NJ 07102
https://www.parentcenterhub.org

Empowering Parents
https://www.empoweringparents.com
From their website: "Empowering Parents has been giving readers 'straight talk and real results' since 2007. We are committed to providing parents and caregivers with sound advice using the same Cognitive Behavioral Therapy principles that The Total Transformation and our other parenting programs are based upon."

March of Dimes
1275 Mamaroneck Avenue
White Plains, NY 10605
https://www.marchofdimes.org
Since 1938, the March of Dimes, a nonprofit organization, has been dedicated to research and advocacy on behalf of infants, including related conditions such as postpartum depression. It was founded by President Franklin D. Roosevelt to deal with polio under the name of the National Foundation for Infantile Paralysis.

Parenting and Childhood Education (P.A.C.E.)
https://www.pacemoms.org
Started in 1973, new parents connect through P.A.C.E. to share information, experiences, and to form friendships with others going through the same life-changing parenting transformation. From the website: "P.A.C.E. is a non-profit organization (501C3) which provides educational & emotional support groups for first and second time moms in DC, NOVA, & Montgomery County, Maryland to promote family well-being. P.A.C.E. does not offer medical, psychological, social work or psychiatric professional services."

UrbanSitter
https://www.urbansitter.com
A service available in over 60 cities that matches babysitters or nannies with parents in need of help. At the website you will find information for parents on how it works and fees, as well as how potential sitters can apply to become part of their roster of available sitters. This San Francisco-based company was founded in 2010.

Family Planning
Planned Parenthood
https://www.plannedparenthood.org/
Founded over 100 years ago, in 1916, Planned Parenthood offers information and direct services in the area of sex education and reproductive health and rights.

National Family Planning & Reproductive Health Association (NFPRHA)
1025 Vermont Avenue NW, Suite 800
Washington, DC 20005
info@nfprha.org
https://www.nationalfamilyplanning.org/
Mission statement: "NFPRHA advances and elevates the importance of family planning in the nation's health care system and promotes and supports the work of family planning providers and administrators, especially those in the safety net."

United Nations Population Fund (UNFPA)
https://www.unfpa.org/family-planning
From the website: "UNFPA works to support family planning by: ensuring a steady, reliable supply of quality contraceptives; strengthening national health systems; advocating for policies supportive of family planning; and gathering data to support this work. UNFPA also provides global leadership in increasing access to family planning, by convening partners–including governments–to develop evidence and policies, and by offering programmatic, technical and financial assistance to developing countries."

Parenting issues such as discipline and education. Certain key listings are only mentioned here with a more complete listing in Chapter 7, Children and Teens:
American Academy of Pediatrics (AAP)
345 Park Boulevard
Itasca, IL 60143
https://www.aap.org
Professional membership organization of 67,000 pediatricians concerned with the total health of infants, children, teens, and young adults.

Child Abuse Prevention Program (CAPP), The New York Foundling
(Do a search at the https://www.nyfoundling.org website for the CAPP program)
Started in 1986, the CAPP program uses puppets to teach children how to recognize and report child abuse so they are able to grow up in the safe environment that every child deserves.

Kids and Cars
https://www.kidsandcars.org
email@kidsandcars.org
For a more complete listing, see the listing in Chapter 8, Consumer Affairs and Safety.
Founded by Janette Fennell, whose family's carjacking was the impetus to her car safety initiatives and the founding of Kids and Cars.

National Parenting Education Network (NPEN)
www.npen.org
Started in 1996, this is a membership organization that offers training and certification to those in the parent education field. State-by-state directory of local parenting education direct help: http://npen.org/professional-development/parenting-education-networks-organizations-and-programs-by-state/.

National Parent Helpline, operated by Parents Anonymous
1-855-4AParent (1-855-427-2736)
Remember their motto: "Asking for Help is a Sign of Strength."
Launched on February 1, 2011 "to provide emotional support and resources to parents and caregivers."
Hours of operation: Monday through Friday, 10 a.m. PST to 7 p.m. PST

New Dream
PO Box 797
Charlottesville, VA 22902
https://newdream.org
Dedicated to emphasizing a non-materialistic approach as reflected in their campaigns, including "Simplify the holidays": https://newdream.org/simplify-the-holidays.

Parents Anonymous
250 West First Street, Suite 250
Claremont, CA 91711
parentsanonymous.org
From their website: "Parents Anonymous Inc. was founded in 1969 through the extraordinary efforts of Jolly K., a courageous and tenacious mother who sought help to create a safe and caring home for her family. Faced with personal traumas and mental health issues of her children she sought help, support, hope and build upon her strengths to foster a brighter future for her family and millions of others. Her tenacity has inspired and encouraged so many families worldwide."
Operates the National Parent Helpline (see separate listing above).

Positive Parenting Solutions
Raleigh, NC
https://www.positiveparentingsolutions.com
Has an informative blog on parenting issues by parenting expert Amy McCready: https://www.positiveparentingsolutions.com/parenting-blog. McCready is the author of If I Have to Tell You One More Time . . . The Revolutionary Program That Gets Your Kids to Listen without Nagging, Reminding, or Yelling (Tarcher, 1994, 3rd edition, 2011).

Raising Children Network
The Australian Parenting Website
raisingchildren.net.au
Launched in 2006, this is a site packed with information on all aspects of parenting including newborns, children, teens, and adults, as well as such topics as language development, discipline, autism, and disability. From their website: "Created by a partnership of member organisations of Australia's leading early childhood agencies, the Raising Children website is produced with the help of an extensive network including the Australian Government." More than 60,000 subscribe to their free parenting newsletter.

Safe Kids Worldwide
1255 23rd Street, NW, Suite 400
Washington, DC 20037-1151
https://www.safekids.org
Founded in 1988. From their website: "Safe Kids works with an extensive network of more than 400 coalitions in the United States and with partners in more than 30 countries to reduce traffic injuries, drownings, falls, burns, poisonings and more."

Stepparenting and blended families:
National Stepfamily Resource Center (NSRC)
www.stepfamilies.info
Stepparenting groups listed by state: http://www.stepfamilies.info/support-groups.php.
     This is a Division of Auburn University's Center for Children, Youth & Families (CCYF) in Auburn, Alabama.

Second Wives Café
https://secondwivescafe.com
Email: mary@secondwivescafe.com
Founded by California-based Mary Kuris. Offers online interaction and support for second wives as well as stepmothers.

The Stepfamily Foundation Inc.
http://www.stepfamily.org/
Jeannette Lofas founded the association in 1976, a year after her book, *Living in Step*, co-authored with Ruth Roosevelt, was published by McGraw-Hill.

StepMom Magazine
www.StepMomMagazine.com
A monthly magazine devoted to the needs of stepmoms.

StepTogether
www.steptogether.org/
This is an online virtual support group since 1998 that includes a Message Board and a Resource section with recommended readings and links to related websites.

Grandparenting:
Ask Granny
https://askgranny.com/
Provides information on various aspects of grandparenting, including cooking with grandchildren, gifts to get, and other issues. Created by Juliet Hambros.

Foster Grandparents
https://www.nationalservice.gov/programs/senior-corps/senior-corps-programs/fostergrandparents
A government program for seniors age 55 and over who want to be part of the Senior Corps in the role of a foster grandparent.
See the complete listing in Chapter 2, Adoption and Foster Care.

GRAND Magazine
4791 Baywood Point Drive S
St. Petersburg, FL 33711
www.grandmagazine.com
Online magazine on grandparenting-related matters including grandparent rights, nicknames, raising grandchildren, relationships, and health and fitness.

Grandparents Rights Organization (GRO)
1760 South Telegraph Road
Bloomfield Hills, MI 48302
https://www.grandparentsrights.org/
From their website: "The Grandparents Rights Organization is a national volunteer nonprofit organization founded in 1984 by founder and executive director, attorney Richard S. Victor. Its purpose is to educate and support grandparents and grandchildren and to advocate their desire to continue a relationship that may be threatened with loss of contact or amputation, usually following: family acrimony; a child being born out of wedlock; the death of one of the child's parents or the divorce of the grandchild's parents."

National Association for Grandparenting
https://grandkidsmatter.org
info@grandkidsmatter.org
A membership organization founded in January 2016 by Ken R. Canfield, PhD, who has ten grandchildren. There are articles at the website as well as a list of stations that carry Dr. Canfield's related radio show.

FAMILY

So much has been written about sibling rivalry that most of us just take it for granted. Maybe that's a good thing because if you just accept that sibling rivalry is a natural phenomenon, it can free you to focus on what is joyful. It's like accepting any reality as a truism. Once you accept it, you can go beyond it instead of judging it, trying to apologize for it, or pretending it does not exist.

You can even verbalize about it and sometimes that can make it less powerful. "I know we may have some sibling rivalry, but . . ." and fill in the blank.

Just like every other relationship in our lives as we age and go through different life cycles, those relationships can change, for better or worse. Your siblings may become very different from the brothers or sisters you grew up with once you're all out of the house, grown up, and living your own adult lives. Especially if you don't live near each other and rarely get together, your siblings may need you to get to know them all over again, learning about each other and how you have each changed or stayed the same.

Probably the biggest mistake that siblings can make in their older years is to take each other for granted or to dwell on the past and not spend time in the present, strengthening and deepening those precious and special sibling bonds. If sharing the same parents was the draw in the adult sibling relationship, especially after one or both parents pass on, it's time to bond to each other as siblings now that your parents can't be the connection.

Extended family has probably had the best benefit from the widespread popularity of Facebook and other social media. These are the aunts and uncles, the first and second cousins, that you probably weren't going to get to see all that much anyway. But at least now, almost like a newsletter for your extended family, you can find out who's getting married and who's died, who's graduating, and where your cousins are vacationing.

But those social media postings still don't take the place of getting together. My parents wrote letters to each other during the years my father was away during World War II, when he was a dentist in the army. I used to enjoy reading those letters as a kid, finding them in the attic. What I learned from those letters was how important cousins and extended family were to my parents and their generation.

My generation, because almost all of my aunts, uncles, and first cousins grew up within one hour of each other in Queens and Long Island, New York, were very close. But my children, growing up hours away from their nearest first cousins, did not have those same experiences. Now that my children are grown, and also because I've become more aware of how much extended family can mean to all of us, I'm trying to make up for lost time. Going to extended family weddings no matter how far away. Taking the time to connect on Facebook with as many extended family members as possible.

Yes, today it seems harder than ever to make the time for extended family since there is only so much time to go around. For most of us, immediate family comes first, along with our jobs, and our friends, but extended families, even if they're spread far away, are part of our key relationships.

Putting together an extended family reunion, whether yearly, biannually, or even every decade, can help aunts, uncles, and cousins to build on those extended family connections and relationships but can be taken for granted. Using videoconferencing to have a remote reunion, although not as good as getting together in person, is an option more and more families are turning to. Free options such as Zoom (https://www.zoom.us), as well as Google Hangouts, Microsoft Teams, Skype, and even FaceTime on your iPhone are ways to strengthen those extended family bonds.

Resources not covered in the above Parenting, Stepparenting, or Grandparenting sections:
23 and Me
Mountain View, CA
https://www.23andme.com/
Fee-based service to have your DNA analyzed to find out about your ancestry. You can also opt into a relative finder option to see if you share the same DNA with others in their database.

Ancestry.com
1300 West Traverse Parkway
Lehi, UT 84043
https://www.ancestry.com/
Fee-based resource for finding out your family history, including seeing what your DNA test reveals. Offers a free 14-day trial.

Center on Children and Families
Brookings Institution

1775 Massachusetts Avenue, NW
Washington, DC 20036
https://www.brookings.edu/center/center-on-children-and-families/
From their website: "The Center on Children and Families studies policies that affect the well-being of America's children and their parents, especially children in less advantaged families. The Center addresses the issues of poverty, inequality, and lack of opportunity in the United States and seeks to find more effective means of addressing these problems."

Extended Family
http://www.extendedfamilyhelp.org/
This organization helps those who have a family member in jail or prison to deal with the experience. See complete listing in Chapter 23, Offenders, Inmates, and Formerly Incarcerated.

Families Forward
https://www.families-forward.org/
See complete listing in Chapter 20, Housing and Homelessness.

My Event
45 Rockefeller Plaza, Suite 2000
New York, NY 10111
https://myevent.com
Since 2002, this site has been helping families to plan reunions. There is a basic free version or you can buy the premium or advanced version with more options for helping you to plan and grow your reunion.

Administration for Children & Families (ACF)
Office of Family Assistance
US Department of Health & Human Services
330 C Street, S.W.
Washington, DC 20201
https://www.acf.hhs.gov/ofa
From their website: "ACF provides states with block grants to design and operate programs to meet Temporary Assistance for Needy Families (TANF) goals": https://www.acf.hhs.gov/ofa/help.

Strong Family Alliance
https://strongfamilyalliance.org/
From their website: "Strong Family Alliance is a non-profit organization focused on supporting parents of children in the LGBTQ+ community. Strong Family Alliance gives parents accurate information, insights, ways to keep their child

safe and healthy, and encouragement to lead with love and solve problems over time." There is a lot of free information at their website for parents who might need assistance in dealing with their LGBTQ child or teen.

For related listings, see Chapter 22, LGBTQ.

Military Families
Blue Star Families
PO Box 230637
Encinitas, CA 92023
https://bluestarfam.org
Started in 2009 by military spouse Kathy Roth-Douquet, this organization has information as well as access to free resources and available services help for those in the military who may frequently move or be deployed.

FOCUS (Families OverComing Under Stress)
760 Westwood Plaza Room, A8-159
Los Angeles, CA 90024
www.focusproject.org
From their website: "Grounded in decades of research on family resilience and prevention programs, FOCUS was adapted for military families by a team from UCLA and Harvard Medical School. Since 2008, FOCUS Program has provided state of the art family resilience services to military families, children and couples. FOCUS is now located at designated Navy, Marine Corps, Army, and Air Force installations, and offered to all military families, including Special Operations Command, through the Department of Defense Office of Military Community & Family Policy." To find the FOCUS program closest to you: https://focusproject.org/contact.

Military Families United
P.O. Box 930073
Wixom, MI 48393
http://www.militaryfamiliesunited.org/
Founded in 2005. From their website: "Military Families United is a not-for-profit 501(c)(3) charitable organization whose mission is to Honor the Fallen, Support Those Who Fight, and Serve Their Families. We are a coalition of Blue Star, Gold Star, Next of Kin, Veterans, and Patriotic American Families who share a deep appreciation for our men and women in uniform and support them in their mission to keep America safe." The website has an extensive Resources section with links to related organizations for everything from education, employment, and moving to kids and teens and physical and emotional support.

Operation Homefront (OH)
1355 Central Parkway S, Suite 100
San Antonio, TX 78232
https://www.operationhomefront.org/
info@OperationHomefront.org
Within 24 to 72 hours, this organization provides emergency funding and other
help to the families of service members and warriors who are wounded.

*Please note: Help for former military families is included in the listings
in Chapter 29, Veterans.*

Reading and Audiovisual Materials

365 Daily Affirmations for Healthy and Nurturing Relationships. Stamford,
   CT: Hannacroix Creek Books, Inc., 2016. Audiobook narrated by
   Lindsay Arber.

Becky Anne Bailey. *Easy to Love, Difficult to Discipline: The Seven Basic
   Skills for Turning Conflict into Cooperation.* NY: Morrow, 2001.

Blended. (2014) Starring Adam Sandler and Drew Barrymore.

Charmaine L. Ciardi. *The Magic of Grandparenting.* NY: Holt, 2014.

Dennis Hevesi. "Police Say Mother Killed Missing Baby." *New York Times,*
   April 22, 1988.

Emily B. Visher. *How to Win as a Stepfamily.* NY: Routledge, 1991.

Evan Thomas. Reporting by Dirk Johnson, Anne Gesalma, Verne E.
   Smith, Elise Pierce, Kevin Peraino, and Andrew Murr. "Motherhood
   and Murder: Andrea Yates was the ultimate caregiver—until
   depression and the strains of raising five children drove her to an
   unspeakable crime. Her descent into darkness." *Newsweek,* 2 July 2001.

Little Miss Sunshine. (2006) Starring Steve Carrell, Toni Collette, and Greg Kinear.

Mayo Clinic Staff. "Postpartum depression." August 11, 2015, Posted at
   their online site.

Parenthood. (1989) Directed by Ron Howard. Starring Steve Martin.

Sal Severe, PhD. *How to Behave So Your Children Will, Too!* NY: Penguin, 2003.

StepMom magazine, https://www.stepmommag.com/

Thomas Insel. "Post by Former NIMH Director Thomas Insel: Spotlight
   on Postpartum Depression." October 28, 2010.

WebMD. "Postpartum Depression." Reviewed by Traci C. Johnson, M.D.
   on April 11, 2018. https://www.webmd.com/depression/guide
   /postpartum-depression#1

CHAPTER 25

Pregnancy and Childbearing

PREGNANCY

One of the most important decisions a woman and her baby's father will make is how and where they want their baby to be delivered. Every aspect of the delivery is a decision and, as much as possible, each key aspect of that decision should be informed: whether the expectant mother will use drugs during the delivery, where the delivery will take place, and of course who will actually deliver. Although usually more of a medical decision than a personal preference, finding out that a cesarean section is necessary, and why, as well as the benefits and recovery aspects of the procedure, not to mention the cost, are all decisions related to pregnancy and childbearing.

Drug-free delivery is a principle of the Lamaze delivery technique. However, even if you plan to ask for drugs to help with your delivery, you may still want to study the Lamaze technique for the help it can offer on relaxation and proper breathing during labor.

Consider taking a childbirth education class if one is offered at the hospital where you will be delivering or at any of the parenting programs sponsored by the YWCAs, parenting or women's centers throughout the country.

American Academy of Pediatrics (AAP)
https://www.aap.org
See complete listing in Chapter 24, Parenting, Stepparenting, Grandparenting, and Family

American College of Nurse-Midwives (ACNM)
8403 Coleville Road, Suite 1550
Silver Spring, MD 20910
www.midwife.org

Professional membership organization of midwives that also provides information on becoming a midwife and referrals to sources of local midwife help.

American College of Obstetricians and Gynecologists (ACOG)
409 Twelfth Street, SW
Washington, DC 20024-2188
http://www.acog.org
Professional membership association of obstetricians and gynecologists that publishes numerous booklets on childbearing issues. Maintains a Directory of Fellows.

Baby Center
https://www.babycenter.com
Information portal on pregnancy and childbearing that was developed through its corporate affiliation with Johnson & Johnson, including a week-by-week brief illustrated guide to pregnancy: https://www.babycenter.com/pregnancy-week-by-week.

The Bump
195 Broadway, Fl. 25
New York, NY 10007
https://www.thebump.com
This site has been created by the company that also developed the popular sites The Knot and The Nest. Includes articles on pregnancy and childbearing as well as a place to have a baby gift registry.

International Cesarean Awareness Network (ICAN)
4975 Wyeth Mountain Road
Gunterville, AL 35976
www.ican-online.org
info@ican-online.org
From their website: "The International Cesarean Awareness Network is a non-profit organization whose mission is to improve maternal-child health by reducing preventable cesareans through education, supporting cesarean recovery, and advocating for vaginal birth after cesarean (VBAC)."

March of Dimes
www.marchofdimes.com
Founded in 1938 under the name National Foundation for Infantile Paralysis, this nonprofit is dedicated to helping to educate the public about the importance of prenatal care for pregnant women and reducing the number of premature births.

National Coalition for Infant Health (NCfIH)
1275 Pennsylvania Avenue NW, Suite 1100A
Washington, DC 20004
www.infanthealth.org
info@infanthealth.org
From their website: "The National Coalition for Infant Health educates and advocates on behalf of premature infants from birth to age two. NCfIH envisions safe, healthy infants whose families can access the information, care and treatment their babies need." Sponsors an annual summit on infant health. Offers an extensive list of resources: http://www.infanthealth.org/resources/.

CHILDBEARING (GIVING BIRTH)

Of course your first source of information on childbearing will be your OB/GYN, as well as trusted family and friends who have given birth. But you may have more general questions that do not require an answer from your physician, or you might want to connect with others who are about to give birth for support or suggestions. For any medical questions, however, make sure you consult with your physician since the listings that follow are for general knowledge only.

American Academy of Pediatrics (AAP)
See complete listing in Chapter 7, Children and Teens.

American College of Obstetricians and Gynecologists (ACOG)
http://www.acog.org
See complete listing above in "Pregnancy."

American College of Nurse-Midwives (ACNM)
www.midwife.org
See complete listing above in "Pregnancy."

Baby Center
https://www.babycenter.com
See complete listing above in "Pregnancy."
Labor and delivery: https://www.babycenter.com/pregnancy-labor-and-delivery. There is also a companion site, Pregnancy.com: https://www.pregnancy.com/labor_delivery.php.

Birth Partner Doulas (Doulas of Connecticut)
https://www.birthpartnersdoulas.com/
Started by Janet Hall Padgett in 1990. Doulas offer emotional and other help during the pregnancy, labor, and delivery that is different from the services of a midwife or the medical expertise of an OB/GYN. FAQ: https://www.birthpart nersdoulas.com/faqs.

Childbirth Connection
1875 Connecticut Avenue NW, Suite 650
Washington, DC 20009
www.childbirthconnection.org
From their website: "Since 1918, Childbirth Connection (known as Maternity Center Association until 2005) has worked on behalf of childbearing women, newborns and families to improve the quality of maternity care through research, education, advocacy and demonstration of maternity innovations." Information on planning a pregnancy, having a healthy pregnancy, and giving birth.

International Childbirth Education Association (ICEA)
110 Horizon Drive, Suite 210
Raleigh, NC 27615
https://icea.org
Membership organization for those interested in childbearing or in the health-care field.

Office on Women's Health
200 Independence Avenue SW
Washington, DC 20201
https://www.womenshealth.gov
At this government portal you will find a section entitled "Labor and birth" with information on the childbearing process: https://www.womenshealth.gov /pregnancy/childbirth-and-beyond/labor-and-birth.

Reading and Audiovisual Materials

Adrian Kulp. *We're Pregnant! The First Time Dad's Pregnancy Handbook.* Emeryville, CA: Rockridge Press, 2018.

Heidi Eisenberg and Sharon Mazel. *What to Expect When You're Expecting.* Fifth edition. NY: Workman, 2016.

Jennifer Lang, MD. *The Whole 9 Months: A Week-By-Week Pregnancy Nutrition Guide with Recipes for a Healthy Start.* Foreword by Jessica Alba. CA: Sonoma Press, 2016.

Myra J. Wick, MD, PhD. *Mayo Clinic Guide to a Healthy Pregnancy.* 2nd edition, revised and updated. Rochester, MN: Mayo Clinic, 2018.

Sheldon H. Cherry, MD. *Understanding Pregnancy and Childbirth.* Fourth edition. NJ: Wiley, 2004.

Woodland Friends. *My Life as a Baby: A First-Year Calendar (with stickers).* Westchester, NY: Peter Pauper Press, 2016.

CHAPTER 26

Relationships: Dating, Singleness, Divorce, Marriage, Friendship, and Work

DATING

With the delaying of marriage, the increase of permanent singleness, and dating because of divorce or widowhood, help with dating concerns is no longer something just for teenagers or those in their twenties. In most cases, help takes the form of suggestions of an app, like Tinder, or a website, like Match.com, and some basic cautionary tales about never giving out your personal information or meeting privately or even alone until you are confident enough to take that next step. Fortunately, the countless joyful stories of couples who meet through online dating sites or apps outweigh the occasional tragedy.

"Stay safe" is the best suggestion for those who are dating, whether you meet someone through a website, a dating app, or the more traditional ways of introductions through a mutual friend or at school or work.

There have always been dating coaches and professional matchmakers, options to consider if the idea of navigating the dating waters on your own is a bit daunting. However, if you have intimacy issues you need to deal with, a dating coach, however, is not a substitute for seeking out professional help from a psychiatrist, psychologist, clinical social worker, or other licensed mental health professional. For help in finding someone with those credentials, please refer to the listings in Chapter 9, Counseling, Depression, and Mental Health.

Elite Singles
https://dating.elitesingles.com
Commercial dating site; check the site for details about how their matching works as well as any fees.

Instantcheckmate
https://www.instantcheckmate.help/
Available on Google Play and the App Store.
Paid subscription service where members can sign up for unlimited access to background check reports.

Intelius
https://www.intelius.com/
Paid background check service that should reveal any arrest and conviction records, weapon permits, and other information from available government data.

Kelleher International
info@kelleher-international.com
Paid matchmaker firm founded in 1986 with locations throughout the US and Canada, headquartered in San Francisco.

Match.com
https://www.match.com/
This site, with its international versions in 24 countries, is one of the oldest online dating site options (since 1995). Check the site for how it goes about making the matches and any fees. A number of popular dating sites are owned and managed by Match.com including Our Time, PlentyofFish (POF.com), and OKCupid.

Our Time
https://www.ourtime.com
Online dating site for those over fifty. (Part of the company that includes various dating websites such as Match.com.)

Relationship Hero
https://relationshiphero.com
contact@relationshiphero.com
This is a phone service that charges by the length of time to talk with your coach. From their website: "We charge an affordable rate of $1.99 / minute to provide you with certified relationship coaching. For your first session, the first 10 minutes are free."

Tinder
https://tinder.com/
Dating app launched in 2012 that suggests potential matches based on whether or not someone falls within the gender and age range that the user has specified as well as other criteria.

Truthfinder
https://www.truthfinder.com
Paid background check service.

Zoosk
https://www.zoosk.com/
Dating app. You can use it for free, but you get more services with the paid subscription version.

Singleness, Including Divorce
(Please note: For help if you are widowed or a widower, please see the listings in Chapter 14, Dying, Death, and Dealing with Grief.)

Dating sites, apps, advice, and background check information are provided in the above "Dating" section. The listings below apply to being single in general, single parents, or those who are coping with the emotional or non-legal aspects of the divorce experience:

National Association of Divorce Professionals
401 E Las Olas Boulevard, #130-646
Fort Lauderdale, FL 33301
https://www.thenadp.com/
A professional association for those who help men and women through the divorce experience.

Parents Without Partners (PWP)
https://www.parentswithoutpartners.org/
This is a membership organization for single parents. It was founded in 1957 in New York City by two parents: a custodial and a non-custodial parent. To find local chapters throughout the US and Canada: https://www.parentswithoutpartners .org/page/FindChapter.

Single Parents Alliance of America
https://www.spaoa.org/
A free membership site with resources and offers for singles provided through Third Party Programs. To be eligible to join you have to be a single parent (male or female) and reside in the US.

MARRIAGE

Here are my ten suggestions that might help to nurture the love between you and your spouse:*

1. Make sexual intimacy a priority and find time for it, no matter how tired or preoccupied you are.
2. Eat dinner together and continue to go out on "dates" with each other on a steady basis, even once you have children.
3. Get off the phone or your computer as soon as your mate walks in the door, not because you are talking about something he or she should not hear, but because it is polite and shows that you care.
4. Don't badmouth your spouse to your friends or relatives. If you're having problems, deal with them in a constructive way, first with each other. If you need outside help, turn to someone you trust such as a religious or marriage counselor, psychologist, or psychiatrist.
5. Compromise, compromise, compromise.
6. Keep your sense of humor and the fun in your relationship and life together as you continue to be each other's best friend.
7. Divide up the necessary domestic chores so neither one feels the burden unfairly falls on her or his shoulders.
8. Make time for what you care about individually, as well as together, such as hobbies, spending time with a special friend, developing new interests, or sports activities.
9. Be positive and supportive. Don't criticize. If you have to be critical, offer what you say as feedback and say it in the gentlest, most nurturing way possible.
10. Actively work to keep the excitement in your relationship by keeping communication open between you and your mate, remembering and making a fuss over birthdays and anniversaries, planning and going on weekends away, excursions, and trips together.

*Reprinted, with permission, from *125 Ways to Meet the Love of Your Life*, 2nd edition, by Jan Yager. These suggestions also served as the basis of a blog post, "10 Tips for a Happy Marriage," available at my website, www .drjanyager.com.

Associations offering referrals to marriage therapists as well as other help available for couples who are married or living together in a committed relationship:

American Association for Marriage and Family Therapy (AAMFT)
https://www.aamft.org/
This is a professional membership association for those who counsel couples and families. Directory of more than 15,000 available therapists: https://www.aamft .org/Directories/Find_a_Therapist.aspx. They hold an annual conference and publish the *Journal of Marriage and Family Therapy*, among other publications.

International Association of Marriage and Family Counselors
http://www.iamfconline.org/
A professional association for those who counsel couples or families.

Marriage 365
270 Baker St E Suite 200
Costa Mesa, CA 92626
https://www.marriage365.org
From their website: "Marriage365 is a nonprofit that provides education for couples from engagement through marriage, from hurting to happy relationships, for all ages, races, religions, and countries."

FRIENDSHIP

More important than the number of friends that anyone has is the quality of those relationships. Feeling worthy of friendship is a necessary first step to developing and maintaining friendships. One of my favorite friendship affirmations is this first one from my friendship affirmation collection: "I am worthy of a positive friendship." (Affirmation #1, *365 Daily Affirmations for Friendship* by Jan Yager)

There are nostalgia friends that you grew up with or went to school with, whom you might cut more slack if they disappoint you than someone you just met within the last year or month. Your friend who cancels getting together a couple of times might seem to have stopped caring about you until you learn there are some health issues in her life that she didn't want to burden you with.

Today, some friends need to be taught how to be a friend by being someone who focuses on what she or he is giving, rather than what she or he is getting in return. There's an old adage, "To get a friend you have to be a friend," and it's as true today as ever.

Campaign to End Loneliness

CAN Mezzanine, Old Street 49-51 East Road
London N1 6AH
United Kingdom
https://www.campaigntoendloneliness.org/
Started in the United Kingdom in 2011, this organization seeks to identify and help those who are lonely, focused on the elderly.

SelfGrowth

www.selfgrowth.com
Co-founded by David and Michelle Riklan, this personal development site offers extensive articles and videos on friendship and other related relationship topics.

UCLA Parenting and Children's Friendship Program

760 Westwood Plaza, Room 27-384
Los Angeles, CA 90095
https://www.semel.ucla.edu/socialskills
Founded in 1982 by friendship expert Fred Frankel, PhD, it offers several programs, including a children's friendship program for first graders.

Girlfriendology

Cincinnati, OH
https://www.pinterest.com/Girlfriendology/
Founded in 2006 by Debba Haupert. Includes a blog, podcast, and community for fostering female friendships.

The Friendship Page

www.friendship.com.au
The Friendship Page, started in 1996 by Australian Bronwyn Polson, includes a friendship chat room and quotes on friendship, as well as highlighting the annual International Friendship Day. Includes a Find a Friend function.

Girlfriend Circles

www.girlfriendcircles.com
A membership friendship networking site started by Shasta Nelson to help women connect locally.

Facebook

www.facebook.com
This free site is usually more of a resource for keeping up with the friends you already have through sharing of status updates, comments, and photos. However, there are certainly countless examples of new friendships that started

on Facebook. (As with all social media, post information about yourself and your loved ones with care.)

Friendship Force International
400 West Peachtree Street Suite #4-980
Atlanta, GA 30308
www.thefriendship-force.org
Friendship Force was established in 1977 and now has chapters throughout the United States and in forty-five countries. Its "citizen ambassadors" travel abroad to live with host families.

International New Friends, Old Friends Week
http://drjanyager/2017/04/08/international-new-friends-old-friends-week-7-days-of-friendship-celebrations/
A week that I founded in 1997 under the previous name, National New Friends, Old Friends Week, to celebrate the friendships in our lives. The week takes place annually beginning on the first Sunday after Mother's Day (in the United States, usually in early May) and ending the following Saturday. Each day has a different theme, although you can just celebrate friendship throughout the week in a more general way.

For more information on this week, and what each day highlights, read my blog, "International New Friends, Old Friends Week: 7 Days of Friendship Celebrations," about this week: https://www.drjanyager.com/international-new -friends-old-friends-week-7-days-of-friendship-celebrations/.

When Friendship Hurts
https://www.whenfriendshiphurts.com
This is the site I created when my book, *When Friendship Hurts*, was published, with excepts from the book as well as original material related to the themes of how to try to salvage a friendship as well as how to break up with a friend. There is also a list of the twenty-one types of potentially negative friends, from Chapter 2.

WORK RELATIONSHIPS

Whether you work with coworkers at a job on site, or you are a self-employed entrepreneur or artist who only interacts with others on an occasional basis, or your employer has asked you to work remotely from home, temporarily or on a permanent basis, work relationships can make or break our careers. Those business connections can also make us feel good about ourselves or depressed and negative. Of course, it would be wonderful if you start a job and, within a few weeks or even months, become friends with one of your coworkers and that friendship is positive and healthy, and not compromising you or your friend at work in any way. But for most, friendship may not happen at work or it might actually complicate your work situation.

If you feel that you are not getting the positive feedback and connections with others that you prefer for your optimal performance at work, stay positive. That will help you to focus on your work and remind yourself that those who may be ignoring you, criticizing you, or even being downright rude have their own problems they're dealing with. It may have little or nothing to do with you if they are not singing your praises or making you feel as cherished and appreciated as you want to be.

Here are six suggestions for getting along better in your work relationships:*

1. Start by looking at your own behavior: are you consciously or unconsciously doing anything to trigger your coworker's behavior toward you? If so, change yourself to help improve things.
2. Think about when you first met this person: were you completely neutral or did you have a strong positive or negative attitude toward him or her from the start? Once you are aware of how you reacted initially you can better understand if your relationship got off to a positive or negative start and what to do now.
3. Give your coworker (boss or employee) the benefit of the doubt, unless of course there is strong evidence that you should be cautious because of documented issues that put you in jeopardy.
4. Try taking your colleague's point of view if you are not seeing eye to eye on something.
5. Agree to disagree so you can get along better at work.
6. Avoid getting into heated debates about politics or religion.

*Excerpted and adapted from *Who's That Sitting at My Desk? Workship, Friendship, or Foe?*, by Jan Yager, PhD.

Resources related to work relationships:
LinkedIn
LinkedIn.com
Popular free social media networking site for business friendships and relationships. In 2020, there were an estimated 610 million members throughout the United States and internationally. There is an optional premium membership version.

Society for Human Resource Management (SHRM)
1800 Duke Street
Alexandria, VA 22314
https://www.shrm.org
Professional membership organization for those working in HR (Human Resources). Has extensive research and reports related to the workplace, including work relationships.

Workplace Bullying Institute (WBI)
PO Box 578
Clarkston, WA 99403
http://www.workplacebullying.org/
Co-founded in 1997 by Gary Namie, PhD, and Ruth F. Namie, PhD. From their website: "WBI is the first and only US organization dedicated to the eradication of workplace bullying that combines help for individuals, research, books, public education, training for professionals-unions-employers, legislative advocacy, and consulting solutions for organizations."

Reading and Audiovisual Materials

AARP and contributors. "The Girlfriend." Weekly newsletter with friendship-related articles for those who are 40+. https://www.thegirlfriend.com/

Alexander Nehamas. *On Friendship*. NY: Basic Books, 2016.

Allie Volpe. "How to Get Your Friends to Stop Treating You Like a Therapist." The *New York Times*, October 19, 2020. Posted at https://www.nytimes.com/2020/10/19/smarter-living/how-to-get-your-friends-to-stop-treating-you-like-a-therapist.html.

David Riesman with Nathan Glazer and Reuel Denney. *The Lonely Crowd*. New Haven, CT: Yale University Press, 1961.

Diane Vaughan. *Uncoupling: Turning Points in Intimate Relationships*. NY: Vintage Books, 1990.

Harriet Lerner, *The Dance of Connection*. NY: HarperCollins, 2001.

—. *Why Won't You Apologize? Healing Big Betrayals and Everyday Hurts*. NY: Simon & Schuster, Inc., Touchstone, 2017.

Heidi Priebe. *This Is Me Letting You Go*. Brooklyn, NY: The Thought & Expression Company, 2016.

Helen Fisher. *Why We Love: The Nature and Chemistry of Romantic Love*. NY: Henry Holt, 2004.

Jan Yager. *125 Ways to Meet the Love of Your Life*. Second edition. Stamford, CT: Hannacroix Creek Books, Inc., 2016. Audiobook version narrated by Karen Commins and Drew Commins.

—. *365 Daily Affirmations for Friendship*. Stamford, CT: Hannacroix Creek Books, 2012. Audiobook version narrated by Tiffany Williams.

—. *365 Daily Affirmations for Healthy and Nurturing Relationships*. Stamford, CT: Hannacroix Creek Books, Inc., 2016. Audio book version narrated by Lindsay Arber, 2016.

—. *Business Protocol*. New York: Wiley, 1991. Second edition, Stamford, Ct: Hannacroix Creek Books, Inc., 2011. With new introduction, Audio book version.

—. *Friendgevity: Making and Keeping the Friends Who Enhance and Even Extend Your Life*. Stamford, CT: Hannacroix Creek Books, Inc., 2021.

—. *Friendshifts: The Power of Friendship and How It Shapes Our Lives*. Second edition. Stamford, CT: Hannacroix Creek Books, Inc., 1999, 1997. E-book version with new Introduction, 2013.

—. *Friendship: A Selected, Annotated Bibliography*. Garland Press, NY: 1985.

—. *When Friendship Hurts*. New York: Simon & Schuster, Inc., Touchstone Books, 2002. Ebook edition with new Introduction, 2010.

—. *Who's That Sitting at My Desk? Workship, Friendship, or Foe?* Stamford, CT: Hannacroix Creek Books, Inc., 2004.

Jennifer Taitz. *How to Be Single and Happy: Science-Based Strategies for Keeping Your Sanity While Looking for a Soul Mate*. NY: TarcherPerigee, 2018.

Karen Lindsey. *Friends as Family*. Boston, MA: Beacon Press, 1981.

Morten T. Hansen. *Great at Work*. NY: Simon & Schuster, 2018.

Murray S. Davis. *Intimate Relations*. New York, NY: The Free Press, 1973.

Natalie Madorsky Elman and Eileen Kennedy-Moore. *The Unwritten Rules of Friendship: Simple Strategies to Help Your Child Make Friends*. NY: Little, Brown, 2003.

Robert D. Putnam. *Bowling Alone*. NY: Simon & Schuster, 2000.

Ronna Lichtenberg. *It's Not Business, It's Personal: The 9 Relationship Principles That Power Your Career*. NY: Hachette Books, 2002.

Rosabeth Moss Kanter. *Men and Women of the Corporation*. New York, NY: Basic Books, 1977.

Shasta Nelson. *The Business of Friendship*. NY: HarperCollins, 2020.

CHAPTER 27

Suicide: Prevention and Related Issues

In 2018, we were shocked to learn of celebrities who seemed to have it all but who, sadly, chose to kill themselves: chef, TV star, and father Anthony Bourdain, 61; Kate Spade, fashion icon and mother, 55; and *Glee* TV star Mark Salling, just 35. They are only three of the faces of suicide in the US in 2018, which claimed 44,965 victims. In 2019, on November 20, nineteen-year-old Johnny Stack, the talented, handsome, and bright son of my colleague Laura Stack, became one of the 47,173 Americans who committed suicide that year, according to statistics provided by the National Institute of Mental Health, a division of the National Institute of Health. Those figures may actually be lower than the deaths due to suicide since the stigma associated with suicide may lead to underreporting. Suicide is a worldwide problem; according to the World Health Organization (WHO) online information, "Mental health, Suicide data," globally an estimated 800,000 people commit suicide each year.

After much consideration, I decided that I want to begin this chapter, an absolutely crucial chapter in *Help Yourself Now*, addressing prevention. You may also want to refer back to Chapter 9, Counseling, Depression, and Mental Health, because we know that there is a definite link among depression and suicide attempts and suicide.

SUICIDE PREVENTION

Getting help before someone succeeds in committing suicide is critical. Whether someone attempts suicide once, many, or dozens of times, preventing suicide is the goal.

The National Institute of Mental Health has a list of signs and symptoms that someone is at risk for suicide. You or your loved ones may find this list useful:

Signs and Symptoms

Source: National Institute of Mental Health website

The behaviors listed below may be signs that someone is thinking about suicide.

- Talking about wanting to die or wanting to kill themselves
- Talking about feeling empty, hopeless, or having no reason to live
- Making a plan or looking for a way to kill themselves, such as searching online, stockpiling pills, or buying a gun
- Talking about great guilt or shame
- Talking about feeling trapped or feeling that there are no solutions
- Feeling unbearable pain (emotional pain or physical pain)
- Talking about being a burden to others
- Using alcohol or drugs more often
- Acting anxious or agitated
- Withdrawing from family and friends
- Changing eating and/or sleeping habits
- Showing rage or talking about seeking revenge
- Taking great risks that could lead to death, such as driving extremely fast
- Talking or thinking about death often
- Displaying extreme mood swings, suddenly changing from very sad to very calm or happy
- Giving away important possessions
- Saying goodbye to friends and family
- Putting affairs in order, making a will

The Mayo Clinic staff, in "What to Do If Someone is Suicidal," suggests that you not leave the person alone and that you call 911 (or your local emergency number) and get immediate help. They also advise: "Or, if you think you can do so safely, take the person to the nearest hospital emergency room yourself."

Helplines (including text lines) dedicated to preventing suicide:

- National Suicide Prevention Lifeline: 1-800-273-TALK (8255) (Available 24 hours a day, 7 days a week.)
- National Hopeline Network: 1-800-SUICIDE (784-2433)
- National Youth Crisis Hotline: 1-800-448-4663
- Crisis Text Line (text HELLO to 741741)

Important Note: If someone you know is in crisis, call 911.

Organizations concerned with suicide prevention:
American Association of Suicidology (AAS)
5221 Wisconsin Avenue NW
Washington, DC 20015
https://www.suicidology.org/
This is a nonprofit membership organization. They also run a dedicated website related to National Suicide Prevention Week, which occurs every September: https://www.aas365.org/ There is also a National Center for the Prevention of Youth Suicide: https://www.suicidology.org/ncpys.

American Foundation for Suicide Prevention (AFSP)
99 Water Street, 11th floor
New York, NY 10028
https://afsp.org/
From their website: "Established in 1987, the American Foundation for Suicide Prevention (AFSP) is a voluntary health organization that gives those affected by suicide a nationwide community empowered by research, education and advocacy to take action against this leading cause of death."

Befrienders Worldwide
https://www.befrienders.org
info@befrienders.org
Provides information on how to set up a helpline as well as a suicide myths quiz. At the top of their front page is a dropdown menu to find a helpline in any country in the world. There is also a useful list of warning signs of suicide: https://www.befrienders.org/warning-signs.

International Association of Suicide Prevention (IASP)
https://www.iasp.info
Sponsors World Suicide Prevention Day in September each year. Suggested activities for that day: https://iasp.info/wspd2018/suggested-activities/.

The Jason Foundation, Inc.
18 Volunteer Drive
Hendersonville, TN 37075
jasonfoundation.com
contact@jasonfoundation.com
Dedicated to preventing teen suicide. Founded by Clark Flatt, who is President, following the July 16, 1997, death by suicide of his youngest son, Jason, who was sixteen years old. The Jason Foundation's efforts have also led to the passage in New Jersey in 2004 of The Jason Flatt Act, which is now in 20 states. It

requires that every year, for teachers to maintain their certification to teach, they are required to take a 2-hour youth suicide awareness and prevention course.

National Suicide Prevention Lifeline
https://suicidepreventionlifeline.org/
24/7 helpline: 1-800-273-8255
This is a national network of more than 170 local crisis centers promoting best practices. It also sponsors the annual National Suicide Prevention Month held every September. SAMHSA (Substance Abuse and Mental Health Services Admnistration), which is part of the US Department of Health and Human Services, funds the Lifeline and it is administered by Vibrant Emotional Health.

Samaritans
41 West Street, 4th Floor
Boston, MA 02111
https://samaritanshope.org/get-help/
Started in 1974 in Boston as the first US-based branch of the international Samaritans suicide-prevention assistance; offers free help by listening to those in danger of committing suicide who call in for help. They can also talk with those who are worried that a friend or relative is at risk for suicide and wonder what to do about it. Includes grief support services for those who have lost some-one to suicide: https://samaritanshope.org/our-services/grief-support-services/

SAVE (Suicide Awareness Voices of Education)
7900 Xerxes Avenue, Suite 810
Bloomington, MN 55431
https://save.org/
In 1989, ten years after Adina Wrobleski lost her daughter to suicide, she and five others founded SAVE. From their website: "SAVE works at the international, national, state and local levels to prevent suicide using a public health model in suicide prevention; concentrating its efforts on education and awareness."

Speaking of Suicide
https://www.speakingofsuicide.com/resources
Site developed and maintained by Stacey Freedenthal, PhD, LCSW, a Denver psychotherapist, suicidologist, and associate professor at the University of Denver Graduate School of Social Work. She is also author of *Helping the Suicidal Person*, published in 2017 by Routledge, an imprint of Taylor & Francis. At Dr. Freedenthal's website, in addition to the resources, you will find a blog with articles about suicide.

Suicide.org
http://www.suicide.org/international-suicide-hotlines.html
This is a nonprofit organization and website founded by Kevin Caruso, who serves as its Executive Director. It offers numerous categories of information related to suicide including bullying and suicide, recommended books, stigma, college students, the elderly and suicide, and much more.

Suicide Prevention Resource Center
43 Foundry Avenue
Waltham, MA 02453-8313
https://www.sprc.org/
This is a federally supported initiative to stop suicide. They offer in-person and online training, articles, and fact sheets.

Information from the key social media sites on suicide prevention:
Facebook.com
https://www.facebook.com/help/suicideprevention

Instagram.com
https://help.instagram.com/553490068054878

One of the many research efforts to try to understand and prevent suicide:
Center for the Study and Prevention of Suicide (CSPS)
University of Rochester Medical Center Department of Psychiatry
601 Elmwood Avenue
Rochester, NY 14642
https://www.urmc.rochester.edu/psychiatry/research/csps
From their website: "The University of Rochester Center for the Study and Prevention of Suicide (UR/CSPS) is dedicated to reducing mortality and morbidity from suicide and attempted suicide."

Help for Families of Those Impacted by Suicide Attempts and/or Suicide

The one universal theme for almost all those whose family member has chosen suicide is the wish that they had made another choice. Since they cannot go back in time and change what happened, they need to find an inner peace with their loved one's decision and their own grief and loss. Support groups with others who have experienced loss from suicide may be helpful for some but not for others. Sharing with friends, family, or even strangers may help some, while others find they prefer to grieve privately and silently. Some find writing in a journal or even writing a letter to the editor of their local newspaper may help somewhat.

I conducted an interview with my colleague, speaker Gina Carr, whose loved one chose suicide. Her teenage son ended his life in 2011. I asked her, "What was the one thing people did after this happened that you found helpful?"

Gina replied, "I think a very helpful thing was people calling or sending me private notes without any expectation that I would get back to them. Just letting me know that they were there to support me and love me if I needed them and that I didn't need to do anything. That was very helpful."

I asked Gina how long it took after her son's death to feel like herself again. She replied, "I would say I think it was about three years before I was feeling like, 'I am going to be okay,' and about five years before I felt somewhat like my normal self. But, I'll never be the same person I was before he passed."

Initially Gina joined a few Facebook groups related to recovering from the loss of a loved one. "I did find them helpful. I guess in the very beginning it was really important that I see the stories of others. People in my 'real life' just couldn't relate to what I was going through. There were a ton of Facebook groups out there for grieving moms. [But] I found the specialized groups about the loss of a child to suicide to be the most helpful."

Gina kindly answered my next question: "Besides missing your son, what's the hardest part of what happened?"

She replied, "The worst part of losing someone close to you to suicide is the constant second-guessing. It's very natural to say, 'What could I have done differently?' That's the hardest thing. If you can help people get through that, that would really be important."

Organizations that help with those who have lost a loved one; some focus only on suicide, also known as suicide bereavement, and some help those who have lost a loved one, regardless of the cause:
A Caring Hand–The Billy Esposito Foundation Bereavement Program
www.acaringhand.org
Offers an eleven-week support group program and other services to help children and teens who have lost a loved one. (See the complete listing in Chapter 14, "Dying, Death, and Delaing with Grief."

Alliance of Hope for Suicide Loss Survivors
http://www.allianceofhope.org/
Founded in 2008 by Ronnie Susan Walker, a licensed clinical mental health counselor whose stepson passed away by suicide in 1995. This is a community of more than 12,000 from around the world who have lost someone to suicide.

American Foundation for Suicide Prevention
199 Water Street, 11th floor
New York, NY 10038
https://afsp.org/
To find a local support group: https://afsp.org/find-support/ive-lost-someone/find-a-support-group/.

Samaritans
Boston and other communities in Massachusetts
Grief support services for those who have lost someone to suicide: https://samaritanshope.org/our-services/grief-support-services/.

Support After Suicide
PO Box 271
Richmond VIC 3121, Australia
http://www.supportaftersuicide.org.au/
Online site for those who have lost someone to suicide to connect with each other for support.

Reading and Audiovisual Materials

A. Alvarez. *The Savage God: A Study of Suicide.* NY: Norton, 1990.

American Foundation for Suicide Prevention. "Suicide Statistics." https://afsp.org/about-suicide/suicide-statistics/

Carla Fine. *No Time to Say Goodbye: Surviving the Suicide of a Loved One.* New York: Harmony, 1999.

Emile Durkheim. *Suicide: A Study in Sociology.* Translated by John A. Spaulding and George Simpson. Originally published in 1897 as *Le Suicide.* NY: The Free Press, 1997.

Francine Klagsbrun. *Too Young to Die: Youth and Suicide.* Boston: Houghton Mifflin, 1976.

Kate Fagan. *What Made Maddy Run: The Secret Struggles and Tragic Death of an All-American Teen.* NY: Little, Brown, 2017.

Kay Renfield Jamison. *Night Falls Fast: Understanding Suicide.* NY: Knopf, 1999.

Laura Stack, "What I Wish I Knew About the Signs of Suicide: Should I Blame Myself?" May 4, 2020 posted at https://johnnysambassadors.org/signs-of-suicide/

Mayo Clinic. "What to do when someone is suicidal." https://www.mayoclinic.org/diseases-conditions/suicide/in-depth/suicide/art-20044707

National Institute of Mental Health. "Suicide Prevention" and "Signs and Symptoms." https://www.nimh.nih.gov/health/topics/suicide-prevention/index.shtml

Rebecca Tervo. *Shattered: From Grief to Joy After My Son's Suicide.* Wandering Poet Publishing, 2017.

"Suicide Bereavement." https://www.lifeline.org.au/get-help/topics/suicide-bereavement

World Health Organization (WHO). "Mental health, Suicide data." Posted at https://www.who.int/mental_health/prevention/suicide/suicideprevent/en/

CHAPTER 28

Transportation, Travel, and Recreation

TRANSPORTATION

Getting around encompasses everything from car, train, or airplane travel to walking and even bike riding. Some key concerns related to transportation, travel, and recreation today include:

- Making sure all forms of public transportation including buses, trains, and airplanes, take the proper precautions to avoid passengers or staff getting sick
- Employee fatigue among long-haul truck drivers
- Having safe infrastructures, such as the bridges, tunnels, and highways which are the cornerstone of transportation
- Safety on the roads, aboard cruise ships, and in all modes of travel, domestic or global
- Advancing transportation and travel so it is more efficient and environmentally friendly, such as the use of electric or hybrid cars
- Increasing the speed of rail travel with the introduction of so-called bullet or high-speed trains
- Continuing to make more rural, suburban, and even urban towns and cities more accessible for walking, running, and bike transportation
- Providing free or low-cost transportation for those who are disabled or for anyone who is unable to drive
- Such developments as self-driving or autonomous cars, as well as flying cars, moving from the drawing board and testing phases to everyday realities

Campaigns to reduce injuries or fatalities because of drowsy, drunk, or drug-related driving are important initiatives that are seeing positive results.

We need to continue to get the message out that texting while driving—whether the vehicle is a car, boat, or train—is dangerous and unacceptable.

Federal agencies concerned with transportation and travel issues:
Federal Railroad Administration (FRA)
US Department of Transportation
1200 New Jersey Avenue, SE
Washington, DC 20590
https://railroads.dot.gov/
From their website: "The Federal Railroad Administration (FRA) was created by the Department of Transportation Act of 1966. It is one of ten agencies within the US Department of Transportation concerned with intermodal transportation."

National Transportation Safety Board (NTSB)
490 L'Enfant Plaza SW
Washington, DC 20594
https://www.ntsb.gov
From the website: "Since its inception [in 1926], the NTSB has investigated more than 132,000 aviation accidents and thousands of surface transportation accidents. On call 24 hours a day, 365 days a year, NTSB investigators travel throughout the country and to every corner of the world to investigate significant accidents and develop factual records and safety recommendations with one aim—to ensure that such accidents never happen again. The NTSB's Most Wanted List of Transportation Safety Improvements highlights safety-critical actions that DOT modal administrations, the USCG, and others need to take to help prevent accidents and save lives."
    The NTSB monitors accidents in the following categories of transportation: aviation, hazardous materials, highway, marine, pipeline, and railroad.

National Highway Traffic Safety Administration (NHTSA)
1200 New Jersey Avenue, SE
Washington, DC 20590
https://www.nhtsa.gov/
This government agency is focused on everything related to automotive travel, including drowsy driving, drug-impaired driving including driving while intoxicated, safety issues such as recalls of defective car parts like air bags, and even bicycle and pedestrian safety.
    To report a safety or vehicle complaint: https://www-odi.nhtsa.dot.gov/Vehicle Complaint/.

For complaints about airlines unrelated to security or safety, write to the Department of Transportation (DOT): https://www.transportation.gov/airconsumer/file-consumer-complaint.

If you are planning an international trip and you are concerned about the safety of your destination, go to this website to see if a travel advisory has been issued:
US Department of State
Bureau of Consular Affairs
https://travel.state.gov
Information on travel advisories: https://travel.state.gov/content/travel/en/travel advisories/traveladvisories.html/.
You put in the country you are traveling to and you will find out what the travel advisory or risk level is pertaining to that country:

1. Exercise normal precautions
2. Exercise increased caution
3. Reconsider travel
4. Do not travel

There is a color-coded map (https://travelmaps.state.gov/TSGMap/) that will tell you what level the US government considers a particular destination. The map is updated daily.

In addition to safety issues related to terrorism threats around the world, you may also find updates on any reported health risks, including the quality of the water or any recent reported contagious illnesses, especially infectious disease outbreaks.

US Coast Guard
Commandant (CG-09232)
US Coast Guard Headquarters Stop 7501
2703 Martin Luther King Jr. Avenue, SE
Washington, DC 20593-7501
http://www.uscgboating.org/
From their website: "The US Coast Guard's Boating Safety Division (CG-BSX-2) is dedicated to reducing loss of life, injuries, and property damage that occur on US waterways by improving the knowledge, skills, and abilities of recreational boaters."

Amtrak
60 Massachusetts Avenue NE
Washington, DC 20002-4285

https://www.amtrak.com
From their website: "Amtrak was originally established [May 1, 1971] by the Congressional Rail Passenger Service Act, which consolidated the US's existing 20 passenger railroads into one." You can sign up for a free Amtrak rewards account so you will be notified about any upcoming discounts. You may also collect points for each trip that you take, points that can be redeemed for free travel, hotel stays, or upgrades.

Rail Passengers Association
https://www.railpassengers.org
Founded in 1967, this organization works for the improvement and expansion of rail travel throughout the US. From their website: "The Rail Passengers Association (formerly NARP) is the only organization that acts as a voice for train passengers–particularly Amtrak customers, but also commuter rail and rail transit riders–on Capitol Hill, before the US Department of Transportation, and before Amtrak management. We are a source of straightforward factual information, presented in layman's terms, that is relied upon by lawmakers' staffs and by reporters."

Your state's Department of Transportation website will have information on transportation and travel issues in your state. For example, http://www.caltrans.ca.gov/ is the state of California's transportation department website. There you will find a wide range of materials—and it will be similar for most states—including how to report a traffic problem, potholes, and even how to apply for jobs at the agency.

Emergency Kit for the Car*
In case you are stranded, keep an emergency supply kit in your car with the addition of these automobile extras:

- Jumper cables
- Flares or reflective triangle
- Ice scraper
- Car cell phone charger
- Cat litter or sand for better tire traction

*This information is from the US Department of Homeland Security: https://www.ready.gov/car.

Prepare Your Vehicle for Emergencies*

Have a mechanic check the following on your vehicle regularly prior to an emergency:

- Antifreeze levels
- Battery and ignition system
- Brakes
- Exhaust system
- Fuel and air filters
- Heater and defroster
- Lights and flashing hazard lights
- Oil
- Thermostat
- Windshield wiper equipment and washer fluid level

*This information is from the US Department of Homeland Security: https://www.ready.gov/car.

Motorcycle Riding
If you ride a motorcycle, you need to be aware of the laws in each state that you will be riding in.
One source of information is the Motorcycle Legal Foundation: https://www.motorcyclelegalfoundation.com/
It has state-by-state information on what is required for anyone driving a motorcycle, such as whether a helmet is required: https://www.motorcyclelegalfoundation.com/state-by-state-guide-to-motorcycle-laws/.

Combating Drunk or Impaired Driving (Drugs or Drowsiness)
Mothers Against Drunk Driving (MADD)
511 E. John Carpenter Freeway
Irving, TX 75062
https://www.madd.org/
The 1980 death of thirteen-year-old Cari Lightner in California, caused by a drunk driver, was the incentive for her mother, Candace Lightner, to found MADD. There are local affiliates throughout the US. MADD is dedicated to making it safer to drive, be a passenger, or even be a pedestrian through its focus on reducing drunk and drugged driving as well as teen drinking. Through its educational campaigns and efforts, MADD claims to have reduced the number of deaths related to alcohol by more than 50%.

National Sleep Foundation Drowsy Driving Prevention Week
https://sleepfoundation.org/drowsy-driving
Sponsors the annual Drowsy Driving Prevention Week in November to draw attention to the preventable cause of injury and death on the road and even at work if someone is operating a dangerous machine.

TRAVEL

States have agencies for tourism that can provide a wealth of free information for any trips that you wish to make. Most countries also have a national tourist agency run by the government. There are also private companies that offer information on particular states, countries, or destinations.

Today, it is easier than ever to plan a trip on your own because of the internet. Airlines and railroad services have their own websites that enable you to book directly, or you can use one of the third-party sites, like Travelocity.com, Kayak.com, Orbitz.com, or Expedia.com, to name just a few. But do you want to do it all yourself or do you want some expert help? That's a question that you need to answer. Sometimes the travel help you seek is actually free because the travel agent is paid by the hotels or airlines that they are affiliated with. You do not have to pay them a commission. Sometimes, even if you have to pay the booking agent a commission or a fee, they may have such deals that are not offered to the general public that you do better using their services. There is also the time and trouble factor to consider. If you are going to a destination for the very first time, and you have little knowledge of the best airline to use, the hotels that will fit in your budget and offer you the best deal, or the restaurants that you should consider including in your itinerary, a travel expert might be worth consulting. There are online, ebook, and print travel guides that you can consult for expert suggestions.

A few of the travel companies you can contact about your upcoming travel plans:
HI USA
8401 Colesville Road, Suite 600
Silver Spring, MD 20910
https://www.hiusa.org
Formerly known as American Youth Hostels, this nonprofit membership organization has a history going back more than eighty years. It is a way for travelers to stay in much lower-cost lodging throughout the US and internationally.

Automobile Association of America (AAA)
1000 AAA Drive, #28
Heathrow, FL 32746
https://www.aaa.com

Founded in 1902. In addition to roadside assistance, AAA offers travel information for its tens of millions of members throughout the US and Canada as well as discounts on a range of services, including movie tickets.

Adventure Cycling Association
150 East Pine Street
PO Box 8308
Missoula, MT 59807
https://www.adventurecycling.org
From their website: "As a nonprofit organization, Adventure Cycling Association's mission is to inspire and empower people to travel by bicycle. Established in 1973 as Bikecentennial, we are the premier bicycle-travel organization in North America with more than 40 years of experience and 53,000 members."

Road Scholar
www.roadscholar.org
Formerly known as Elderhostel, a not-for-profit travel organization that promotes international opportunities for education, travel, and friendship. They sponsor intergenerational national and international trips.

For information on volunteering internationally, go to Chapter 30, Volunteerism.

Professional association for travel agents:
American Society of Travel Advisors
https://www.asta.org/
Founded in 1931. There are numerous events throughout the year, including the annual ASTA Global Convention, for members and related sponsors to attend.

RECREATION

We all know that taking breaks, including short day or weekend trips or longer one- or two-week or even longer vacations, if you can get the time off, can boost your productivity, improve your worker satisfaction, and, ideally, make your family and even your friendship relationships stronger and closer.

The pandemic of 2020 caused untold millions to learn how to entertain themselves while staying home due to recommended or mandatory "sheltering in place" orders or lockdowns. The weeks, and sometimes even months, when going on a trip, except perhaps to the local grocery store or pharmacy, became impossible, necessitated finding new ways to relax and de-stress. For so many, in addition to working remotely from home or distance learning, having an extended staycation, rather than the one- to two-week trip, became the norm.

Once travel becomes a possibility, every state and most countries have a tourism office, where you can find information that will help you in planning a trip. You will learn about any upcoming events that might assist you in your preparations as well as additional seasonal information. Sometimes the best sources of information about where to go next, or activities to pursue, are from the referrals your friends, colleagues, or relatives share with you. Posts and photographs on social media sharing about a particular destination, hotel, or restaurant could be your starting point for your next trip.

National Park Service
US Department of the Interior
https://www.nps.gov
There are more than 2,000 federal recreation sites throughout the United States. Military personnel and selected other groups can apply for a free annual pass. Seniors can purchase an annual pass at a reduced rate. See https://www.nps.gov/planyourvisit/passes.htm for details.

Meetup
632 Broadway
New York, NY 10012
https://www.meetup.com/
Launched in 2002 by Scott Heiferman and four others, Meetup is a way for those with similar interests to connect by registering at the website. There are currently millions of users and tens of thousands of different groups in 180 countries arranging meetings for those with a shared interest to get together for everything from film, cooking, or politics to training for a marathon, hiking, or creating an app. The site is available in English and twelve other languages. If you do not see a local group that addresses one of your interests, you can start a group and become its organizer. In 2017, the company WeWork acquired Meetup.

The Three Tomatoes
http://thethreetomatoes.com/
tomato@thethreetomatoes.com
A popular and successful online newsletter, started in New York City, sharing information and creating events. Their tag line is, "The Insider's Guide for

Women Who Aren't Kids." Co-founded by Cheryl Benton and Roni Jenkins, New York City is still a strong emphasis in their online newsletter, but they now also have sister newsletters, and events, in Los Angeles and San Francisco.

Young Men's Christian Association (YMCA)
http://www.ymca.int/ (international)
www.ymca.net (for USA)
Started in 1844, the YMCA–often referred to only as the "Y"–operates in 119 countries and according to their website, reaches 58 million members. The first YMCA in the US was founded in Boston in 1851. Each Y offers its own programs which range from activities for children, teens, or adults as well as summer camp, swimming lessons, gymnastics, personal training, health and wellness lectures, and exercise machines.

Young Women's Christian Association (YWCA)
https://www.ywca.org/
Started in 1855 as a place for women to pursue recreational activities as well as develop relationships and learn about their current initiatives to fight racism, eliminate violence, and improve the opportunities available to women. Find your local YWCA at support.ywca.org/ywca-map.

Young Men's and Young Women's Hebrew Association (YM-YWHA)
Jewish Community Center
There is no national site, but search either of the above terms and your state to find a local center for recreation, education, cultural activities and events, and building relationships. Many YM-YWHAs have after school programs as well as day camps for children and teens during the summer months.

Reading and Audiovisual Materials

Daskal, Lolly. "4 Scientific Reasons Vacations Are Good for Your Health." Posted at Inc.com, June 13, 2016.

Ferris Jabr. "You Need More Downtime Than You Think." Posted at Salon .com, October 16, 2013, originally published by Scientific American.

Florence Williams. *The Nature Fix: Why Nature Makes Us Happier, Healthier, and More Creative.* NY: Norton, 2018.

Lonely Planet. *Amazing Train Journeys.* Lonely Planet, 2018.

Michael Shapiro. *A Sense of Place: Great Travel Writers Talk About Their Craft, Lives, and Inspiration.* Travelers' Tales, 2004.

National Geographic. *Destinations of a Lifetime: 225 of the World's Most Amazing Place.* National Geographic, 2015.

Patricia Schultz. *1,000 Places to See Before You Die: Revised Second Edition*. NY: Workman, 2015.

Steven B. Stern. *Stern's Guide to the Cruise Vacation*. Gretna, 22nd edition. LA: Pelican Publishing Company, Inc., 2011.

CHAPTER 29

Veterans

In 2016, there were an estimated 20.4 million veterans in the United States. By "veteran," I am referring to anyone who has previously served in any branch of the armed services—Navy, Army, Marines, Air Force—but who is no longer serving (what the military refers to as being "separated" from the military).

This chapter explores services that are available to veterans as well as their family members. There has been a lot of press over the last few years about the long waits that veterans have had to endure to get treatment within the VA healthcare system. There seem to have been some improvements in recent years, but more work is needed to help veterans and their families get service in a timelier fashion.

A key issue that definitely needs to be highlighted is the higher rate of suicide among veterans, an increase that has been linked to the greater prevalence of PTSD (Post-Traumatic Stress Disorder) related to serving in combat, returning home with life-changing major injuries, or even serving in the military without going to a war zone or personally getting injured. The higher rate of homelessness among veterans is another priority issue.

There is one benefit to veterans that I wish I had known about when my father, a captain in the army during World War II, passed away from a brain tumor at the age of eighty, twenty-four years ago. I witnessed it when the husbands of two of my friends passed away last summer and the military sent a current soldier to play taps and drape the flag over the coffin. The flag was then folded and presented to my friends at the end of the ceremony. In both cases it was a very humbling and meaningful ceremony, and a tribute to the years of service to their country that both men had given. It would have been nice to have a military tribute to my father as well, if I had only known about that free benefit.

Please note that this chapter covers help for those who previously served in the armed forces and their families. Help for military families of those currently serving is covered in Chapter 24 under the "Family" category, as well as in the "Employment" section of Chapter 6, Business, Entrepreneurship, and Employment.

Federal agency whose sole purpose is taking care of American veterans:
US Department of Veterans Affairs
810 Vermont Avenue NW
Washington DC 20420
https://www.va.gov
This site will tell you more about eligibility requirements as well as the health, education, and other benefits available to you and your family if you meet the prerequisites. The Explore VA site (https://explore.va.gov) will help you with that process.

To find the nearest veterans hospital, go to https://www.va.gov/directory/guide/home.asp.

VA health information: https://www.va.gov/health/.

There is a PTSD program in practically every state. To find the nearest program: https://www.va.gov/directory/guide/PTSD.asp.

National Center for PTSD
https://www.ptsd.va.gov/
Government agency offering information and referrals related to PTSD for veterans, as well as advice for how their family and friends may help.

Please note: if you or your loved one are in crisis and need immediate help, call 911, or 1-800-273-TALK/8255 and press 1, which is the Veterans Crisis Line.

Most states have their own department of Veteran Affairs. If possible, it is usually best to work with your state agency if you have questions or need to file a claim, rather than the federal agency in Washington, DC, because the federal agency is so huge and often has a backlog of claims. If you work with your state agency, you may even be able to talk with a specific employee whom you might be able to meet with in person to help you with any applications you might be submitting for various benefits. You can find a link to your state's veterans affairs office at https://www.va.gov/statedva.htm.

Private national organizations offering help to veterans and their families:

Air Force Aid Society (AFAS)
https://www.afas.org/
Started in 1942. From their website: "AFAS works to support and enhance the USAF mission by providing emergency financial assistance, educational support and community programs."

American Legion
https://www.legion.org/
Founded in 1919, this national veteran's membership organization offers help in a range of areas including homeless veterans and a family support network. They have branches–called Posts–throughout the US.

DAV
Disabled American Veterans
https://www.dav.org/
Helping veterans since 1920. From their website: "We are dedicated to a single purpose: Empowering veterans to lead high-quality lives with respect and dignity."

Gary Sinise Foundation
PO Box 368
Woodland Hills, CA 91365
https://www.garysinisefoundation.org
Founded in 2011 by actor Gary Sinise, who found it his mission to help wounded veterans and their families. Just one of its many accomplishments has been to adapt 70 homes for severely wounded veterans.

Military Officers Association of America
http://www.moaa.org/
Serves those who are retired as well as surviving spouses. There is career information at their website for those in pursuit of jobs outside the military.

Paralyzed Veterans of America (PVA)
https://www.pva.org/
Offering help since 1946 for veterans who have been paralyzed by spinal cord injury or dysfunction.

Veterans of Foreign Wars (VFW)
https://www.vfw.org/

Started at the end of the nineteenth century, following the Spanish-American War and the Philippine Insurrection, chapters were formed in Ohio, Colorado, and Pennsylvania. There are chapters throughout the US now, and the website lists its current membership in VFW and its Auxiliary at 1.7 million. To find a local post: https://www.vfw.org/find-a-post.

Wounded Warrior Project
https://www.woundedwarriorproject.org/
This project helps in the areas of mental and physical wellness, getting connected, providing career and VA benefits counseling, and aiding veterans on their journey to independence.

Reading and Audiovisual Materials

Claudia Zayfert and Jason C. DeViva. *When Someone You Love Suffers from Posttraumatic Stress.* NY: Guilford Press, 2011.

Jack Canfield, Mark Victor Hansen, and Sydney R. Slagter. *Chicken Soup for the Veteran's Soul.* Cos Cob, CT: Backlist, LLC, 2012.

Kayleen Reusser. *We Gave Our Best: American World War II Veterans Tell Their Stories (WWII Legacies)* (Volume 3). Bluffton, IN: Kayleen Reusser Media, 2018.

Kristen Bialik. "The changing face of America's veteran population." November 10, 2017. http://www.pewresearch.org/fact-tank/2017/11/10/the-changing-face-of-americas-veteran-population/

Mark I. Nickerson and Joshua S. Goldstein. *The Wounds Within: A Veteran, a PTSD Therapist, and a Nation Unprepared.* NY: Skyhorse Publishing, 2015.

Michael Morris and Dick Pirozzolo. *Escape from Saigon: A Novel.* NY: Skyhorse Publishing, 2017.

CHAPTER 30

Volunteerism

Although this chapter focuses on organizations and associations that are specifically tied to volunteerism, you could contact practically any resource listed in this book and see if they want your volunteer help.

With countless Baby Boomers retiring from work daily, those who may find—especially after the first year or two—that not having a routine or work-related connection in their lives is disappointing, being a volunteer could be the answer. Yes, it requires the same time and commitment as a job, or at least a part-time one. The responsibility of showing up and doing excellent work is just as real.

You could volunteer related to a cause that you care about, such as a health-related issue, where an organization has paid staff but relies on volunteers to augment what they do, especially for fund-raising walks or runs or galas and the related silent or charity auctions. Or you could volunteer related to an interest or hobby that you have. If you are still active in your profession, whether retired or not, many professional associations rely on volunteers to deal with member-related concerns, such as membership drives; arranging guest speakers for monthly luncheons; developing, updating, or maintaining the association's or organization's website; or generating publicity about the association and its membership.

You probably already know this, but the good news is that volunteering is good for the volunteer! As reported by Stephanie Watson, executive editor of the *Harvard Women's Health Watch*, in "Volunteering may be good for body and mind," the benefits are not just social—they are medical. A Carnegie Mellon study found that volunteers are more physically active than they would be without volunteering. Volunteer work also reduces stress; 200 hours annually of volunteering was associated with lower blood pressure.

But volunteering is most definitely not just for the retired or semi-retired. The researchers behind a longitudinal federally funded project called "Helping Others Stay Sober" at Case Western Reserve University School of Medicine, Department of Psychiatry, Division of Child Psychiatry, researching what helps someone to stay sober, found this about teens: "Our results show that helping others helps adolescent helpers reduce their craving for alcohol and drugs. Examples of this would be service-related tasks in AA [Alcoholics Anonymous] such as making coffee or simply assisting someone with a task like carrying their heavy bags." Yes, volunteering to help others at AA meetings had the dramatic benefit of actually reducing their alcohol and drug cravings!

At any age, volunteering also opens up the opportunity to connect with others who share a similar interest or concern. It is a way to meet new people and to interact regularly with those you meet through your volunteer activities. Over the years, I have also heard many examples of those who found that the skills they mastered through their volunteer work helped them in landing a paid job, sometimes even at the very place where they started off as a volunteer.

Government-funded volunteer programs:
AmeriCorps NCCC
https://www.nationalservice.gov/programs/americorps/americorps-programs/americorps-nccc
From their website: "AmeriCorps NCCC is a full-time, residential, team-based program for young adults, age 18–24 (with no upper age limit to serve as a team leader). Members develop leadership skills and strengthen communities by completing service projects and gaining life experience. Teams, comprised of 8–10 members, complete multiple projects that address essential community needs throughout the United States. During the 10-month service term, members receive lodging, transportation, uniform and meals. Upon the completion of the program, members are eligible to receive the Segal AmeriCorps Education Award equal to the maximum Pell Grant amount: $6095, as of Oct. 1 2018."

AmeriCorpsVISTA
https://www.nationalservice.gov/programs/americorps/americorps-programs/americorps-vista
From their website: "Since 1965, over 220,000 VISTA members have served with the mission to strengthen organizations that alleviate poverty. VISTA serves in

each of the 50 US States and in all US Territories. VISTA members go where they are needed and make a difference through volunteering and the mobilization of resources." VISTA volunteers are paid a small living allowance. You have to be at least eighteen years old. At the end of your service, you will be offered either an education award of up to $5,920 or an $1,800 cash stipend.

Foster Grandparents
Corporation for National and Community Service (CNCS)
1201 New York Avenue NW
Washington, DC 20525
http://www.seniorcorps.gov/about/programs/fg.asp
Established in 1993, the Foster Grandparents program is part of this government-funded effort to provide service to children "with exceptional or special needs." Those fifty-five and over who have limited income and meet the income eligibility requirement may apply to be a Foster Grandparent. If accepted into the program, they will be volunteers, but they will receive a nominal stipend, assistance with payment of their meals related to their services, and reimbursement for transportation to the foster child or children that they are assigned to.

Peace Corps
https://www.peacecorps.gov/
Envisioned by President John F. Kennedy, who formalized the Peace Corps in an executive order on March 1, 1961, there are currently over sixty countries where their volunteers are serving. Peace Corps volunteers are provided with housing and a stipend that enables them to live in a similar way to those they are serving. The Peace Corps takes care of the flight to and from the country where you are serving. Each month, volunteers are given two vacation days, which you can use to travel to neighboring countries or to return home for a visit (at your own expense). At the end of your two years of service, you will be provided with $8,000 to use however you choose to help you transition back to whatever job or lifestyle that you will return to. If any emergencies arise during your two years of service, you can get paid leave.

Volunteers must be US citizens and at least eighteen years of age. Couples who want to serve together will have to be in separate houses during the pre-service training so they will adequately immerse themselves in the language and the culture, but during their two years of service, they will live together in their own apartment. Peace Corps volunteer openings: https://www.peacecorps.gov/volunteer/volunteer-openings/. You can only have one active application at a time, so make a careful choice about what you want to apply for.

RSVP

https://www.nationalservice.gov/programs/senior-corps/senior-corps-programs/rsvp

For seniors fifty-five and over. From their website: "RSVP volunteers choose how, where, and how often they want to serve, with commitments ranging from a few hours to 40 hours per week. Volunteers receive pre-service orientation, training from the organization where they will serve, and supplemental insurance while on duty. RSVP volunteers do not receive monetary incentives, but sponsoring organizations may reimburse them for some costs incurred during service." Typical volunteer programs available to those who participate in RSVP:

- Organizing neighborhood watch programs
- Tutoring and mentoring disadvantaged or disabled youth
- Renovating homes
- Teaching English to immigrants
- Assisting victims of natural disasters

Senior Companions

https://www.nationalservice.gov/programs/senior-corps/senior-corps-programs/senior-companions

From their website: "Senior Companions are volunteers 55 and over who provide assistance and friendship to seniors who have difficulty with daily living tasks, such as shopping or paying bills. The program aims to keep seniors independent longer, and provide assistance to family caregivers. Senior Companions serve 15 to 40 hours per week helping an average of two to four adult clients live independently in their own homes. Volunteers receive pre-service orientation, training from the organization where they serve, supplemental insurance while on duty, and may qualify to earn a tax-free hourly stipend . . . Last year, roughly 220,000 Senior Corps Volunteers volunteered at 25,000 unique sites across the country."

To find out more about what Senior Companions are doing in your state, go to https://www.nationalservice.gov/impact-our-nation/state-profiles .

National and even international organizations and associations to contact for volunteer opportunities:
Canadian Parks and Recreation Association (CPRA)
1180 Walkley Rd
Ottawa, ON K1V 2M5
Canada
https://www.cpra.ca/
info@cpra.ca (to inquire about any volunteer opportunities)

A membership association of Canada's parks and recreation centers and related service providers. From their website: "As a national organization, CPRA welcomes the creativity, energy and expertise of volunteers in order to make a difference for the parks and recreation sector. We welcome volunteers in a variety of areas including communication, research, advocacy, administration, strategic development and IT."

Eye Heroes CIC
www.eyeheroes.org.uk
According to coordinator Caroline Campbell, "Eye Heroes is a British child-led campaign to tackle avoidable sight loss. Volunteers are recruited to run free workshops, in schools and other educational settings, to train children to carry the eye health message to their local community." Those interesting in volunteering should contact Caroline at coordinator@eyeheroes.org.uk

National Runaway Safeline
https://www.1800runaway.org
The Safeline (free telephone service) is available 24 hours a day, 7 days a week. For information on how to become a hotline volunteer counselor, go to https://www.1800runaway.org/support-youth-in-crisis/volunteer/.

Opening Hearts
30 Corinaldo Drive
Hamilton, Ontario, L8W3J7
Canada
www.openinghearts.ca
This charity supports families that have children with special needs. They need volunteers to help them to run several fundraisers each year.

Do Something
19 West 21st Street, 8th Floor
New York, NY 10010
www.dosomething.org
From their website: "DoSomething.org is mobilizing young people in every US area code and in 131 countries! Sign up for a volunteer, social change, or civic action campaign to make real-world impact on a cause you care about."

Global Volunteers
375 East Little Canada Road
St. Paul, MN 55117-1628
http://www.globalvolunteers.org

Coordinates trips to their seventeen service programs abroad, lasting one to three weeks. Fees range from $1,000 to $3,000 to cover housing, food, and related costs.

Help Abroad
106 E. Sixth Street Suite # 900
Austin, TX 78701
https://www.helpingabroad.org
This is not a free volunteer program, but it does help volunteers to assist around the world by matching volunteers up with programs keeping the fees to $99/week as an average cost to the volunteer. From their website: "Based in Kathmandu, Nepal, Helping Abroad has grown to become one of the leading and most affordable volunteer abroad programs. Since 1998, thousands of promising volunteers have participated with us in our programs across 19 countries."

Idealist
389 5th Ave, 9th Floor
New York, NY 10016
https://www.idealist.org
From their website: "Idealist is all about connecting idealists–people who want to do good–with opportunities for action and collaboration." At the part of their website related to volunteering it says: "Find the perfect opportunity to change the world."

All for Good
https://www.allforgood.org
From their website: "All for Good is a digital hub for volunteerism and community engagement, and a service of Points of Light. Volunteer opportunities from many sites around the web are pulled into All for Good by feeds to provide the most comprehensive database of volunteer opportunities around the world."

Points of Light
600 Means Street, Suite 210
Atlanta, GA 30318
http://pointsoflight.org/
info@pointsoflight.org
At the website there are three sections for each of these groups: volunteers, nonprofits, and companies. Go to http://pointsoflight.org/for-volunteers to search for volunteer opportunities and also to read volunteer stories, among other related topics. The history of Points of Light includes the calls to action of President George H.W. Bush beginning with his 1989 inaugural address advocating Americans helping each other.

MADD (Mothers Against Drunk Driving)
511 E. John Carpenter Freeway
Irving, TX 75062
https://www.madd.org/
A nonprofit organization founded in 1980 by Candy Lightner, whose thirteen-year-old daughter, Cari, was killed that year by a drunk driver. MADD has helped educate the public about the hazards of drunk driving. This organization is considered one of the prime factors in getting the number of fatalities from drunk driving cut in half since its founding. For more information on their call for volunteers and what volunteers do for the association, go to https://www.madd.org/volunteer/.

National Ability Center
www.discovernac.org
From their website: "We need your help to provide life-changing activities to people of all abilities. From lending a hand on the slopes, in the pool or on a bike, to helping in the office or at one of our events, we have many indoor and outdoor volunteer opportunities to suit your passion, abilities and recreational interests."
See listing in Chapter 13, Disabilities.

Rotary International
One Rotary Center
1560 Sherman Avenue
Evanston, IL 60201
https://myrotary.org
Founded in 1905 by Chicago attorney Paul Harris, Rotary International is headquartered in Illinois, with six offices around the world. It reportedly has 35,000+ local clubs whose causes include fighting disease, growing local economies, providing clean water, hygiene, and sanitation, promoting peace, and other concerns, as indicated at their website.

SCORE
1175 Herndon Parkway, Suite 900
Herndon, VA 20170
https://www.score.org/
From their website: "SCORE is volunteer business people helping small business people solve business problems. Volunteers give freely of their time, energy and knowledge to help others. SCORE volunteers donate over 1 million hours of their time each year to support their communities . . . 11,000+ volunteers helped create more than 54,000 new businesses in 2016." Mentoring by senior volunteers

is provided in person or through email, phone, or video interviews. Volunteers also offer seminars or workshops on business topics. Mentors provide three or four hours of assistance to new or current small business owners who need advice to get started or to grow their business.

To find a local SCORE, go to https://www.score.org/find-location. To become a volunteer, go to https://www.score.org/volunteer. To request a mentor, go to https://core.score.org/mentoring/request .

Together We Can Change the World (TWCCTW)
http://twcctw.org/
Founded in 2008 by speaker/singer Jana Stanfield and speaker/author Scott Friedman. Their group of volunteers travels to South East Asia several times a year to work on projects to help disadvantaged children, especially orphans, and women to have an improved daily existence, educational opportunities, and future.

Tunnel to Towers Foundation
2361 Hylan Boulevard
Staten Island, NY 10306
https://tunnel2towers.org/
info@Tunnel2Towers.org
Firefighter Stephen Siller was the youngest of seven children. He was thirty-four years old on September 11, 2001. He had already ended his shift but he chose to go back to help out. He didn't survive in the South Tower. Every year, family and friends of Stephen Siller and, now, total strangers from throughout the US and internationally honor him and raise money to help others when they repeat his run through the Brooklyn Battery Tunnel on the last Sunday in September. Since the foundation was started, they have raised millions of dollars to help those who are less fortunate, such as providing a mortgage-free home to a widow with two children whose husband died serving his country.

To find out more about how volunteers help the foundation, and how you can help too, go to https://tunnel2towers.org/get-involved/volunteer/

United Planet
Boston Harbor Shipyard and Marina
256 Marginal Street
Boston MA 02128
https://www.unitedplanet.org
quest@unitedplanet.org
Organizes one- to twelve-week international volunteer trips in thirty-five countries.

VolunteerMatch
409 13th Street, Suite 800
Oakland, CA 94612
https://www.volunteermatch.org
From their website: "VolunteerMatch matches inspired people with inspiring causes."

VolunTourism
http://www.voluntourism.org/
From their website: "In the broadest sense, Voluntourism represents voluntary service experiences that include travel to a destination in order to realize one's service intentions."

Some of the many local programs that are looking for volunteers:
Retired and Senior Volunteer Program (RSVP)
Community Service Society
633 Third Avenue, 10th Floor
New York, NY 10017
http://www.cssny.org/programs/entry/retired-and-senior-volunteer-program
From their website: "Created in 1966 by the Community Service Society, the Retired and Senior Volunteer Program (RSVP) recruits, trains, and places volunteers at community-based organizations throughout the five boroughs of New York City."

St. John's Bread & Life
795 Lexington Avenue
Brooklyn, NY 11221
https://www.breadandlife.org
From their website: "Since 1982, St. John's Bread & Life has worked to alleviate hunger and poverty in Brooklyn and Queens. We serve nearly 3,000 meals to hungry New Yorkers every day." Volunteers serve food, work in the pantry, and attend events.

Volunteering to help the formerly incarcerated:
Fortune Society
29-76 Northern Boulevard
Long Island City, NY 11101
https://fortunesociety.org
The Fortune Society is looking for volunteers. For more information, go to https://fortunesociety.org/volunteer-or-intern-with-us/.

To volunteer to help those still incarcerated:
The Innocence Project
New York, NY
Founded 25 years ago at Cardoza Law School, the project works to get those wrongly convicted freed through DNA evidence. Here is the sign-up sheet for those interested in volunteering: https://www.innocenceproject.org/volunteer/. See complete listing in Chapter 23, "Offenders, Inmates, and the Formerly Incarcerated"

Volunteer Services Coordinator
Contact the Department of Corrections in your state for a referral to the volunteer coordinator at the state correctional facilities. If there is a federal correctional facility in your state, you could contact that facility to see what volunteer opportunities are available in the federal prison.

Lionheart Foundation
PO Box 170115
Boston, MA 02117
https://lionheart.org
questions@lionheart.org
From their website: "Volunteers are often in demand at the Lionheart office to reach out to programs nationwide and introduce them to our programs and offer free resources. Internet savvy and a pleasant telephone manner is all it takes. We also have a need for administrative and development support. The Lionheart office is located in Dedham, Massachusetts."

Reading and Audiovisual Materials

Arthur I. Blaustein. *Make a Difference: America's Guide to Volunteering and Community Service*. Revised and updated edition. San Francisco, CA: Jossey-Bass, an imprint of Wiley, 2003.

Dawn C. Carr, MGS, PhD. "5 Reasons Why You Should Volunteer." Posted May 12, 2014 at PsychologyToday.com.

Dillon Banerjee. *The Insider's Guide to the Peace Corps: What to Know Before You Go*. Berkeley, CA: Ten Speed Press, 2009, 2000.

Jack Canfield, Mark Victor Hansen, and Arline McGraw. *Chicken Soup for the Volunteer's Soul*. Backlist LLC, 2012.

Stephanie Watson. "Volunteering may be good for body and mind." *Harvard Women's Health Watch*, June 26, 2013, updated October 29, 2015. https://www.health.harvard.edu/blog/volunteering-may-be-good -for-body-and-mind-201306266428

CHAPTER 31

World Wide Web, the Internet, and the Media

WORLD WIDE WEB AND THE INTERNET

According to Statista, in 2019, more than four billion people were using the Internet which means that literally half the world's population is connected to the Internet and the other half is not. Why does that statistic matter? In a simplistic way, it is dividing the world into the "haves" and the "have nots" with the "have" part whether or not someone has access to the information, and resources, that the Internet offers. When the pandemic of 2020 forced so many to work from home as well as to study online, including college students, relying on an Internet connection so they could access their teachers, professors, and courses, just how pivotal the Internet has become to communication and the dissemination of knowledge became clearer than ever.

For so many, the Internet and all that it offers is taken for granted. I can remember, however, when I got a computer with access to the World Wide Web and the Internet for the first time in the mid-1990s. What a wonder it was to be able to find so much information out without having to go to a physical library or to connect with people around the world in an instant without having to make a phone call or send a letter through the regular mail.

The University of Alabama at Birmingham, in its article, "World Wide Web vs. Internet: What's the Difference?" posted at the website for its Bachelor of Science in Information Systems degree program, discusses how these two phenomena differ. Stated simply, "As the Mozilla Foundation notes in its documentation for developers, the web is one of the applications build on the internet" and "The internet is the network of networks that provides the basis for the web." Websites are still one of the main ways that the internet is accessed, especially for companies or associations. But other ways of accessing the Internet, including e-mail, using mobile apps, or instant messaging "are not necessarily web functions." But they also point out that if someone is using Gmail.com to send an e-mail, "you are using both the internet and the web."

Elsewhere in *Help Yourself Now* you were directed to agencies or associations that deal with one of the downsides of the Internet, namely, cybercrime. For example, illegal cyber activity is investigated by the FBI (https://www.fbi.gov). (Please refer to the section on cybercrime in the chapter on crime victims.) There is also something known as the dark web. These websites are not indexed by search engines and in a study by researchers Daniel Moore and Thomas Rid of King's College in London, as reported on by Darren Guccione, in classifying the contents of 2,723 live dark web sites over a five-week time period in 2015, they discovered that 57 percent contained illicit material. No one wants their personal information on the dark web; that is where hackers can buy usernames and passwords as well as buying drugs and even guns.

On a more positive note, there are so many helpful uses of the Internet such as the discussion groups that revolve around issues or concerns that private mailing lists like ListServ handle; information shared through electronic magazines, newspapers, or blogs; looking for a job through classified ads as well as online only sites that share about job openings, including Indeed.com, Entertainmentcareers.net, and Linkedin.com, to name just a few; online shopping where you can buy practically anything and you can now even pick up those items at a local location if that is your preference over shipping directly to you; electronic mail; conducting research; downloading files; taking online educational courses; playing an interactive game; finding friends or romantic partners; and even just finding out what time it is in another part of the world (www.timeanddate.com).

So you have to be careful about what websites you access, as well as protecting your personal information when you shop online. It is usually advised that you use a credit, not a debit, card for shopping online. If you have more than one credit card, keep track of the credit card you used to make an online purchase so you can more easily monitor your monthly statement for any unusual charges that might indicate that your information has been accessed and you need to immediately alert your credit card company and/or the bank that issued the card.

I am certainly not an expert on the internet, the World Wide Web, or cybersecurity, but one thing I have learned over the years is that "https" is a more secure distinction, for your own sites or for the ones that you visit and use, than "http." So keep that in mind if you are designing or redesigning your site, or when you are visiting and using websites on the internet. This brings up an excellent point about websites and the internet. Yes, you can build your own site and there are many web-building programs, often free for the basic version, that you could rely upon. But building, and maintaining and hosting, a website may be beyond your capabilities. So consider hiring and working with a seasoned web designer and web hosting service.

Although some are gravitating from their own website for their company or business to having their company or service posted for free through Facebook or even LinkedIn, for others, having a dedicated website is still seen as an essential part of the business plan. Even if you are still on the fence about whether you want a dedicated site or not, consider buying the domain name for your name, or the name of your product, business, association, or company, so it is available to you when and if you do decide to develop that site. There are many services you can turn to for that domain name purchase. One of the biggest and better known, with reasonable rates and a range of available services, is Go Daddy (www.godaddy.com).

Organizations, agencies, and companies involved with the World Wide Web and the Internet:
Internet Society (The)
11710 Plaza America Drive, Suite 400
Reston, VA 20190
https://www.internetsociety.org
In 1992, The Internet Society was founded by two of its early pioneers, Vint Cerf and Bob Kahn. There are offices in the US and Switzerland with regional contacts on other continents. Members include individuals, companies, and special interest groups.

World Wide Web Foundation
1110 Vermont Avenue, NW Suite 500
Washington, D.C. 20005
https://webfoundation.org
In 2009, the World Wide Web Foundation was founded by web inventor, Sir Tim Berneres-Lee, and Rosemary Leith, with the goal, as stated at its website, "to advance the open web as a public good and a basic right."

SEARCH ENGINES

Everyone knows that Google has become the biggest player in the search engine world but there are other search engines you should know about and even consider trying, if you have not already done so. Also, be careful that you totally rely on putting a keyword, company, organization, or agency, into a search engine and that is as far as your search goes. You can try different key words and you can also consider such old-fashioned but still effective ways of searching such as asking for referrals by e-mail, text, or phone of experts or even family, friends, or colleagues (who might have suggestions that a search engine might not even consider), doing your own research and following up on the leads that you uncover, or following up on the suggestions for additional information that you find listed in books, scholarly or popular articles, or even blogs by well-regarded authors, consultants, or executives, from trusted sources, or through the online resources posted at the websites for companies, agencies, or associations.

Here are search engines that you can use to find out information on a wide range of consumer, health, education, and other concerns:
Ask
https://www.ask.com/
You can put a question in the search engine and see what answer you get.

Bing
https://www.bing.com/
The search engine developed and operated by Microsoft.

Google
https://google.com
Founded in 1998 by Larry Page and Sergey Brin, this multi-billion dollar California-based technology company has grown from a search engine to an international company with more than 100,000 employees.

DuckDuckGo
https://duckduckgo.com/
Gabriel Weinberg founded this search engine in 2008 with the unique feature that they do not store any of the personal information that you might inadvertently share when you do a search.

Yahoo!
https://search.yahoo.com
Founded in 1994, Yahoo! is now owned by Verizon Media. It is a search engine as well as a directory of websites on the World Wide Web.

THE MEDIA

As more and more parts of the media find its way to the internet, the lines between the internet and the media become increasingly blurred. Print newspapers and magazines, and even movies released in brick-and-mortar movie theaters, are increasingly vanishing. Newspapers and magazines are available simultaneously online in electronic versions and, in decreasing frequency, also available in a print version, as movies increasingly announce that new releases will be available through a streaming service simultaneously with a release into the physical movie theaters, or exclusively through internet streaming services and downloads.

Whether media is the so-called traditional media of television, cable, or radio, or the newer media, or podcasts available exclusively online, sharing information in as truthful a way or opinions as long as its recognized as such is still the media's goal. Like the organizations, associations, or other sources of information that you can access online, it is up to you to judge whether you feel confident about the impartiality of the media that you are watching. Does a particular reporter have an axe to grind against whatever individual or product that he or she is criticizing? How is funding that media's platform so you can assess if there might be a conflict of interest in what they are reporting? How do they gather their information? What are their sources?

One of the biggest stories of 2020, after the pandemic of course, was the awareness that traditional and social media might have been censoring what information was being made available to the American public. These accusations, whether proven or not, still highlighted the necessity of getting your information from trusted sources as well as from multiple sources. Although books are not as quickly disseminated as information posted on the internet, shared through TV/cable or radio/podcast interviews, or in social media posts on Twitter, LinkedIn, Facebook, or videos posted to YouTube or Instagram, since publishing a book can be accomplished literally overnight these days, well-researched books should not be overlooked as a contemporary and noteworthy source of information.

As with any information that you access from the online or social media, be a smart consumer of the books you choose to read. Who published a particular book? It is unnecessary for a book to be published by one of the five huge conglomerate commercial houses in the US for it to be worthwhile. There are literally thousands of independent publishing companies as well as university presses that have stellar reputations and excellent books. Once you feel confident in the book's publisher, now consider, if it is nonfiction, what are the credentials of the author? Even if its fiction, or a children's book, are there hidden messages or an agenda that the author is pushing that you need to be aware of?

Several media-related unions, associations, or organizations were previously listed, and described, in the Arts chapter, such as the Writers Guild of America East, Writers Guild of America West, and The Newspaper Guild. In this section you will find the listing for the US government watchdog on the media as well as listings for fact checking services, network and cable stations, social media sites, and wire services.

These agencies or organizations are concerned with the media's accountability to the public:
Federal Communications Commission (FCC)
https://www.fcc.gov/
The FCC's mission (*from the website): "The Federal Communications Commission regulates interstate and international communications by radio, television, wire, satellite, and cable in all 50 states, the District of Columbia and U.S. territories. An independent U.S. government agency overseen by Congress, the Commission is the federal agency responsible for implementing and enforcing America's communications law and regulations."

Here are several sites that are fact checking enterprises:
FactCheck.org®
https://www.factcheck.org/
A Project of The Annenberg Public Policy Center
Their mission (from the website): "We are a nonpartisan, nonprofit "consumer advocate" for voters that aims to reduce the level of deception and confusion in U.S. politics. We monitor the factual accuracy of what is said by major U.S. political players in the form of TV ads, debates, speeches, interviews and news releases. Our goal is to apply the best practices of both journalism and scholarship, and to increase public knowledge and understanding."

FAIR: Fairness and Accuracy in News Reporting
https://fair.org/
FAIR, a non-profit organization started in 1986, describes itself as "the national media watch group, has been offering well-documented criticism of media bias and censorship."

PolitiFact
https://www.politifact.com/
PolitiFact is owned by the nonprofit Poynter Institute for Media Studies and functions as a not-for-profit national news organization. As noted at the website, "PolitiFact partners with Facebook and TikTok to help try and slow the spread of misinformation online." But the social media sites make the determination about what action, if any, they will take about a particular fact/post.

NETWORK STATIONS
ABC (American Broadcasting Company)
https://abc.com/
Founded in 1943 as a radio network, it is one of the four leading network stations.

CBS (Columbia Broadcasting System)
https://www.cbs.com/
Began in 1927 as the United Independent Broadcasters radio network.

FOX (Fox Broadcasting Company)
https://www.fox.com/
In 1986, the newest network station began.

NBC (National Broadcasting Company, Inc.)
https://www.nbc.com/
Founded in 1926 as a broadcasting network.

CABLE STATIONS
CNBC
https://www.cnbc.com/
Started in 1989, the parent company is NBC.

CNN (Cable News Network)
Ted Turner and Reese Schoenfeld founded CNN as a 24-hour cable all-news station in 1980.

Fox Business Network
https://www.foxbusiness.com/
The cable channel was launched in 2007.

MSNBC
https://www.msnbc.com/
Founded in 1996, it is owned by NBC.

NEWSMAX
https://www.newsmax.com/
Founded in 1998, this is a news media company which publishes Newsmax.com and also has a TV network.

SOCIAL MEDIA
Facebook
https://www.facebook.com/
Free website founded by Mark Zuckerberg in 2004 with more than two million subscribers globally.

Instagram
https://www.instagram.com/
Founded in 2010 and bought by Facebook in 2012 with a billion MAUs (Monthly Active Users).

WhatsApp
https://www.whatsapp.com/
Owned by Facebook, users can make calls, send messages, or images throughout the world.

Parler
https://parler.com/
@ParlerSupport
Subscriber-based social media app founded in 2018 by John Matze and Jared Thomson. Considered by some as a microblogging alternative to Twitter.

Pinterest
https://www.pinterest.com/
Founded in 2009, there are approximately 250 million MAU (Monthly Active Users) sharing images and messages.

Snap Inc.
https://www.snapchat.com/
Launched in 2011. More than 250 million MAUs (Monthly Active Users).

Tumblr
https://www.tumblr.com/
Founded in 2007, this microblogging site has more than 600 million MUVs (Monthly Unique Visitors).

Twitter
https://twitter.com/home
Founded in 2006, this microblogging site has more than 300 million MAUs (Monthly Active Users).

YouTube
https://www.youtube.com/
Founded in 2005, this video-sharing platform is one of Google's subsidiaries. There are close to two billion MAUs (Monthly Active Users).

WIRE SERVICES
Associated Press (AP)
https://www.ap.org/
Founded in 1846, the AP is "an independent global news organization dedicated to factual reporting." Their journalists are reporting from 250 locations around the world.

Reuters
https://www.reuters.com/
Founded in 1851, Reuters is a news organization company headquartered in London.

Reading and Audiovisual Materials

Edward Yourdon. *Death March: The Complete Software Developer's Guide to Surviving "Mission Impossible" Projects.* Upper Saddle River, NJ: Prentice Hall PTR, 1997.

J. Clement. "Internet usage worldwide—statistics & facts." Posted at Statista.com. October 26 2020.

Jan Yager. *Delivering Time Management for IT Professionals: A Trainer's Manual.* Birmingham, UK: Packt Publishing Limited, 2015.

John Battelle. *The* Search: How Google and Its Rivals Rewrote the Rules of Business and Transformed Our Culture. New York: Penguin Books, 2005.

Larissa Hjorth and Sam Hinton. *Understanding Social Media.* 2nd Edition. Los Angeles, CA: SAGE, 2019.

Network. Movie directed by Sydney Lumet and written by Paddy Chayefsky about the media Released in 1976. Faye Dunaway, Beatrica Straight, and Peter Finch all won Oscars with Finch's being award posthumously.

Nicolas Carr. *The Shallows: What the Internet Is Doing to Our Brains*. New York: Norton, 2020.

Sharyl Attkinson. *Slanted: How the News Media Taught Us to Love Censorship and Hate Journalism*. New York: Harper, 2020.

Tim Berners-Lee. *Weaving the Web: The Original Design and Ultimate Destiny of the World Wide Web*. New York: HarperBusiness, 2000.

The Truman Show. This 1998 gem of a movie, starring Jim Carrey, was prophetic in its premise as reality TV still dominates so much of television today. Directed by Peter Weir and co-starring Ed Harris.

University of Alabama at Birmingham, Bachelor of Science in Information Systems program. "World Wide Web vs. Internet: What's the Difference?" Posted online. n.d.

How I Went About Researching This Book

The original *The Help Book* was the starting point for the new *Help Yourself Now*. I attempted to contact resources listed in the first help book to see if they were still relevant and, if still viable, to do any necessary updating. I added the related website and a physical address, if available.

In addition, since I usually included a resource section in the non-fiction books I have authored or co-authored, I had those organizations and related bibliographic information to start from on such topics as the criminal justice system and crime victims (*Victims*); relationships (*Friendgevity; When Friendship Hurts; Friendshifts; 365 Daily Affirmations for Healthy and Nurturing Relationships; Single in America*); sleep and sleep disorders (*Sleeping Well*); business (*Business Protocol; Productive Relationships*); money (*21 Ways to Financial Freedom*); careers (*Career Opportunities in the Publishing Industry; Career Opportunities in the Film Industry*); time management (*Work Less, Do More; Put More Time on Your Side; How to Finish Everything You Start*); and more. I was also a weekly columnist for six months for consumeraffairs .com, writing a column called "Boomerific," which covered everything from caring for your aging parents, avoiding Ponzi schemes, and heart health to friendship after fifty, finding a job, and keeping your brain in shape. Every one of those twenty-six articles concluded with where to get help as well as additional related reading material.

To research *Help Yourself Now*, I also attended conferences or presentations on a range of topics, such as dealing with active shooter situations or online or phone counseling, and conducted interviews and collected 90 detailed questionnaires through surveymonkey.com for those who offer, or obtain, help. More than 200 help providers, and those getting help, responded to my various queries in HARO (Help-A-Reporter Out), sharing about their organization, company, or series, or disclosing their stories, and providing links to websites or suggestions for related books and other resources for me to review and consider for inclusion.

This book is also the essence of what I have learned about getting and giving help, as well as the knowledge I have gained over the many years of research related to the various topics covered in *Help Yourself Now*. It draws upon the courses I have taken or taught including Drugs and Society; Family; Race, Class, and Gender; Forensic Health, the Law, and the Criminal Justice System; Sociology of Health; Victimology; Penology; Intro Sociology; Criminology; International Criminology; Nonfiction Writing; Crisis Intervention; Public Speaking; and Sociology of Deviance.

Permissions

For the overview at the beginning of the following chapters, I edited and updated information from several introductions from my previous book, *The Help Book*, by J. L. Barkas (aka Jan Yager), including: Adoption and Foster Care; Aging; Animal Rights and Care; Arts; Courts; Emergencies and Disasters; Health; and Housing. Revised and reprinted by permission of the copyright holder, Jan Yager.

The introduction to Chapter 26, Relationships, is based on an edited and updated introduction to my book, *365 Daily Affirmations for Healthy & Nurturing Relationships*, published by Hannacroix Creek Books, Inc.

The beginning of the "Employment" section of Chapter 6 is an edited and updated version of my article, "What to Do If You're Fired," that was previously published in *Parade* magazine.

Thanks to the following individuals for allowing me to publish their material in *Help Yourself Now*: to criminal defense attorney Kevin Gres, for permission to reprint his seven tips if you are pulled over, originally published in his May 2017 newsletter, with limited distribution, and to Dr. Stephanie Benjamin (thirdyear.org), author of *Love, Sanity, or Medical School: A Memoir* (2019), to publish her disaster preparedness tips. I also appreciate permission to include excerpts from my interviews with Gina Carr, in Chapter 27, Stephanie Taylor, in Chapter 1, Matt Pinsker, in Chapter 21, Julio Briones, in the Introduction, Pastor Mike Casey, in Chapter 1, Robert Sollars, in Chapter 11, and Irwin Zucker, in Chapter 3.

Acknowledgments

Thank You

First, I want to thank Tad Crawford, founder and Editorial Director of Allworth Press, an imprint of Skyhorse Publishing. Tad asked me to write *Help Yourself Now,* and I am grateful to him for this opportunity to follow up on my popular *The Help Book.* Thanks to Chamois Holschuh, former Project Editor at Skyhorse, as well as editor Caroline Russomanno.

Second, every person who responded to my various HARO (Help a Reporter Out) queries has my thanks. Whether you made it into the final book or not, please know that your input is deeply appreciated.

Third, thanks to my family, friends, and colleagues at the colleges where I teach for your support as I researched and wrote this book.

Fourth, I want to thank four for-credit college interns from Adelphi University for their help with fact checking the typeset manuscript: Ashley Hazan, Carson Bailey, Emily Flint, and Rebecca Justiniano.

Thank you for reading *Help Yourself Now.* I hope you have found it an informative and useful guide to getting, or even giving, help. A book like this is never really finished since new organizations or government or company-initiated programs are founded, and others are halted, or change their focus or direction. There may also even be new concerns that have to be addressed. *Help Yourself Now,* however, is a self-help book that I hope you will refer to again and again. I welcome hearing from you with your comments, feedback, or suggestions for future editions, although a personal reply cannot be guaranteed. Use the form at the back of the book, or fill out the Contact form at my website, www.drjanyager.com, or fill out the confidential survey at https://www.surveymonkey.com/r/D7S6F6H

About the Author

Jan Yager, PhD, the former J. L. Barkas, is the author of *The Help Book*, which was featured in the *New York Times* and by the Associated Press, and more than fifty additional nonfiction, fiction, children's, and poetry books. Her award-winning nonfiction books in the areas of business, time management, money, careers, relationships, crime, and health include *Business Protocol*; *When Friendship Hurts*; *Productive Relationships*; *Work Less, Do More*; *365 Daily Affirmations for Happiness*; *Grow Global*; *Friendshifts*; *Put More Time on Your Side*; *How to Finish Everything You Start*; *21 Ways to Financial Freedom*; *Sleeping Well*; *Career Opportunities in the Publishing Industry*; and *Victims*; with translations into thirty-four languages.

Since 2014, Dr. Yager has been an Adjunct Assistant Professor (now Associate) in the Department of Sociology at John Jay College of Criminal Justice. Other colleges and universities where she has taught include Baruch College, Iona College, William Paterson University, the University of Connecticut, the New School, Penn State, and New York Institute of Technology. Previously, she was head of the Crime Prevention Resource Center at Marymount Manhattan College and worked as a crime victim hotline counselor, among other jobs. Her articles have appeared in the *New York Times, Redbook, Harper's, Family Circle, Woman's Day, Parade, Newsday, Glamour, Seventeen, Inc.*, and other publications.

The author's academic credentials include a BA in fine arts from Hofstra University, an MA in criminal justice from Goddard College Graduate Program, a PhD in sociology from City University of New York Graduate Center, and a year of graduate work in psychiatric art therapy at Hahnemann Medical College.

Dr. Yager has been interviewed on such major talk shows as *Today, Good Morning America, CBS This Morning, CBS Sunday Morning, ABC Nightline*, and CNN. She is a coach, entrepreneur, consultant, professional speaker, and trainer. To book Dr. Yager as a speaker, contact your favorite speaker bureau or write directly to her at jyager@aol.com. For more information on the author, go to http://www.linkedin.com/in/drjanyager or her main website, https://www.drjanyager.com.

Selected Other Books by Jan Yager, PhD

Nonfiction

21 Ways to Financial Freedom
125 Ways to Meet the Love of Your Life (2nd edition)
365 Daily Affirmations for Friendship
365 Daily Affirmations for Happiness
365 Daily Affirmations for Healthy and Nurturing Relationships
365 Daily Affirmations for Time Management
Business Protocol
Career Opportunities in the Film Industry (with Fred Yager)
Career Opportunities in the Publishing Industry (with Fred Yager)
Creative Time Management
Creative Time Management for the New Millennium
Delivering Time Management to IT Professionals: A Training Manual
Effective Business and Nonfiction Writing
The Fast Track Guide to Losing Weight and Keeping It Off
The Fast Track Guide to Speaking in Public
Foreign Rights and Wrongs
Friendgevity
Friendshifts
Grow Global
The Help Book
How to Finish Everything You Start
Idiot's Guide: Social Security (with Fred Yager)
Productive Relationships
Put More Time on Your Side (2nd edition)
Road Signs on Life's Journey

The Vegetable Passion: A History of the Vegetarian State of Mind
Victims
When Friendship Hurts
Who's That Sitting at My Desk? Workship, Friendship, or Foe?
Work Less, Do More: The 7-Day Productivity Makeover

Fiction
Just Your Everyday People (with Fred Yager)
On the Run
The Pretty One
Untimely Death (with Fred Yager)

Children's Picture Books
(Illustrated by Mitzi Lyman)
The Cantaloupe Cat
The Quiet Dog
The Reading Rabbit

Index

Survey Link and/or Suggestion for Entry

Please visit the following link if you wish to complete the confidential survey on giving, or receiving, help: (alternatively, you could fill out the form below):
https://www.surveymonkey.com/r/D7S6F6H

SUGGESTION FOR AN ADDITIONAL ENTRY/RESOURCE

(If this is a library book, please make a copy of the information requested and email or mail that completed form to the address below.)

Please note: If this is a library book, or a staff copy, and you do not want to write in this information, please photocopy this form and/or use it as a model of the kind of information you should include. Then send it by email (jyager@aol.com) or regular mail (Dr. Jan Yager, 1127 High Ridge Road, #110, Stamford, CT 06905 USA) (or include this information on the Contact Form at drjanyager.com) for consideration for the next edition of *Help Yourself Now.*

Name of organization, agency, or company: _____
Address (line 1): _____
Address (line 2): _____
City, State, Zip: _____
Country: _____
Website address: _____
Phone number: _____
Work phone number: _____
Cell phone number (optional): _____

Email address (for information inquiries): _____

Description of services, information, or products offered: _____

_____

_____

_____

State or states that are served: _____

Check off what applies to this organization:

- ☐ National
- ☐ Federal
- ☐ Statewide
- ☐ Nonprofit
- ☐ Not-for-profit
- ☐ For-profit company
- ☐ Other (please list): _____

Please provide a brief description of the services, information, or products that your organization offers as well as any issues that it is concerned with:

_____

_____

_____

_____

What year was your organization or company founded?: _____

In twenty words or less, please describe your organization: _____

_____

_____

Please list any publications that your organization publishes: _____

Please list any resources that your organization recommends for inclusion in *Help Yourself Now* (which you did not find in the current edition), along with the website address and/or email of that organization for possible follow-up:

_____

_____

_____

_____

This information will not be published but is requested for any follow-up related to your recommended entry:

Your name: _____

Your title: _____

Your email: _____

Any additional comments: _____

_____

_____

Books from Allworth Press

Boost Your Career
by Sander Flaum and Mechele Flaum (5½ × 8¼, 208 pages, paperback, $16.99)

The Copyright Guide (Fourth Edition)
by Lee Wilson (6 × 9, 304 pages, hardcover, $24.99)

Feng Shui and Money (Second Edition)
by Eric Shaffert (6 × 9, 256 pages, paperback, $19.99)

Fund Your Dreams Like a Creative Genius™
by Brainard Carey (6⅛ × 6⅛, 160 pages, paperback, $12.99)

How to Survive and Prosper as an Artist (Seventh Edition)
by Caroll Michels (6 × 9, 368 pages, paperback, $24.99)

Legal Forms for Everyone (Sixth Edition)
by Carl Battle (8½ × 11, 280 pages, paperback, $24.99)

Legal Guide to Social Media
by Kimberly A. Houser (6 × 9, 208 pages, paperback, $19.95)

Living Trusts for Everyone (Second Edition)
by Ronald Farrington Sharp (5½ × 8 ¼, 192 pages, paperback, $14.99)

Love & Money
by Ann-Margaret Carrozza (6 × 9, 240 pages, paperback, $19.99)

The Money Mentor
by Tad Crawford (6 × 9, 272 pages, paperback, $24.95)

The Patent Guide (Second Edition)
by Carl Battle and Andrea Small (6 × 9, 356 pages, hardcover, $24.99)

Protecting Your Assets from Probate and Long-Term Care
by Evan H. Farr (5½ × 8¼, 208 pages, paperback, $14.99)

Scammed
by Gini Graham Scott, PhD (6 × 9, 276 pages, paperback, $14.99)

The Secret Life of Money
by Tad Crawford (5½ × 8½, 304 pages, paperback, $19.95)

Sell Online Like a Creative Genius™
by Brainard Carey (6⅛ × 6⅛, 160 pages, paperback, $12.99)

The Smart Consumer's Guide to Good Credit
by John Ulzheimer (5½ × 8¼, 216 pages, paperback, $14.95)

Starting Your Career as a Freelance Writer (Third Edition)
by Moira Allen (6 × 9, 368 pages, paperback, $19.99)

Starting Your Career as a Professional Blogger
by Jacqueline Bodnar (6 × 9, 192 pages, paperback, $19.95)

The Trademark Guide (Third Edition)
by Lee Wilson (6 × 9, 272 pages, hardcover, $24.99)

Your Architecture Career
by Gary Unger (6 x 9, 288 pages, paperback, $19.99)

To see our complete catalog or to order online, please visit *www.allworth.com*.